J. Eric Smithburn

JUDICIAL DISCRETION

A Text

THE NATIONAL
JUDICIAL COLLEGE

NJC

Est. 1963

ISBN 0-9788287-0-4
ISBN 978-0-9788287-0-7

Printed in U.S.A.

For any inquiry:

Order Fulfillment
The National Judicial College
Judicial College Building/358

Reno, Nevada 89557
Tel: 800-255-8343
Fax: 775-327-2161
E-mail: pubs@judges.org

PREFACE

In the early 1980s, I accepted an invitation to speak on decision-making in juvenile and family court to a group of Nebraska judges at a conference in Fort Robinson. I flew into Scotts Bluff, Nebraska (my first trip to the state), rented a car and drove two hours or so to Fort Robinson. I had never seen such open spaces- mile after mile of sand hills with few fences in sight. It was this journey through the wide-open terrain of northwest Nebraska and my arrival at a fenced-in former military fort that provided me with the metaphor I needed to discuss the nature of judicial discretion in trial court proceedings. This and other metaphors have been helpful during the twenty-five years that I've lectured to judges, lawyers, probation officers, child welfare case managers and law students about a central aspect of judicial decision-making – the exercise of discretion.

Judicial Discretion: A Text follows my two earlier casebooks, *Judicial Discretion* (1980) and *Judicial Discretion: Successor Edition* (1991), both published by the National Judicial College. Organized in four chapters, this *text* continues the exploration of cases and secondary authorities, which analyze discretion as a jurisprudential concept, together with consideration of other basic questions. These issues include why the trial judge has discretion; how much discretion the judge has (or should have) under various circumstances; and discretion as a review-restraining device, using the abuse of discretion standard.

In addition to its use in the education of judges, this text will be useful in law school curricula as a part of the study of judicial decisions and the different standards of appellate review.

I began in the late 1970s having conversations and exchanging correspondence with Felix F. Stumpf of the National Judicial College about the nature of judicial discretion, how discretion differs from the judge's inherent power and the scholarship in these areas. Our scholarly collaboration and Felix's encouragement provided the genesis for my earlier writing on judicial discretion and this text as well, and for his support I'm most grateful. I also want to thank my research assistant, Matthew Grantham J.D.2005, for his substantial assistance with case selection, research and drafting of the text. Thanks also to my secretary, Sharon Loftus, for typing and proofreading the manuscript, along with help from Keoini Haynes, J.D. 2006, and to Jenny Jones for preparing the Index. Finally, my thanks to Margaret Anne Walz and her assistant Jaclyn Walz for thier patience and skill in preparing the manuscript for publication.

J. Eric Smithburn

FOREWORD

The National Judicial College is honored to make available to the judiciary this monumental work of Professor J. Eric Smithburn. In addition to his "day job" as one of America's most respected professors of law, Professor Smithburn has, for many years, been an important contributor to the education and enlightenment of the men and women of the judiciary. An alumnus of The National Judicial College, he has served on the NJC's faculty since 1978.

This text on judicial discretion fills a void in existing judicial literature and provides guidance on a foundational subject that goes to the core of the art of judging. The National Judicial College's Felix F. Stumpf, who coordinated the publication of this book, believes "it is the first major treatment of this subject in over 70 years".

One can reasonably argue that judicial discretion is the heart and soul of the decision-making process that seeks to provide individual but equal justice. Judicial discretion is the mechanism by which meaning is given to legal precedence in the application of law to the facts.

This text provides a scholarly yet practical examination of the meaning of discretion, why discretion exists, the levels of discretion, and the standard by which to define and review the abuse of discretion. While judges and legal scholars will continue to wrestle with the appropriate use of discretion, this unprecedented work will be a timely resource to guide any analysis and application of discretion. On behalf of all who believe in the rule of law, we sincerely thank Professor Smithburn for his service to justice through this text.

William F. Dressel
President, The National Judicial College

ABOUT THE AUTHOR

J. Eric Smithburn is a Professor of Law at Notre Dame Law School, where he teaches Appellate Review, Family Law, Comparative Family Law, Juvenile Law and Evidence. Professor Smithburn was engaged in general law practice before serving as a trial court judge in Plymouth, Indiana. He is author of eleven books and numerous law review and journal articles in the areas of evidence, trial advocacy and practice, criminal procedure, family law, juvenile law and the judicial process.

A practicing member of the Indiana Bar since 1974, Professor Smithburn has served as judge pro tem and special judge in the Circuit, Probate and Superior Courts of St. Joseph County in South Bend, Indiana, and Attorney for the St. Joseph County Office of Family and Children in South Bend, Indiana. He was called to the Bar of England and Wales, as a barrister and member of the Middle Temple, in 1989. As a door tenant with 1 Hare Court in London, Professor Smithburn consults with chambers in the area of international child abduction under the Hague Convention.

He is a regular member of the faculties of The National Judicial College, The National College of Juvenile and Family Justice of the National Council of Juvenile and Family Court Judges, the National Association of Counsel for Children and the National Institute for Trial Advocacy.

Professor Smithburn was appointed by the Indiana Supreme Court to serve on the Indiana Evidence Committee, which was responsible for drafting a new code of evidence rules for Indiana trial courts. During the Spring of 2000 and Summers of 2001 and 2002, Professor Smithburn served as a Visiting Scholar of Wolfson College at the University of Oxford and as a Visiting Fellow at the Centre for Socio-Legal Studies at Oxford.

Since 2001, Professor Smithburn has served as a Senior Judge of the St. Joseph Probate Court in South Bend. In 2002, he was appointed to the National Association of Counsel for the Children Juvenile Attorney Certification National Advisory Board. In 2003, Professor Smithburn was elected to membership in the American Law Institute(ALI).

DEDICATION

To Hon. Peter J. Nemeth
with gratitude

TABLE OF CONTENTS

1

The Meaning of Discretion

§ 1.1. Discretion as a Jurisprudential Concept: The Courts

Reviewing a motion for a new trial, based on juror misconduct, the Supreme Court of Kansas summarized the different approaches courts might take to "judicial discretion" as a jurisprudential concept as follows:

> The granting of a new trial or recalling the jury to answer for misconduct is within the sound discretion of the trial court.

> Discretion is the freedom to act according to one's judgment; and judicial discretion implies the liberty to act as a judge should act, applying the rules and analogies of the law to the facts found after weighing and examining the evidence—to act upon fair judicial consideration, and not arbitrarily. When so acting in a matter committed to the discretion of the court by the law the judgment ought not to be overruled by a reviewing court, for to do so would be to deny the right to exercise the discretion given by the law itself.

> ....

2

It is regrettable, though a fact, that the term judicial discretion has become so deeply embedded in legal nomenclature that any attempt to dislodge it would be futile. It is an anonym to be endured and dealt with and explained in the unnumbered instances where, on account of merely an unhappy phraseology definitive of certain judicial powers administrative in their character, both courts and practitioners have been led into paths of rather uncertain reasoning. There is in reality seldom a pure strict sense that implies a power of decision in every phase, uncontrolled and uncontrollable by any supervisory authority. And while appellate courts are teeming with expressions to the effect that certain enumerated matters were in the discretion of the trial court, and therefore, would not be reviewed or disturbed, yet what is in fact meant is that such matters have been reviewed and that the decision of the trial court was right under the particular circumstances and consequently the decision would be permitted to stand.

Legal discretion is a readily comprehended concept. It means nothing more than the application of statutes and principles to all of the facts of a case. Discretion in performing an act arises when it may be performed in [more than one-way, any] of which would be lawful, and where it is left to the will or judgment of the performer to determine in which way it shall be performed....[1]

---

[1] *Saucedo v. Winger*, 850 P.2d 908, 917–18 (Kan. 1993). The highest court in Maryland once indicated that the meaning of "discretion" may depend on the type of case. Quoting a prior ruling from a lower appellate court, the court stated:

> The two discretions enjoyed by the trial court, the one to permit the moving party to reopen its case to introduce evidence adducible in chief, and the other, to determine whether evidence offered to rebut is truly rebuttal evidence, are separate and distinct. As to both, of course, the evidence must be competent, relevant and material. With respect to reopening the case, the judge must consider whether the State deliberately withheld the evidence proffered in order to have it presented at such time as to obtain an unfair advantage by its impact on the trier of facts. To this end the judge must see whether the proposed evidence is merely cumulative to, or corrobative of, that already offered in chief or whether it is important or essential to a conviction. With respect to rebuttal evidence, the judge must consider whether the evidence explains, or is a direct reply to, or a contradiction of, any new matter that has been brought into the case by the accused. Thus, the considerations involved in the exercise of the two discretions are materially different. The sound exercise of discretion to allow the State to reopen its case provides no basis for finding that evidence meets the definition of rebuttal evidence, and vice versa.

State v. Hepple, 368 A.2d 445, 449 (Md. 1977).

a) Discretion as Choice

The Washington Court of Appeals in *In re Marriage of Stuart* upheld the trial court's discretionary decision denying a father attorney fees based on his intransigence and financial need.[2] Father's daughter had accused father of sexual misconduct, but the trial court in subsequent dependency proceedings found no credible evidence of such. Father moved for attorney fees after the ruling modifying the parenting plan to account for the daughter's emotional problems and strong aversion to her father. Under the modified plan, the daughter would live with her mother and seek therapy until she could maintain a more normal relationship with her father. Although the court implied that it was sympathetic to the father's position, it nonetheless upheld the trial court's decision:

> On these same facts, the trial court could, as easily, have ruled the other way, and we might have done so. However, the test for abuse of discretion is not whether the appellate court might or even would have ruled the other way. The test is whether the trial court based its decision on tenable grounds and reasons. As explained by one commentator, the central idea of discretion is choice: the court has discretion in the sense that there are no "officially wrong" answers to the questions posed. On these facts, we conclude that there is no "officially wrong" answer to the question posed.[3]

Nevertheless, the appellate court awarded the father attorney's fees associated with pursuing his appeal, noting that "the parameters of attorney fee awards based on intransigence, and the limitations of trial-court discretion in that regard, are still being developed" by Washington appellate courts.[4]

The Washington court's commitment to the "choice" definition of discretion is not absolute. In *Brewer v. Tanner*, the court reviewed the trial court's decision denying a medical malpractice plaintiff's motion for a continuance.[5] The trial court's docket calendar required plaintiffs to disclose lay and expert witnesses by May 12, 2003. After defendant filed a motion for summary judgment on June 26, plaintiffs filed a motion for continuance on August 1, identified an expert witness, and offered the expert's testimony by affidavit. The trial court denied the motion for continuance and granted the defendant's motion to strike the affidavit. Because the plaintiffs, therefore, had no evidence in support of their contentions, the trial court granted the defendant's motion for summary judgment. In finding that the trial court erred by striking the affidavit and, consequently, granting the defendant's motion for summary judgment, the court stated:

---

[2] No. 50515-7-I, 2003 WL 22766033, at *3 (Wash. Ct. App., Nov. 24, 2003).
[3] *Id.* at *5.
[4] *Id.* at *8 ("Even though we have deferred to the trial court's discretion in this instance, the appeal is far from frivolous.").
[5] *See generally* No. 22433-3-III, 2004 WL 2445666 (Wash. Ct. App. Nov. 2, 2004).

The [trial] court struck the affidavit only because of their untimely disclosure of the doctor as an expert witness under the case schedule order. We review its ruling on the motion to strike for an abuse of discretion. Because of the court's strict adherence to the time limitations in the case schedule order that caused it to strike the expert witness' affidavit, [plaintiffs] had nothing left with which to oppose the defendant's summary judgment motion. The rules should be interpreted to allow a decision on the merits and to do justice. The trial court's decision does neither. Moreover, there is no showing of any prejudice to the defendants other than a possible delay in the trial date.... [W]e fail to see how justice is served by the draconian application of time limitations here. By failing to exercise any discretion, the trial court abused its discretion.[6]

As will be discussed in Chapter 4, the Michigan courts have defined abuse of discretion to mean a decision "palpably and grossly violative of fact and logic."[7] In *Stamp v. Hagerman*, the court reviewed a trial court's discretionary decision not to award attorney fees to defendants in order to determine whether the denial was "in the interest of justice."[8] In dicta, the court explained its own difficulty with the "palpably and grossly violative" standard, which the court claimed rested on the presumption that discretion itself was a "choice" between equally legitimate courses of action:

> We are, however, of the opinion that what constitutes "in the interest of justice" must be decided on a case-by-case basis. While not controlling, a trial court may properly consider the good faith or reasonable conduct of the parties in resolving whether attorney fees are appropriate. We believe that our holding comports with the decisions in other cases involving court rules that require a court to consider the interest of justice in making discretionary decisions as involving a balancing of the interests of both parties. Discretion itself involves the idea of choice.

> "The term discretion itself involves the idea of choice, of an exercise of the will, of a determination made between competing considerations. In order to have an abuse in reaching such determination, the result must be so palpably and grossly violative of fact and logic that it evidences not the exercise of will but perversity of will, not the exercise of judgment but defiance thereof, not the exercise of reason but rather passion or bias" "*People v. Talley*, 410 Mich. 378, 387, 301 N.W.2d 809 (1981)"....

---

[6] *Id.* at *2.

[7] *Stamp v. Hagerman*, 448 N.W.2d 849, 852 (Mich. Ct. App. 1989).

[8] *Id.* at 852.

This standard for discretionary decisions was originally established in *Spalding v. Spalding*, 355 Mich. 382, 384–385, 94 N.W.2d 810 (1959)....

> Even in a civil case, not all courts have agreed on whether the *Spalding* standard is appropriate. Justice Levin, in his concurring opinion in *Talley*, described the *Spalding* standard as "simplistic and misleading," and thereafter proceeded to express his approval of the more balanced view of judicial discretion in *Langnes v. Green*, 282 U.S. 531 (1931), wherein it was stated:

"The term discretion denotes the absence of a hard and fast rule.... When invoked as a guide to judicial action it means a sound discretion, that is to say, a discretion exercised not arbitrarily or willfully, but with regard to what is right and equitable under the circumstances and the law, and directed by the reason and the conscience of the judge to a just result."

Members of this Court have also expressed discomfort with the standard set forth in *Spalding*.... One member of this panel, Judge Shepherd, was on the panel in *Muntean v. Detroit*, 372 N.W.2d 348 (1985), wherein it was stated "[w]hether we apply the nearly insurmountable test of *Spalding*... or the more balanced view suggested in *Langnes*..., the concept of discretion denotes the absence of a single, correct result.

More recent decisions of our Supreme Court have not alleviated the problem with *Spalding*. Justice Riley, writing for the majority in *Bosak v. Hutchinson*, 375 N.W.2d 333 (Mich. 1985), referred to both definitions of judicial discretion in *Langnes* and *Spalding* and then went on to quote, with apparent approval, from Justice Levin's concurring opinion in *Talley* that, despite our Supreme Court's references to *Spalding*, our Supreme Court has continued to give full-fledged review to discretionary decisions by carefully weighing the various rights and considerations involved in each type of discretionary decision. This is so despite her concurrence in the majority opinion of *Marrs v. Bd. of Medicine*, 375 N.W.2d 321 (Mich. 1985), wherein it is stated that the *Spalding* standard regarding the abuse of discretion remains "essentially intact."...

We make these observations only to highlight the difficulty in reviewing discretionary decisions under the *Spalding* test. In the present case, however, the discretionary decision in question is safeguarded against arbitrary decisions by the presence of a discernable standard which must be followed by the trial court, specifically, the refusal to award attorney fees must be in the interest of justice. This "interest of justice" standard is, as we previously noted, a standard which itself requires a balancing of competing interests. Whether we apply the *Spalding* test or the *Langnes* test, our decision to affirm the trial court's decision under these circumstances would be the same.[9]

The discretionary choices of trial court are not necessarily impervious to review.[10] In rejecting a *de novo* standard of review for preliminary injunction orders when the trial court heard no live testimony, the Second Circuit took the opportunity to clarify what it meant when it states that the trial court "abused its discretion."[11] The court first distinguished the *de novo* standard of review as "review without deference."[12] The court also distinguished clear error review as a highly deferential standard governing appellate review of the trial court's findings of fact.[13] Turning to the abuse of discretion standard, a "more complicated species of deferential appellate review," the court stated that when "a district court is vested with discretion as to a certain matter, it is not required by law to make a *particular* decision."[14] The court continued, "Rather, the district court is empowered to make a decision—of *its* choosing—that falls within a range of permissible decisions."[15] In a subsequent footnote, the court stated further:

> ...Discretion is said to be "abused" ("exceeded" would be both a more felicitous and correct term) when the decision reached is not within the range of decision-making authority a reviewing court determines is acceptable for a given set of facts. This determination that the range of acceptable decision-making has been exceeded in a particular case is assuredly one of law, but it is analytically distinct from a determination that a legal standard applicable to a generality of fact situations has been ignored, incorrectly applied, or inadequately applied in a particular case.[16]

---

[9] *Id.* at 852–53 (internal quotations omitted).

[10] *See, e.g., United States v. Pierson*, 419 F.2d 1020, 1022 (7th Cir. 1970) ("The term discretion means only that no hard and fast rules are laid down. It does not mean that the trial court's decision is immune from review.").

[11] *Zervos v. Verizon New York, Inc.*, 252 F.3d 163, 168 (2d Cir. 2001).

[12] *Id.* ("When we review a district court's decision *de novo*, we take note of it, and study the reasoning on which it is based.") ("However, our review is independent and plenary; as the Latin term suggests, we look at the matter anew, as though it had come to the courts for the first time.").

[13] *Id.* (explaining that clear error "is a deferential standard of review grounded, *inter alia*, on the belief that district courts have a good deal of expertise when it comes to fact-finding) ("A finding is clearly erroneous when although there is evidence to support it, the reviewing court on the entire evidence is left with the definite and firm conviction that a mistake has been committed.").

[14] *Id.* at 168–69.

[15] *Id.* at 169.

[16] *Id.* at 169 n.6 (citing to various authorities that describe discretion as "a decision" "lawful at any point within the outer limits of the range of choices appropriate to the issue

A leading "informed choice" case is *Johnson v. United States*.[17] Reversing a trial court's ruling denying a motion to sever in an attempted murder trial, the District of Columbia Court of Appeals described discretion thus:

> Discretion signifies choice. First, the decision-maker exercising discretion has the ability to choose from a range of permissible conclusions. The decision-making activity is not immaterial and the various elements of the problem do not preordain a single permissible conclusion. Second, the decision-maker can rely largely upon his own judgment in choosing among the alternatives.
>
> Although the act of choosing will be guided by various legal and other considerations, the decision-maker, and not the law, decides. In this sense, the core of discretion as a jurisprudential concept is the absence of a hard and fast rule that fixes the results produced under varying sets of facts.
>
> The trial court nevertheless must choose wisely so that its judgment reflects a discretion exercised not arbitrarily or willfully but with regard to what is right and equitable under the circumstances and the law, and directed by the reason and conscience of the judge to a just result. This is to say neither that a determination committed to the trial court's discretion is freed from the restraints of fact and the reasoned dictates of law nor that judgment and choice play no part in a trial court's determination of law and fact in a case. The one proposition is untenable; the other is unrealistic. As in its other decision-making activity, the court's substantial freedom of choice in an exercise of discretion must be tempered by rationality.
>
> The concept of exercise of discretion is a review-restraining one. The appellate court role in reviewing the exercise of discretion is supervisory in nature and deferential in attitude.
>
> Consequently, when the primary focus of the trial court's role shifts from the facts and law to the sound exercise of judgment, the appellate court, in its review capacity, does not render its own decision of what judgment is most wise under the circumstances presented. Rather, it examines the record and the trial court's determination for those indicia of rationality and fairness that will assure it that the trial court's action was proper.[18]

---

at hand" and as a "range" of choices "determined by the number of permissible courses of action that exist").

[17] 398 A.2d 354 (D.C. 1979).

[18] *Id.* at 361–62 (discussing also the reasons for conferring discretion on the trial court, which are discussed further in Chapter 2). The District of Columbia

8

The District of Columbia Court of Appeals followed *Johnson* in a recent case involving a guardianship.[19] Quoting *Johnson*, the *Orshansky* court reiterated that it "does not render its own decision of what judgment is most wise under the circumstances presented" but that "it examines the record and the trial court's determination for those indicia of rationality and fairness that will assure it that the trial court's action was proper."[20] The court concluded that in order to determine whether the *Johnson* test had been satisfied, it would inquire as to whether there was "a sufficient factual predicate in the record for the determination that the trial court made" and as to whether the trial court's action and reasoning feel "within the range of permissible alternatives under the law and given the facts presented."[21]

b)   Discretion as a Means to Justice

Reversing a trial court's order dismissing plaintiff's personal injury case for failure to prosecute, the Supreme Court of Appeals of West Virginia identified justice as the proper end of the trial court's discretionary decisions:

> The power to resort to the dismissal of an action is in the interest of orderly administration of justice because the general control of the judicial business is essential to the trial court if it is to function. To this extent, Rule 41(b) is still good law in that granting authority to trial judges to control their dockets through dismissals is consistent, not debilitative, of sound judicial administration....
>
> The extent of discretionary authority, however, must be delimited with care, for there is always the unseemly danger of overreaching when the judiciary undertakes to define its own power and authority. Guided by this limitation, we have suggested that circuit court's sanction authority be a reasonable response to the problems and needs that provoked its use. In other words, a court's authority to issue dismissals as a sanction must be limited by the circumstances and necessity giving rise to its exercise. The sanction of dismissal with prejudice for lack of prosecution is most severe to the private litigant and could, if used excessively, disserve the dignitary purpose for which it is invoked. It remains constant in our jurisprudence that the dignity of a court derives from the respect accorded its judgment. Too often, that dignity is eroded, not enhanced, by too free of a recourse to rules foreclosing considerations of claims on the merit[s].
>
> ....
>
> It is our task to supervise the administration of justice in the circuit courts, and to that end, we must ensure that fair standards of

---

[19] *See In re Orshansky*, 804 A.2d 1077, 1092 (D.C. 2002)
[20] *Id.* at 1092.
[21] *Id.* at 1092–93.

procedure are maintained. Judicial supervision and responsibility implies the duty of establishing and maintaining civilized standards of procedure and evidence. Our supervisory and rulemaking authority extends to issuance of sanctions under Rule 41(b), particularly when we are dealing with a procedure for which a uniform practice is desirable. As suggested below, other appellate courts have found that exercise of their authority is appropriate when needed to guarantee litigants fair access to the courts to have their grievances heard on the merits. Of course, our supervisory and rulemaking authority is not a form of free-floating justice, untethered to legal principle. Attempts by an appellate court, for example, to use broad supervisory and rulemaking authority as a way to control the properly vested discretion of the trial court should be squarely rejected. But, on occasion, and we think this is one, we must act to secure rightness and fairness when we are persuaded a procedure followed in a trial court is wrong.[22]

c) **Due Process Distinguished**

Reversing the trial court's denial of a continuance to a mother involved in parental termination proceedings, the Connecticut Court of Appeals noted that in a parental termination proceeding, a denial of a continuance could result in the denial of the parent's due process rights.[23] In this case, the trial court denied a continuance to the mother. The mother had moved for a continuance because the lawyer and guardian *ad litem* for her children died during an extended recess of the trial. Admitting that a "reviewing court ordinarily analyzes a denial of a continuance in terms of whether the court has abused its discretion,"[24] the court explained the role judicial discretion plays in a case such as the one before it:

> If, however, the denial of a continuance is directly linked to the deprivation of a specific constitutional right, some courts analyze the denial in terms of whether there has been a denial of due process.
>
> Even if the denial of a motion for a continuance on the ground of lack of due process can be directly linked to a claim of a denial of a specific constitutional rights, if the reasons given for the continuance do not support any interference with the specific constitutional right, the court's analysis will revolve around whether the trial court abused its discretion. In other words, the

---

[22] *Dimon v. Mansy*, 479 S.E.2d 339, 344–45 (W. Va. 1996) (holding that Rule 41(b) dismissals for failure to prosecute require that the non-movant have notice and an opportunity to be heard prior to dismissal).

[23] *In re Shaquanna M.*, 767 A.2d 155, 162 (Conn. App. Ct. 2001).

[24] *Id.* at 162 ("This is so where the denial is not directly linked to a specific constitutional right.").

constitutional right alleged to have been violated must be shown, not merely alleged.

As we have noted, many cases involving motions for a continuance do not divorce a claim of a denial of due process from one claiming an abuse of discretion and discuss both. In this case, we analyze the respondent's claim in terms of a denial of dues process for the following reasons.

Discretion involves choice by a court to do or not to do something that one cannot demand as an absolute right. Courts exercise discretion in cases where impartial minds could hesitate, which exercise usually entails a balancing of the relative gravity of the factors involved. An abuse of discretion exists when a court could have chosen different alternatives but has decided the matter so arbitrarily as to vitiate logic, or has decided it based on improper or irrelevant factors. Some cases involving motions for a continuance analyze the facts in terms of discretion and then state that some denials are so arbitrary as to violate due process.... An abuse of discretion occurs when an injustice has been done. Discretion implies the absence of a hard and fast rule or a mandatory procedure regardless of the circumstances.

A denial of constitutional due process, when shown by the particular facts, does not involve discretion because due process is an absolute right guaranteed by the constitution and allows the court no choice. "Due process" may be a phrase impossible of precise definition, but when an act is shown by reliable facts to affect a specific constitutional right, such as the constitutional interests of parents in their children, the analysis should turn on whether a due process violation exists rather than whether there has been an abuse of discretion. A discretionary act and an act requiring due process are mutually exclusive.[25]

d) Discretion as Judgment Guided by Law

The leading case espousing this description of discretion is *Langnes v. Green.*[26] Adding its own gloss to the Supreme Court's holding, the Maryland Court of Appeals quoted *Langnes* approximately ten years ago in a case involving a trial judge's order directing a juvenile delinquent to pay restitution:

The term discretion means the absence of a hard and fast rule [citing *Langnes*]. Judicial discretion has been defined as follows:

---

[25] *Id.* at 162–64.
[26] 282 U.S. 531, 544 (1931).

Judicial discretion is a composite of many things, among which are conclusions drawn from an objective criteria; it means a sound judgment exercised with regard to what is right under the circumstances and without doing so arbitrarily or capriciously. Where the decision or order of the trial court is a matter of discretion it will not be disturbed on review except on a clear showing of abuse of discretion, that is, discretion manifestly unreasonable, or exercised on untenable grounds, or for untenable reasons.[27]

Reversing a trial court's rejection of a plea agreement for an abuse of discretion, the Appellate Division of the New Jersey Superior Court has described discretion as follows:

While it is certainly true that a trial court has wide discretion in deciding whether to accept a plea, it must be a "sound discretion." Judicial discretion is not unbounded and it is not the personal predilection of the particular judge.

Not long after adoption of the current state constitution, Judge Jayne, sitting with Judge McGeehan and then Judge William J. Brennan, Jr., had occasion to consider the nature of judicial discretion:

It has been said that judicial is that discretion which is not and cannot be governed by any fixed principles and definite rules because the possible eventualities to be dealt with in the exercise of that power cannot be specifically catalogued. Such a definition obviously offends accuracy. Chief Justice Marshall in his decision rendered in *Osborn* stated: Judicial power is never exercised for the purpose of giving effect to the will of the judge; always for the purpose of giving effect... to the will of the law.

Lord Mansfield had said in *Rex v. Wilkes* that judicial discretion means sound discretion, guided by law. It must be governed by rule, not by humour. It must not be arbitrary, vague and fanciful, but legal and regular. Perhaps a more accurate composite definition is that judicial discretion is the option which a judge may exercise between the doing and the not doing of a thing which cannot be demanded as an absolute legal right, guided by the spirit, principles, and analogies of the law, and founded upon the reason and conscience of the judge, to a just result in the light of the particular circumstances of the case.

---

[27] *In re Don Mc.*, 686 A.2d 269, 272 (Md. 1996).

> And so it is universally recognized that the authority to exercise judicial discretion is not an arbitrary power of the individual judge, to be exercised when, and as, his caprice, or passion, or partiality may dictate, or forsooth as his vindictiveness or his idiosyncrasies may inspire. [*Smith v. Smith*, 85 A.2d 523 (N.J. Super. App. Div. 1951)]

> Similar thoughts have been expressed in other decisions. In *Wasserstein v. Swern & Co.*, 84 N.J. Super. 1, 6, 200 A.2d 783 (App. Div. [1964]), we said:

> Preliminary, it may be said that judicial discretion means *legal* discretion in the exercise of which the court must take account of the law applicable to the particular circumstances of the case and be governed accordingly. Implicit is conscientious judgment directed by law and reason and looking to a just result. Consequently, if the trial judge misconceives the applicable law or misapplies it to the factual complex, in total effect the exercise of discretion lacks a foundation and becomes an arbitrary act. When this occurs it is the duty of the reviewing court to adjudicate the controversy in the light of the applicable law in order that a manifest denial of justice be avoided.

> Our concern in the present case arises from the insufficient factual underpinning for the trial court's and the legal mistakes in the court's rationale....[28]

The court concluded that the trial court had abused its discretion in rejecting the plea because, in the appellate court's view, "the facts presented a classic case for an aggravated manslaughter plea" and the trial court apparently rejected the plea because "a jury could also" have found "defendant guilty of murder as a result of the knowing infliction of serious bodily injury."[29]

An earlier case before the same court, this time reviewing a trial court's judicial review of a police department's disciplinary decision against one of its officers, distinguished between discretion that leads to a "dispositional result" in a case from discretion stemming from "procedural considerations":

> The... trial court's power to modify the [police department's] sanction has consistently been regarded as self-evident, with only one limitation thus far declared: that the penalty imposed on the municipal level may not be increased or enhanced on judicial review.

---

[28] *State v. Madan*, 840 A.2d 874, 881–82 (N.J. Super. Ct. App. Div. 2004).

[29] *Id.* at 882 ("The possibility of a defendant being found guilty of a greater offense, however, does not, in and of itself, provide a basis for rejecting a plea.").

Notwithstanding the scope of its authority, the trial court is not a free agent in this regard, however. While the determination of the sanction to be applied where a dereliction of duty has been found is, to a great extent, a discretionary exercise, judicial discretion is not unguided or uncontrolled.

Judicial discretion, sound discretion guided by law so as to accomplish substantial justice and equity, is a magisterial, not a personal discretion. It is legal discretion, in which the judge must take account of the applicable law and be governed accordingly. If the judge misconceives or misapplies the law, his discretion lacks a foundation and becomes an arbitrary act. When that occurs, the reviewing court should adjudicate the matter in light of the applicable law to avoid a manifest denial of justice.

There are, to be sure, at least two distinct categories of judicial discretion. The first involves the latitude to reach a dispositional result based upon facts found from the evidence. The second is associated with the court's authority to manage the conduct of cases and to make rulings, even those with substantive effect, that stem from procedural considerations or reflect the manner in which the parties have litigated the case.

With respect to the latter category, we are enjoined to accord substantial deference to such rulings of trial judges and not to invalidate such determinations merely because from our examination of the record we believe that we would have decided differently. Even with regard to the former, just as we are obliged to consider [f]indings [of fact to be] binding on appeal when supported by adequate, substantial and credible evidence, we are charged to accord substantial regard to the conclusions of trial judges and to discretionary determinations that flow from them. Mandates of deference do not apply when issues of law are involved, however.[30]

After discussing the meaning of discretion generally, the court described how its discussion would apply to the review of the trial court's decision in the case before it:

Although the statute governing judicial review of disciplinary proceedings against police employees in non-civil-service municipalities, [the relevant statute] is couched in terms that confer decisional discretion upon the trial judge[;] that discretion, too, must be exercised in conformity with applicable rules of law

---

[30] *Cosme v. Borough of E. Newark Twp. Comm.*, 698 A.2d 1287, 1292–93 (N.J. Super. Ct. App. Div. 1997).

14

grounded either on clear statutory declarations or upon the types of policy considerations that inform case law standards which are not based on explicit statutory criteria. The determination whether or not a trial judge has pronounced judgment agreeably with the applicable rule of law, is, in this connection, as in all others, one to be made independently by an appellate court, unfettered by principles of decisional deference.

We are called upon to determine not only whether the trial judge's discretion to modify the penalty imposed on the municipal level a fair and equitable result that flowed logically from the record before him, but also whether, as a matter of law, the particular result reached was one that is or ought to be available in the circumstances. After examining all the available arguments and authority so ably provided by counsel for the parties and discovered independently, we conclude that in ordering a one-year suspension from plaintiff's employment, the trial judge applied a mistaken view of the law.[31]

The Ninth Circuit added a gloss on the "judgment guided by law" description of judicial discretion by pointing out that the key question is not the trial court's judgment itself but the extent to which and appellate court will tolerate that judgment.[32] In *Harman*, the appellate court considered whether to apply a *de novo* or and abuse of discretion standard of review to a trial court's decision to remand a social security case to the administration as opposed to ordering the immediate payment of benefits.[33] The court first distinguished "matters of discretion" from "questions of law" and "questions of fact" and noted that the parties contested whether the trial court's decisions was a question of law or a matter of discretion.[34]

---

[31] *Id.* at 1293–94.

[32] *Harman v. Apfel*, 211 F.3d 1172, 1176 (9th Cir. 2000).

[33] *Id.* at 1175 ("Here, the task of divining a fruitful analytical framework is particularly difficult because other questions which intuitively seem likely subjects for appellate review have been addressed by the courts only rarely and, moreover, have yielded conflicting results.").

[34] *Id.* at 1175 The court explained further the difference between the two standards of review:

> In their treatise on federal standards of review, Childress and Davis suggest that the abuse of discretion label appears to describe a *range* of appellate responses with varying degrees of deference handed down. Normally, the decision of a trial court is reversed under the abuse of discretion standard only when the appellate court is convinced firmly that the reviewed decision lies beyond the pale of reasonable justification under the circumstances. In contrast, in undertaking *de novo* review, the appellate court accords no deference to the trial court, but rather determines for itself whether the administrative decision should be reversed on the ground that it is arbitrary, capricious, an abuse of discretion, or contrary to law.

The court concluded its discussion of discretion by noting the difficulty of distinguishing between *de novo* and abuse of discretion review:

> While the distinction between these standards seems clear enough in the abstract, in practice the distinction often begins to blur as a body of appellate case law begins to develop with respect to issues which frequently are the subject of appeals. Under either standard of review, the case law eventually creates a template which may be placed over trial court decisions as a matter of law fall inside or outside the guidelines of permissibility.
>
> In such situations, perhaps the most important difference between the two standards has to do with which court's judgment is paramount. In the context of *de novo* review, a trial court's error, or lack thereof, is defined by the *appellate court's* exercise of judgment. With abuse of discretion review, error is defined by the appellate court's tolerance for the trial court's judgment. In determining the proper standard of review in this case and other like it, we must decide whether the task of reviewing a decision to remand a cause for further proceedings rather than for immediate payment of benefits tests our facility for judgment or our capacity for tolerance.[35]

e)   Discretion as Decision Guided by What is Right and Equitable

After Vermont charged defendant Hunt with first-degree murder, defendant sought to plead guilty.[36] Vermont at the time had a system in which two non-lawyer assistant judges could consider the plea along with the presiding judge, who had a legal education and training. In the present case, the presiding judge had accepted the plea agreement but the two lay judges had effectively overruled the presiding judge and rejected the plea. Defendant argued (1) that the lay judges did not possess jurisdiction over the acceptance of rejection of plea agreements and (2) that the lay judges' rejection of the plea agreement violated defendant's due process rights.[37] The core of defendant's argument (to which the state apparently conceded) was that the lay assistant judges had impermissibly decided a question of law when ruling on his plea agreement.[38] The court rejected this argument, stating that the rejection of a plea agreement was within the trial court's discretion.[39] The court explained:

---

[35] *Id.* at 1176.

[36] *See generally State v. Hunt*, 485 A.2d 109 (Vt. 1984).

[37] *Id.* at 111.

[38] *Id.* at 112. The court characterized the argument as follows:

> Although disputes of fact and of law may very have been the impetus for plea bargaining between the parties, the Agreement itself, which was the culmination of those negotiations, contained no legal issues for the trial court to resolve in conjunction with its acceptance or rejection....
>
> Nevertheless, the State and the defendant contend that acceptance or rejection of the Agreement calls upon the ability of the lay

As previously noted, *Dunkerley* only limited assistant judges from ruling on legal issues raised during a criminal trial; it did not address issues calling for resolution by the exercise of judicial discretion. Therefore, *Dunkerley* is not controlling and imposes no limitations on the assistant judges' exercise of judicial discretion in passing on the acceptance or rejection of the Agreement proffered to the full court in this case. [Vermont procedural Rule 54(c)] tracks *Dunkerley*, but goes one step further and permits the assistant judges to participate with the presiding judge in determining the facts involved in mixed questions of law and fact, [however] *[a]pplication of the law to the facts so found* shall be determined by the Presiding Judge in each instance. (Emphasis added by the court). Thus, in order for [Rule 54(c)] to govern a particular situation, there must be *facts* to find and *law* to apply. This is not the case in accepting or rejecting the Agreement here. Neither the State nor the defendant has suggested that the court should have made findings of fact when the Agreement was offered and rejected. Similarly they have nowhere suggested that any conclusions of law then be derived from facts found [Rule 54(c)] applies to situations such as a motion to suppress evidence where first facts must be found and then law applied. Accepting or rejecting the Agreement in the case at hand involves nothing of this sort and therefore, is not subject to the dictates of [Rule 54(c)].

....

In this context, [the judges'] rejection of the Agreement was an exercise of judicial discretion. Neither the State nor the defendant argues that [Rule 54(c)] or *Dunkerley* precludes the assistant judges from exercising judicial discretion.

....

"Discretion of course means sound discretion, not discretion exercised arbitrarily, but with due regard for that which is right and

---

assistant judges to recognize and understand the impact on this case of relevant case law, statutes, and federal and state constitutional standards. In addition, they argue, the lay judges must be able to evaluate the State's ability to prove the defendant's guilty beyond a reasonable doubt as well as to evaluate the merits of defendant's plea of not guilty and his defense of insanity or diminished mental capacity. Because of the complexity of these evidentiary and constitutional issues, both the State and the defendant insist that only a lawyer trained judge would be able to weigh intelligently the propriety and fairness of the Agreement.

[39] *Id.* at 113 ("Neither the litigants nor the amicus briefs have cited any instance where the assistant judges have been excluded from participating in sentencing procedures which required the exercise of judicial discretion.").

equitable under the circumstances, and dictated by reason and conscience to a just result"....[40]

With respect to defendant's argument that the assistant judges had no jurisdiction to reject his guilty plea, the court concluded:

> When the presiding judge in the case before us spoke of the rejection of the Agreement, he spoke for a majority of the court. A ruling such as this should reflect the discretion of the majority of the court unless specifically prohibited by the rule. Had the assistant judges decided a question of law, we would have an issue to decide under the rule. But the record reveals no rulings by the assistant judges on questions of law. Just because the presiding judge had reservations about the validity of some of his previous legal rulings at suppression hearings, we cannot conclude that [Rule 54(c)] barred the exercise of judicial discretion by the full court.
>
> In exercising judicial discretion in accepting or rejecting a plea bargain agreement, the presiding lawyer trained judge and the lay assistant judges each registers his or her independent judgment, based upon heritage, environment, education and a myriad of other influences including the Agreement itself and the record before the court. There is nothing in the legal training of the presiding judge which makes him or her more qualified than a lay judge to exercise discretion in considering a plea bargain agreement.[41]

The court also rejected defendant's due process argument, concluding the "availability of appeal," "the presence of the lawyer trained presiding judge below" and "the limits on the authority" of the assistant judges gave defendant sufficient protections to safeguard his due process rights.[42]

Judge Peck dissented, arguing that the majority had "fled back across the Rubicon" by expanding the powers of assistant judges who "were not trained or qualified" to review plea agreements.[43] In doing so, the dissent—citing to multiple authorities—attacked the court's definition of "judicial discretion" on the grounds that it did not account for the "legal aspects of discretion":

> The majority undertakes to define "judicial discretion" by accepting, without analysis, the statement of a federal district court in 1964.... This definition is appropriate enough in the context of the case in which it appears. There was no need to address the legal

---

[40] *Id.*
[41] *Id.* at 114–15.
[42] *Id.* at 117.
[43] *Id* at 118 (Peck, J., dissenting).

aspects of judicial discretion; it was not an issue, and certainly it did not involve lay judges....

No less a tribunal than the United States Supreme Court had occasion to recognize that "law" is an integral part of judicial discretion. Stating a definition, virtually identical to the definition relied on by the majority, except for the element that is the true key to the case at bar, the Supreme Court said:

"When invoked as a guide to judicial action it [discretion] means a sound discretion, that is to say, a discretion exercised not arbitrarily or willfully, but with regard to what is right and equitable under the circumstances *and the law*, and directed by the reason and conscience of the judge to a just result."

....

In an early opinion written by Chief Justice John Marshall, the United States Supreme Court held:

"Courts are the mere instruments of the law, and can will nothing. When they are said to exercise a discretion, it is a mere legal discretion, a discretion to be exercised in discerning the course prescribed by law; and, when that is discerned, it is the duty of the Court to follow it. Judicial power is never exercised for the purpose of giving effect to the will of the Judge; always for the purpose of giving effect to the will of the Legislature; or, in other words, to the will of the law."

[D]iscretion means *legal* discretion, in the exercise of which the trial judge must take account of the law applicable to the particular circumstances of the case and be governed accordingly. Discretion contemplates a conclusion based on a logical rationale founded upon proper *legal standards*. Discretion means a *legal discretion* to be exercised in discerning the course prescribed by law *according to principles established by the adjudicated cases*. It means a *legal discretion*, controlled and limited by sound *principles of law applied to the facts*. Discretion is a *legal discretion*, guided and controlled by fixed *legal principles*. It is not a personal discretion, but a legal discretion exercised according to principles of law. Discretion means a judicial discretion calling for the invocation by a *trained mind* producing a result in conformity to law. The exercise of discretion means *the application of statutes and legal principles to all of the facts of a case*.[44]

---

[44] *Id.* at 118–19 (Peck, J., dissenting).

The court concluded that "the vast majority of courts, and probably all courts now" "agree that judicial discretion means legal discretion," which both "contemplates the understanding and application of legal standards, principles of law, and of adjudicated decisions" and "envisions the exercise" of discretion "by a law-trained judge."[45]

The dissent also argued that by not treating a plea agreement as a mixed question, the court had failed "to understand the nature of mixed questions of law and fact":

> They are not like apples and oranges mixed together in a basket, each unit of which may be identified as one or the other and separated out. A mixed question is analogous to a crossbred animal. In the latter instance there is but one animal, not two. In the former there is but one question, although it contains elements of law and elements of fact. That, I think, is what the parties are arguing, and they are right. Quite apart from the nature of judicial discretion itself, when the question before the court was whether to accept or reject the agreement, that question in itself was an inseparable mixture of the standards and principles of law to be applied to the fact of the proposed agreement and other surrounding facts. Therefore, the fact that the ruling was discretionary is immaterial. The ruling embraced a question of law; therefore, the action of the assistant judges was beyond their jurisdiction.[46]

f)   Discretion and the Conscience of the Judge

Although the Maryland Court of Appeals' holding in *City of Bowie v. Prince George's* County pertained to a decision of the local land-use planning board, the court in dicta described discretion as an exercise of the governmental actor's "conscience."[47] The court first reiterated its distinction between a governmental agency's "ministerial" functions and "quasi-judicial" functions that "are not purely

---

[45] *Id.* at 119 (Peck, J., dissenting). The dissent continued:
> The assistant judges, who are neither trained nor qualified, were confronted here with the determination and application of the law and legal standards and principles. Not only did they participate in the ruling, they overruled the presiding judge. In asserting a jurisdiction they never had, they violated the defendant's fundamental constitutional right to due process. Discretion in the judicial sense does not exist in a vacuum; it is inextricably bound up with the law and the application of the legal standards and principles as the cases cited above indicate.

Id. at 120.
[46] *Id.*
[47] 863 A.2d 976, 991 (Md. 2004).

20

and completely judicial or legislative in nature, but have qualities or incidents resembling them."[48] The court explained the distinction further:

> Ministerial acts are objective in nature and include, for example, the issuance of a building permit, predicated upon presentation of final plat approval, as in the case *sub judice*. On the other hand, quasi-judicial functions employ the use of discretion, a term which denotes freedom to act according to one's judgment in the absence of a hard and fast rule. When applied to public officials, discretion is the power conferred upon them by law to act officially under certain circumstances according to the dictates of their own judgment and conscience, and uncontrolled by the judgment or conscience of others. While it may be said that [i]n a strict sense, every action of a government employee, except perhaps a conditioned reflex action, involves the use of some degree of discretion, the act of determining conformance of a final plat to a preliminary plat, as in the case *sub judice*, involves no application of discretion in respect to facts.[49]

g)   Equitable Discretion and Summary Judgment

In *M.D. Fleetwood v. Med Center Bank*, the Texas Court of Appeals held that a trial court had improperly granted summary judgment in an equitable proceeding relating to a land foreclosure.[50] In doing so, the court distinguished between cases governed by legal principles and cases governed by equitable principles.[51] In the former case, a trial court "need only review the summary judgment evidence and, on the basis of established rules of relevancy, decide if that evidence establishes the

---

[48] *Id.*

[49] *Id.* (quoting *Schneider v. Hawkins*, 16 A.2d 861, 864 (Md. 1940). The *Schneider* court described the discretion of a probate court thus:

> The term discretion denotes freedom to act according to one's judgment in the absence of a hard and fast rule. When applied to public officials, discretion is the power conferred upon them by law to act officially under certain circumstances according to the dictates of their own judgment and conscience and uncontrolled by the judgment or conscience of others. Judicial discretion is defined as the power of a court to determine a question upon fair judicial consideration with regard to what is right and equitable under the law and the circumstances, and directed by reason and conscience to a just result. When a court has authority to act within its discretion, it is vested with power to decide as it considers proper, and its discretion is not subject to review by the Court of Appeals.

16 A.2d at 864.

[50] 786 S.W.2d at 550, 557 (Tex. App. 1990) ("For all of the foregoing reasons, we conclude that the present record does not show there is no genuine issue as to any material fact, nor does it show that Med Center is entitled to judgment as a matter of law.").

[51] *Id.* at 556.

fact... as a matter of law."[52] "In a case governed by equitable principles, on the other hand, there are no such clear guidelines for determining what is a material fact."[53] The court noted that "in an equitable action," a trial court must "often take into consideration a myriad of circumstances and factors that would be immaterial in a legal action."[54] The court then discussed the role judicial discretion plays in a trial court's decision to award summary judgment in an equitable action:

> Further, trial courts have a measure of discretion in all cases governed by equitable principles. "Discretion" has been said to arise when an act may be performed in one [of] two or more ways, either of which would be lawful, and where it is left to the will or judgment of the performer to determine in which way it shall be performed.
>
> The notion of discretion is not altogether consistent with the concept of summary judgment, the purpose of which is to eliminate patently unmeritorious claims and untenable defenses. As one noted Texas jurist stated,
>
> "If there is a range of equitable discretion within the authority of the trial judge apart from his authority to find facts, reviewable only for abuse of discretion, the matters which may be so determined are more nearly analogous to fact inferences to be drawn from the entire record than to conclusions of law resulting from application of established rules to undisputed facts. Consequently, such discretion should not be exercised without development of the evidence at a full trial. It cannot properly be exercised on affidavits and other summary-judgment evidence designed to show that the moving party is entitled to judgment as a matter of law. Summary judgment is proper only when the summary-judgment proof shows that no question of equitable discretion exists."
>
> To the extent that Judge Guittard may have been asserting that summary judgment is *never* proper in equity cases, we are constrained... to disagree. His logic applies, strongly, however, in cases such as the present one, where the summary judgment record does not fully develop the facts on which the trial court's equitable discretion must be exercised, and where the facts that are developed, though uncontroverted, can give rise to more than one reasonable inference. Trial courts should, therefore, be even more

---

[52] *Id.*

[53] *Id.*

[54] *Id.* ("This places an extraordinary burden on litigants in attempting to show—and courts in purporting to conclude—that there is no genuine issue as to any material fact.").

cautious than usual before granting summary judgments in equitable actions.[55]

h)   Discretion and the Burden of Proof

The Colorado Supreme Court has stated that neither party has the burden of persuasion when a matter is committed to the discretion of the trial court.[56] Petitioner Riggs, who had been acquitted of murder due to insanity, requested that the trial court allow his "temporary removal... for treatment and rehabilitation."[57] Upon the state's objection, the trial court conducted a hearing, and ultimately denied defendant's release. The intermediate court reversed because the state did not prove by "preponderance of the evidence that such removal was unwarranted."[58] Reversing the intermediate appellate court, the court first pointed out that "the statutory language strongly implies that the decision" whether to allow temporary removal "is a matter of trial court discretion."[59] The court found the discretionary nature of the trial court's decision dispositive of the case:

> In its abstract sense, judicial discretion implies the absence of any settled legal standard that controls the controversy at hand. Judicial discretion therefore means that the court is not bound to decide the issue one way or another, but has the power to choose between two or more courses of action and is not bound in all cases to choose one over the other. Because there is no single correct answer, under any given set of facts, the outcome is never predetermined by the failure of either party to shoulder a burden of persuasion, and review of the court's decision is limited to an inquiry into whether the court abused its discretion in making the choice that it did. Discretionary decisions will not be disturbed unless the court's action was manifestly arbitrary, unreasonable, or unfair.[60]

The court also emphasized the "public safety" aspect of the trial court's decision:

> While the temporary removal provisions may not specify particular factors upon which the court's approval should be based, the entire statutory scheme of automatic commitment and conditional release

---

[55] *Id.* at 556–57.

[56] *People v. Riggs*, 87 P.3d 109, 114 (Colo. 2004) The court's holding was that "the court of appeals erred in imposing [a preponderance] burden of proof on what is a matter of discretion for the district court." *Id.* at 110–11.

[57] *Id.* at 111.

[58] *Id.* at 112.

[59] *Id.* at 114 (noting that the relevant statute requires the trial court's "approval" of temporary removal). ("The very act of approval imports the act of passing judgment, the use of discretion, and the determination as a deduction therefrom unless limited by the context of the statute.").

[60] *Id.*

leaves no doubt that the court's overriding concern in dealing with the release of insanity acquittees must be one of public safety. Permitting the removal of an insanity acquittee from confinement without proper supervision, before he is able to satisfy the statutory prerequisites for release, arguably poses an even greater threat to public safety than release without adequate terms and conditions to prevent relapse. Although an insanity acquittee has a limited right to treatment, he has no right to treatment outside the institution in which he has been placed, except with the approval of the court. Because the court is not itself granted the authority to impose conditions on such treatment, it must therefore satisfy itself that any proposal for removal for treatment and rehabilitation will be consistent with the safety of both the public and the acquittee....[61]

i)   Using "Discretion" to Determine the Appropriate Standard of Review

An opinion of the Maryland Court of Appeals, a court that apparently discusses the meaning of discretion frequently, illustrates nicely how an appellate court will use the concept of "discretion" to determine the appropriate standard of review in a given case.[62] Reviewing both an order enjoining a landowner's building housing on

---

[61] *Id.* at 114–15. *See also In re D.T.*, 818 N.E. 2d 1214, 1221 (Ill. 2004) (state's petition for parental termination). With respect to discretion and the burden of proof, the *D.T.* court stated:

> Although we agree that determination of a child's best interests presents a difficult and delicate task, requiring a nuanced analysis of the statutory factors, we disagree that the difficulty of the task facing the trial court justifies relieving the [State] of its burden to demonstrate its entitlement to the relief it seeks. We also disagree with the suggestion that "sound discretion" is some sort of "nontraditional" standard of proof—traditional, nontraditional, or otherwise....
>
> ...Sound discretion says nothing about the degree of confidence the trial judge must have in the correctness of his or her factual conclusions concerning the child's best interests. Rather... sound discretion implies the degree of deference the trial court's decision will be given by a reviewing court. Thus, sound discretion is tied to the standard of review; it does not identify a standard of proof.

Id. at 1222–23. The *D.T.* court went on to hold that abuse of discretion—which the court called "the most deferential standard of review" and "next to no review at all" should not apply in a parental termination case. It found that the abuse standard was more appropriate "for decisions made by a trial judge in overseeing his or her courtroom or in maintaining the progress of the trial." *Id.* at 1223 (finding no "analysis as to the origin or reason behind the appellate court's application of" an abuse of discretion review in the cited authorities) ("Mere repetition of a purported rule of law does not establish its validity."). Justice Garman, writing in dissent, pointed out that abuse of discretion review also applies to substantive matters, such as the sentencing of a criminal defendant. *Id.* at 1230 (Garman, J., dissenting).

[62] *See J.L. Matthews, Inc. v. Maryland-Nat'l Capital Park & Planning Comm'n.*, 792 A.2d 288, 300.

24

its property and an *in limine* order excluding evidence showing how construction would affect the fair market value, the court first determined the appropriate standards of review. It concluded that is should employ *de novo* review with respect to both issues.[63] The court explained its decision thus:

> Appellate review of a trial court ruling on the admissibility of evidence often is said to be based on the standard that such a ruling is left to the sound discretion of the trial court, so that absent a showing of abuse of that discretion, its ruling will not be disturbed on appeal. Application of that standard, however, depends on whether the trial judge's ruling under review was based on a discretionary weighing of relevance in relation to other factors or on a pure conclusion of law. When the trial judge's ruling involves a weighing, we apply the more deferential abuse of discretion standard. On the other hand, when the trial judge's ruling involves a legal question, we review the trial court's ruling *de novo*. Likewise, if a court's ruling constitutes a conclusion of law based upon the facts of a case, the court's interpretation of the law enjoy[s] no presumption of correctness on review and is not entitled to any deference.
>
> In this case, it is clear the trial judge based its grant of Respondent's second motion *in limine* on a conclusion of law. The lower court found that the presentation of evidence of what Petitioner could have done, but for the injunction, and how that might have affected fair market value was not permissible in a condemnation trial. Because it was based on the trial judge's interpretation of the scope of condemnation proceedings, it constituted a legal conclusion. Therefore, we review the trial court's ruling *de novo*.
>
> Likewise, although the decision to issue or not issue injunctive relief obviously implicates a court's equitable powers, for which an abuse of discretion standard would be applied ordinarily on appellate review of the exercise of that power, the nature of the underlying cause of action in the present case, the collateral role played by the injunctive relief in the action and the purely legal question presented by the clash between Petitioner's constitutionally-grounded rights to just compensation and to make a lawful use of its property and Respondent's attempted substitution of injunctive relief for its inability to use "quick-take" condemnation authority, lead us to conclude that *de novo* review is the proper standard to apply to Petitioner's threshold question.[64]

---

[63] *Id.* at 301.
[64] *Id.* at 300–01.

§ 1.2. Discretion as a Jurisprudential Concept: The Literature

a) Discretion Defined

Bouvier's *Law Dictionary* defines discretion thus:

> That part of the judicial function which decides questions arising in the trial of a cause, according to the particular circumstances of each case, and as to which the judgment of the court is uncontrolled by fixed rules of law.

> The power exercised by courts to determine questions to which no strict rule of law is applicable but which, from their nature, and the circumstances of the case, are controlled by the personal judgment of the court.

> Discretion when applied to a court of justice means sound discretion guided by law. Judicial discretion is a mere legal discretion–a discretion in discerning the course presented by law; and what that has discerned it is the duty of the court to follow. The discretion is not willful or arbitrary, but legal [to set aside a judicial sale], and though its exercise be not purely a matter of law, yet it involves a matter of law or legal inferences. A legal discretion is one that is regulated by well known and established principles of law.

> Bishop on Mar. & Div. § 830, defines it as "denoting a sort of individual liberty, a sort of liberty in the collective judges and an adherence to legal principles blended in such a way as shall constitute an established course of justice bending to the circumstances of the case instead of requiring the cases to bend to it."

> But if the word discretion in this connection [injunction] is used in its secondary sense, and by it is meant that the chancellor has the liberty and power of acting, in finally settling property rights, at his discretion, without the restraint of the legal and equitable rules governing those rights [then that power is to be denied]

> It would tend to clearness and exactness if discretion were used only with reference to those matters where the action of the trial judge is final.

> Whether or not a particular question is one of discretion is in almost every case a matter of settled law, and the individual court or judge has no power to place it within or without that category. It is only when a question arises which, according to precedent, is

treated as such that the judicial discretion is invoked and its exercise cannot be reviewed.

> The discretion of a judge is said by Lord Camden to be the law of tyrants: it is always unknown, it is different in different men; it is casual, and depends upon constitution, temper, and passion. In the best, it is oftentimes caprice; in the worst, it is every vice, folly, and passion to which human nature is liable. But the prevailing opinion is that discretion must not be arbitrary, fanciful, and capricious; it must be legal and regular, governed by rule, not by humor....[65]

Professor Bower's early treatise on judicial discretion offered a similar definition:

> In all cases courts must exercise a discretion in the sense of being discreet, circumspect, prudent, and exercising cautious judgment. But that is a duty generally laid upon all officers as well as private individuals. Judicial discretion, in its technical sense, means something more. It is that power of decision, exercised to the necessary end of awarding justice, and based upon reason and the law, but for which decision there is no special governing statute or rule. It is obvious that if a special statute prescribes the decision, there is in all instances coming within its purview a restraint upon the judge that precludes the exercise of discretion by him; for the very word, "discretion" implies the absence of restraint. This statement is only apparently at variance with the oft-quoted statement of Lord Mansfield that "Discretion, when applied to a court of justice, means sound discretion guided by law. It must be governed by rule, not by humor; it must not be arbitrary, vague, and fanciful, but legal and regular."... Judicial power, as contra-distinguished from the power of the law, has no existence. Courts are the mere instruments of the law, and can will nothing. When they are said to exercise a discretion, it is a mere legal discretion, discretion to be exercised in discerning the course prescribed by law; and, when that is discerned, it is the duty of the court to follow it. Judicial power is never exercised for the purpose of giving effect to the will of the judge; always for the purpose of giving effect to the will of the legislature; or, in other words, to the will of the law." Such expressions as those quoted do not mean that Courts must search for and find some statute or rule prescribing the manner of doing every act of theirs in the furtherance of proceedings before them. What is meant is that every act of the court, whether or not under the prescription of a rule, must be in accordance with, and sanctioned by, reason and the law. If there be an authoritative command for performance in a particular way, obedience must follow; if not, discretion must be exercised. Whenever a clear and

---

[65] Bouvier's Law Dictionary 884–85 (3d ed. 1914).

well-defined rule has been adopted, not depending upon circumstances, the court has parted with its discretion as a rule of judgment. Discretion may be, and is to a very great extent, regulated by usage or by principles which courts have learned by experience will, when applied to a great majority of cases, best promote the ends of justice, but it is still left to the courts to determine where a case is exactly like in every color, circumstance, and feature to those upon which the usage or principle is founded, or in which it has been applied. Discretion implies that in the absence of positive law or fixed rule, the judge is to decide by his view of expediency or of the demands of equity and justice. By discretion-judicial-discretion-we mean the exercise of final judgment by the court in the decision of such questions of fact as from their nature and the circumstances of the case come peculiarly within the province of the presiding judge to determine, without the intervention and to the exclusion of the functions of a jury. Such discretion must and should be performed in every case with such conscientious intelligence as belongs to the judge, and that is the best that can be done in any case where he is called upon to discharge that duty. While judicial discretion, therefore, denotes power in a court to make decision upon a given phase of procedure untrammeled by a statute or rule prescribing it, the power is never based upon a wild, unbridled license for the assumption of autocratic authority in the particulars acted upon; but there must always be some underlying principle of law as a foundation for the decision. As has been said of such a discretion as the law sanctions: "It is not arbitrary, vague, or fanciful, nor is it to be controlled by humor or caprice, but to be governed by principle and regular procedure for the accomplishment of the ends of right and justice. If errors of law are relied upon, then the judgment of the court is required as to the right rule of law to be applied, and the questions are strictly of legal cognizance." The discretion intended, however, is not a capricious or arbitrary discretion, guided and controlled in its exercise by no fixed legal principles. It is not a mental discretion, to be exercised *ex gratia*, but a legal discretion to be exercised in conformity with the spirit of the law and in a manner to subserve and not to impede or defeat the ends of justice. In a plain case this discretion has no office to perform, and its exercise is limited to doubtful cases where an impartial mind hesitates....[66]

Bowers concluded that the term "judicial discretion" was a misnomer insofar as it implies that the trial court has the final word on discretionary decisions.[67] Although Bowers notes that "appellate courts are teeming with expressions to the effect that certain enumerated matters were in the discretion of the trial court and, therefore,

---

[66] Renzo D. Bowers, The Judicial Discretion of Trial Courts § 10 (1931).
[67] *Id.* at § 11.

would not be reviewed or disturbed," he concludes that "what is in fact meant is that such matters have been reviewed and that the decision of the trial court was right under the particular circumstances and consequently the decision would be permitted to stand."[68]

b)   Rosenberg

Most commentators on judicial discretion cite to one of Maurice Rosenberg's articles on the subject.[69] Although one can find the impressions of Rosenberg's thought on many scholars of judicial discretion, one of his most important contributions is his analytical framework distinguishing primary discretion from secondary discretion:

> If the word discretion convey to legal minds any solid core of meaning, one central idea above all others, it is the idea of *choice*. To say that a court has discretion in a given area of law is to say that it is not bound to decide the question one way rather than another. In this sense, the term suggests that there is no wrong answer to the questions posted-at least, there is no *officially* wrong answer.
>
> Lawyers are instinctively drawn to this meaning of discretion, which is correct as far as it goes. But it is incomplete and, besides,

---

[68] *Id. Bowers* continued:

> Such a discretion as is said to be conferred upon a trial court in passing upon a question of procedure is not different from that abiding in the appellate court in reviewing the decision made. It is merely the capacity of the judge presiding over a particular court to perceive and apply the law of the land to the particular facts as that in each case the legal rights of the parties may be declared and enforced according to the law of the land. An appeal to a judge's discretion is an appeal to his judicial conscience. The discretion must be exercised, not in opposition to, but in accordance with, established principles of law. It is not an arbitrary power, but one which must be exercised wisely and impartially. In its practical application... judicial discretion is substantially synonymous with judicial power.

Id. For an overview of different definitions of discretion, see Ben F. Overton, *The Meaning of Judicial Discretion, in* Judicial Discretion 3 (Smithburn 1991).

[69] *See, e.g.*, Maurice Rosenberg, *Judicial Discretion of the Trial Court, Viewed from Above*, 22 Syracuse L. Rev. 635 (1971). (Excerpts are reprinted with permission of the Syracuse Law Review.) Rosenberg was aware of the inherent complexity of his subject:

> To speak of discretion in relation to law is to open a thousand doorways to discussion. The concept is pervasive and protean, with intimations of both power and responsibility. Even when confined to judicial settings, it manifests itself in numberless ways. Whatever the court, wherever it sits, the judge soon finds himself talking, wondering, and, at times, thinking about discretion and its implications.

Id. at 635.

it conceals a confusing duality by lumping together two distinct types of judicial discretion. They can usefully be referred to as *primary* and *secondary*.

When an adjudicator has the primary type, he has decision-making discretion, a wide range of choice as to what he decides, free from the constraints which characteristically attach whenever legal rules enter the decision process. When the law accords primary discretion in the highest degree in a particular area, it says in effect that the court is free to render the decision it chooses; that decision-constraining rules do not exist here; and that even looser principles or guidelines have not been formulated. In such an area, the court can do no wrong, legally speaking, for there is no *officially* right or wrong answer.

The other type of discretion, the secondary form, has to do with hierarchical relations among judges. It enters the picture when the system tries to prescribe the degree of finality and authority a lower court's decision enjoys in the higher courts. Specifically, it comes into full play when the rules of review accord the lower court's decision an unusual amount of insulation from appellate revision. In this sense, discretion is a review-restraining concept. It gives the trial judge a right to be wrong without incurring reversal.

One source of confusion in treating the subject is that courts tend to use the two types of discretion indiscriminately, interchangeably and without marking the distinction....

That casual conjunction of the two meanings of the concept impedes analysis. Courts at every level of the system are given scope for exercise of primary discretion. For instance, when a statute declares that a decree or order in respect to a particular matter... may be made "in the discretion of the court" and this language is construed as applying to each court in the appellate hierarchy, we have an example of primary discretion. Precise norms are not laid down, decision is intended to pivot on the circumstances of the particular case, and each court along the route is free to reach an independent conclusion as to the result called for by its own sound exercise of discretion. Primary discretion bestows *decision-liberating* choice.

By contrast, secondary discretion is, for practical purposes, confined solely to trial courts, and is essentially a *review-limiting* concept....[70]

---

[70] *Id.* at 636–38. Rosenberg proceeded to compare a trial judge's exercise of secondary discretion to a college football official's (*i.e.*, no instant replay) calls on the field.

30

In a later article, Rosenberg succinctly traced four means by which trial courts come to enjoy some degree of judicial discretion:

> All appellate Gaul, the trial judge would say, is divided into three parts: review of facts, review of law, and review of discretion....
>
> Discretion is a pervasive yet elusive concept.... Despite its pervasiveness, it is hard to grasp hold of just what it means in day-to-day practice....
>
> Let me give... four examples, each chosen because of the source in law, or the place where the bestowal of discretion is embedded or implied. First, so far as federal appellate judges' work is concerned... after a certification is made by the district judge that the three necessary conditions for interlocutory review are satisfied, the statute goes on to say that the court of appeals may thereupon "in its discretion" permit an appeal. Presumably there are standards and guidelines which the appellate court invokes in exercising its discretion to allow an appeal... once the three necessary matters have been certified by the district judge. At all events, the point I want to underscore is that discretion can be accorded at times in the "secondary" or procedural sense by statutory provision.
>
> At other times it occurs as an express provision of a rule rather than in a statute. There are many examples of this. One of them is furnished by Rule 39(b) of the Federal Rules of Civil Procedure, which allows a party, who has missed the boat by failing to make a timely demand for trial by a jury, to catch the next boat by making a tardy request for a jury. The rule says that "despite the failure of a party to demand a jury in an action in which such a demand might have been made as a matter of right, the court 'in its discretion' upon motion may order a trial by jury of any or all issues."... When appellate judges find themselves reviewing an order of the district court granting or denying a trail by jury under Rule 39(b), does it make any difference that the rule specifically uses the words "in its discretion" instead of reading, as it might: "Despite the failure of a party to demand jury trial in an action in which such a demand might have been made as a matter of right, the court upon motion for good cause shall allow the trial by jury"? Would the substitution of the words "for good cause," or "in the interest of justice," or some similar phrase, change the mode of reviewing the district court's order; in short, is there magic in the word "discretion"?

Although the official may make a call that is clearly wrong under an established rule of the game, it will stand.

A third way to raise the issue of review of discretion is to find a procedural rule in which appellate decisions have interpolated the idea of discretion. I once searched the Federal Rules of Civil Procedure from start to finish to discover how many times the word "discretion" occurs. It turned up only ten times. Yet if one reads the decisions of the United States Courts of Appeals and reviews the major treatises, one finds at least forty procedural situations in which the courts of appeals have construed a rule to grant discretion to the district court. The decisions have recognized discretion in the ten rules in which it explicitly appears and additionally in at least three times as many rules in which there is no reference to the word. That would lead [one] to think that it is not important whether discretion is expressly written into the rule or not. Rather, it depends on whether the appellate courts think it should have been there.

Finally, there are situations in which there is no formulary rule governing the situation or the issue, and yet judicial decisions have established that discretion over the matter is lodged in the trial judge....

What all this amounts to is that one can support the existence of discretion in the procedural review sense by referring to express language in statues and rules, by judicial interpretation of rules that are silent on the matter, and by decisions in common law areas that are not subject to formal rules....[71]

c)   The Judicial Hunch

A leading article on judicial discretion by Professor Yablon argues that the historical methods of describing judicial discretion are inadequate.[72] Approaching the problem from a realist's perspective, Yablon first suggested that "judicial intuition" rather than a "legal rule structure" determines the outcome of discretionary decisions:

Jerome Frank's 1932 article, *What the Courts Do in Fact*, provides a good example of the centrality of the judicial hunch in the jurisprudence of the Realists. As its title indicates, Frank's article is intended as an objective empirical description of the activities of trial court judges from the point of view of the practicing lawyer or litigant. From this perspective, Frank derides the notion that

---

[71] Maurice Rosenberg, *Appellate Review of Trial Court Discretion*, 79 F.R.D. 173, 173–75 (1978). (Reprinted with permission of Thomson West.)
[72] *See generally* Charles M. Yablon, *Justifying the Judge's Hunch: An Essay on Discretion*, 41 Hastings L.J. 231 (1990) (discussing historical descriptions of judicial discretion). (©1990 by University of California, Hastings College of the Law. Excerpts reprinted from Hastings Law Journal, Volume 41 Number 2, January 1990, 231,1, by permission.)

lawyers, merely because of their knowledge of legal rules, can predict judicial actions with any degree of certainty. He argues that the legal rules are of marginal importance in most trials, particularly jury trials....

Thus, Frank concludes, the primary determinant of the judicial decision is not the legal rule structure but the "personality of the judge" or the "judicial intuition," that is, the whole set of characteristics that lead the judge to perceive the world, including the plaintiffs, the defendants, and the witnesses, in a particular way. Frank is quite aware of the vagueness of this concept. As he says:

> "The personality of the judge" is a phrase which too glibly describes an exquisitely complicated mass of phenomena. The phrase "judicial hunch" is likewise beautifully vague. But those phrases will do for present purposes. Be it noted that "the personality of the judge" and the "judicial hunch" are not and cannot be described in terms of legal rules and principles.

For Frank and for other Legal Realists, the vagueness of the "judicial hunch" concept was part of its appeal. It helped shake lawyers out of a mind set in which every legal problem had a deductively demonstrable "right answer." This notion that legal certainty could be achieved by careful study of legal rules and concepts was the prime focus of the Realist attack.[73]

Yablon quite rightly acknowledges that other jurisprudential schools would describe the role of judicial discretion differently. Hart, for example, acknowledges "no uniquely discretionary form of decisionmaking, no magical judicial hunch" because "discretion is simply what occurs when the guidance of authoritative legal rules run out" and the judge must supply a new one.[74] Likewise, Dworkin "denies that discretion in any 'strong sense' ever enters into judicial decisionmaking."[75] Yablon explains Dworkin's distinction between judicial discretion in the "strong sense" and the "two weaker senses of discretion":

> Dworkin's "strong sense" of discretion appears equivalent to the freedom a legislator has to promulgate new laws on any basis he deems appropriate. Dworkin carefully notes that exercises of strong discretion can be criticized as unwise or ill considered, but he does not think the term "abuse of discretion" can be applied appropriately to such actions.

---

[73] *Id.* at 237–38.

[74] *Id.* at 239 ("The judge then has the authority and role of a legislator.").

[75] *Id.* at 241.

Dworkin distinguishes strong discretion from two weaker senses of discretion, termed "discretion as judgment" and "discretion as finality," which are found in judicial decisionmaking. "Discretion as judgment" occurs when a judge, in order to apply the rule, must utilize her own evaluative powers and judgment. Dworkin's example is a sergeant ordered to take his five most experienced soldiers on patrol. Obviously, the sergeant must make an evaluation of his soldiers in terms of the somewhat nebulous concept of "experience," and different sergeants may select somewhat different groups. Nonetheless (and this is of key importance to Dworkin) such a decisionmaker is still following a rule, though a somewhat vague and "open textured" one, because the decisionmaker still seeks to conform his conduct to the authoritative norm of "experience."[76]

Turning away from jurisprudence and toward the "practical implications" as to how a discretionary "decision is made, constrained, and reviewed," Yablon concludes that it is "not surprising" "that some legal scholars have chosen to analyze discretion as a characteristic of power relationships in certain institutional arrangements."[77] He concludes this because, in the real world of the courtroom, a "decisionmaker with discretion has power to decide either way, without fear that the decision will be nullified or reversed, unless that discretion is 'abused'."[78] Yablon first discusses in tandem the work of Thurman Arnold (*The Role of Substantive Law and Procedure in the Legal Process*) and Kenneth Culp Davis (*Discretionary Justice: A Preliminary Inquiry*, a leading work an administrative discretion):

> Proceeding from the assumption that discretion as exercised by courts is not fundamentally different from that exercised by bureaucrats, Arnold argues for a discretion that is publicly recognized and acknowledged, exercised by those with expertise in the subject, open to public criticism, and subject to modification if subsequent conditions warrant. One does not find any reverence in Arnold for the magical judicial hunch. Rather, he argues that courts simply do covertly, with little understanding, what bureaucrats do

---

[76] *Id.* at 241–42.

[77] *Id.* at 244.

[78] *Id.* Yablon continues:

> These scholars generally share three characteristics: (1) concern with discretion as a matter of power, often focusing on the institutional arrangements, if any, that constrain or limit that power; (2) greater emphasis on the practical problems of decisionmaking (proceduralists tend to analyze and cite actual case more frequently than the jurisprudes who are often content with a few paradigmatic examples or thought experiments); and, (3) constant awareness of (and often great frustration with) the desire for predictable and general rules of conduct and its inevitable conflict with the needs of individual justice in particular cases.

34

openly and often with greater expertise. Arnold, in short, argues for the creation of the bureaucratic state.[79]

Davis is well aware that a change in the form of [legal] rules would not be a panacea and that rules can often be bent or ignored. Operating under a clearer and more explicit set of rules, however, would nonetheless change the attitudes administrative decisionmakers have toward their role and the decisions they are called upon to make, leading a greater responsibility and equality of treatment. Davis is making the other side of... Arnold's argument. Whereas Arnold thought that describing the judicial process in terms of practical matters of procedure would lead to a more flexible and discretionary attitude on the part of judges, Davis believes that describing the administrative process in terms of clear and explicit rules would shift the attitude of administrators toward greater consistency and equal treatment.

Though both arguments are valid, they rely on a particular set of assumptions about the relationship of decisionmakers to legal language and rules—relationships that are assumed but never delineated. Indeed, Davis' book reveals the difficulties of analyzing and critiquing discretion as a matter of process, without the theoretical framework of the jurisprudes. His call for an end to "unnecessary" discretion invites discussion of the role of law in society and what it means to say that a certain legal arrangement is "necessary." His description of certain discretionary decisions as illegal, despite the fact that they are permitted by the institutional power arrangements, calls for a discussion defining the "law." Most importantly, the notion that it is sometimes desirable to move discretion to different levels in the system points out the need for a theory of institutional competence, an account of why certain decisionmakers are most appropriate to make certain decisions.[80]

Although Yablon acknowledges that Rosenberg's work marks the "beginnings of" "an institutional competence theory" and that it "builds on Davis' and seeks to supply some of the theoretical framework that Davis lacks," he criticizes "Rosenberg's strong separation of internal and external perspectives of decisionmaking."[81] Yablon writes:

Rosenberg's article is a first step toward a theory of institutional competence, and he sets forth criteria for determining when trial judges, rather than appellate courts, should receive deference in the decisionmaking process. Yet, while his criteria are clearer and

---

[79] *Id.* at 245.
[80] *Id.* at 248–49.
[81] *Id.* at 249–50.

more theoretically grounded than Davis' criteria, they still rest on vague and sometimes dubious jurisprudential assumptions. Rosenberg provides three grounds for conferring discretion on the trial judge: (1) when it is "impracticable" to formulate a rule of decision; (2) when the issue before the court is new or unsettled; and, (3) when circumstances critical to the decision are "imperfectly conveyed" by the record on appeal. But because of Rosenberg's purely external, institutional perspective, he fails to deal with the internal jurisprudential issues raised by his criteria. For example, is there a correct response to a discretionary decision when it is impracticable to formulate a rule of decision or when the issue is new or unsettled? There would not seem to be, yet if that is the case, then how can they be reviewed for "abuse of discretion?"[82]

Yablon finds the jurisprudes' understandings of discretion inadequate for two reasons: (1) they assume that "discretionary decisionmaking has a single set of distinguishing characteristics that can be analyzed and described" and (2) they assume that the "analysis can be done solely from the internal perspective of the decision maker."[83] The heart of Yablon's critique, however, lies in the fact that contemporary jurisprudence does not take adequate account of the "judicial hunch":

By seeking a single account of discretionary decisionmaking, the jurisprudential question assumes that discretion is a single thing that can be described or, more precisely, that there are at least some attributes that all discretionary decisions share that may be usefully described at the appropriate level of generality. But as we have seen, the shared presumption of the jurisprudes is a negative one, that not all valid decisions are logically derivable from preexisting rules. It does not support the *positive* assumption that these other valid decisions, lumped together as "discretionary," share any common distinguishing features or characteristics that make possible a positive account of "discretion."...

Such an assertion calls for an analysis of the language of lawyers to determine what kinds of actions by legal decisionmakers are actually referred to as "discretionary." Only against this baseline of actual usage could one begin to examine whether such discretionary decisions share common characteristics. As we have seen, however, the jurisprudes, by and large, tend to eschew such a perspective. They prefer to begin from a theoretical or ideal form of judging and then to identify what aspect of that decisionmaking

---

[82] *Id.* at 250–51 ("Nonetheless, Rosenberg's article represents an important first step in the attempt to combine jurisprudential and institutional perspectives on discretion. This Article will expand on this attempt.").
[83] *Id.* at 256.

process is appropriately labeled "discretionary" within the confines of the theory. Any claims made about usage are accordingly self-fulfilling and are refuted easily (as Greenawalt refutes Dworkin) by reference to external usages that do not comport with the theory.[84]

After criticizing the "proceduralist perspective" for its lack of a "normative theory" of judicial discretion,[85] Yablon attempts to formulate alternative descriptions of the concept. In doing so, he seeks to answer two questions (to which he respectively refers as the "old problem" and the "new problem"): (1) How may a judge "act appropriately within the legal system even though the judge is free (in that she will not be reversed) to give differing, even contradictory answers?, and (2) "What distinguishes instances of doctrinally recognized discretion... from other judicial activities, like statutory or constitutional interpretation in which judges may also decide in contradictory ways?"[86]

In answer to these two questions, Yablon offers several models of judicial discretion. The first model, which he calls "discretion as skill," involves "the exercise of a practice that is neither reducible nor justifiable in terms of a rule."[87] Yablon finds this model "particularly appropriate for decisions" "in which the decisionmaker has a large, but not an exhaustive set of options."[88] He explains "discretion as skill" thus:

[I]n that [the] decision largely is insulated from appellate review, the justification for the freedom assumes not that the judge is acting without constraint, but that she is exercising skillful, practical judgment to "tailor" the most appropriate sentence for that particular case.

The justification of discretion in such cases, the deference to trial court decisions, rests on a claim that the trial judge has special knowledge that enables her to achieve an answer better than any that could be obtained by simply following rules laid down by a higher court or legislature. Trial court opinions involving the appropriateness of criminal sentences differ strikingly from other judicial opinions in their lack of any attempt to apply rules to the sentencing determination. Other than the statutory minima and maxima, traditionally there have been no rules for sentencing, so justification based on rules is not possible.[89]

Yablon's "discretion as skill" model assumes that the decisions before the court involve the court's validly choosing "among a large but not exhaustive set of

[84] *Id.* at 253–54.
[85] *Id.* at 256.
[86] *Id.* at 257.
[87] *Id.* at 262.
[88] *Id.*
[89] *Id.*

outcomes, such as sentencing, setting bail and bonds, and determining what kind of injunction to issue after trial."[90] Yablon acknowledges that many "trial court decisions normally called discretionary have only two possible outcomes, which together constitute not merely the permissible zone of discretion but exhaust the possible outcomes."[91] For such decisions, which "themselves often contain indications of tentativeness or uncertainty," Yablon proposes a "discretion as expediency" model.[92] He explains:

> Rather, it is the tentativeness of such decisions, the fact that they are made under conditions of uncertainty, that provides the underlying institutional justification for trial court discretion. The decisions are justified, not on the grounds that they represent the correct answer, but because they are the best approximation possible under the circumstances. If, indeed, no better answer is possible, then deference to the trial court is justified, not so much on the basis of its presumed superior skill, but on institutional considerations like the need for speed, finality, and predictability. Thus, I refer to this model as "discretion as expediency."
>
> The assumptions underlying this justification are the reverse of those in the first model. It assumes the existence of a presumptively controlling doctrinal rule to which the decision should conform, a "right answer" in theory. It also assumes that at the level of practice, the judge can do no more than approximate the theoretical right answer. The legal rules may give judges a clear and precise theoretical answer as to when to grant a preliminary injunction or exclude certain types of evidence but these rules, though theoretically precise, provide only a rough guide as to how to act in practice. Discretionary decisions of this kind are justified not because they are correct, but because they are close enough, and making a finer determination is either not possible or not worth the time and effort.[93]

Finally, Yablon discusses his model "discretion as creativity," which he describes as "the heroic judge who, through her intuitive grasp of the felt necessities of time and her judicial craft in interpreting existing precedents, is a powerful force for creative social change."[94] Yablon acknowledges that the appellate court exclusively employs this model of discretion when creating new rights or correcting social maladies and questions whether such action is "discretion" at all, as opposed

---

[90] *Id.* at 268.
[91] *Id.* (noting that such decisions "seem to be bipolar, yes or no determinations, no different from most others made by courts").
[92] *Id.* at 269.
[93] *Id.* at 269–70.
[94] *Id.* at 274 (noting that the "creativity" model does not have "substantial influence in Anglo-American law") ("Discretion, in this sense, is quite different form the institutional notion of discretion characterized by appellate deference to trial judge decisionmaking.").

38

to rulemaking or interpretation.[95] Nevertheless, Yablon finds a trial-court "analogue" to creative discretion in "doctrines traditionally associated with equity practice."[96] He writes:

> This kind of discretion seems to be closely analogous to the "heroic" discretion of appellate court judges.... In both cases the judges break out of preexisting rule structure to create a result that looks "wrong" in terms of prior precedent and expectation yet seems "right" in terms of broader societal concerns. When such a ruling is made by the highest court, it becomes a new rule and can have vast societal implications. When such a ruling is made by a trial court, it generally is treated as the exercise of equitable discretion in the individual case, and has little effect on the preexisting rule structure. Thus, considering such decisions discretionary in an institutional sense serves both to authorize trial judges to take such actions occasionally and to limit their impact on the preexisting rules. This is the modern version of the old function of equity courts, which were both outside of and unconstrained by the system of law, yet thereby helped to preserve it.

> Decisions of this kind are not justified, as are the first two models, by reversing the appellate court's assumptions about its institutional competence to review trial court determinations. Rather, they are justified like ordinary legal decisions, by persuading the appellate courts that they are "correct," in that the appellate court would have decided the issue the same way. The difference is that the trial court, in attempting to persuade the appellate court, does not apply the preexisting legal rule, but rather appeals to factors outside the scope of that rule.[97]

d)   Difficulty of Precise Definition

An Ohio appellate judge, (and his law clerk), attempting to determine what "abuse of discretion" should mean under Ohio law, discussed as an initial matter the difficulty that both courts and scholars have in determining what "judicial discretion" means.[98] According to the authors, some courts, perhaps out of confusion as to the nature of discretion, believe that judicial discretion amounts to immunity from review:

> "The judge, even when he is free, is still not wholly free. He is not to innovate at pleasure. He is not a knight-errant, roaming at will in

---

[95] *Id.* at 274–75.

[96] *Id.* at 275.

[97] *Id.* at 276.

[98] *See generally* Mark P. Painter and Paula L. Welker, *Abuse of Discretion: What Should It Mean under Ohio Law?*, 29 Ohio N. U. L. Rev. 209 (2002). (Reprinted with permission of the Ohio Northern University Law Review.)

pursuit of his own ideal of beauty or of goodness. He is to draw his inspiration from consecrated principles. He is not to yield to spasmodic sentiment, to vague and unregulated benevolence. He is to exercise a discretion informed by tradition, methodized by analogy, disciplined by system, and subordinated to the primordial necessity of order in the social life. Wide enough in all conscience is the field of discretion that remains."

As recognized by then New York Court of Appeals Justice Benjamin Cardozo, when a matter is committed to a trial judge's discretion, that discretion is limited and must be exercised in a disciplined and rational manner. If the trial judge does not exercise his or her discretion in a reasoned manner, the trial judge should be reversed on appeal. Unfortunately, counsel and judges at all levels perceive a grant of discretion as immunity from reversal and treat it as such.[99]

Beyond exercising judgment "in a reasoned manner," the authors concede that discretion is "an elusive concept that is very difficult to analyze, because it operates so differently from person to person and from situation to situation."[100] What makes precise definition of "discretion" even more difficult are the differing "gradations of discretion," which this book discusses in detail in Chapter 3.[101] Regarding the different gradations and the difficulties they present, the authors write:

Scholars recognize—although reviewing courts rarely do—that there are gradations of discretion, which require differing amounts of deference. How much deference should be given to the trial judge's exercise of his or her discretion is directly related to why the trial court was given discretion in the first place.

Some exercises of discretion "are so constricted by guidelines or ways to decide that it is stretching the word to even call them discretionary." An example of this type of discretion is found in cases where either by statute or case law the trial judge is required to consider a list of factors and apply them to the facts of the case....

Reviewing courts should afford less deference to trial court judgments in these situations because case law, rules, or statutes have set out clearly established principles, rules, or factors to

---

[99] *Id.* at 209.

[100] *Id.* at 212 ("Judicial discretion has been defined as 'choice.' Choice occurs where, between 'two alternatives or among a possibly infinite number,' there is 'more than one possible outcome, with the selection of the outcome left to the decisionmaker.'") ("However, the concept of discretion or choice defies uniform application [in] all situations.").

[101] *Id.*

consider. Less deference is necessary because a reviewing court is in just as good a position as the trial judge to determine whether the trial judge considered the principles, rules, or factors correctly, considered inappropriate factors or principles, or misapplied the law.[102]

On the other end of the continuum are exercises of discretion that are almost unrestrained. A trial judge is vested with discretion "in supervising his [or her] court, the progress of the trial, the litigation process, and the general operations of the judicial system.... This type of discretion is seemingly unfettered, and a trial court is rarely reversed for abusing its discretion.[103]

Turning to the origins of judicial discretion, the authors contend that at times a grant of discretion is presumed simply on account of the inherent power of a court or because of certain words in a statute:

Where does the trial court obtain its discretion? Discretion may be inherent in the trial judge's role as supervisor of the litigation and manager of his or her courtroom. The ability of a trial court to exercise discretion may be granted, knowingly or unknowingly, by the drafters of legislation and rules. Frequently, courts interpret the word "may" as used in statutes and procedural rules as a magic wand bestowing unlimited discretion on the trial court. Other discretionary-bestowing magic words include "in the interests of justice," "on terms and conditions that are just," and "if justice so requires."

Professor Rosenberg warns that a grant of discretion should not be presumed. "Discretion is a powerful judicial medicine and draftsmen and judges should not be cavalier in strewing it about or finding it implied. Terms such as may or in the interest of justice should not be treated as synonymous with an explicit grant of review-restraining discretion." Accordingly, reviewing courts should look closely at the intent or policy behind legislation or rules to ascertain whether a statute or rule that uses discretionary-sounding language really grants or limits a court's discretion.[104]

Adding to the difficulty in formulating a definition for discretion, the authors discuss how Ohio courts have in the past distinguished "legal discretion" from "arbitrary and uncontrolled discretion."[105] With regard to "legal discretion," Ohio courts have acknowledged that the trial court does not have unlimited authority to act:

---

[102] *Id.* at 212-13.
[103] *Id.* at 213.
[104] *Id.* at 215.
[105] *Id.* at 216.

[The Ohio Supreme Court] determined that the latitude of discretion granted a court by a statute was limited by the constitution. The court concluded that such statutory discretion was "not absolute, or its exercise a finality. It is a sound legal discretion and can be reviewed." The court determined that, although the trial judge followed the letter of the law, he "overlooked [the statute's] principle, and confounded the impartiality required by the constitution with the ability of the juror, not withstanding his prejudice, to render an impartial verdict." Chief Justice Johnson, dissenting from that part of the majority's holding that the trial court abused its discretion stated, "[t]his discretion is sound legal discretion, which this court cannot review, unless it is clear to the reviewing court that there has been a manifest abuse of that discretion."....[106]

"Uncontrolled discretion" initially presented an entirely different set of issues, as the Ohio courts had described it as "controlled by no fixed rule" and an "uncertain judicial discretion, too unlimited and too various to furnish a just and safe guide, and which every cautious and prudent judge desires to avoid."[107] The authors explained:

The [Ohio Supreme Court] recognized a distinction between legal discretion and absolute and uncontrolled discretion and cited to a South Carolina appellate decision, *Reynolds v. State*. The Georgia Supreme Court had defined legal "discretion as discretion that must be exercised in conformity to known rules." Arbitrary discretion is but another name for caprice, or favour. Under its exercise, the boldest may tremble, and the free be made slaves. It is better therefore to act upon a fixed rule, even if it should now and then enable the guilty to escape, than to act without a rule, to the terror and danger of the innocent.[108]

Fortunately, the authors point out that although Ohio courts now use the term "judicial discretion," the meaning of "discretion" in Ohio law follows what the Ohio courts once called "legal discretion."[109]

e)   **Why Not Create Additional Rules and Eliminate Discretion?**

Because appellate courts obviously have authority to make rules and to interpret statutes, one can ask why an appellate court would want to confer discretion on a

---

[106] *Id.* at 217 (quoting *Palmer v. State*, 42 Ohio St. 596 (1885)).

[107] *Id.* (noting that in such cases an appellate court will often exercise its rulemaking authority to limit the trial court's discretion).

[108] *Id.* at 217–18 (quoting *Reynolds v. State*, 14 Ohio 295 (1846)) (internal quotes omitted).

[109] *See id.* at 218.

42

trial court in the first place.[110] Rosenberg himself articulated several reasons against

---

[110] *See, e.g.,* Martin B. Louis, *Allocating Adjudicative Decision Making Authority Between the Trial and Appellate Levels: A Unified View of the Scope of Review, the Judge/Jury Question, and Procedural Discretion,* 64 N.C. L. Rev. 993 (1986). Despite the title, Louis devotes relatively little attention to the trial court's judicial discretion, preferring instead to discuss how the appellate court limits that discretion. *See id.* at 1945 ("In short, it may be more accurate to divide certain complex procedural determinations into their component parts and to characterize the scope of review of the parts separately."). He described the functions of the appellate court thus:

> The trial [court's] function is to exercise discretionary power of one kind or another as defined by and within the limits set by law. The appellate function is to establish the relevant definitions and limits through the exercise of lawmaking power, carried out principally through the free review of questions of law. For discussion purposes, the lawmaking power of the appellate courts can be subdivided into three subsidiary powers: (1) the law declaration power, which is the power to declare the law and thus to impose on the trial level decision maker general rules affecting all cases that come within the rules' terms; (2) the supervisory power, which is the power to state as a matter of law, generally through rulings on the sufficiency of the evidence, that a particular trial level finding of historical or ultimate fact exceeds the limits of the discretion conferred; and (3) the classification power, which is the power to withdraw particular mixed law/fact questions from the discretionary power of the trial level by classifying them as questions of law or as constitutional or jurisdictional facts. Through these three powers appellate courts define the trial level's discretionary power, set the outer limits thereto in specific fact situations, and occasionally take the power for themselves.

Id. at 1017. Louis later elaborates on the broad scope of the appellate court's rulemaking authority:

> The law-declaring power, of course, includes more than these minimal uses. It includes the recognition of new common-law claims and defenses, the identification of the legislative purposes of new claims and defenses created by statute, the ascertainment of the essential elements of all claims and defenses, the development of appropriate definitions or tests for these elements, the identification of the factors that may or may not be considered in determining the existence of an essential element, the assignment of the appropriate weight to be given relevant factors, the identification of the party with the burden of proof, the degree of proof required, and, when appropriate, the development of presumptions or other guides to decision. Together these facets of law declaration can be employed to elaborate law in such detail that fact-finder discretion is substantially narrowed. Appellate courts do not regularly assay such heavy-handed elaboration. In *The Common Law,* however, Oliver Wendell Holmes urged courts to act vigorously in accordance with the "fair teaching of experience." He believed that in recurring situations courts should use the law-declaring power both to codify consistent jury

conferring judicial discretion on trial courts.[111] For one, "even though the constitution does not spell out an obligation to grant appeals," the "right to appeal has been traditional in this country's judicial process."[112] Adherence to a "deep sense of fitness" to appeal "in our view of the administration of justice" explains why our society remains "committed to the practice of affording a two-tiered or three-tiered court system, so that a losing litigant may obtain at least one chance for review of each significant ruling made at the trial-court level."[113] Moreover, Rosenberg points out that "trial judges are manned by a single judge and appellate courts are collegial"; thus, Rosenberg argues, appellate review offers "safety in numbers."[114] Most importantly, the idea that a judge could potentially ignore the rule of law in the exercise of his or her discretion makes "discretion a four-letter word in many legal circles."[115] Rosenberg is not so alarmed, but still urges caution in this regard:

> Lord Camden called discretion the law of tyrants. He said that "in the best it is oftentimes caprice"; and in the worst, every vice, folly and passion to which human nature can be liable. Discretion has been said to promote a government of men, not laws. These and other strictures have been summed up in an acrid epigram which asserts: "That system of law is best which confides as little as possible to the discretion of the judge...."

> Of course, nothing so roundly vilified could be all bad. The element of flexibility and choice in the process of adjudicating is precisely what justice requires in many cases. Flexibility permits more compassionate and more sensitive responses to differences which ought to count in applying legal norms, but which get buried in the gross and rounded-off language of rules that are directed at wholesale problems instead of particular disputes. Discretion in this sense allows the individualization of law and permits justice at times to be hand-made instead of mass-produced.

> ....

> determinations and to resolve inconsistent ones by making choices themselves; experienced judges could sometimes elaborate the law independently because they would know the sense of the community as well as or better than would an average jury... (Reprinted with permission of the North Carolina Law Review.)

Id. at 1021–22.

[111] *See* Rosenberg, *supra* note 68, at 641.

[112] *Id.*

[113] *Id.* at 642.

[114] *Id.* ("The idea that incantations about discretion can invest a single judge with the final say in important cases makes many people restless.").

[115] *Id.* ("The thought that in some areas of law judges are liberated from legal rules can take their choice in deciding goes down hard.").

Of course, a judge's total freedom to follow his own desires in deciding issues would raise the risk of a government of men if he were not under any constraints at all. But he is under at least one bond that, struggle as he will, he cannot break. It is, as Lord Mansfield observed in John Wilkes' case, the constraint of consistency....

That unwritten command binds the common law judge even in areas where the existence of discretionary power seemingly gives him choice. "Act in your considered judgment, with a resolve to decide in the same way if the issue arises again." That is the unspoken but inescapable silent command of our judicial system. To the extent that judges hear and obey this command, the potential for abuse of discretionary decisional power is tempered.

The dilemma is how judges can be at the same time sensible to the need for even-handedness and constancy in their behavior and sensitive to the value of wielding judicial power flexibly. Is it realistic to suppose they can be made captives of a law-minded tradition that constrains them to decide in one way, when the insistent voice of their discretionary power impels them to decide in another way? Very probably only the slow process of absorbing year after year of the common law's values and ideals can produce the subtle blend of power and restraint they need....[116]

Judge Friendly took a less optimistic view of judicial discretion than Rosenberg, asking whether it was "time to think seriously about our widespread use of single judges to decide issues" via their discretion.[117]   Judge   Friendly   first

---

[116] *Id.* at 642–43 (internal quotations omitted). (Reprinted with permission o fhte Syracuse Law Review.)

[117] Henry J. Friendly, *Indiscretion About Discretion*, 31 Emory L. J. 747, 755 (1982). Later in his comment, Judge Friendly states his proposal more directly:

> A presumptively strong case for a broad reading of "abuse of discretion"—more accurately, for complete appellate abdication—is the situation where there is no law to apply. Very few cases, however, fall into this category. Even when a statute or rule expressly confers discretion or uses the very "may" or some similar locution, there is still the implicit command that the judge shall exercise his power reasonably. This principle must lie at the root of a series of decisions that even in a field long thought to be archetypical for the discretion of the trial judge.... Professor Rosenberg cites as an example of a situation where there is no law to apply, the decision whether or not to allow jurors to take notes during the course of a trial. But why not establish some, as many states have done?

Id. at 765. (All excerpts of Judge Friendly's article of this as well as those that follow are reprinted with permission of the Emory Law Journal.)

distinguished "discretion" as a review-restraining concept from discretion as a normative concept opposed to the rule of positive law:

> A good deal of confusion has been generated by failure to distinguish between two uses of the word "discretion." The one with which I primarily concern myself today, namely how far an appellate court is bound to sustain rulings of the trial judge which it disapproves but does not consider to be outside the ball park—a question of allocation of an admitted power within the judicial system—is quite different from the question whether, as a normative matter, it is wise for lawmakers to insist on rigid rules in the interest of certainty, no matter how harshly these may operate in some cases, and whether it is not better to prescribe accordion-like standards that afford the courts some dispensing powers to accomplish what they perceive to be justice. To say the latter does not necessarily entail that such discretionary power should be vested predominantly in the trial court rather than in the entire judicial system. If we have been moving increasingly in the direction of seeking justice in the individual case by more general rules and grants of dispensing power, as a noted scholar believes has happened in England, restrictions upon review of such decisions made by courts of first instance are increasingly unacceptable....[118]

Judge Friendly does not base his desire for less discretion on the abilities of an appellate judge vis á vis that of a trial judge.[119] Nor does he advocate allowing appellate courts to intrude on the trial court's findings of fact.[120] Rather, Judge Friendly sees discretion as an obstacle to the uniformity in decisionmaking for which common law courts strive:

> In most cases there is, or at least ought to be, more time for research and deliberation.... Counsel will have had more

---

[118] *Id.* at 754–55.

[119] *Id.* at 757 ("My belief in the general desirability of at least one appellate review does not reflect a view that an appellate judge is inherently more able than a trial judge.") ("The advantages of the appellate tribunal lie primarily not in the personal qualities of its members but elsewhere.").

[120] *Id.* at 759. Judge Friendly explains:

The most notable exception to full appellate review is deference to the trial court's determination of the facts. The trial court's direct contact with the witnesses places it in a superior position to perform this task. For this reason and others, the Seventh Amendment decrees that "no fact tried by a jury, shall be otherwise re-examined in any Court of the United States, than according to the rules of the common law." This is read to mean that a federal appellate court may not reverse a judgment founded on a jury verdict if, with all questions of credibility resolved in favor of the appellee, there was a rational basis for the jury's conclusion.

opportunity to develop their arguments. In many cases the trial judge's opinion will help to focus the controversy. While the trial judge usually knows more about the particular case, the appellate judge is likely to have decided more cases in the same field. One member of a panel may bring an entirely fresh insight not shared by the trial court or by counsel. Assuming that all panel members take seriously their responsibility for independent exercise of judgment, the give and take of discussion may produce a result better than any single mind could reach. Finally, collegial review tends to eliminate or curtail decisions based on impermissible factors. I am not thinking of the rare cases of venality or of prejudice in its most perjorative sense, but rather of the subconscious mind-set from which few judges are immune.

Beyond all this, broad judicial review is necessary to preserve the most basic principle of jurisprudence that "'we must act alike in all cases of like nature.'" As Professor Rosenberg suggests, that constraint should operate to provide consistency among decisions of a single judge even without appellate review. However, it does not assure consistency among decisions of different trial judges, of whom there are now over five hundred in the federal system alone. It is no answer that the restrictions on review of determinations of trial judges imposed by the discretion principle exist only when cases are not exactly alike. The jurisprudential rule of like treatment demands consistency not only between cases that are precisely alike but among those where the differences are not significant.[121]

Judge Friendly does not totally discount the beneficial role that trial-court discretion plays in the justice system, and, in fact, appears to welcome it in certain instances. He acknowledges that discretion is useful when the decisionmaker must weigh a large number of factors that could compel multiple results.[122] Judge Friendly also acknowledges the "limit on the capacity of the judicial system to entertain appeals and afford retrials"[123] and concedes that too "perfectionist an attitude with respect to many sorts of claims of trial error involves a prospect of infinite regress" from trial to appeal, back to trial, then a second appeal, and so forth.[124]

In Judge Friendly's final analysis, however, the "case for full appellate review is particularly strong when a settled practice has developed in cases of the type sub judice and the trial court has departed from it."[125] Because the "rulemakers gave the district courts discretion" in the first place, once enough trial courts have

---

[121] *Id.* at 757–58.

[122] *See id.* at 760.

[123] *Id.* at 761.

[124] *Id.* at 762.

[125] *Id.* at 771.

"decided always to exercise it the same way, a way that the court of appeals" deems "appropriate," "the channel of discretion" narrows, "and a court of appeals should keep a judge from steering outside it rather than allow disparate results on the same facts."[126] Judge Friendly concludes:

> The main thrust of this lecture is that there is not just one standard of "abuse of discretion" on the part of the trial judge. In those situations "where the decision depends on first-hand observation or direct contact with the litigation," the trial court's decision "merits a high degree of insulation from appellate revision." At the other extreme, when Congress has declared a national policy and enlisted the aid of the courts' equity powers in enforcement, the Supreme Court has said that the fact that "the [trial] court's discretion is equitable in nature... hardly means that it is unfettered by meaningful standards or shielded from thorough appellate review." In some instances the need for uniformity and predictability demand thorough appellate review. In short, the "abuse of discretion" standard does not give nearly so complete an immunity bath to the trial court's rulings as counsel for appellees would have reviewing courts believe. An appellate court must carefully scrutinize the nature of the trial court's determination and decide whether that court's superior opportunities of observation or other reasons of policy require greater deference than would be accorded to its formulations of law or its application of law to the facts. In cases within the former categories, "abuse of discretion" should be given a broad reading, in others a reading which scarcely differs from the definition of error. Above all, an appellate court should consider whether the lawmaker intended that discretion should be committed solely to the trial judge or to judges throughout the judicial system.

> A good note on which to end is Chief Justice Marshall's statement in the Burr case that discretionary choices are not left to a court's "inclination, but to its judgment; and its judgment is to be guided by sound legal principles." Although Marshall was there talking to himself as the trial judge, his remark embodies an appropriate standard of review for many discretionary determinations often claimed to lie beyond meaningful appellate scrutiny.[127]

Discussing the role of judicial discretion in statutory interpretation, Professor Cleveland offered a more recent critique of judicial discretion as opposed to deference to the legislative rulemaker:

---

[126] *Id.* at 772 ("When the rulemakers have another go at the rule, as they should periodically, they can either adopt the construction or reject it. Meanwhile, parties will know where they stand and consistency will have been achieved.").

[127] *Id.* at 783–84.

Familiar arguments suggest that there should be appropriate limits on judicial discretion, so only three are presented here. First, the Framers entrusted Congress with the role of assessing the people's needs and preferences and drafting legislation to fulfill those needs and preferences. Relative to Congress, the judiciary is institutionally incompetent to assess and fulfill those needs and preferences for which legislation was enacted, and thus could not pick up the interpretive gauntlet when challenged.

Second, members of a collective body may not act with a single purpose. Though a bill must be supported by majorities in the House and Senate, the reasons that individual members support a bill may not coincide. The purpose of a statute, as articulated by one member of Congress, may not command the necessary support for enactment. Thus, to ensure enactment, different purposes, each supported by individual members of Congress, may be bundled. Of course, the language of a bill must command the necessary support for enactment, but the language itself may support various purposes. Consequently, the selection of a single purpose—and particularly one at a high level of generality—permits the injection of judicial preference into the analysis. The search for a single purpose may be futile and may be an inquiry so malleable that the judiciary ceases to interpret the law and instead creates it.

Third (though related to the second), questions of purpose invite framing issues. The manner in which a question is framed impacts the answer. Each party invariably will frame an issue in hopes of influencing a court to reach an interpretative conclusion that favors that party. The framing contest will not be limited to the principal issue, but may also touch upon the purpose of the statute. Disputes as to the purpose of the statute, however, may further the principal inquiry with which the court struggles little, if at all. If a court gives credence to arguments relating to the purpose of the statute, the court signals to future litigants that such arguments may persuade, perhaps providing signals that should not be sent.[128]

---

[128] Steven J. Cleveland, *Judicial Discretion and Statutory Interpretation*, 57 OKLA. L. REV. 31, 33–34 (2004). (Reprinted with the permission of Professor Cleveland and the Oklahoma Law Review.) *See also, c.f.,* Todd D. Peterson, *Restoring Structural Checks on Judicial Power in the Era of Managerial Judging*, 29 U.C. Davis L. Rev. 41 (1995) (arguing that the onset of managerial judging has compromised the structural checks on judicial discretion that the Framers established) (proposing, *inter alia* that managerial matters should be left to magistrates, who are subject to the plenary review of the district court).

f)   Judicial Discretion and the Rule of Law

A student note appearing in the Southern Methodist University Law Review discusses several jurisprudential approaches to judicial discretion in the context of the relationship between law and equity.[129] After reviewing the history of both law and equity and their relatively contemporary merger, the author concludes that the "current jurisprudence of judicial decision making is the child" of the "systematic confusion" between law and equity following the merger of the two.[130] She concludes further that "each of the major modern theories of judicial discretion making blurs the ideological distinction underlying law and equity" and that the "result of this blurring is an unchecked discretion and an end to the rule of law as traditionally conceived."[131]

Turning to the "major modern theories," the author divides "the modern jurisprudential theories of judicial discretion" into "four basic elements: positivism, moralism, formalism, and realism."[132] She then discusses how the "norms and attitudes borrowed from equity define our legal landscape" no matter which of the four elements is controlling in a given case.[133] Each theory leaves little room for the rule of law and plenty of room for broad judicial discretion.

To a traditionalist, law is "the command of the sovereign,"[134] whereas equity, as the "realm of the conscience" "was necessarily dynamic and constrained only by the bounds of the public trust."[135] The author notes that the "merger of law and equity has blurred the distinction between equity in the system (provisions authorizing equitable relief) and equity of the system (the diffuse concept of fairness)" and concludes that the merger caused a "jurisprudential fog" that in turned spawned the modern concept of judicial discretion.[136]

Contemporary legal realists and adherents of the Critical Legal Studies school of thought would view judicial discretion favorably, as an appropriate rejection of the "rule of law" in the strict sense.[137] To a realist, "what the law 'says'

---

[129] *See generally* Kelly D. Hine, Comment, *The Rule of Law Is Dead, Long Live the Rule: An Essay on Legal Rules, Equitable Standards, and the Debate over Judicial Discretion,* 50 S.M.U. L. Rev. 1769 (1997). (Excerpts originally appearing in Vol. 50, of the SMU Law Review and reprinted with permission from the SMU Law Review and the Southern Methodist Univerity School of Law.)

[130] *Id.* at 1779.

[131] *Id.*

[132] *Id.* ("Positivism and moralism are diametrically opposed. Likewise, formalism and realism are polar opposites.").

[133] *Id.* at 1780.

[134] *Id.* ("Whether expressed through the judicial common law or through legislative statutory enactment, the law was a set of positive rules for ordering human conduct.").

[135] *Id.*

[136] *Id.* at 1781.

[137] *See id.* ("To proponents of traditional realism and Critical Legal Studies, the "law" is what the law says. Judicial pronouncements and legislative directives provide the building blocks for judicial decision making.").

50

is unclear" because "[a]mbiguities, contradictions, and exceptions in the positive law leave room for (and indeed invite) selective interpretation."[138] The author explains:

> This belief in the indeterminacy of legal decision making leads "realist" scholars to reject the rule of law. One scholar summarized the "realist" argument as follows: (1) all values except personal liberty are subjective; (2) to maximize personal liberty (the only universal value), the legislature promulgates general laws; but (3) because all values are subjective, judges cannot neutrally interpret and apply the law. This discretionary application prevents the "law" from being prospectively knowable. Rather, legal decision making results in a retrospective promulgation of the law by those charged with applying it.
>
> ….
>
> If there is no positive law, then personal morality, in one form or another, provides the only standards available for judicial decision making....[139]

According to the author, the neo-positivist theory of Lon Fuller reaches the same result. The author explains:

> Fuller's "neo-positivism" is, in fact, neither new nor positivist. For Professor Fuller, the "law" encompasses much more than merely what the law says. In his opinion, the law must incorporate notions of morality: "law must represent some general direction of human effort that we can understand and describe, and that we can approve in principle even at the moment when it seems to us to miss its mark."...
>
> Although Fuller decries the formalism of traditional positivists, his "neo-positivist" theory also strives for a formalist application. Fuller professes that the fusion of morality and law makes legal outcomes self-determinative. To be morally sound, a legal system must do justice in the performance of its duties. To do justice, the system must be properly ordered. Proper order requires reference to "good" morality. And because good morality is more coherent than evil morality, rational "neo-positivist" judges will always find the good. Therefore, given a set of facts and the proper moral "law," the just outcome is assured.[140]

---

[138] *Id.* ("For these scholars, the ultimate application of law is dynamic and indeterminate.").

[139] *Id.* at 1782.

[140] *Id.* at 1783.

The author implies that Dworkin's jurisprudence marks an unsuccessful attempt to undercut the importance of judicial discretion.[141] She focuses her critique not on the run-of-the-mill cases in which the result "is the product of existing political rights" but on so-called hard cases:

> But in a complex legal system such as ours, it is common to have cases in which the legal rules conflict, so called "hard cases." In the face of conflicting legal rules, the Dworkinian judge must formulate the argument that best explains and harmonizes existing precedent, gives effect to the most weighty underlying principles (morals), and then writes off the least possible precedent as mistake. Upon completion of this Herculean task, the judge applies the "best" legal argument to the facts. Application is straight forward. If the judge's analysis was correct, he mechanically vindicates the pre-existing right.

> But despite this exceedingly well-reasoned procedure, Dworkinian analysis falls victim to the same basic problem undercutting "neo—positivism"—it assumes that a "best" moral theory exists. To be more exact, Professor Dworkin assumes, first, the existence of a normative "best" morality and, second, that this normative "best" morality is empirically significant. He assumes that in every hard case a judge can not only discover the "proper" harmonizing of precedent, weighting of morality, and discounting of mistake, but also that enough of society would agree with the judge's formulation to make the formulation worth while.

> These assumptions are at best troubling and at worst completely bogus. First, although the esoteric concept of a normative "best" morality is not without merit, Professor Dworkin fails to provide a practical procedure for discerning it. Dworkinian theory lacks an overriding "metaprinciple" for use in determining the proper relative weights of competing principles. Lacking ultimate guidance, a Dworkinian judge is forced to rely on personal morality to determine these relative weights. And because judicial outcomes rest on the balance of these weights, Dworkinian analysis slips into the void of moral relativism.

> Second, even assuming the existence of a normative "best" theory, there is no guarantee that such theory would be empirically meaningful. Like a line of best fit through a scattergram of random dots, the Dworkinian theory may be the finest explanatory device available and still be irreconcilably poor. Nothing guarantees the

---

[141] *See id.* at 1784 ("For Professor Dworkin, one party to a dispute, even in 'hard' cases, is always entitled to judgment. This entitlement is the product of existing political rights. The role of the legal decision maker is to formulate the 'best' [most correct and principled] legal argument available in defense of these pre-existing rights.").

social or judicial acceptance of any theory and Professor Dworkin admits as much in his assertion that "judges often disagree not simply about how some rule or principle should be interpreted, but whether the rule or principle one judge cites should be acknowledged to be a rule or principle at all. If the best possible theory is, for all intents and purposes, no better than any other theory, application of all theory becomes arbitrary.[142]

Answering the question: "Why does it matter if what we currently call legal decision making really amounts to no more than equitable discretion?,"[143] the author concludes that although under any modern jurisprudential theory "the rule of law is dead," a "simple return to a jurisprudence embracing the original ideological distinction between legal rules and equitable discretion would suffice" to avoid the dangers of latent discretion exercised under the label "rule of law."[144] She explains:

A return to the rule of law under such a system would provide both tangible and esoteric benefits to society. Consistently applied rules make the law knowable within society, and known rules eliminate the need to advert to basic principles during judicial decision making....

Recognizing and permitting the exercise of equitable discretion would mitigate the problem of over inclusiveness in the positive law. Preserving the ability of judges to treat the differently situated differently would ensure fairness within the system. Keeping the exercise of discretion in the open ensures the ability to monitor discretion and to keep the exercise of discretion above board.

This last point is really the most important. Having "neither purse nor sword," the judiciary depends on the voluntary compliance of those who come before it. All that ensures compliance is a finite reservoir of respect for our legal institutions and for the people running them. Honesty and candor in judicial decision making are essential to maintaining this respect — the trustee who is less than truthful is undeserving of trust....[145]

g)   Judicial Discretion as the Exercise of Skill

One scholar advocates what she calls a "paradigm of discretion" as the "skill" of a "self-conscious" decisionmaker who clearly addresses "the contextual and

---

[142] *Id.* at 1784–85.

[143] *Id.* at 1785.

[144] *Id.* at 1787.

[145] *Id.* at 1787–88.

subjective elements of their sanction decisions."[146] At the outset, Armour explains her use of the term "skill" to describe judicial discretion:

> The purpose of the Article… is not simply to describe the courts' current practices. Rather, the goal is to develop the normative assumptions of the paradigm of discretion as "skill" that are used to justify its use by the courts in their sanctions practice. This Article takes the paradigm and fleshes it out using both case law and commentary in order to establish its normative contours. Only then can the fit between the paradigm and the courts' practice be evaluated at both the trial and appellate level.
>
> Discretion is not an abstraction to a judge, [*sic*] it is part of her daily life. To a sitting jurist, the paradigm of judicial discretion as "skill" has its own internal logic. If the matter is delegated to the trial courts' discretion because of their perceived skill and institutional competence, a legitimate exercise of that discretion requires the courts to exercise that skill and expertise rather than engage in highly subjective, idiosyncratic decisionmaking….
>
> Analyzing the courts' discretion in this way points out an important distinction between criticisms aimed at improving the courts' sanctions practice and criticisms that challenge the practice on its face. Even if particular instances of the courts' sanctions practice adhere to the criteria of a skillful sanctions decision, the practice itself can be criticized by reference to values and norms which are recognized as relevant to judging the practice as a whole…. Critics of Rule 11 have routinely challenged the assumption that a sanctions practice shaped by the paradigm of discretion as "skill" can yield fair results. In effect, these criticisms reflect a desire for a more doctrinally circumscribed, rule-based sanctions practice that adheres more explicitly to the adjudicative norms of the "legal paradigm," thereby restraining the courts' exercise of discretion. There critics reject the normative assumptions that shape the paradigm of discretion as "skill" and justify its application in the Rule 11 arena as a legitimate exercise of judicial discretion.[147]

Armour later describes her proposed paradigm specifically:

---

[146] Maureen N. Armour, *Practice Makes Perfect: Judicial Discretion and the 1993 Amendments to Rule 11*, 24 Hofstra L. Rev. 677, 782 (1996) (discussing judicial discretion and Rule 11 sanctions). Armour states the purpose of the article is not only to discuss discretion in the Rule 11 context but also "to develop a larger perspective from which to approach the question of how to define the court's evolving Rule 11 practice, and how to analy[z]e the problem of discretion, decisionmaking, and sanctions." *Id.* at 709–10. (Excerpts of Professor Armour's article are reprinted with the permission of the Hofstra Law Review Association.)

[147] *Id.* at 686–87.

54

...[I]t is possible to develop a descriptive paradigm of the court's discretion defined as its skill and institutional expertise. This paradigm of discretion is characterized primarily by an emphasis on the individualized facts of the case, the specialized expertise and "situatedness" of the decisionmaker, and the broad delegations of discretion afforded to the decisionmaker to exercise that expertise in fashioning an individualized response. This paradigm of judicial discretion is further shaped by the institutional context within which it is exercised. The questions to be considered is whether the court is looking at a managerial problem, attempting to resolve a procedural issue with a substantive impact, or attempting to render a decision on the merits. This institutional context largely defines the goals of the practice and the decisionmaking norms to be applied.[148]

Near the conclusion of her article, she offers a practical test as to whether the trial court followed her paradigm:

This Article is not recommending that a court of appeals merely substitute its judgment for that of the trial court. However, the policy of deferring to the trial court's skills should adhere to the logic of the skill paradigm. Accordingly, the court of appeals should scrutinize the trial court's decisions to sanction for the elements of skill discussed above. Were the facts developed? Does the court's selection of a context reflect the underlying normative and legal issues involved in the sanctions? Has the court adequately outlined applicable doctrine and any other factors on which it relied? And has the court defined the specialized skill and institutional perspective brought to bear? Courts should no longer rely on a peculiarly personal or self-referring definition of their discretion; nor should they hide behind a highly fact specific analysis. Having to explain the decision is one way to make the trial courts accountable and ensure that the rule is properly interpreted and applied. Having something more than a perfunctory appellate review of the sanction decision is another way. The appellate court should determine if the decision is one with which other skilled practitioners would agree. In addition, the appellate court should determine if the trial court has constructed an opinion that adequately addresses the important legal question: Do the practices at issue in the particular case exceed the bounds of acceptable advocacy?[149]

---

[148] *Id.* at 710–11.
[149] *Id.* at 781.

Armour proposed her "skill" paradigm as a response to what she calls a "reductive approach" to judicial discretion in the Rule 11 context.[150] She criticizes the reductive approach because "it inevitably interweaves different senses of judicial discretion in a single term."[151] Armour then explains the distinction between the "different senses of judicial discretion" further:

> From the judge's perspective, it is possible to identify two models of decisionmaking, the "legal" paradigm and the paradigm of discretion as "skill." These are explicitly referred to in the case law, including Rule 11 case law, and the courts consciously use these two paradigms to justify their exercise of decisionmaking authority or discretion. Implicit in the courts' view that their decisionmaking needs to be explained or justified is an awareness that all judicial decisions raise concerns about the human element—the judge—and the institutional commitment to produce decisions based on law. Thus, the fact and process of justification, the explication and explanation of a decision, is an integral part of the judicial system and the courts' decisionmaking activities....[152]

Armour asserts that the "historical trend in procedural reform" (in which the Advisory Committee to the Federal Rules of Civil Procedure plays its role in encouraging) "increasingly relies upon the courts' specialized skills and unique institutional competence to implement procedures for the courts, and manage dockets and pending litigation through the trial."[153] Armour argues further that this trend does not involve only procedural matters:

> This trend toward delegating the practice of legal problem-solving to the trial courts' discretion extends beyond the procedural arena. Increasingly when the formal adjudicative process of the courts is invoked, the resulting substantive legal decisions are made expressly contingent upon, or otherwise limited in their impact to, the unique facts of the particular case at hand, foreclosing any broad or formal hortatory role for the adjudicative process. This highly contextual or "situationalist" approach to resolving legal problems is also reflected in the courts' reliance upon legal standards and norms that are in their application fact specific, grounded in the particular context of the individual case, and

---

[150] *Id.* at 706. ("The Civil Rules have generally favored judicial discretion as a means to secure just results and have avoided procedural rigidity. On the other hand, indeterminacy in the sanctions rules can weaken their instructive value.").

[151] *Id.* ("If the term discretion simply describes the personal input of decisionmakers, what results is a discussion at cross purposes. Is discretion an essential dimension of judicial decisionmaking under the Rule or do courts only have discretion when the Rule fails to adequately constrain their decisionmaking?").

[152] *Id.* at 706–07.

[153] *Id.* at 707–08 ("This trend in the procedural arena has been aptly denoted... 'pragmatic proceduralism.'").

expressly limited to the court's exercise of their specialized skill and expertise. A diverse array of critics has challenged this trend toward pragmatic decisionmaking on the grounds that it creates power without guidelines or procedural restraints, erodes traditional due process safeguards, and threatens the tradition of judicial objectivity and impartiality with regard to litigants, individual attorneys, and their cases....[154]

Nevertheless, she suggests that her paradigm would alleviate any concern that a trend toward judicial discretion would confer too much power on a trial court:

The paradigm of discretion as "skill" contrasts sharply with the traditional "legal" paradigm of judicial discretion. The successful outcome of this decisionmaking process-has traditionally been measured by the specificity of its fact findings and the clarity of its legal reasoning in the interpretation and application of law to fact. This paradigm of judicial discretion focuses in part on the success with which the court resolves the dispute before it. However the court's decision is not evaluated primarily by how well it provides "individualized" justice to the parties, but by how well it states, clarifies, and applies the law ensuring its future development. This paradigm is also shaped by the institutional context. In the adjudicative arena, the courts' use of the paradigm of legal decisionmaking emphasizes the public dimension of adjudication—the forma, state-sanctioned resolution of controversies involving conflicting legal rights. The goal of adjudication, as a normative theory or model of decisionmaking, is to produce uniform results in similar cases in a manner that demonstrates consistency and predictability in the courts' application of the law. By way of contrast, the successful application of the paradigm of discretion as "skill," whether in the managerial or adjudicative arena, is measured primarily by criteria that focus on individualized outcomes. Here the primary concern is whether the solution is skillfully tailored to the unique facts and circumstances of the case, and the extent to which it successfully resolves the litigants' immediate problem.

The two paradigms differ in another important way. The "legal" paradigm approaches decisions with the normative assumption that there is always a best or right answer, a correct application of law to facts. There is an obvious parallel here between the internal logic of the "legal" paradigm and the adjudicative function and institutional role of the court. The "fit" between the two is not inadvertent. If the goal of adjudication is to produce uniform results in similar cases in a way that affirms and develops the law, it is not

---

[154] *Id.* at 708–09.

surprising that variability in outcomes is seen as problematic when the "legal" paradigm is applied in the adjudicative context. In the paradigm of discretion as "skill," there is no expectation that similar cases will necessarily produce observably similar results precisely because of the fact-sensitive nature of the courts' judgments and intuitions involved in the decisionmaking. The goal of the paradigm is to produce "skillful" decisions, a decisional norm that clearly tolerates wider variability in outcomes.

The paradigm of discretion as "skill" has obvious utility in the managerial and procedural context. It is equally true, conceptually, that using the "legal" paradigm to address issues of substance or merit poses few problems for decisionmakers. There is a clear institutional reluctance, however, to use this narrower, more demanding decisionmaking paradigm to address issues of court management or procedural questions other than those raising important substantive issues. The more problematic situation involves the application of the paradigm of discretion as "skill" when issues of substance are raised in an adjudicative context. Here the internal logic of the paradigm appears to be at odds with the decisional norms and institutional goals that largely define this type of decisionmaking....[155]

In a subsequent article, Armour appears to back away from her paradigm.[156] Again discussing the role of judicial discretion in the context of Rule 11 sanctions, Armour questions whether discretion is nothing more than "a range of tolerable, but variable outcomes."[157] She writes:

Numerous commentators' attempts to grapple with judicial discretion should serve as a warning to anyone undertaking that task. The term judicial discretion is used in so many different ways by courts and commentators alike that it is easy to understand the attraction of a simple, reductive approach. The implicit ambiguity in the term discretion, and the fact that its specific meaning or scope is subject to change depending upon the context, makes its use subject to confusion. Confusion, however, is not always inadvertent: "[C]ertain confusions about that concept . . . and in

---

[155] *Id.* at 711–15. For an Aristotelian gloss on Armour's "discretion as skill" model, see generally Rebecca S. Henry, *The Virtue in Discretion: Ethics, Justice, and Why Judges Must Be "Students of the Soul"*, 25 N.Y.U. Rev. L. & Soc. Change 65 (1999) (arguing that judges must rely on virtue [*virtus* literally means "skill"] in order to exercise their discretion properly).

[156] *See generally* Maureen Armour, *Rethinking Judicial Discretion: Sanctions and the Conundrum of the Close Case*, 50 S.M.U. L. Rev. 493, 521 (1997). (Orginally appearing in Vol 50, No. 5 of the SMU Law Review. Excerpts are reprinted with permission from the SMU Law Review and the Southern Methodist University School of Law.)

[157] *Id.*

58

particular a failure to discriminate different senses in which it is used, account for the popularity of the doctrine of discretion." While a few commentators have attempted to pull together a variety of perspectives on the topic of judicial discretion in an attempt at analytic coherence, the general field is still wide open....

...Numerous theorists conceptualize the limits of that judicial discretion by reference to the restraints imposed by the operative legal norms: Discretion, like the hole in a doughnut, does not exist except as an area left open by a surrounding belt of restriction. It is therefore a relative concept. It always makes sense to ask, "Discretion under which standards?" or "Discretion as to which authority?"

Many theorists look at discretion as what is left after the explicitly articulated rules have been applied, while others look at discretion as what is left, not only after the "black letter" of the law has been applied, but also after any other applicable guides or norms as well. For these latter theorists, discretion lies in large part in the court's ability to pick and choose the "other" gap-filling norms or to reach a "principled" decision, one in which all of the applicable legal norms are articulated. Regardless of the view adopted, it is logical to treat this discretion as a conscious dimension of judicial decision making, just as the courts do when discussing the close or hard case.[158]

Nevertheless, Armor concludes that her paradigm of discretion as skill—which relies on the presumption that the trial judge has the greatest expertise with respect to certain decisions—is reconcilable with the notion of a discretion as a "zone of possibilities":

If discretion in a close case can be defined as the articulation of acceptable alternatives or range of possibilities, then a choice from within that zone can be viewed as a consciously self-limiting decision. Such a decision defines the zone of possibilities by posing alternative or opposite outcomes as their primary decisional guidelines. Approaching discretion from this perspective focuses on discretion as a range of conscious judicial action and on the close case as a decisional guideline defining the zone of those possibilities. This approach facilitates the merging of the logic of discretion with the decision maker's perspective in order to create a decisional methodology that is grounded in the reality of adjudication.[159]

---

[158] *Id.* at 520–21.
[159] *Id.* at 544.

h)   Procedural and Substantive Discretion Distinguished

Professor Richard Marcus has argued that, although the federal appellate courts are conferring more discretion on the district courts, this trend is not as alarming as critics of judicial discretion might suggest.[160] Marcus first distinguishes between procedural and substantive discretion, calling the latter "more unsettling" "in the abstract."[161] He explains that substantive discretion in its purest form could "give the adjudicator complete discretion to resolve each case any way she saw fit."[162] Marcus also groups the common-law judge's power to create substantive rules of law and to apply established law to the facts of the case as examples of judicial discretion.[163]

Noting a trend toward curbing the trial judge's substantive discretion,[164] Marcus describes procedural discretion as a type of discretion "decoupled" from substantive discretion "for most of the life of the American federal courts."[165] Marcus noted the trial court's traditional power to establish procedures to govern its cases.[166] Even under a legislatively enacted procedural code (or one imposed by the higher courts, for that matter), to the extent that the code prescribes standards as opposed to hard-and-fast rules, the discretion of the trial court will remain intact.[167] Marcus then devoted much of his discussion to areas in which contemporary trial judges enjoy a great deal of procedural discretion.[168]

Marcus describes his attitude toward the contemporary trend as one of "guarded optimism."[169] He notes first that a trial judge's procedural discretion does not raise the same specter of rule by judicial fiat as does broad substantive discretion.[170] Although he acknowledges that "the exercise of procedural discretion

---

[160] Richard L. Marcus, *Slouching toward Discretion*, 78 Notre Dame L. Rev. 1561, 1564 (2003).

[161] *Id.* at 1571 ("The precise dividing line between substance and procedure is sometimes in doubt, but one anxious to appreciate the importance of procedural discretion should start with some appreciation of the possibility of substantive discretion.")

[162] *Id.* ("One is reminded, for instance, of the Biblical tale of King Solomon's judgment when presented with competing claims of motherhood of a child.").

[163] *Id.* at 1568–69.

[164] *See id.* at 1569 ("In the United States, common-law crimes have been supplanted by legislation in almost all jurisdictions due to a conscious legislative decision that judges should not have the power to declare conduct criminal.").

[165] *Id.* (noting that the "current concern about procedural discretion is whether unconstrained discretion about procedure could subvert substantive justice") ("Procedure—and therefore procedural discretion—may be conceived as dedicated to accomplishing the purposes of the substantive law.").

[166] *Id.* at 1572.

[167] *Id.* at 1574.

[168] *See generally id.* at 1581–1604 (discussing examples of the modern trend toward judicial discretion).

[169] *Id.* at 1605.

[170] *See id.* ("Any common-law system accords some substantive discretion to the judicial branch.... At least from the perspective of the federal courts... that substantive discretion

60

can be colored by substantive concerns," such as judicial management of class action and of discovery, Marcus concludes that "the sorts of determinations that come within procedural discretion are less freighted with substantive overtones"[171] generally, and that there "hardly seems a widespread uprising of lawyers asserting that federal judges as a group are regularly using their procedural discretion to advance their substantive preferences."[172] Marcus points out further that the appellate courts do intervene often in matters committed to the trial court's procedural discretion, such as class actions.[173] Moreover, writing judicial opinions enables the appellate courts to "stake out limits on the exercise of trial court discretion" by adopting rules to govern the particular situation.[174]

Turning to policy concerns, Marcus concedes that the increase in procedural discretion vested in the trial court curtails the "freedom of movement" by lawyers.[175] He argues, however, that limited freedom of movement is not necessarily a bad thing:

> So long as [judicial] oversight is not tinged with a substantive bias, the fact that it involves substantial primary and secondary procedural discretion for the trial court judge is not inherently too disturbing. It is certainly true that lawyers who find themselves under the hand of a firm judge are more likely than others to object that the judge has not given them enough time or latitude to complete their preparation. But it must be true that most of these attitudes flow actually from concerns quite different from substantive bias. And it must be confessed that judicial intervention can have adverse results, requiring extra effort that provides no advantages. So it is not necessarily such a good thing as the proponents urge. But that is not because it is discretionary.... In a number of ways, individual tailoring (judicial discretion) may be superior to across-the-board timetables administered by clerks who lack discretion to modify the prescribed schedules.[176]

Marcus also points out the drawbacks of alternatives to broader procedural discretion. He points out first that involving "a second level of judges in case management would be likely to lead to unacceptable delays without promising

---

has been curtailed, if not abolished, by the need to follow the dictates of state law on issues not governed by federal law.")

[171] Id. at 1606.

[172] Id. at 1607.

[173] Id. at 1608.

[174] Id. ("Increasingly, the appellate courts are also insisting on a full record on which to base [their] review.").

[175] Id. at 1609.

[176] Id. at 1610 (noting also that "it is striking how often lawyers beseech judges to provide more 'adult supervision' of their cases.") (Reprinted with permission © by Notre Dame Law Review, University of Notre Dame. The publisher bears responsibility of any errors, which have occurred in reprinting or editing.)

significant improvements."[177] On the other hand, Marcus argues, the "turmoil about the federal Sentencing Guidelines" demonstrates the dangers of "calibrating too precisely" procedural decisions better left to the trial judge.[178]

i)   Judicial Discretion and the Personal Biases of the Trial Judge

Obviously, not everybody is a fan of broad judicial discretion. Reviewing the legal efforts of the Mexican-American community to secure greater equality, Professor Martinez concluded that "courts generally exercised their discretion by taking a position against Mexican-Americans on key issues."[179] Although Martinez argues that trial courts, acting within their discretion, "could have done significantly more to help establish the rights of Mexican-Americans," he also concludes that there is "hope of racial reform" even though trial courts will no doubt continue to make discretionary decisions.[180] Martinez bases his hope on a view of judicial discretion influenced by critical race jurisprudence:

> The view that judicial decision-making is highly influenced by the perspective and preconceptions of the judge, and that the perspective of the dominant group may present a barrier to racial reform, finds substantial support in the recent revival of pragmatism in legal philosophy. Pragmatists treat "thinking as contextual and situated." Thinking is "always embodied in practices—habits and patterns of perceiving and conceiving." Thus, pragmatists have recognized that one cannot view the world except through one's preconceptions. Applying this notion to legal decision-making, they have emphasized the importance of context and perspective to the act of judging. Significantly, pragmatists also have recognized that the dominant perspective can stand in the way of racial reform. Both critical race scholars and pragmatists offer a similar explanation for why the dominant perspective may inhibit reform. The general idea is that the dominant perspective or mindset makes current social and legal arrangements seem fair and natural. Bringing this mindset to the bench, judges may commit moral error in civil rights cases because narrow habits of perceiving lead them to believe that the way things are is inevitable or just.
>
> One way to help judges break down mindset, broaden their perspectives, and promote justice in civil rights cases, is to provide counterstories-i.e., explain how decisions were not inevitable. Through this process judges can overcome ethnocentrism and the unthinking conviction that their way of seeing the world is the only

---

[177] *Id.* at 1611.
[178] *Id.* at 1611–12.
[179] *See generally*, George Martinez, *Legal Indeterminacy, Judicial Discretion and the Mexican-American Litigation Experience*, 27 U.C. Davis L. Rev. 555, 611 (1994).
[180] *Id.* at 612-13.

one—that the way things are is inevitable, natural, just, and best and thereby avoid moral error when deciding any civil rights case. Similarly, pragmatists have stressed that justice may be advanced only if judges try to grasp the world from perspectives that run counter to the dominant perspective. In particular, some pragmatists have urged judges to try to grasp the world from the perspective of the dominated or the oppressed. As Martha Minow has explained, the effort to take the perspective of another may help us see that our perspective is limited and that the status quo is not inevitable or fair....[181]

Taking a position similar to that of Martinez's, Professor Lahav described discretion in terms of the trial judge's character.[182] Although Lahav calling abuse of discretion "a mark of bad character" might surprise some, it is not as controversial when one considers what Lahav means by character: "Robert Nagel took character to mean moral fortitude and rectitude. But one may also understand character as neutral concept, designating different temperaments or personality types."[183] After concluding that no one factor, such as lack of experience or old age, constituted a *sine qua non* of the trial judge's controversial decision, Lahav explained how several psychological and cultural forces could contribute to the judge's decision:

I am not arguing that judicial experience, political partisanship, social class, age, or awareness of the public aspects of one's job are irrelevant attitudes to character formation. I would even add to this checklist ethnic background and the particular position in the judicial hierarchy. Where one is a trial judge facing events as they unfold, or sitting on appeal reflecting on past events, is also relevant. Any biographer knows that these factors are influential in salient as well as subtle ways. I am arguing that these cannot, by themselves, account for the interaction between character and law. Rather, there must be something deeper at work here, which affects the legal decision-making process, and which in turn may be nourished and shaped by factors such as experience, social class, and so on. One may call this "something else" the essence of character, or personality. Character, interacting with and nurtured by these other factors, as well as life experience, leads to a certain understanding of the situation, a certain interpretation of law and ethics, that encourages a preference for action, and that is what was at stake here.

---

[181] *Id.* at 613–15. (Reprinted with permission. This work, copyrighted 1994 by George Martinez was originally published in the UC Davis Law Review, Vol. 27, pg. 553-611, copyright 1994 by the Regents of the University of California. All rights reserved.)

[182] Pnina Lahav, *The Chicago Conspiracy Trial: Character and Judicial Discretion*, 71 U. Colo. L. Rev. 1327, 1338 (2000) (discussing a federal district court's 1969 decision to order a defendant involved with the student protest movement bound and gagged in the courtroom).

[183] *Id.*

I suggest that Judge Hoffman possessed what is known as an authoritarian personality and that this propensity led him to his decision, which in fact turned all of his expectations upside down.[184]

After citing several instances from the record that supposedly demonstrated the judge's authoritarian personality, Lahav concluded that by virtue of his character, the only consideration relevant to the judge in making his discretionary decision was whether the decision had substantial support in case law:

> According to Judge Hoffman, the legality of the decision to bind and gag was itself a sufficient justification to order Seale bound and gagged. The facts that it could be perceived as constitutionally controversial, or that it might be morally objectionable, were not relevant in this context. Seale refused to accept the court's decisions that he could not represent himself and that Kunstler should act as his lawyer. Seale's insistence on his rights did not allow the trial to progress properly. These circumstances, Judge Hoffman believed, called for a drastic means, and that drastic means, approved by *Allen v. Illinois*, was binding and gagging.

> At this point, we may return to Justice Brandeis's poetic defense of freedom in *Whitney v. California*. The secret of freedom, said Brandeis, was the open mind. Deliberation, consideration, a willingness to re-evaluate time-honored principles, a readiness to engage with those we distrust and dislike—these were the guarantees of a robust society capable of growth and change. Transferred to the context of the trial, the Brandeis theorem would mean a more intense judicial attention to defendants' rights despite the distaste the judge was feeling towards the defendants and his suspicion of their motives.[185]

---

[184] *Id.* at 1341–42. (Excerpts reprinted with permission of the University of Colorado Law Review.)

[185] *Id.* at 1353–54. *See also* Nicholas L. Georgakopoulos, *Discretion in the Career and Recognition Judiciary*, 7 U. Chi. L. Sch. Roundtable 205, 223 (2000) (arguing that in a recognition judicial system, in which judges assume the bench after distinguishing themselves as lawyers and often remain on the same bench for a long time, judges will tend to resort to judicial discretion more frequently)

> If, nevertheless, a reduction of judicial discretion is desired in a recognition system, it could be achieved by means of adopting some of the attributes of the career system. Judges should only be appointed to higher courts from the lower courts, perhaps even on a pure seniority system. This would also revoke the apparent license to exercise one's judicial philosophy. A norm that judges should be selected from a narrow subset of the legal profession, such as litigators, would tend to reduce judicial discretion, as would the requirement of a technical

j)   The Omega Point of Judicial Discretion: The Appellate Court's Rulemaking

Professor Martha Davis, who has written extensively on discretion and standards of review, described how discretionary decisions eventually become established rules of law subject to plenary review by an appellate court.[186] Once the legislature or the higher court has the opportunity to impose "guiding factors" on a particular decision, Davis argues that "the question no longer is an application of personal judgment to supervisory facts and issues, but a broader legal determination of what facts and issues should determine generically this category of overall choice."[187] Davis explains:

> Discretion is one of the most exercised and least understood of trial court or agency activities—a very basic activity that must be understood in all areas of decisionmaking and administrative, criminal, and civil appeals, and one of the most difficult to address rationally. The need for discretion arises because there are areas in which the trial court or agency must exercise a certain measure of judgment in reaction to its "on the scene" presence at trial, or because Congress and the courts have given no guidelines for deciding the issue, or because the issue is one that is so novel or vague that there is no way to measure the "correctness" of the trial court's decision....[188]

> The question of course, is not whether [the United States Supreme] Court, or whether the Court of Appeals, would as an original matter have dismissed the action; it is whether the District Court abused its discretion in so doing. The highly deferential review indicated... is not the level of deference always accorded to decisions labeled "discretionary." Frequently, when an issue of law is new to a jurisdiction, the reviewing court is more focused on the developing factors and considerations than on the actual decision itself. This kind of deferential review may continue for some time in order to allow appellate or trial courts to develop the factors that

---

> examination. Discretion would also tend to be reduced by placing impediments on judges' realizing their prestige. A norm of unsigned opinions would prevent judges from achieving recognition and enjoying reputation; a revocation of their authority to determine trial procedure would have a similar effect, as would the implementation of trials by record, as opposed to oral trials.

[186] *See generally* Martha S. Davis, *Standards of Review: Judicial Review of Discretionary Decisionmaking*, 2 J. App. Prac. & Process 47 (2000). Davis, Discretionary Decision making. Supra, n. 185 at 51. For another example of Davis's work, see Steven Alan Childress & Martha S. Davis, *Federal Standards of Review* (2d ed. 1992).

[187] *Id.* At 49-51.

[188] Id. (footnotes omitted) (quoting *National Hockey League v. Metrolpolitain Hockey Club*, 427 U.S. 639, 642 (1976)).

should be considered when exercising discretion, as well as the balancing of those factors. Eventually, for issues as to which rules can be developed, the appellate body, as part of its law-making function and after having further redefined the factors, will specify those factors and considerations that will thereafter be required to make the decision. The end result is usually more a question of law than an exercise of discretion. During the time that the decision remains an actual discretionary exercise of judgment [however], the decision of one district court on the issue should have no broad control over the same decision by another district court.[189]

After reviewing both academic discussions of judicial discretion and cases in which courts have wrestled with the same concept, Davis offers the following advice to appellate practitioners:

Thus the successful practitioner must approach each issue with sensitivity to the level of deference afforded the issue itself and the factors the court must consider in making its choice. Counsel should direct the appellate court's attention to the judge's decision below with an eye toward exploring *generally* what kind of discretionary decision was made there, in a way that aids the reviewing court in understanding properly why, and how much, deference should or should not follow. Appellate courts, in turn, should frame their review by issue, factors, reasoned analogy, and degree of discretion, providing general guidance on the evolving concept of discretion as well as the specific application at hand. At the very least, the court or counsel should consider four questions:

1. Has this decision been given to the discretion of the trial court? If so, why? That is, is there law to apply, a framework of legal standards to contain possible discretion, factors to guide the exercise of the discretion, but nevertheless no actual rule of law, so that the trial court is best positioned to exercise the necessary discretion?

2. If the decision to be made has a framework of legal standards or factors to guide the trial judge's exercise of discretion, has the judge stayed within the framework and properly considered the factors?

3. If this is a discretionary decision that is in the evolutionary process, is there enough precedent to show a pattern of decision and, if so, what is that pattern?

---

[189] *Id.* at 49-51.

4. Has the appellate court indicated in this or analogous issues that it is ready to state a rule of law based on that pattern? [190]

§ 1.3. The Evolving Nature of Discretion: Sentencing

Traditionally, a trial court has broad discretion to sentence a criminal defendant. Matters collateral to sentencing can also fall within the trial court's broad discretion.[191] On account of the rapidly changing and confusing relationship between sentencing and judicial discretion, it is important to trace the recent case law in this area, particularly with respect to the intersection between discretionary sentencing and the Sixth Amendment rights to trial by jury and conviction upon proof beyond a reasonable doubt.[192]

Before the enactment of the federal sentencing guidelines, trial courts enjoyed virtually unfettered discretion in sentencing, so long as they adhered to the limits imposed by the relevant statute.[193] Under the sentencing guidelines, federal district judges had discretion to sentence within a narrow range prescribed by an administrative sentencing commission.[194] However, the guidelines allowed the trial judge to depart from the prescribed range upon a finding of compelling reasons to do so.[195]

---

[190] *Id.* at 82–83.

[191] *See, e.g., United States v. Powell*, 57 Fed. Appx. 959 (3rd Cir. 2003) *available at* 2003 WL 214773 at **2 (citing *United States v. Babich*, 785 F.2d 415, 416–17 (3rd Cir. 1986)). The *Babich* court held that a trial court acted within its discretion when it revoked defendant's supervised release simply for failing to get in touch with his probation officer upon being arrested. 785 F.2d at 418.

[192] For an excellent discussion of the relevant case law, see Katie M. McVoy, Note, *"What I Have Feared Most Has Now Come To Pass": Blakely, Booker, and the Future of Sentencing*, 80 Notre Dame L. Rev. 1613 (2005).

[193] *See, e.g., Apprendi v. New Jersey*, 530 U.S. 466, 481 (2000) ("[O]ur periodic recognition of judges' broad discretion... has been regularly accompanied by the qualification that that discretion was bound by the range of sentencing options prescribed by the legislature.").

[194] *See id.* at 550 (O'Connor, J., dissenting).

[195] *See, e.g., United States v. Booker*, 125 S.Ct. 738, 746 (2005) ("The judge, however, held a post-trial sentencing proceeding and concluded by a preponderance of the evidence that Booker had possessed and additional 566 grams of crack and that he was guilty of obstructing justice.") ("Thus, instead of the sentence of 21 years and 10 months that the judge could have imposed on the basis of the facts proved to the jury beyond a reasonable doubt, Booker received a 30-year sentence.). For a review of similar guideline systems enacted by the states, see Richard S. Frase, *Is Guided Discretion Sufficient? Overview of State Sentencing Guidelines*, 44 ST. Louis U. L. J. 425 (2000) (arguing *inter alia* that some states' experiments with "voluntary" guideline systems have been successful in accomplishing the goals of the determinate sentencing movement).

The court first cast doubt on whether the sentencing guidelines were constitutional in *Jones v. United States*.[196] Although *Jones* dealt with the statutory interpretation of a federal carjacking statute, the court discussed sentencing in the context of its one of its longstanding canons of construction: that of interpreting statutes in such a manner so as to ensure that they pass constitutional muster.[197] The court concluded that the government's interpretation of the carjacking statute would "be open to constitutional doubt in light of a series of cases over the past quarter century, dealing with due process and the guarantee of trial by jury."[198] The Court worried that a state might "manipulate its way out" of the requirement that it prove all elements of a crime beyond a reasonable doubt if the Court assumed "Sixth Amendment indifference to treating a fact that sets [a] sentencing range as a sentencing factor, not an element" of the offense.[199] Reviewing the history of the judge's and jury's respective roles in sentencing, the Court concluded that "the history" of sentencing showed not "accepted tolerance for exclusively judicial factfinding to peg penalty limits."[200]

Justice Kennedy dissented and expressed great "concern" over the court's "constitutional discussion."[201] One of his concerns were that states seeking to foster greater uniformity in sentencing would be whip-sawed between what the state might perceive as two equally unattractive choices: (1) broad trial court discretion that renders sentencing an unpredictable and inconsistent art, and (2) and "unexpected rule mandating that what were once factors bearing upon the sentence now must be treated as offense elements for determination [beyond a reasonable doubt] by the jury."[202] Justice Kennedy pointed to the efforts some states had taken to avoid the first unattractive choice:

> The rationale of the Court's constitutional doubt holding makes it difficult to predict the full consequences of today's holding, but it is likely that it will cause disruption and uncertainty in the sentencing systems of the States. Sentencing is one of the most difficult tasks in the enforcement of the criminal law. In seeking to bring more order and consistency to the process, some States have sought to move from a system of indeterminate sentencing or a

---

[196] *See generally* 526 U.S. 227 (1999).

[197] *Id.* at 239. The Court stated the doctrine:
> Any doubt that might be prompted by the arguments for that other reading should, however, be resolved against it under the rule, repeatedly reaffirmed, that where a statute is susceptible of two constructions, by one of which grave and doubtful constitutional questions arise and by the other of which such questions are avoided, our duty is to adopt the latter.

[198] *Id.* at 240.

[199] *Id.* at 243.

[200] *Id.* at 244.

[201] *Id.* at 264 (Kennedy, J., dissenting).

[202] *Id.* at 271 (Kennedy, J., dissenting).

grant of vast discretion to the trial judge to a regime in which there are more uniform penalties, prescribed by the legislature.[203]

In the next term, the Court held, "other than the fact of a prior conviction, any fact that increases the penalty for a crime beyond the prescribed statutory maximum must be submitted to a jury, and proved beyond a reasonable doubt."[204] Defendant Apprendi had been convicted of several firearms charges related to an incident in which he fired several rounds into a neighbor's house. The residents of the home were African - American. Following Apprendi's plea, the prosecutor moved to enhance Apprendi's sentence under New Jersey law because of evidence that Apprendi committed the crime on account of racial animosity toward his neighbors. The trial judge concluded on a preponderance of the evidence that Apprendi had acted with racial bias, enhanced his sentence beyond the 10-year maximum, and sentenced him to 12 years in prison on one firearms count.[205]

The Court based its holding in part on the fact that, historically, a trial judge had no discretion to impose a sentence; once the jury determined that the state had proven its case, the law provided a mandatory sentence:

> Any possible distinction between an "element" of a felony offense and a "sentencing factor" was unknown to the practice of criminal indictment, trial by jury, and judgment by court as it existed during the years surrounding our Nation's founding. As a general rule, criminal proceedings were submitted to a jury after being initiated by an indictment containing "all the facts and circumstances which constituted the offense... *that there may be no doubt as to the judgment which should be given*, if the defendant be convicted." The defendant's ability to predict with certainty the judgment from the face of the felony indictment flowed from the invariable linkage of punishment with crime....
>
> Thus, with respect to the criminal law of felonious conduct, "the English trial judge of the later eighteenth century had very little explicit discretion in sentencing. The substantive criminal law tended to be sanction-specific; it prescribed a particular sentence to

---

[203] *Id.* (Kennedy, J., dissenting).

[204] *Apprendi*, 530 U.S. at 490 (adopting the constitutional discussion in *Jones* as law).

[205] *Id.* at 474. The Court stated the issue of the case thus:

> The constitutional question, however, is whether the 12-year sentence imposed on count 18 was permissible, given that it was above the 10-year maximum for the offense charged in that count. The finding is legally significant because it increased—indeed, it doubled—the maximum range within which the judge could exercise his discretion, converting what otherwise was a maximum 10-year sentence on that count into a minimum sentence.

Id. Note that the trial judge had *statutory* authority under New Jersey law to enhance the sentence.

each offense. The judge was meant simply to impose that sentence (unless he thought in the circumstances that the sentence was so inappropriate that he should invoke the pardon process to commute it)."[206]

Although the Court acknowledged the trial court's broad discretion to sentence within statutory limits,[207] it concluded,

> The historic link between verdict and judgment and the consistent limitation on judges' discretion to operate within the limits of the legal penalties provided highlight the novelty of a legislative scheme that removes the jury from the determination of a fact that, if found, exposes the criminal defendant to a penalty *exceeding* the maximum he would receive if punished according to the facts reflected in the jury verdict alone.[208]

Justice O'Connor dissented, contending that the "Our Court has long recognized that not every fact that bears on a defendant's punishment need be charged in an indictment, submitted to a jury, and proved by the government beyond a reasonable doubt."[209] In her dissent, Justice O'Connor questioned the relevance of the fact that trial judges historically had no discretion in imposing a sentence and argued that the majority itself had rejected "its relevance to the constitutional question presented here due to the conflicting American practice of judges exercising sentencing discretion and our decisions recognizing the legitimacy of that American practice."[210] Turning to what she called the "constitutional principle underlying" the Court's reasoning, she announced that she would reject "any such principle" that would require any fact that could increase the maximum sentence to be proven to a jury beyond a reasonable doubt.[211] She wrote:

> [I]t is inconsistent with our precedent and would require the Court to overrule, at a minimum, decisions like *Patterson* and *Walton*. More importantly, given our approval of—and the significant history in this country of—discretionary sentencing by judges, it is difficult to understand how the Fifth, Sixth, and Fourteenth Amendments could possibly require the Court's or Justice Thomas' rule. Finally, in light of the adoption of determinate-sentencing schemes by many States and the Federal Government, the consequences of the Court's and Justice Thomas' rules in terms of

---

[206] *Id.* at 479 (Emphasis added).

[207] *Id.* at 482.

[208] *Id.* at 482–83.

[209] *Id.* at 524 (O'Connor, J., dissenting).

[210] *Id.* at 535 (O'Connor, J., dissenting) ("Indeed, the Court does not even claim that the historical evidence of nondiscretionary sentencing at common law support its 'increase in the maximum penalty' rule.").

[211] *Id.* at 543–44 (O'Connor, J., dissenting).

sentencing schemes invalidated by today's decision will likely be severe.

As the Court acknowledges, we have never doubted that the Constitution permits Congress and the state legislatures to define criminal offenses, to prescribe broad ranges of punishment for those offenses, and to give judges discretion to decide where within those ranges a particular defendant's punishment should be set. That view accords with historical practice under the Constitution." From the beginning of the Republic, federal judges were entrusted with wide sentencing discretion. The great majority of federal criminal statutes have stated only a maximum term of years and a maximum monetary fine, permitting the sentencing judge to impose any term of imprisonment and any fine up to the statutory maximum. Under discretionary-sentencing schemes, a judge bases the defendant's sentence on any number of facts neither presented at trial nor found by a jury beyond a reasonable doubt. As one commentator has explained:

"During the age of broad judicial sentencing discretion, judges frequently made sentencing decisions on the basis of facts that they determined for themselves, on less than proof beyond a reasonable doubt, without eliciting very much concern from civil libertarians.... The sentence in any number of traditional discretionary situations depended quite directly on judicial findings of specific contested facts ... Whether because such facts were directly relevant to the judge's retributionist assessment of how serious the particular offense was (within the spectrum of conduct covered by the statute of conviction), or because they bore on a determination of how much rehabilitation the offender's character was likely to need, the sentence would be higher or lower, in some specific degree determined by the judge, based on the judge's factual conclusions."

Accordingly, under the discretionary-sentencing schemes, a factual determination made by a judge on a standard of proof below "beyond a reasonable doubt" often made the difference between a lesser and a greater punishment.

....

Under our precedent, then, a State may leave the determination of a defendant's sentence to a judge's discretionary decision within a prescribed range of penalties. When a judge, pursuant to that sentencing scheme, decides to increase a defendant's sentence on the basis of certain contested facts, those facts need not be proved to a jury beyond a reasonable doubt. The judge's findings, whether by proof beyond a reasonable doubt or less, suffice for purposes of the Constitution. Under the Court's decision today, however, it appears that once a legislature constrains judges' sentencing discretion by prescribing certain sentences that may only be imposed (or must be imposed) in connection with the same determinations of the same contested facts, the Constitution requires that the facts instead be proved to a jury beyond a reasonable doubt. I see no reason to treat the two schemes differently.[212]

Arguing *a fortiori*, Justice O'Connor also concluded that the majority's holding in effect limited the efficacy of determinate sentencing schemes whereas indeterminate sentencing schemes raised far more serious Sixth Amendment concerns:

Consideration of the purposes underlying the Sixth Amendment's jury trial guarantee further demonstrates why our acceptance of judge-made findings in the context of discretionary sentencing suggests the approval of the same judge-made findings in the context of determinate sentencing as well. One important purpose of the Sixth Amendment's jury trial guarantee is to protect the criminal defendant against potentially arbitrary judges. It effectuates this promise by preserving, as a constitutional matter, certain fundamental decisions for a jury of one's peers, as opposed to a judge. For example, the Court has recognized that the Sixth Amendment's guarantee was motivated by the English experience of "competition... between judge and jury over the real significance of their respective roles, and measures [that were taken] to diminish the juries' power[.]" "We have also explained that the jury trial guarantee was understood to provide" an inestimable safeguard against the corrupt or overzealous prosecutor and against the compliant, biased, or eccentric judge. If the defendant preferred the common-sense judgment of a jury to the more tutored but perhaps less sympathetic reaction of the single judge, he was to have it. "Blackstone explained that the right to trial by jury was critically important in criminal cases because of" the violence and partiality of judged appointed by the crown... who might then, as in France or Turkey, imprison, dispatch, or exile any man that was obnoxious to the government, by an instant declaration, that such is their will and pleasure." Clearly, the concerns animating the Sixth Amendment's jury trial guarantee, if they were to extend to the sentencing context at all, would apply with greater strength to a discretionary-sentencing scheme than to determinate sentencing. In the former scheme, the potential for mischief by an arbitrary judge is much greater, given that the judge's discretion of where to set the

---

[212] *Id.* at 544–46 (O'Connor, J., dissenting).

72

defendant's sentence within the prescribed statutory range is left almost entirely to discretion. In contrast, under a determinate-sentencing system, the discretion the judge wields within the statutory range is tightly constrained. Accordingly, our approval of discretionary-sentencing schemes, in which a defendant is not entitled to have a jury make factual findings relevant to sentencing despite the effect those findings have on the severity of the defendant's sentence, demonstrates that the defendant should have no right to demand that a jury make the equivalent factual determinations under a determinate—sentencing scheme.[213]

In conclusion, Justice O'Connor warned that the Court's "decision [would] likely have an even more damaging effect on sentencing conducted in the immediate future under current determinate-sentencing schemes."[214]

In a separate dissent, Justice Breyer emphasized the importance of understanding "how a judge traditionally determined which factors should be taken into account for sentencing purposes."[215] Noting the many different factors that potentially account for a given sentence, Justice Breyer concluded,

In principle, the number of potentially relevant behavioral characteristics is endless. A judge might ask, for example, whether an unlawfully possessed knife was "a switchblade, drawn or concealed, opened or closed, large or small, used in connection with a car theft (where victim confrontation is rare), a burglary (where confrontation is unintended) or a robbery (where confrontation is intentional)." Again, the method reflects practical, rather than theoretical, considerations. Prior to the Sentencing Guidelines, federal law left the sentencing judge free to determine which factors were relevant. That freedom meant that each judge, in an effort to tailor punishment to the individual offense and offender, was guided primarily by experience, relevance, and a sense of proportional fairness.[216]

Responding to Justice Breyer's conclusion, Justice Scalia, concurring, criticized Justice Breyer's "admirably fair and efficient scheme designed for a society that is prepared to leave criminal justice to the State [i.e., a judge paid by the federal government]."[217] In doing so, he called into question the notion that judges should enjoy broad sentencing discretion:

In Justice Breyer's bureaucratic realm of perfect equity, by contrast, the facts that determine the length of sentence to which

---

[213] *Id.* at 547–49 (O'Connor, J., dissenting).
[214] *Id.* at 551 (O'Connor, J., dissenting).
[215] *Id.* at 558 (Breyer, J., dissenting).
[216] *Id.* (Breyer, J., dissenting).
[217] *Id.* at 498 (Scalia, J., concurring).

the defendant is exposed will be determined to exist (on a more-likely-than—not basis) by a single employee of the State. It is certainly arguable... that this sacrifice of prior protections is worth it. But it is not arguable that, just because one thinks it is a better system, it must be, or is even more likely to be, the system envisioned by a Constitution that guarantees trial by jury....[218]

Justice Scalia also concurred in *Ring v. Arizona*, in which the Court held that, in light of *Apprendi*, a court could not sentence a defendant to death when the court—as opposed to the jury—finds an aggravating factor meriting the death penalty.[219] In it, he defended the province of the jury against what he found to be unwarranted intrusion by legislatures and federal judges exercising their sentencing discretion:

> Second, and more important, my observing over the past 12 years the accelerating propensity of both state and federal legislatures to adopt "sentencing factors" determined by judges that increase punishment beyond what is authorized by the jury's verdict, and my witnessing the belief of a near majority of my colleagues that this novel practice is perfectly OK, cause me to believe that our people's traditional belief in the right of trial by jury is in perilous decline. That decline is bound to be confirmed, and indeed accelerated, by the repeated spectacle of a man's going to his death because *a judge* found that an aggravating factor existed. We cannot preserve our veneration for the protection of the jury in criminal cases if we render ourselves callous to the need for that protection by regularly imposing the death penalty without it.[220]

The same day it decided *Ring*, the Court held in *Harris v. United States* that a mandatory minimum sentencing scheme passed constitutional muster, even though the judge had to find an additional fact before the mandatory minimum went into effect.[221] The majority first explained that a fact "affecting the defendant's punishment" is not an element of an offense when the judge imposes "a sentence within a range provided by statute."[222] Presumably, the relevance and weight of such facts reside in the discretion of the trial judge, as guided by the legislature.[223] Characterizing a mandatory minimum scheme is nothing more than an effort on the

---

[218] *Id.* (Scalia, J., concurring).

[219] 536 U.S. 584 (2002). As discussed, Justice Breyer dissented from *Apprendi* itself based in part on the fact that numerous factors figure in to imposing a sentence, and those factors could produce a number of different results. Here, the Arizona trial court needed only find one aggravating factor in order to impose the death penalty. In the absence of that factor, however, the court had no other choice but to impose life in prison. Justice Breyer concurred in the judgment in *Ring* on Eighth Amendment grounds.

[220] *Id.* at 611–12 (Scalia, J., concurring).

[221] 536 U.S. 545 (2002).

[222] *Id.* at 549.

[223] *See id.*

74

part of the legislature to guide the court's discretion, the Court held that "[w]ithin the range authorized by the jury's verdict, however, the political system may channel judicial discretion—and rely upon judicial expertise—by requiring defendants to serve minimum terms after judges make certain factual findings.[224] The majority explained its reasoning earlier in the opinion:

> In sustaining the [mandatory minimum] statute the *McMillan* Court placed considerable reliance on the similarity between the sentencing factor at issue and the facts judges contemplate when exercising their discretion within the statutory range....

> ....

> In response to the argument that the Act evaded the Constitution's procedural guarantees, the Court noted that the statute simply took one factor that has always been considered by the sentencing court to bear on punishment... and dictated the precise weight to be given that factor.

> That reasoning still controls. If the facts judges consider when exercising their discretion within the statutory range are not elements, they do not become as much merely because legislatures require the judge to impose a minimum sentence when those facts are found—a sentence the judge could have imposed absent the finding. It does not matter, for the purposes of constitutional analysis, that in [certain statutes] the State provides that a fact shall give rise both to a special stigma and to a special punishment. Judges choosing a sentence within the range do the same, and [j]udges, it is sometimes necessary to remind ourselves, are part of the state. These facts, though stigmatizing and punitive, have been the traditional domain of judges; they have not been alleged in the indictment of proved beyond a reasonable doubt. There is no reason to believe that those who framed the Fifth and Sixth Amendments would have thought of them as the elements of the crime.[225]

The difference in opinion between Justice O'Connor and Justice Scalia came to a head in *Blakely v. Washington*, which struck down a portion of Washington's sentencing guidelines as unconstitutional.[226] In a dissent that in many ways echoed her dissent in *Apprendi*, Justice O'Connor argued that the court had told legislatures that if they wanted "to constrain the sentencing discretion of judges

---

[224] *Id.* at 567.
[225] *Id.* at 559–60.
[226] *Blakely v. Washington*, 542 U.S. 296 (2004) (holding that the statutory maximum for *Apprendi* purpose is the maximum sentence that a court can impose without finding additional facts).

and bring some uniformity to sentencing" they would pay a price.[227] Justice O'Connor's criticized the "unguided discretion" of the sentencing court, which she argued the majority's opinion had resurrected:

> This system of unguided discretion inevitably results in severe disparities in sentences received and served by defendants committing the same offense and having similar criminal histories…. Indeed, rather than reflect legally relevant criteria, these disparities too often were correlated with constitutionally suspect variables such as race.
>
> ….
>
> Far from disregarding principles of due process and the jury trial right, as the majority today suggests, Washington's reform has served them. Before the passage of the Act, a defendant charged with second degree kidnapping, like petitioner, had no idea whether he would receive a 10-year sentence or probation. The ultimate sentencing determination could turn as much on the idiosyncrasies of a particular judge as on the specifics of the defendant's crime or background. A defendant did not know what facts, if any, about his offense or his history would be considered relevant by the sentencing judge or by the parole board. After passage of the Act, a defendant charged with second degree kidnapping knows what his presumptive sentence will be; he has a good idea of the types of factors that a sentencing judge can and will consider when deciding whether to sentence him outside the range; he is guaranteed meaningful appellate review to protect against an arbitrary sentence. Criminal defendants still face the same statutory maximum sentences, but they now at least know, much more than before, the real consequences of their actions.
>
> Washington's move to a system of guided discretion has served equal protection principles as well. Over the past 20 years, there has been a substantial reduction in racial disparity in sentencing across the State.
>
> ….
>
> The costs are substantial and real. Under the majority's approach, any fact that increases the upper bound on a judge's sentencing discretion is an element of the offense. Thus, facts that historically

---

[227] *Id.* at 314 (O'Connor, J., dissenting) ("Congress and States, faced with the burdens imposed by the extension of *Apprendi* to the present context, will either trim or eliminate altogether their sentencing guidelines schemes and, with them, 20 years of sentencing reform.") ("The 'effect' of today's decision will be greater judicial discretion and less uniformity in sentencing.").

have been taken into account by sentencing judges to assess a sentence within a broad range—such as drug quantity, role in the offense, risk of bodily harm—all must now be charged in an indictment and submitted to the jury simply because it is the legislature, rather than the judge, that constrains the extent to which such facts may be used to impose a sentence within a pre-existing statutory range.[228]

---

[228] *Id.* at 315-318.

2

Reasons Trial Court Has Discretion

§ 2.1.   Overview

Maurice Rosenberg's well-known article on judicial discretion set out five reasons that appellate courts use to justify their deference to the trial court's discretion in certain contexts:

> One is the plain urge to economize on judicial energies. Appeal courts would be swamped to the point of capsizing if every ruling by a trial judge could be presented for appellate review.... With the explosion of the caseload of many of the busiest courts, this understandable instinct for self-preservation becomes an even more potent argument for according the final word to trial courts on many questions within their purview. But which? The argument for economizing appellate energies does not help us to identify the issues that should be committed to trial judges for final or presumptively final determination. It advances a persuasive reason for often making the first court effectively the court of last resort, but is undiscriminating in selecting the issues that are to be unreviewable....
>
> A second reason is maintaining morale. A trial judge might become dispirited if he had the sense that every rapid-fire ruling he makes at trial is to be fully reviewable by a clutch of appellate judges who can study, reflect, hear and read carefully assembled arguments, consult their law clerks, debate among themselves and, after close analysis, overturn his ruling. He would have an oppressive sense that appellate Big Brothers were ever watching, peering over the trial bench, waiting for the harried and hurried trial judge to lapse into mortal fallibility.
>
> ....
>
> That reason, worthy and compassionate as it is, again falls short of telling which of the rapid-fire trial rulings are to be immune from review and which not....
>
> The third reason for hands-off review is finality. The more reverse-proof the trial judge's rulings, the less likely the losing attorney is to test them on appeal and the sooner the first adjudication becomes accepted and the dispute tranquilized. Delay would surely result, and injustice might result, if every trial court order could be dragged up the appellate ladder with some fair hope of reversal. Except where restrained by the final judgment principle, the party with the deeper pocket might try to wear down his adversary by challenging every uncongenial ruling, whether made in the

pleading, discovery, trial or post-trial phases of the litigation. Conferring near-finality on trial court orders by restrictive review practices dampens the possibility of that sort of abuse. But once again, the reason is non-selective. It fails to offer criteria indicating which lower court rulings are shielded by discretion and which are not, and it also fails to indicate how firm the hands-off policy is in the particular instance....

....

One of the "good" reasons for conferring discretion on the trial judge is the sheer impracticability of formulating a rule of decision for the matter in issue. Many questions that arise in litigation are not amenable to regulation by rule because they involve multifarious, fleeting, special, narrow facts that utterly resist generalization—at least, for the time being. Whether a witness may be called out of regular sequence, the scope of cross-examination in many circumstances, enlarging time, ordering special hearings, requiring special memoranda, and a host of other trial administration issues, are obviously unamenable to hard and fast legal rules. When the ruling under attack is one that does not seem to admit of control by a rule that can be formulated or criteria that can be indicated, prudence and necessity agree it should be left in the control of the judge at the trial level. That is true when the circumstances which rationally deserve attention are so infinitely variable that it is hopeless to try to cover them by general propositions.

On occasion, the difficulty is the novelty of the situation rather than the multifarious minuteness of its circumstances. When the problem arises in a context so new and unsettled that the rule-makers do not yet know what factors should shape the result, the case may be a good one to leave to lower court discretion. Actually, this may be a form of primary or free-form discretion, but the point is that it permits experience to accumulate at the lowest level before the appellate judges commit themselves to a prescribed rule....

....

The final reason—and probably the most pointed and helpful one—for bestowing discretion on the trial judge as to many matters is, paradoxically, the superiority of his nether position. It is not that he knows more than his loftier brothers; rather, he sees more and senses more. In the dialogue between appellate judges and the trial judge, the former often seem to be saying: "You were there. We do not think we would have done what you did, but we were not present and we may be unaware of significant matters, for the record does not adequately convey to us all that went on at the trial. Therefore, we defer to you."[1]

Our analysis of the reasons for trial court discretion follows Rosenberg's closely. We begin by discussing those situations in which the appellate courts defer to the trial court because of the trial court's "superior vantage point" over the issue. Because there is little case law discussing the "morale of the trial court" as a justification for discretion, we include it as part of our "superior vantage point" discussion. The second section identifies those situations in which appellate courts, unable or unwilling to articulate "hard—and—fast rules" to govern an issue, defer to the trial court's discretionary judgment. As Rosenberg suggests, there may be many more examples of this justification for discretion (e.g., the court's control of its calendar with respect to the parties) that are so rarely appealed that the case law is scarce. Finally, we discuss the rule "efficiency and economy" have in determining the extent of trial court discretion. We also include in this section a brief discussion of "finality" and trial court discretion.

§ 2.2. Superior Vantage Point of Trial Judge

a) Mistrial

Appellate courts often uphold the discretion of the trial court either to grant or deny a motion for a mistrial "because the trial court is in the best position to gauge the surrounding circumstances of the event [giving rise to a motion for a mistrial] and its impact on the jury."[2] Defendant Ritchie was convicted of the murder of a police officer and sentenced to death. During the guilt phase of the trial, the prosecutor referred to a tattoo on defendant that depicted the numbers "3" and "7."[3] Defendant moved for a mistrial. Although defendant claimed the tattoo referred to the badge number of the victim, the record did not show that the jury would be aware of that fact.[4] The court therefore defined the issue as "solely whatever effect [defendant's] having a tattoo might have on the jury."[5]

Acting pursuant to the abuse of discretion standard, the court declined to disturb the trial court's ruling denying defendant's motion for a mistrial. In doing so, however, the court addressed two collateral matters. First, the trial judge had granted defendant's motion *in limine* to prohibit the state from referring to the tattoo during the guilt phase of the trial.[6] The court did not address the state's apparent violation of the *in limine* order, stating instead that the "issue before this [c]ourt is

---

[1] Maurice Rosenberg, *Judicial Discretion of the Trial Court: Viewed from Above*, 22 Syracuse L. Rev. 635, 660–63 (1971). (Reprinted with permission of the Syracuse Law Review.)

[2] *See, e.g.*, *Ritchie v. State*, 809 N.E.2d 258, 270 (Ind. 2004).

[3] *Id* at 269.

[4] *Id.*

[5] *Id.* at 269.

[6] *Id.* at 269.

whether the misconduct requires a retrial, not whether it violates a trial court order."[7] Second, in its dicta, the court discouraged trial courts from simply granting a mistrial without considering less drastic remedies for misconduct, stating that "the trial court must determine that no lesser step could have rectified the situation."[8]

The New Hampshire Supreme Court stated as a general principle that mistrial is only a "proper remedy" for prosecutorial misconduct when that conduct is "not merely improper, but also so prejudicial that it constitutes an irreparable injustice that cannot be cured by jury instructions."[9] However, the court leaves it to the discretion of the trial judge to "determine what remedy will adequately correct the prejudice created by a prosecutor's remarks" and will uphold the trial court's decision "absent an unsustainable exercise of discretion."[10]

A trial court's decision to grant (or deny) a mistrial on account of other irregularities in the trial process are also subject to the abuse of discretion standard.[11] In *Griffin*, the Eleventh Circuit considered whether the trial court abused its discretion by denying a mistrial when one of plaintiff Griffin's witnesses began crying during her testimony. Plaintiff alleged that the defendant, her ex-boss and the former city manager of Opa-Locka, had repeatedly harassed her at work and had raped her in her home. Before breaking down, plaintiff's witness testified that defendant had repeatedly harassed her while she worked under defendant in Florida City.[12] Rather than granting defendant's request for a mistrial, the trial court first instructed the jury to ignore the witness's crying and eventually struck the entirety of witness's testimony.[13] On appeal, defendant claimed that the witness's testimony had deprived him of his right to a fair and impartial jury. Upholding the trial court's discretion, the Eleventh Circuit concluded that the trial court responded sufficiently to the crying by instructing the jury and ultimately striking the witness's testimony.[14]

Addressing an issue involving an individual juror's second-guessing of the jury panel's verdict for death in the penalty phase of a capital double murder case, the Ohio Supreme Court applied reasoning similar to that of the *Griffin* court.[15] The jury had already convicted the defendant of murder; if the judge declared a mistrial in the penalty phase, the judge would sentence defendant to life imprisonment.

---

[7] *Id.*

[8] *Id.*

[9] *State v. Hearns*, 855 A.2d 549, 555 (N.H. 2004).

[10] *Id.*

[11] *See, e.g.*, *Griffin v. City of Opa-Locka*, 261 F.3d 1295, 1302 (11th Cir. 2001) (so holding).

[12] *Id.*

[13] *Id.*

[14] *Id.*

[15] *See State v. Brown*, 796 N.E.2d 506, 517 (Ohio 2003) ("In deciding whether there has been an abuse of discretion, we are cognizant of the fact that the trial judge remains in the best position to view the demeanor and actions of the juror to determine whether further questioning is necessary.")

After lengthy deliberation, the jury had returned to the courtroom and had recommended death for one of the murders and life imprisonment for the other. When polled, one juror said that she had "compromised" with the other jurors and that the jury verdicts were not her verdicts.[16] The court reread the penalty instructions and sent the jurors away for further deliberations but denied defendant's motion for a mistrial. On appeal, defendant contended that the court should have questioned the hesitant juror more thoroughly once the court knew she had "compromised."[17]

The court acknowledged that "the better practice would be for the trial judge to conduct further inquiry of a dissenting juror" but held that neither Ohio criminal procedure nor state statutes mandate further questioning.[18] Moreover, the court held that the juror's expressing reservation does not require a mistrial *per se*.[19] The court noted that in *Hessler* the trial court had questioned the juror in chambers subsequent to her hesitation; however, the court concluded that because the juror in the present case had willingly returned to deliberations and made no further signs of hesitation, the trial court had not abused its discretion by not pursuing the matter further than it had.[20]

On a related note, appellate courts have afforded "a great latitude of discretion" to trial courts "in determining whether and to what extent the [civil] verdict was supported by the evidence" and thus whether remittitur is appropriate.[21] Reviewing defendant's argument on appeal that the trial court did not allow further *remittitur* of the jury's verdict, the court noted that a "trial court abuses its discretion when the remitted judgment remains grossly excessive so as to shock the conscience of the appellate court."[22] The court cautioned trial courts only to interfere with a jury judgment with hesitation and only when the verdict is "manifestly unjust."[23]

---

[16] *Id.* at 516.

[17] *Id.* at 517.

[18] *Id.* at 517.

[19] *Id.* (citing *State v. Hessler*, 734 N.E.2d 1237 (Ohio 2000), a case upholding the trial court's decision not grant a mistrial even though one juror, upon signing a penalty form, began to cry and refused to enter the courtroom).

[20] *Id.* at 518 ("Had [juror] expressed further reservation about her verdict or about further deliberating, then it may have been necessary to conduct an inquiry."). The court went on to discuss the process of reaching a unanimous verdict as "a difficult and emotional undertaking." *Id.* The court stated that "[h]eightened emotions and intense feelings are part and parcel of this process. Experience tells us that during deliberations, it is not unusual to find heavy-handed influencing, browbeating, and even bullying to a certain extent."

[21] *Gomez v. Construction Design, Inc.*, 126 S.W.3d 366, 376 (Mo. 2004) (holding that the "trial court's superior vantage point warrants a great latitude in discretion").

[22] *Id.* at 375.

[23] *Id.*

b)   Evidentiary Matters

Federal Rules of Evidence 403 provides that otherwise relevant evidence "may be excluded if its probative value is substantially outweighed by the danger of unfair prejudice, confusion of the issues, or misleading the jury, or by considerations of undue delay, waste of time, or needless presentation of cumulative evidence."

> Given "the superiority of his nether position"... a trial judge is given broad discretion to weigh these competing interests because he is in a superior position to evaluate all of the circumstances connected with them, since he sees the witnesses, defendant, jurors, and counsel, and their mannerisms and reactions.[24]

The *Jamil* court however, listed some considerations under which would review the trial court's Rule 403 decision: (1) The trial court does not have unfettered discretion; the appellate court will reverse if the trial court acts "arbitrarily or irrationally"; (2) the trial court must specify its reasons for excluding evidence under rule 403 on the record "so the counsel can, if possible, obviate the objection"; (3) the trial court must use the Rule 403 power sparingly and only after a "conscientious assessment of whether unfair prejudice outweighs probative force."[25]

The evidence at issue in *Jamil* was a tape recording taken by a government informant. At the time of the recording, defendant Jamil was under a federal investigation for selling military equipment without a license. The government knew Jamil was represented by counsel when it supplied a recording device to its informant. The tape recording contained some evidence of a shipment of military equipment to Beirut, and it appears from the recording that defendant had not acquired the necessary licenses. Subsequently, the government indicted defendant and defendant moved to dismiss the indictment on the grounds that the tape violated his rights under Fifth and Sixth Amendments. The trial court rejected defendant's constitutional arguments but ultimately suppressed the evidence under Rule 403.

On appeal, the court reconsidered all of the interests that Rule 403 enumerates. The court conceded that the recording would prejudice the defendant, but held that there was no unfair prejudice to the defendant. The court focused first on the fact that an informant's tape could paint defendant as someone ever under the watchful eye of the authorities (and, thus, suspicious), but the court declined to describe that as "unfair" because if it did so, the court reasoned that all such evidence would be "inherently inadmissible, simply because it connoted interest in the person by [enforcement] officers."[26] The court then turned to the fact that

---

[24] *United States v. Jamil*, 707 F.2d 638, 642 (2d Cir. 1983).
[25] *Id.*
[26] *Id.* at 644.

84

defendant's counsel's voice also appeared on the tape. The court declined to decide whether defendant's counsel would be unable to represent defendant because of the recording (which would possibly compel counsel to testify) because defendant could "seek to have the tape redacted, or seek some stipulation from the government about it, or allow the entire tape to be played."[27] The court also concluded that the ethical problems of admitting the statements of defendant's counsel into evidence did not "provide a sufficient basis for the Rule 403 ruling."[28] The court concluded that the trial judge's 403 findings were "unsupported by the record" and that the exclusion of the tape was "arbitrary" and "constituted a clear abuse of discretion."[29]

Some appellate courts have used the superior position of the trial judge to uphold judicial discretion even when the trial judge makes a decision of constitutional import or a decision touching on deeply held values in our legal system, such as respecting the privileged nature of certain relationships. The Minnesota Supreme Court has held that a trial court "is in the best position to appraise the claim of [Fifth Amendment] privilege" and will not overturn a trial court's decision to allow a witness to assert that privilege when the record does not show an abuse of discretion.[30] Defendant had been convicted of first-degree murder. During *voir dire*, a potential defense witness appeared through counsel and asserted his Fifth Amendment right not to testify. Defense counsel requested that the court make a preliminary inquiry to determine whether the witness had validly asserted a Fifth Amendment privilege.[31] The witness's counsel declined to state the reasons why the witness had invoked the Fifth Amendment, citing attorney-client privilege.[32] The trial court declined to inquire further and excused the witness. The court left open the question as to whether the trial court would receive the same deference had it determined that the witness would be required to testify despite the Fifth Amendment claim.

The Hawaii Supreme Court had to balance the right of a defendant (accused of molesting a child) to confront his accuser against the accuser's privileged

---

[27] *Id.*

[28] *Id.* at 645.

[29] *Id.* at 646–47. Appellate courts will also consider the trial judge's superior vantage point an important reason to uphold trial court discretion when there are no ethical issues lurking in the shadows of the case. *See United States v. Thomas*, 377 F.3d 232, 240 (2nd Cir. 2004) (trial judge's superior vantage point as to whether or not evidence is admissible applies to trial court decision to restrict cross-examination); *State v. Hubbard*, 48 P.3d 953, 959 (Utah 2002)

> We have not adopted a per se rule of inadmissibility of expert testimony regarding eyewitness identification. Instead, we recognize that whether to allow proffered expert testimony regarding eyewitness identification testimony is a matter best left to the trial court's discretion because of the trial court's superior position to judge the advisability of such testimony.

[30] *State v. Manley*, 664 N.W.2d 275, 286 (Minn. 2003) ("Trial courts have broad discretion in deciding whether a claim of privilege is valid.").

[31] *Id.* at 285.

[32] *Id.*

communications with her therapist.[33] Defendant Peseti's *hanai* (trans., "adopted" or "foster") daughter accused Peseti of molesting her in the back of a pickup truck on New Year's Day of 1998. Following the incident, some evidence emerged that complainant told her therapist that the truck incident never happened. During pretrial discovery, defendant subpoenaed the state Children's Protective Service (CPS) requesting complainant's records. The trial court inspected the records *in camera* and redacted all but a few pages of police reports.[34] The trial court noted defendant's objection to that action. Later, during defendant's cross-examination of complainant, defendant asked complainant if she told her therapist that the incident really did not happen. The state objected on grounds of patient-therapist privilege, and the trial court sustained the objection even though the question went to the credibility of the complaining witness.

The court affirmed the discretionary decision of the trial court to redact the records based on patient-therapist privilege but reversed the trial court on the grounds that defendant had a constitutional right to ask complainant whether she had told her therapist that the incident never happened.[35] With respect to the redacted records, the court concluded that defendant's due process right to gather exculpatory evidence had not been violated because the court had examined the records *in camera*.[36] In doing so, the court reasoned that the trial court was in the best position to "determine the optimal time for evaluating the relative significance of proffered exculpatory but otherwise privileged material."[37] The court distinguished defendant's limited interest in "general pretrial discovery," which could well result in defendant's roving through privileged information, from defendant's interest in showing that a particular piece of pretrial information could influence the outcome of the trial.[38]

A trial court also has the discretion to determine when a "misimpression" exists for the purposes of the opening-the-door doctrine.[39] "The 'opening-the-door' doctrine permits a trial judge, in his or her discretion, to admit otherwise inadmissible evidence to rebut prejudicial evidence that has been admitted."[40] In the present case, defendant Goodman was convicted of criminal threatening and second-degree assault after he said he would kill the victim and later threatened her with a knife. After the victim testified as to her fear of defendant, defense counsel

---

[33] *State v. Peseti*, 65 P.3d 119, 131 (Hawai'i 2003).

[34] *Id.* at 121.

[35] Although the court strongly implied that the trial court had abused its discretion by limiting defendant's cross-examination, its discussion focused on the legal question as to when a defendant's right to confront trumps complainant's privileged communication with her therapist. *Id.* at 127.

[36] *Id.* at 133.

[37] *Id.*

[38] *Id.* (concluding further that the trial judge is in the best position to balance these competing interests.)

[39] *State v. Goodman*, 764 A.2d 925, 927 (N.H. 2000) (noting that the opening-the-door doctrine can apply only when the opposing party created a misimpression.)

[40] *Id.* at 926.

cross-examined her and elicited that she had consensual relations with defendant on the night of the threat and did not take any action following the first threat. The state then argued, and the trial court found, that defendant had "created a misimpression that the victim was not afraid of the defendant and that she could have left him at any point during the evening."[41] The victim then testified about "defendant's aggressive acts during the week prior to the charged incidents."[42] The court upheld the trial court's decision, noting also that defendant's opening statement alleging that victim's supposedly inconsistent behavior amounted to her not really being afraid of defendant.[43]

c)   Case Management

"[C]onsiderable deference is given the trial judge's determination regarding the default judgment since he is the person most familiar with the circumstances of the case and, thus, is in the best position to evaluate the good faith and credibility of the parties at the hearings."[44] Plaintiffs (native Nigerians) sued defendant Babcock and Ross School of Aviation (of which Babcock is owner and president). Plaintiffs prepaid their tuition only to see the school close before they could arrive in Tulsa to begin pilot-training classes. Plaintiffs served defendant by certified mail March 1, 1984 and received a return receipt marked "refused." Babcock took no further action in his defense, and plaintiffs received compensatory and punitive damages by default judgment. Three months after that judgment, Babcock moved to set aside default pursuant to Rule 60(b)(4). After three evidentiary hearings, the trial judge denied Babcock's motion, concluding that Babcock had been apprised of the lawsuit.[45]

The court upheld the trial court's discretion on two grounds. In response to defendant's claim that he had not been served, the court concluded that "there was clearly ample evidence that allowed the trial court to adduce that (1) Babcock or his wife refused service, and (2) Babcock was simply endeavoring to avoid service of process."[46] Defendant also argued that the process did not comply strictly with the Oklahoma statute requiring a return receipt "from addressee only" and therefore was defective. Noting the distinction between "refused" service and papers that are lost or unclaimed, the court concluded that the fact defendant had tried to avoid process justified the trial court's decision.[47]

An appellate court "generally defers to the decision of a trial court regarding sanctions for failure to comply with discovery procedures because the trial court is in the best position to assess whether parties are disregarding the rights

---

[41] *Id.*

[42] *Id.*

[43] *Id.* at 927.

[44] *Nikwei v. Ross Sch. of Aviation*, 822 F.2d 939, 941 (10th Cir. 1987).

[45] *Id.* at 941.

[46] *Id.* at 942.

[47] *See id.* at 944 ("Finally, and most importantly, in none of the above cited cases where service was invalidated was the defendant ever accused of attempting to avoid process.")

of opposing parties in the course of litigation and to determine which sanctions for such conduct are most appropriate."[48] Plaintiff Hawkins sued defendant veterinarians for breach of an implied contract to perform competent veterinary services on her dog. (Her dog, affectionately referred to as "Laddie," suffered injuries in a vehicle accident. Defendants cared for the wounded canine until they discovered he had injuries outside their scope of expertise. The dog was paraplegic for the rest of his life.) During discovery, defendants submitted an interrogatory to plaintiff requesting that she provide information on any expert she expected to call at trial. Plaintiff answered the interrogatory, "[n]ot determined," and defendants asked for a supplemental answer, which the court subsequently required of plaintiff no later than December 31, 2001. On December 28, 2001, plaintiff provided the name and address of veterinarian in Oklahoma. Defendants filed a motion to compel discovery and moved for sanctions. Plaintiff later submitted one page of information on her expert witness, but the trial court found that answer insufficient and sanctioned plaintiff by barring her expert and dismissing the case.

Analyzing the trial court's decisions "in light of the underlying policies of Rule 26,"[49] the court asked whether plaintiff's answer served to "eliminate surprise" and "to promote effective cross-examination of expert witnesses."[50] The court concluded that plaintiff's answer did both, since it listed the name, address, education, and employment of plaintiff's expert and also described the fact and opinions to which he would testify and on what grounds those opinions rested.[51] The court also noted that, although it did not "condone" plaintiff's "tardiness," defendant still had time either to prepare cross–examination and/or to depose plaintiff's expert.[52] The court concluded that the trial court "abused its discretion when it determined that Hawkins did not provide an adequate response.[53] Based on that conclusion, the court also concluded that the trial court abused its discretion when it imposed sanctions against plaintiff for a discovery violation she did not commit.[54]

In Georgia, a trial court hearing a divorce case decided to skip the parties' closing arguments, saying "Y'all have about worn me out. I don't think I want to hear any closing arguments."[55] Wife appealed from the final divorce decree, claiming that she had a right to make a closing argument and that the denial of that right was reversible error.

The majority of the court alluded to a split among jurisdictions regarding whether parties in a civil, nonjury action have a right to make closing arguments.[56] It

---

[48] *Hawkins v. Harney*, 66 P.3d 305, 310 (Mont. 2003).
[49] *Id.* at 309.
[50] *Id.* at 310.
[51] *Id.*
[52] *Id.*
[53] *Id.*
[54] *Id.*
[55] *Wilson v. Wilson*, 596 S.E. 2d 392, 393 (Ga. 2004)
[56] *Id.*

88

indicated that although in Georgia there is no absolute right to closing argument, closing argument even in a civil, nonjury action is not purely discretionary.[57] The court reiterated its prior holding that the trial judge can dispense with closing arguments when the parties waive them or when "no factual issues exist" or when the proceeding is interlocutory.[58] Because the case at bar fell into none of these categories, the court reversed the trial court's decision.

Chief Justice Fletcher dissented, claiming first that there was "no evidence that the trial judge's decision not to hear closing arguments in this case harmed either of the parties...."[59] The dissent also argued that "[t]he trial judge, having heard the evidence presented by the parties, is in the best position to know whether closing argument is necessary to reach a decision in the case."[60] It concluded that "the trial judge is in the best position to determine the necessity of closing argument in a non-jury civil trial" and that "this Court [should not] compel him to do so, absent a showing that he abused his discretion and thereby unfairly prejudiced one of the parties."[61]

The superior vantage point of a trial judge may cause an appellate court to defer to the trial court even when the trial court's management of a case has constitutional ramifications. Defendant Algee claimed that a federal district court deprived him of his constitutional rights when it disqualified his attorney of choice.[62] The district court had disqualified defendant's attorney (despite defendant's waiver of any conflict) because the attorney had represented a codefendant who later gave a taped confession implicating defendant. The Sixth Circuit upheld the trial court's decision as a legitimate exercise of discretion, affording it "substantial latitude" "because of the dangers associated with multiple representation."[63] The Sixth Circuit compared the case before it with the Supreme Court's decision in *Wheat v. United States*, a case in which the defendant requested an attorney "who had previously represented two other defendants charged in the same criminal conspiracy."[64] The *Wheat* court reasoned that if the defendant's coconspirators testified at trial, the defendant's "chosen counsel would have been unable ethically to provide vigorous cross-examination."[65] Noting that the *Wheat* court had acknowledged "that the trial court was in the best position to evaluate the facts and circumstances of each case," the Sixth Circuit extended the trial court's

---

[57] *Id.*

[58] *Id.*

[59] *Id.* at 396 (Fletcher, C. J., dissenting).

[60] *Id.* at 397.

[61] *Id.*

[62] *United States v. Algee*, 309 F.3d 1011, 1013 (6th Cir. 2002).

[63] *Id.* at 1014 ("It is well-settled, however, that a criminal defendant's right to his chosen attorney may be outweighed by a serious potential for conflict due to the attorney's prior representation of other defendants charged in the same criminal conspiracy.").

[64] *Id.* (citing 486 U.S. 153 (1988)).

[65] *Id.* (citing 486 U.S. at 164).

discretion to include cases in which the defendant's attorney of choice had represented a person who had implicated defendant. [66]

A divided Washington Supreme Court held that a trial judge had discretion to decide whether a criminal defendant voluntarily waived his right to appear at trial (although it also held that the trial judge had abused that discretion).[67] State police arrested defendant Garza following a high-speed chase and charged with attempting to elude a pursuing police vehicle. During pretrial, the trial judge admonished defendant for repeated tardiness and told him not to be late for further proceedings. On June 19, 2000, the day of the trial, defendant failed to appear. Defense counsel told the trial court that defendant had called counsel to explain that he was running late. After waiting five minutes, the court found defendant voluntarily absent and allowed the jury trial to proceed without defendant. After waiting two hours and allowing defendant's counsel to attempt to contact defendant, the court reiterated that defendant was voluntarily absent and issued a bench warrant. Defendant was convicted the following day. A week later, defendant filed a motion for a new trial, alleging that the trial court had deprived him his Sixth Amendment right to be present at his trial. Defendant stated that he had been arrested on his way to court based on an outstanding warrant in another county. He also stated that he asked the arresting officer to contact the court and explain that defendant would not be able to attend his trial. He was released on bail the evening of June 19, after testimony in his trial had ended. The trial court denied defendant's motion for a new trial.

Noting a "dispute" regarding the appropriate standard of review, the trial court determined that the Ninth Circuit's *de novo* standard for Sixth Amendment questions would not apply to defendant's case because the Ninth Circuit "did not determine a question of whether a trial court's finding of waiver violated the defendant's Sixth Amendment right to be present at trial."[68] The majority stated further that the "*de novo* standard is better applied when the appellate court is in the same position as the trial court and may make a determination as a matter of law."[69] Because the case at bar involved a trial court's factual finding of waiver, the majority concluded that the "abuse of discretion standard" was "appropriate" as the trial court was "in the best position to a make a factual determination" as to whether defendant had waived his Sixth Amendment right to be present.[70] Applying the abuse standard, the court concluded that the trial court had abused its discretion because the trial court failed to determine that the "circumstances justify a renewed finding of voluntary absence."[71]

---

[66] *Id. Aglee* 309 F.3d at 1014.

[67] *State v. Garza*, 77 P.3d 347 (Wash. 2003).

[68] *Id.* at 350 (citing *Guam v. Palomo*, 35 F.3d 368 (9th Cir. 1994)).

[69] *Id.*

[70] *Id.*

[71] *Id.* at 352 (requiring a trial court to "inquire into the circumstances surrounding the absence). "The trial court must give a defendant the opportunity to explain the absence." *Id.* "If the absence was due to incarceration, there must be a showing that the defendant could not, or tried but failed to, contact the court." *Id.*

Justice Sanders concurred. He argued that although the majority acknowledged "a defendant's Sixth Amendment right to be present at trial" as a "fundamental right," it "jeopardized" that "fundamental constitutional right" because it adopted "the deferential abuse of discretion standard."[72] Judge Sanders also argued that the Ninth Circuit's *de novo* standard was supported by United States Supreme Court precedent and was therefore mandatory authority over the Washington courts.[73]

The Supreme Court of Florida restored a trial court's decision to award a new trial based on a verdict against the clear weight of the evidence.[74] The intermediate appellate court had held that a trial court could only grant a motion for a new trial "when it is clear, obvious, and indisputable that the jury was wrong."[75] The court concluded that the appellate court had applied a "substantial, competent evidence standard that was issued prior to this Court's rejection of that standard in Cloud."[76] The court offered the following explanation:

> The trial judge's discretionary power to grant a new trial on the grounds that the verdict is contrary to the manifest weight of the evidence is the only check against a jury that has reached an unjust decision on the facts. This discretionary power emanates from the common law principle that it is the duty of the trial judge to prevent what he or she considers to be a miscarriage of justice. The role of the trial judge is not to substitute his or her own verdict for that of the jury, but to avoid what, in the judge's trained and experienced judgment, is an unjust verdict. Thus, the trial judge does not have broad discretion to enter a judgment for a litigant or to deny a litigant a jury trial. As our cases illustrate, this discretionary authority of a trial judge to order a new trial when the verdict is contrary to the manifest weight of the evidence has been applied to the benefit of both plaintiffs and defendants who have been victimized by unjust verdicts.[77]

The court then discussed its decision in *Cloud v. Fallis*:

---

[72] *Garza*, 77 P.3d at 352–53 (Sanders, J., concurring).

[73] *Id.* at 353. For an example of another case in which an appellate court found an abuse of discretion in a criminal matter, see *State v. Boyd*, 846 So.2d 458, 460 (Fla. 2003) (holding that the trial court had abused its discretion when it "summarily denied" a motion to extend petitioner's time to file for post-conviction relief) ("We emphasize that an extension of time under rule 3.050 is not designed to indefinitely expand the two-year deadline, but only to afford a defendant a short period of extra time to file the motion where good cause is shown.").

[74] *Brown v. Estate of Stuckey*, 749 So. 2d 490 (Fla. 1999) (quashing the intermediate appellate court's decision reversing the trial court for abuse of discretion).

[75] *Id.* at 494.

[76] *Id.*

[77] *Id.* at 495.

This Court's seminal decision in *Cloud v. Fallis*, 110 So. 2d 669 (Fla. 1959), governs the broad discretion of a trial judge to grant a new trial when the verdict is contrary to the manifest weight of the evidence.... The district court opted to follow the broad discretion doctrine and it affirmed the trial court's order of a new trial. The district court's decision was appealed and this Court determined that the issue was whether the so—called broad discretion rule or the so-called substantial, competent evidence rule should be applied in this state. *Cloud*, 110 So. 2d at 671. This Court upheld the district court's decision, stating, "We adhere to the early rule placing in trial courts broad discretion of such firmness that it would not be disturbed except on clear showing of abuse...." Id. at 672 (emphasis added). The *Cloud* Court explained the trial judge's duty in considering a motion for a new trial based on the verdict being against the manifest weight of the evidence:

When a motion for a new trial is made it is directed to the sound, broad discretion of the trial judge, who because of his contact with the trial and his observation of the behavior of those upon whose testimony the finding of fact must be based is better positioned than any other one person fully to comprehend the processes by which the ultimate decision of the triers of fact, the jurors, is reached.

When the judge, who must be presumed to have drawn on his talents, his knowledge and his experience to keep the search for the truth in a proper channel, concludes that the verdict is against the manifest weight of the evidence, it is his duty to grant a new trial, and he should always do that if the jury has been deceived as to the force and credibility of the evidence or has been influenced by considerations outside the record.[78]

The court concluded that "[w]hen reviewing the order granting a new trial, an appellate court must recognize the broad discretionary authority of the trial judge and apply the reasonableness test to determine whether the trial judge committed an abuse of discretion."[79] Applying its exposition of the *Cloud* holding to the facts in front of it, the court concluded that the intermediate court had intruded upon the trial court's discretion to grant a new trial based on a verdict against the manifest weight of the evidence.[80]

Judge Pariente dissented on the grounds that the *Cloud* decision never discussed the meaning of "manifest weight of the evidence" and that the intermediate court's use of a "clear, obvious, and indisputable test" went to what constituted "manifest weight," not abuse of discretion.[81] Judge Pariente also pointed

---

[78] *Id.* at 495–96.
[79] *Id.* at 497–98.
[80] *Id.* at 498.
[81] *Id.* at 499 (Pariente, J., dissenting).

to the lack of explanation as to "how the jury was deceived about the force of the evidence" or how the damages awarded were "duplicative."[82] Judge Pariente concluded that "the trial court simply disagreed with the jury's assessment of damages and did no more than impermissibly sit as a seventh juror, thereby usurping the jury's fact-finding function."[83]

Courts have reserved questions of other long-established (albeit subconstitutional) rights to the discretion of the trial court as well. The Massachusetts Supreme Judicial Court reserved the question as to whether to terminate an impoundment order to the discretion of the trial court.[84] The underlying case involved a civil action against a Catholic priest alleging that the priest had molested plaintiff. A newspaper company sought access to court records impounded since the accused priest had been subject of a murder investigation. In connection with a search warrant executed in the course of that investigation, a trial court had in 1993 impounded a police officer's affidavit and supporting documents, legal memoranda, and parts of the trial court's decision on the search warrant that referenced "sensitive material."[85] At the newspaper's request, another judge modified the impoundment order in 1996 and released all material, "subject to redaction of certain personal information."[86] In 2003, a trial judge modified the order again, releasing all the material except "the names and addresses of private individuals who furnished highly personal information to the investigators."[87] The state eventually appealed the 2003 modification to the Supreme Judicial Court.

After discussing the public's interest in having access to judicial records, the court stated that the "public's right of access to judicial records, including transcripts, evidence, memoranda, and court orders, may be restricted, but only a showing of 'good cause.'"[88] The court state further that the "burden of demonstrating the existence of good cause always remains with the party urging their continued impoundment."[89] Although the trial court summarized its finding that the state could not longer sustain that burden, the appellate court deferred to the trial court because of its "meticulous in camera inspection of the impounded material" and because of several other factors (*e.g.*, widespread media exposure of priests' sexual misdeeds) that had rendered outdated the thirty-year-old impoundment order.[90]

---

[82] *Id.* (Pariente, J., dissenting).

[83] *Id.* (Pariente, J., dissenting).

[84] *Republican Co. v. App. Ct.*, 812 N.E.2d 887 (Mass. 2004).

[85] *Id.* at 890.

[86] *Id.*

[87] *Id.*

[88] *Id.* at 892.

[89] *Id.* at 892.

[90] *Id.* at 894.

d)   Jury Matters

The superior vantage point of the trial court justifies its discretion in a variety of matters pertaining to the management of the jury. A more common one of these matters is whether to excuse a juror for cause. In *State v. Taylor*, the Missouri Supreme Court, sitting en banc, reaffirmed a prior holding that the "trial court is in the best position to evaluate a venireperson's commitment to follow the law and is vested with broad discretion in determining the qualifications of prospective jurors."[91] Defendant, on trial for capital murder, had objected to the state's motion to strike for cause. The state had moved to strike because a venireperson had stated she would only vote for the death penalty in a case of "something like at the [Twin] Towers" and that defendant's prior conviction for murder would not change her position.[92] The trial court overruled defendant's objection. The Supreme Court found the record sufficient to establish that the prospective juror had "equivocated" about her ability to follow the law and had indicated hesitation at the thought of having to sign a verdict for death.[93]

The trial judge also has discretion in dealing with possible jury taint once the panel is chosen. In *United States v. Ramos*, several jurors expressed concern that an associate (and supplemental witness) of one of the defendant's was following them. One juror admitted that she "would not vote someone guilty if I think it's going to affect my family."[94] The judge reassured the panel and recessed early for the weekend. After the trial resumed, defense counsel moved that the juror be replaced. In chambers, the juror stated that she would be able to remain impartial so long as she was not followed again. Based on the juror's testimony, the trial court denied defendant's motion to remove the jury. The trial court also denied defendant's motion to question the rest of the panel.

On appeal, defendant argued that the trial court had to "presume" that the incident had prejudiced the jury, and the trial court's limited questioning of one juror was an insufficient safeguard of defendant's due process rights.[95] The court first cited United States Supreme Court precedent identifying the "remedy" for jury taint as a "hearing in which the defendant has the opportunity to prove actual bias."[96] The Fifth Circuit did not construe *Smith* "to require a full-blown evidentiary hearing in every instance in which an outside influence is brought to bear upon a petit jury."[97] Rather, the court noted its precedents that "allow the trial judge the flexibility, within broadly defined parameters, to handle such situations in the least

---

[91] 134 S.W.3d 21, 29 (Mo. 2004) (quoting *State v. Smith*, 32 S.W.3d 532, 544 (Mo. 2000)).

[92] *Id.* at 30.

[93] *Id.* (relying on *Smith*, 32 S.W.3d at 544).

[94] 71 F.3d 1150, 1152 (5th Cir. 1995) (upholding trial court's discretion to determine the effect of outside influence on the jury).

[95] *Id.* at 1153.

[96] *Id.* (quoting *Smith v. Phillips*, 455 U.S. 209 (1982)).

[97] *Id.*

94

disruptive manner possible."[98] The court applied an abuse of discretion review (the same it applied when the trial court bypassed a hearing altogether) on the grounds that the trial court was in a "better position to judge the mood at trial and the predilections of the jury."[99]

In another case dealing with jury bias, the Ohio Supreme Court held that the trial court has discretion whether to allow jurors to question witnesses during trial.[100] An Ohio trial court convicted defendant Fisher of felonious assault with a firearm following a jury verdict of guilty. The court announced at the beginning of trial that the jurors could ask the witnesses questions, but that they would have to submit their questions in writing to the bailiff so that the attorneys could review the questions at sidebar. The trial court would then read all admissible questions aloud to the witness. The jurors submitted twenty-three questions altogether, five of which the trial court disallowed on evidentiary grounds and two of which the trial court rephrased for clarity. Defendant raised a continuing objection to the "general practice of allowing jurors to submit questions."[101] Defendant renewed that argument on appeal. The intermediate appellate court certified the following question to the Ohio Supreme Court: "Is the practice of a trial court of allowing members of a jury to submit questions to the court and attorneys for possible submission to witnesses *per se* prejudicial to a criminal defendant?"[102]

The Ohio Supreme Court first dissected the language of the certified question, reasoning that it could be interpreted in two ways: (1) that juror questioning "*always* affects the outcome of the trial," or, (2) that "juror questioning, although not always affecting the outcome of the trial, should give rise to a *conclusive presumption* of prejudice as a matter of law."[103] Under the first interpretation, the court concluded that the answer to the certified question would be "no" because defendant conceded on appeal that juror questioning does not cause "prejudice in each and every situation."[104] The court concluded that the real issue behind the second interpretation of the certified question was whether juror questioning was grounds for reversal regardless of whether defendant could show actual prejudice to his cause.[105]

The court began its analysis by noting that the majority of jurisdictions commit the matter of juror questioning to the discretion of the trial court in some degree.[106] Nevertheless, the court independently inquired as to (1) whether trial courts in Ohio should have discretion to allow juror questioning, and (2) what extent

---

[98] *Id.*
[99] *Ramos*, 71 F.3d at 1153 (internal quotation omitted).
[100] *State v. Fisher*, 789 N.E.2d 222 (Ohio 2003)
[101] *Id.* at 224.
[102] *Id.*
[103] *Id.* at 225 (original emphasis).
[104] *Id.*
[105] *Fisher*, 789 N.E.2d at 226 (applying the structural error doctrine).
[106] *Id.*

the appellate courts should defer to the trial courts.[107] The court first noted that while every federal circuit affords the trial courts some discretion in the matter of juror questioning, many discourage the practice.[108] The court also reviewed state authority, and with the exception of five states that restrict the practice, found that most states have traditionally endorsed juror questioning within the discretion of the trial court.[109]

The Ohio court then noted several policy considerations in favor of allowing juror questioning. These considerations included: (1) juror questioning affords counsel additional insight as to the jurors' thought processes about the case;[110] (2) juror questioning "provides for two-way communication through which jurors can more effectively fulfill their fundamental role as factfinders";[111] (3) jurors are more attentive when allowed to ask questions and usually feel more satisfied both with their service and their verdict.[112]

Defendant raised several policy concerns regarding juror questioning, including (1) the possibility of asking inadmissible questions; (2) counsel's fear of objecting to juror questions because of possible jury alienation; (3) interruptions for jury questions might disrupt the trial; and (4) juror questions compromise the jury's impartiality.[113] The court did not find the first three concerns present in this case because the trial court provided adequate procedural safeguards to mitigate them.[114] The court found that defendant's fourth concern rested "on the erroneous premise that one must be passive to be impartial."[115] The court concluded,

> The issue of whether juror questions are aimed at advocacy rather than clarification cannot be answered in the abstract, but instead requires courts to examine the nature of each question in the overall context of a trial. We conclude that the trial court is in the best position to render such a determination and, within its sound discretion, disallow improper juror questions.[116]

e) **Note on Sentencing**

Trial courts have traditionally had broad discretion in sentencing because of their familiarity, relative to the appellate court, with the circumstances surrounding both

---

[107] *Id.*

[108] *Id.*

[109] *Id.* 226–27 (noting further that some jurisdictions require the trial court to employ "procedural safeguards" when allowing juror questioning).

[110] *Id.* at 228.

[111] *Id.* ("The hallmark of the American trial is the pursuit of truth.").

[112] *Id.* at 228–29.

[113] *Id.* at 229.

[114] *Id.* ("In the instant case, the procedural safeguards applied by the trial court operated to circumvent many of the foregoing dangers.").

[115] *Id.* at 229 (citing state evidentiary rule that allows the factfinder to question witnesses).

[116] *Id.* at 229.

the crime and the defendant.[117] With the advent of statutory sentencing guidelines, one might question the continuing viability of this discretion, especially in light of the Supreme Court's recent holdings requiring that a judge not depart from the sentencing guidelines except when an additional aggravating factor justifying departure is found by a jury beyond a reasonable doubt.[118] Sentencing was discussed in Chapter 1 at §1.3.

§ 2.3.   Absence of Hard–And–Fast Rules

a)   Meaning

An appellate court will defer to the discretion of the trial court when it is impracticable or otherwise extremely difficult to formulate a bright-line rule to govern a particular issue. In *Dudley v. East Ridge Dev. Co.*, the Wyoming Supreme Court addressed as a matter of first impression whether it would allow oral testimony at a summary judgment proceeding.[119] Adopting the holdings of other jurisdictions, the appellate court declined to balance the parties' interest in not being subject to surprise against the court's interest in having probative testimony before it.[120] Moreover, the court juggled two conflicting facets of the problem: (1) that the rule authorizing summary judgment did not allow for the practice (but did not prohibit it) and (2) that summary judgment is a motion and counsel are allowed to present oral arguments on motions.[121] The court concluded that the issue would best be left to the state trial courts, and decided that the trial court acted within its discretion by not allowing oral testimony because there was "no indication in the record that the appellant made an offer of proof at the summary judgment hearing regarding the proposed testimony of the two witnesses."[122] (The court did *not* state that they were upholding the trial court because appellant failed to preserve the error below.)

Some courts go one-step further than the Wyoming court and define "discretion" as the absence of hard–and–fast rules.[123] The Seventh Circuit defined discretion as such when considering whether to uphold the trial court's discretionary decision admitting evidence of a prior wrong of defendant Fierson under pursuant to

---

[117] *See, e.g., Commonwealth v. Mouzon*, 812 A.2d 617, 620 (Pa. 2002) (reaffirming that "the trial court is in the best position to determine the proper penalty for a particular offense based upon an evaluation of the individual circumstances before it") (internal quotation omitted).

[118] *See, e.g., Blakely v. Washington*, 524 U.S. 296 (2004).

[119] 694 P.2d 113, 114 (Wyo. 1985).

[120] *Id.* at 115.

[121] *Id.* (internal citation omitted)

[122] *Id.*

[123] *See e.g., United States v. Fierson*, 419 F.2d 1020, 1022 (7th Cir. 1969) ("The term 'discretion' means only that no hard and fast rules are laid down. It does not mean that the trial court's decision is immune from review."); *State v. Shirley*, 6 S.W. 3d 243, 247 (Tenn. 1999) (motion to sever offenses) ("Discretion essentially 'denotes the absence of a hard and fast rule'").

F.R.E. 404(b).[124] Fierson had allegedly seized a car by representing himself as an F.B.I. agent and faced charges stemming from that conduct. Over objection, the trial court admitted the testimony of a witness who claimed that eleven months prior to the conduct in issue, defendant had demanded his car and had represented himself as an F.B.I. agent. The court noted that "[a]dmissibility of this type of evidence is subject to knowable, yet necessarily imprecise standards" and that "[a]t its roots the problem is one of balancing probative value against prejudice."[125] The court noted the similarity of the "other wrong" to the conduct in issue but also noted that defendant had not put his intent in issue because he denied altogether that he had impersonated a federal officer.[126] The court concluded that the trial court had abused its discretion by admitting the evidence because the evidence had been offered for the purpose of proving intent and intent was not in issue in the present case.[127] As such, the evidence "was purely cumulative" and inadmissible.[128]

Judge Cummings dissented on the grounds that (according to the jury instructions) one of the elements in defendant's indictment was whether defendant had done "such act or acts willfully and with the intent to deceive or defraud another."[129] Defendant did not object to the jury instruction. Judge Cummings concluded that the instruction showed that "this case was tried on the theory that the Government had to show defendant had acted 'willfully and with the intent to deceive or defraud another.'"[130] The prosecution also referred to the intent element during closing argument. Because intent was an element of the offense, Judge Cummings concluded that the trial court had acted within its discretion by allowing proof of the other wrong.[131]

The concept of an "indefinable" problem may also apply to those cases in which a party may find it nearly impossible to satisfy a clear rule of law. In a dispute involving the chain of custody of a car tire belonging to a defendant in a sexual assault case,[132] the Connecticut Supreme Court reaffirmed its prior holding that no rule requires the prosecution to "exclude or disprove all possibility that the article or substance has been tampered with; in each case the trial court must satisfy itself in reasonable probability that the substance had not been changed in important

---

[124] Fed. R. Evid. 404(b) provides:
> Evidence of other crimes, wrongs, or acts is not admissible to prove the character of a person in order to show action in conformity therewith. It may, however, be admissible for other purposes, such as proof of motive, opportunity, intent, preparation, plan, knowledge, identity, or absence of mistake or accident....

[125] Fierson, 419 F.2d at 1022.
[126] Id. at 1023.
[127] Id.
[128] Id.
[129] Id. at 1024 (Cummings, J., dissenting).
[130] Fierson, 419 F.2d at 1024 (Cummings, J., dissenting).
[131] Id. at 1024 (Cummings, J., dissenting).
[132] Apparently, the prosecution offered the tire to prove that the defendant was at the scene of the assault.

respects...."[133] The appellate court found that the trial court had not abused its discretion by admitting the tire because three witnesses had testified that (1) the "defective tire marked as an exhibit corresponded to the vehicle at the time of purchase," (2) the tire tread was about 50 % worn, the tire in question typically had twenty thousand miles of tread life, and the truck from which the tire was seized had about ten thousand miles on it , and 3) the tire defect was "extremely unusual" and would have made a distinct print at the time of the crime.[134]

An indefinable problem may also include those areas in which the trial court gives strong consideration to the equities of a particular case. The Ninth Circuit explained the "lack of hard and fast rules" in the area of preliminary injunctive relief precludes a rule requiring that a preliminary injunction simply restore the status quo.[135] The court reaffirmed a trial court's discretion in "fashioning relief" in an equitable action, even when that relief "disturbed the status quo."[136] The court did note, however, that "it is not usually proper to grant the moving party, on a temporary basis, the full relief to which he might be entitled if successful at trial."[137]

b)   Indefinability and the Constitution

The difficulty appellate courts have in articulating hard—and—fast rules can leave trial courts deciding questions of constitutional importance. In *Committee for Voluntary Prayer v. Wimberly*, the District of Columbia Court of Appeals upheld the trial court's decision to review a proposed ballot initiative for constitutional defect before the initiative came to vote.[138] The proposed ballot initiative would have permitted "non—sectarian, non-proselytizing student-initiated voluntary prayer, invocations and/or benedictions" during school events.[139] Opponents of the initiative challenged the measure on constitutional grounds. Relying on prior case law from the appellate court, the trial court concluded that the case presented "one of those few extreme situations" in which it had discretion to "determine that a proposed measure was not a proper subject for initiative because it [was] patently, obviously, and unquestionably unconstitutional."[140] The trial court proceeded to strike the prayer initiative from the ballot on constitutional grounds.

Although the appellate court noted that pre-review of ballot measures was "imprudent," it concluded that… "it was appropriate for the trial court to consider whether this matter fell into one of those 'extreme cases' permitting pre-election

---

[133] *State v. Pollitt*, 530 A.2d 155, 169 (Conn. 1987) (internal quotation omitted).
[134] *Id.*
[135] *United States v. Barrows*, 404 F.2d 749, 752 (11th Cir.1968).
[136] *Id.*
[137] *Id.*
[138] *Comm. Voluntary Prayer v. Wimberly*, 704 A.2d 1199 (D.C. Ct. App. 1997).
[139] *Id.* at 1200.
[140] *Id.* at 1201 (internal quotations omitted).

constitutional review, and to conclude that pre-election review was necessary."[141] In a footnote, the court addressed appellant's contention that the case law upon which the trial court relied pertained to a statute that was "patently unconstitutional" and that as a rule, the trial court could not conduct preballot review of the prayer initiative because it was not patently unconstitutional.[142] The court rejected this argument, saying that the "patently unconstitutional" standard was "not presented necessarily as the *sole* standard for pre-election constitutional review of a proposed initiative."[143] The court expressed concern that adopting the "patently unconstitutional" standard "might leave no choice with the trial court, and thus, might be inconsistent with the notion of discretion."[144]

Courts will often reverse in criminal cases on constitutional grounds even while acknowledging the absence of a bright-line rule governing the matter. Following a jury trial, a federal district court convicted defendants Riggi and Timpani (both affiliated with the mob) of extortion charges.[145] At the beginning of trial, the court "announced a blanket rule that there would be no recross-examination."[146] Defendants objected. The trial court eventually backed away from its blanket prohibition, but only after thirteen witnesses had testified. One witness, a former mob affiliate turned FBI informant, testified to two "new matters" during the government's redirect examination: (1) that because he distanced himself from the mob, he lost his family and his normal way of life and (2) that defendant Riggi was "the boss or the acting boss of the DeCavalcante family."[147] Following witness's testimony, defendant objected to the "no recross" rule on the grounds that defendant could impeach witness based on his "new" testimony and that he had the right to challenge witness's assertion about defendant Riggi's role in organized crime.[148] The trial court did not permit recross.

Defendants claimed on appeal that the trial court's restrictions on recross deprived them of a fair trial under the Sixth Amendment's Confrontation Clause. The appellate court initially found that the witness appeared reliable and credible and that his testimony likely had an impact on the jury's guilty verdict.[149] The appellate court also noted that the court had not made its policy clear to defense

---

[141] *Id.* at 1202 (stating that "the proposed prayer initiative raises constitutional issues on its face").

[142] *Id.* at 1202, n.6.

[143] *Id.*

[144] *Id.* Another area that often raises both federal and state constitutional issues is the doctrine of "prudential standing," under which a court may decline to review certain matters. *See e.g.*, *Missoula City-County Air Pollution Control Bd. v. Bd. Enviro. Rev.*, 937 P.2d 463, 466 (Mont. 1997).

[145] *United States v. Riggi*, 951 F.2d 1368 (3rd Cir. 1991).

[146] *Id.* at 1372.

[147] *Id.* at 1372–73.

[148] *Id.* at 1373.

[149] *See id.*

counsel until after the prosecution had conducted redirect; thus, defendant had no opportunity to object to the witness introducing new material on redirect.[150]

Having stated those initial facts, the appellate court discussed the law and policy behind cross-examination. The appellate court acknowledged that the "exercise of the court's discretion" in allowing new material to come into evidence on cross "necessarily operates not as a hard and fast rule, but according to the actual development of the case."[151] The court also acknowledged that trial courts, in similar fashion, can limit the scope of redirect so as to prevent new material from coming before the jury.[152] Nevertheless, the court concluded that "[w]hen material new matters are brought out on redirect examination, the Confrontation Clause of the Sixth Amendment mandates that the opposing party be given the right of recross—examination on those new matters."[153] The appellate court pointed to both "well settled" doctrine and "essential" role cross-examination serves in ensuring a fair trial as "the principal means by which the trustworthiness of a witness is tested."[154] The court concluded that "[t]he reversible error in this case was the district court's absolute ban on recross-examination, an error which the [trial] court itself eventually recognized and ameliorated before testimony was completed."[155]

The dissent agreed with the majority that "[w]hen new evidence is raised on redirect examination, the trial court must give the opposing party an opportunity to cross examine on the new matter"; however, the dissent disagreed that the problematic testimony in the case was "new matter."[156] The dissent pointed both to the testimony of other witnesses and the *direct* examination testimony of the witness in question for evidence that the redirect did not introduce new evidence.[157] Although the dissent acknowledged that the defendant did not know the full implications of the trial court's "no recross" rule, the dissent concluded that defendant did have the opportunity to *cross* on the issues that the redirect highlighted.[158] The dissent concluded that the "district court did not abuse its discretion when it refused to give the defendants another opportunity to challenge the witness."[159]

---

[150] *See id.*, at 1374.

[151] *Id.* at 1375.

[152] *Id.*

[153] *Id.*

[154] *Id.* at 1376.

[155] *Riggi*, 951 F.2d at 1376.

[156] *Id.* at 1378 (Nygaard, J., dissenting).

[157] *Id.* at 1379 (Nygaard, J., dissenting).

[158] *Id.* (Nygaard, J., dissenting).

[159] *Id.* at 1380 (Nygaard, J., dissenting). The Supreme Court of Arkansas has held that although "there is no hard and fast rule on when a refusal to grant a continuance will amount to abuse of discretion," a trial court deprived defendant of her right to counsel by making her proceed with trial on the same day that she terminated her attorney's services. *Murdock v. State*, 722 S.W.2d 268, 270 (Ark. 1987).

In a case involving juror prejudice, the Supreme Court of Rhode Island refused to lay down a blanket constitutional principle but decided that "in the context of the facts" of the case before it, the trial court abused its discretion by refusing to pass a case because "the cautionary instructions given by the trial court were insufficient to free the minds the jury from the prejudice which results when jurors learn that the individual on trial before them has committed other unlawful acts."[160] During initial questioning of prospective jurors, defendant Massey learned that a juror had been at the scene of a stabbing that gave rise to the charges against defendant. Juror had arrived on the scene shortly after the stabbing and watched part of the police investigation. Juror admitted discussing the stabbing as he watched, testifying that he had said at the time, "I'll bet it was a Massey."[161] After the trial court excused juror, defendant moved to pass the case. The trial judge denied the motion on the ground that other members of the Massey family were at the scene of the stabbing, but he "asked the prospective jurors if any of them felt his judgment would be prejudiced by that remark."[162] The juror returned a guilty verdict against defendant, and defendant appealed.

On appeal, the court reaffirmed its precedent "that a defendant is denied a fair trial when evidence of other separate and distinct crimes is erroneously put before the jury."[163] Although the juror did not make a "direct statement implicating defendant in a separate and distinct crime," the court concluded that "no less harm resulted to defendant" because defendant "was placed in a position of having to defend himself against not one specific additional charge but rather the inescapable implication that had been left with the jurors that his family was always in trouble with the law."[164] Because the court could not "say that the procedures adopted by the trial justice were sufficient to cure the taint," the court concluded that "defendant was denied his right to trial by an impartial jury" and that the trial court abused its discretion by letting the trial proceed as the court did.[165]

Judge Kelleher, joined by Judge Joslin, dissented. The dissent examined the United States Supreme Court's holding in *Marshall v. United States*,[166] which the majority cited in support of the proposition that some "prejudicial information" has such a powerful impact on a jury that the trial court must declare a mistrial, or, for that matter, pass the case.[167] The dissent stated that the *Marshall* court reversed a jury verdict because the jury had access to newspapers that described the

---

[160] *State v. Massey*, 382 A.2d 801, 802–03 (R.I. 1978).

[161] *Id.* at 802.

[162] *Id.*

[163] *Id.* at 803.

[164] *Massey*, 382 A.2d at 803 ("The basic underpinnings of the rule prohibiting the use of evidence of other crimes against a defendant include the undue burden imposed upon the defendant of defending himself against another charge and the introduction of prejudice and confusion into the minds of the jury.")...

[165] *Id.* at 804 ("This court has noted that there is no fixed formula by which we can determine whether a particular statement is prejudicial.... Every case must be decided on its own facts. The one before us is certainly not free of doubt.").

[166] 360 U.S. 310, 313 (1959).

[167] *Massey*, 382 A.2d at 804.

defendant's prior drug convictions.[168] The dissent noted the "large measure of discretion" *Marshall* afforded trial courts "in disposing of contentions that an accused's right to a fair trial [had] been prejudiced" and stated that *Marshall* "also stressed that there is no hard–and–fast rule for determining prejudice, as each case must be resolved on its own particular facts."[169]

After arguing that the trial court had considerable discretion, the dissent concluded that the "measures taken by the trial judge were sufficient to disabuse the jury's mind of the prejudicial effect of the objectionable evidence."[170] He noted that the trial court conducted an extensive voir dire on each juror (which lasted a total of two days) and impressed upon the jury "that every litigant is entitled to a fair and impartial trial."[171] The dissent also pointed to the evidence that some of the jurors did not hear the remark at issue, and many of those jurors that heard them expressed doubt that the remark was even accurate, much less an influence on their decision.[172]

c)   Eyewitness Testimony

The Supreme Court of Washington, reviewing a defendant's rape conviction that was based in large part on the eyewitness testimony of the victim, held that the trial court had not abused its discretion when it disallowed defendant's expert testimony to the effect that the victim's eyewitness identification was unreliable.[173] The trial court had determined that the expert testimony "would not be helpful to the trier of fact" and that the defendant could use cross-examination to test the reliability of the victim's identification.[174] The court began by reaffirming that "the question of admissibility of eyewitness identification is within the discretion of the trial court" but by acknowledging that under the intermediate court's *Moon* test, "an abuse of discretion in excluding testimony on eyewitness identification may be found where the identification is the main issue at trial, the defendant presents an alibi defense,

---

[168] *Id.* at 806 (Kelleher, J., dissenting).

[169] *Id.* (Kelleher, J., dissenting).

[170] *Id.* (Kelleher, J., dissenting).

[171] *Id.* (Kelleher, J., dissenting).

[172] *Id.* at 807 (Kelleher, J., dissenting). For a case in which in which the court rejected an Eighth Amendment argument and upheld a trial court's discretion to set bail, *see State v. Foy*, 582 P.2d 281, 286 (Kan. 1978). On a related note, at least one court has classified mootness as an issue in which there are few hard and fast rules: "The question of mootness is one of convenience and discretion and is not subject to hard-and-fast rules." *Exeter Hosp. Med. Staff v. Bd. Trs. Exeter Health Res.*, 810 A.2d 53, 58 (N.H. 2002) ("We generally will refuse to review a question that no longer presents a justiciable controversy because issues involved have become academic or dead, but may review a question that has become moot if it involves a significant constitutional question or an issue of significant public concern.").

[173] *State v. Cheatam*, 81 P.3d 830, 842 (Wash. 2003) (stating that expert testimony would be of "only marginal relevance and would have been of debatable help to the jury") ("Therefore, refusal to admit expert testimony on this point was not so untenable as to constitute an abuse of discretion.").

[174] *Id.* at 839.

and there is little or no other evidence linking the defendant to the crime."[175] The court also acknowledged precedent from the lower courts suggesting that in cases involving "close and confusing facts," such as when the eyewitness testimony is conflicting, the trial court should be more inclined to allow expert testimony to explain the eyewitness identification.[176]

The court agreed with the intermediate appellate court in declining to follow *Moon* in the circumstances of the case at bar:

> First, while *Moon* suggests that its three-factor analysis is derived from other cases using the same or a similar analysis, that is not exactly the case. Instead, it appears largely based on the particular facts of one of the cases cited.... Second, the mere fact that the defendant presents an alibi defense, in and of itself, is a doubtful reason to more readily admit such testimony. Third, the test itself is too restrictive of the trial court's discretion, is evidence by numerous qualifications added to it. Fourth, a trial court may have good reason for excluding such testimony on some subjects the expert would testify to, regardless of the other evidence in the trial or the presence of an alibi defense. That is, a court can legitimately conclude that some subjects are a matter of common sense, for example, that a witness will have more difficulty identifying an individual seen in a dark alley than one seen in broad daylight, while other subjects are not so readily matter of common sense, for example, that lay people may not be as aware of the malleability of eyewitness confidence or weapon focus. The *Moon* three-factor test does not account for these distinctions.

> Finally, a criminal defendant has the right to offer the testimony of his or her witnesses in order to establish a defense. The *Moon* test's emphasis on whether the defense presents an alibi defense does not accord with this right, given that the expert's testimony may be just as relevant and helpful to the jury where the defendant raises a defense of mistaken identification, for example. It is also troubling that admission of the expert testimony hinges on the strength of the State's case on identity, making it appear that the defendant's right to present a defense is contingent on the weakness of the State's case.

> We decline to adopt the *Moon* test. We conclude, instead, that where eyewitness identification of the defendant is a key element of the State's case, the trial court must carefully consider whether expert testimony on the reliability of eyewitness identification would assist the jury in assessing the reliability of eyewitness testimony. In making this determination the court should consider

---

[175] *Id.* at 841.
[176] *Id.*

the proposed testimony and the specific subjects involved in the identification to which the testimony relates, such as whether the victim and the defendant are of the same race, whether the defendant displayed a weapon, the effect of stress, etc. This approach corresponds with the rules for admissibility of expert testimony under ER 702 in particular. After reviewing this record we find that excluding the expert's testimony in this case was not an abuse of discretion.[177]

Judge Chambers' concurring opinion emphasized that "it is not this court's duty to supplant the trial court's discretion with our own" and that "trial courts must be afforded an amount of discretion in these matters because the line between that which is helpful and that which is unhelpful cannot be 'very accurately drawn.'"[178]

Judge Sanders dissented. He accused the majority of centering the "heart" of its analysis on the "trial court's discretion to admit or reject evidence" and failing to consider "the *lack* of trial discretion to refuse *relevant* evidence, especially when a defendant's constitutional right to present a defense is at issue, as well as the obvious relevance of this particular testimony."[179] Justice Sanders explained further:

> The trial court may have discretion to determine what *is* relevant evidence, but it has *no* discretion to disallow evidence that *is* relevant. And discretion exercised may be abused. This is especially true in criminal trials where a person's life, liberty, and property can be taken. The United States Supreme Court has said as much, noting that a defendant has an absolute right to present a defense, including one's own witnesses for one's defense. We have followed this rule. Refusing relevant evidence denies the defense its right to call a witness on its behalf and its right to argue the facts and circumstances of the case to the jury as they may have been developed through the testimony of the excluded witness.
>
> The problem with the majority's analysis is that it attacks the *persuasiveness* of Dr. Loftus's testimony, not its relevance. Dr.

---

[177] *Id.* at 841–42.

[178] *Id.* at 845 (Chambers, J., concurring) (quoting *State v. Smails*, 115 P. 82 (Wash. 1911)). Quoting *Smails*, Judge Chambers continued:

> The line of demarcation between matters that fall within the knowledge of mankind generally and matters that are the subject of special and peculiar knowledge cannot, from the nature of things, be very accurately drawn. The one, of necessity, shades into the other, and hence, even though the extremes of the opposing rules may be definitely marked and error predicated thereon easy of determination, the trial judge must have something of discretion whether he will or will not admit opinion evidence when the line of demar[c]ation between these rules is approached.

Id. at 846.

[179] *Id.* at 849 (Sanders, J., dissenting).

Loftus would have testified that (1) stress and violence, (2) weapon focus, (3) lighting, and (4) cross-racial identification all could have rendered M.M.'s memory less accurate. In this case there was: (1) a violent rape, (2) with a weapon, (3) that occurred during darkness, and (4) by a person of the opposite race. Where M.M. had a clear recollection of her assailant, never focused on the knife, viewed her assailant from close range, or gave a description with a very strong resemblance to Cheatam all go to the persuasiveness of Dr. Loftus or lack thereof. While I have no doubt the prosecution could make a strong argument that M.M.'s identification was, all considered, reliable, it was an argument for the *prosecution* to make—not the court. But, persuasiveness has no bearing on relevance. If Dr. Loftus's testimony would have had *any tendency* to make [M.M.'s eyewitness account], more probable *or less probable* that it would be without the testimony, it was relevant and the trial court had a duty to admit it. Dr. Loftus's testimony was unquestionably relevant under ER 401 and I do not read the majority to say it would have been error to admit it, only that it would prefer to abdicate its responsibility to be the final arbiter of the law in deference to the trial court. The right to appeal becomes a hollow one if our function is merely to rubber stamp.[180]

d)   Remoteness of Convictions

Courts do not define a precise limit on how far back in time a party can go to bring forth evidence of a prior conviction otherwise admissible under the law of evidence. Reviewing for plain error only, the Texas Court of Criminal Appeals found that the trial court had acted within its discretion when it allowed the prosecution to impeach a testifying defendant with a twenty–five–year old burglary conviction in a case involving the burglary of a retail store.[181] Although the court reaffirmed that remoteness is not a doctrine amenable to clear rules, the court concluded that the rule of remoteness did not apply because (1) "there was evidence of a lack of reformation," and (2) defendant had "subsequent felony convictions."[182]

The same court had an opportunity to consider remoteness from a different angle in *Gordon v. State*.[183] The trial court convicted defendant Gordon of burglary and sentenced him to ten years in prison. Defendant appealed on the grounds that

---

[180] *Id.* at 849–50 (Saunders, J., dissenting). Judge Saunders continued:
> I opine, however, that this court must be ever vigilant in its duty to protect the accused's constitutional right to present a complete defense, and that this court must be equally vigilant *not* to intrude upon the province of the jury, which is and should be the ultimate decider of persuasiveness of relevant expert testimony.

Id. at 850, n.8.

[181] *Rascon v. State*, 496 S.W.2d 99 (Tex. Crim. App. 1973) (Onion, J.).

[182] *Id.* at 101–02.

[183] 651 S.W.2d 793 (Tex. Crim. App. 1983) (en banc).

the trial court allowed the state "to impeach him with a prior conviction over ten years old."[184] That conviction was for possession of marijuana. The majority concluded in a brief opinion that defendant had waived the issue because he admitted that he was guilty of the burglary during the sentencing stage of the trial.[185] Judge Teague's concurrence "put defendants and counsel on notice" that admitting guilt during the punishment stage of a bifurcated trial would amount to a guilty plea and "suffers the consequences that a plea of guilty has, as to the preservation of any error that may have occurred during the guilt stage of trial."[186]

Judge Onion concurred in part and dissented in part. He dissented from the majority's holding that defendant had waived the issue, citing evidence that defendant retracted his admission of guilt during the punishment phase upon cross-examination. He distinguished the situation in which a defendant does not testify at the guilt stage and then testifies at the punishment stage from the situation at bar, in which the defendant testifies both at the guilt and punishment stage.

Turning to the merits of defendant's argument, Judge Onion first notes that "[w]hile the admission of a prior conviction for impeachment is within the discretion of the trial judge, in determining whether a prior conviction is too remote it has generally been held that if the witness has been released from prison within 10 years of his trial testimony, the conviction is not too remote and evidence of conviction is admissible."[187] Judge Onion clarified that the ten-year threshold is "not the correct rule" because "facts of the case must be looked to and considered in determining the question of remoteness."[188] Judge Onion concluded that the trial judge had not "under the facts and circumstances" "abused its discretion" and concurred in the majority's disposition of the case.[189]

Judge Clinton dissented on the grounds that although marijuana possession is technically a felony under Texas law, a legislative mandate had clarified that the crime was not necessarily one of "moral turpitude."[190] The judge reasoned that the state could only offer crimes of "moral turpitude" in to evidence for impeachment purposes.[191] The judge concluded that "[c]oupled with [the conviction's] remoteness, permitting the State to use the prior conviction to attack [defendant's] credibility is such an egregious error against appellant that his trial was fundamentally unfair."[192] Judge Clinton also dissented with respect to the waiver issue.

---

[184] *Id.* at 793.
[185] *Id.*
[186] *Id.*
[187] *Id.* at 795 (noting that convictions otherwise too remote may still be admissible "if it is shown he has not reformed").
[188] *Gordon*, 651 S.W.2d at 796.
[189] *Id.*
[190] *Id.* at 797.
[191] *Id.*
[192] *Id.*

A remoteness issue can also arise when the state offers specific instances of the defendant's bad character in response to a defendant's character witness. During trial of a voluntary manslaughter case, a character witness on behalf of defendant Cross testified that defendant had a "drinking problem" but was a "fine fellow," honest, and nonviolent.[193] Defendant stood accused of stabbing his roommate in the course of a robbery. The state offered a 1958 Michigan conviction for robbery with an automatic weapon in order to prove knowledge, intent, and lack of mistake, to which the defendant objected as irrelevant and too remote in time. The court took the matter under advisement. Following the character witness's testimony on direct, the state asked the following on cross: "I'll just ask you this, Mr. Watson. Would it change your mind any if you knew this man had been convicted of armed robbery with an automatic weapon in the State of Michigan?"[194] Defendant objected, and the prosecutor argued that defendant had opened the door by calling a character witness. The court later advised that it would admit evidence of a prior condition "as proof of motive, intent, and lack of mistake or accident."[195] Defendant renewed his remoteness and relevance objections. The court prevented the state from cross-examining defendant on the prior conviction on the grounds that it was fifteen years old, but stated that it would allow the state to cross—examine if defendant brought up the prior conviction on direct.

The appellate court first noted that "[t]he relevancy of a prior conviction to the offense charged is linked to the similarity of the two offenses."[196] The court explained further that "the remoteness in time of a prior conviction if otherwise admissible affects the weight of the prior conviction rather than its admissibility."[197] Applying the rule, the court concluded that the "authenticated copy of the conviction did not show the facts, circumstances or nature of the robbery" and that it "was admitted in evidence because 'the document speaks for itself.'"[198] The appellate court then acknowledged that there "is no hard and fast rule by which it can be determined when evidence of other crimes, if otherwise admissible, becomes irrelevant because of intervening time and the matter is largely left to the discretion of the trial judge."[199] Nonetheless, the appellate court reversed the trial court because the remoteness of the crime, combined with the fact that the present case presented little evidence of a robbery, rendered the "prejudicial impact of the prior conviction" "far out of proportion to its probative value."[200]

---

[193] *State v. Cross*, 532 P.2d 1357, 1360 (Kan. 1975).

[194] *Id.*

[195] *Id.*

[196] *Id.* at 1363.

[197] *Id.* at 1364 (explaining that as the remoteness in time of a prior conviction increases, the weight of that evidence decreases).

[198] *Cross*, 532 P.2d at 1365 ("No effort was made by the prosecution to establish the facts, circumstances or nature of the prior offense.").

[199] *Id.*

[200] *Id.*

108

e)   Impeachment

The majority of courts have abandoned the "orthodox rule" prohibiting parties from impeaching their own witness.[201] The Missouri Supreme Court followed this trend in *Rowe v. Farmers Insurance Co.* The court noted that, unlike bygone days in which witnesses were carefully selected "'oath helpers'" to a party, today "parties may not know their witnesses or be familiar with their honesty and credibility."[202] The court concluded that it seemed "foolish to talk about a party guaranteeing the credibility of his witness," even though the voucher rule was a traditional justification for the ban on impeaching one's own witness.[203]

Judge Blackmar, concurring in the judgment, emphasized that "[o]ur ultimate faith, nevertheless is in the ability of jurors to separate the sound evidence from the infirm."[204] He differed somewhat with the majority on another issue addressed in the case but agreed that the law should allow a party to impeach its own witness, implying that the orthodox rule may "punish the diligent" and that "[n]either certainty nor absence of possibility of abuse is required as a condition of admissibility."[205]

Judge Billings, dissented, accused the majority of practicing "judicial legislation" and of exercising rulemaking authority "contrary to the Constitution of Missouri."[206] Judge Billings expressed a firm belief that "Missouri's common law rule [against impeaching one's own witness] operates fairly and effectively and in no way impedes the ascertainment of truth."[207] He first noted that Missouri's common law had never laid down a bright-line rule regarding impeachment of one's own witness.[208] He then noted several exceptions to the general ban: (1) the rule does not apply to adverse or hostile witnesses, (2) the rule will allow a party to refresh the memory of one's own witness, and (3) a party may impeach his or her own witness in the event of surprise and entrapment.[209] Taken together, Judge Billings concluded that the "precise contours of the rule" both account for modern trial circumstances while preventing "a party from setting up straw men" and "from bringing in the back door unreliable hearsay evidence."[210]

---

[201] *Rowe v. Farmers Ins. Co.*, 699 S.W.2d 423, 425 (Mo. 1985) (en banc) (holding that a party may use a prior inconsistent statement to impeach his or her own witness).
[202] *Id.* at 424.
[203] *Id.*
[204] *Id.* at 428–29 (Blackmar, J, concurring).
[205] *Id.* at 428–29, and n.1 (Blackmar, J., concurring).
[206] *Rowe*, 699 S.W.2d at 433 (Billings, J, dissenting).
[207] *Id.* (Billings, J., dissenting).
[208] *Id.* at 437 (Billings, J., dissenting).
[209] *Id.* at 438 (Billings, J., dissenting).
[210] *Id.* at 437–38 (Billings, J., dissenting) (noting also that of the jurisdictions that majority cited as having abandoned the common-law rule, only two had done so by judicial decision).

f)   *Voir dire*

"The scope of voir dire examination of jurors is within the discretion of the trial judge."[211] "*Voir dire* affords attorneys an opportunity to elicit sufficient information to develop a rational basis for excluding veniremen whether for cause or by peremptory challenges."[212] The Michigan Supreme Court had to balance these two principles in *People v. Harrell*. Defendant Harrell, a young black man, was tried and convicted of assaulting a police officer and of evading a police officer because of an encounter between defendant and a group of mostly white police officers. On *voir dire*, defendant submitted 120 questions, mostly dealing with possible racial prejudice. The court used seven of defendant's questions "to cover any bias or racial prejudice in the proposed jurors."[213] Defendant appealed the trial court's decision.

The Michigan Supreme Court acknowledged defendant's Fourteenth Amendment right "to interrogate jurors upon the subject of racial prejudice after the defendant's timely request," but concluded that the trial judge does not as a rule have to "ask every question dealing with racial prejudice that the defense might wish to be heard."[214] All the constitution requires, the court reasoned, was "an assessment of whether under all of the circumstances presented there was a constitutionally significant likelihood that, absent questioning about racial prejudice, the jury would not be impartial."[215] Applying the abuse of discretion standard to the facts of the case, the court concluded that the trial court's seven questions "sufficient to afford defense counsel information necessary to challenge prospective jurors" and that "many [of the 120 questions] [were] repetitive of the Court questionnaire and many [were] not proper for voir dire."[216]

Judge Levin, joined by two others, dissented. He first pointed out the "significant racial overtones which would be operative throughout trial." and that the "emotionally charged atmosphere" required, as defense counsel suggested, "an extensive and probing *voir dire*."[217] From the facts, the dissent concluded that the case presented a situation where limiting voir dire allowed "the state or a wealthy litigant [to] enjoy an overwhelming advantage due to superior resources for pre-trial investigation of the panel," leading to what in this case would amount to racial discrimination.[218] The dissent concluded further that the questions the trial court asked were too conclusory to protect "the right of a litigant to probe below the

---

[211] *People v. Harrell*, 247 N.W.2d 829, 830 (Mich. 1976).

[212] *Id.*

[213] *Id.*

[214] *Id.*

[215] *Id.* at 831.

[216] *Id.* at 832.

[217] *Id.* at 833 (Levin, J., dissenting) (noting "the alignment of witnesses along racial lines").

[218] *Id.* at 837 (Levin, J., dissenting).

110

surface for attitudes which could provide a basis of challenge for cause, or peremptorily...."[219]

g)   Warrants

Criminal defendants have a qualified right "to a hearing on the veracity of statements made in a warrant affidavit" in order to prevent police abuse.[220] On the other hand, informants upon whom the state relies to obtain search warrants communicate on a privileged basis to authorities, so that the informant can give valuable information to the government without fear of reprisal.[221] The Supreme Judicial Court of Massachusetts described this problem as a "question of how to balance the public interest in protecting and encouraging informants against the public interest in deterring police misconduct."[222] Applying for a search warrant, Commonwealth claimed that it received a tip from an anonymous "reliable informant" that defendants had drugs in their apartment. Based on the tip, Commonwealth obtained a search warrant, searched the suspected premises, and discovered illegal drugs. An indictment followed. Defendants each moved to suppress evidence seized pursuant to the search warrant, and one defendant moved the court to require Commonwealth to disclose information about the informant. Defendant filing the motion for disclosure alleged that the informant had never previously provided helpful tips to the police with respect to drug activity. The motion court denied the motion to suppress and refused to require release of the informant's name, but it ordered Commonwealth to disclose in greater detail which (if any) of the informant's tips had been helpful to law enforcement. When Commonwealth refused, the court suppressed the evidence on the grounds that defendants had made a preliminary showing that the state's "reliable informant" claim was a "material misstatement" that would invalidate the warrant.

On Commonwealth's appeal, after finding that the warrant affidavit was sufficient on its face to establish probable cause, the Supreme Judicial Court turned to the question of whether the informant's interest in secrecy or the court's interest in preventing the police's abuse of power should prevail.[223] As an initial matter, the court declined to establish "a hard and fast rule prohibiting disclosure in all warrant affidavit cases no matter what the circumstances" but left "disclosure to the sound discretion of the judge hearing the motion."[224] Reviewing relevant law under the federal constitution, the court concluded "that the public interest in deterring police

---

[219] *Id.* (Levin, J., dissenting). For another case describing the trial court's discretion to regulate voir dire, see *United States v. Bascaro*, 742 F.2d 1335, 1350–51 (11th Cir. 1984)) (so describing).
[220] *Commonwealth v. Amral*, 554 N.E. 2d 1189, 1193 (Mass. 1990) (noting also that defendants have "no constitutional right to suppression" of a warrant).
[221] *Id.*
[222] *Id.*
[223] *Id.* (noting that a defendant "has no constitutional right to suppression"). "Suppression is a remedy designed by the courts, as a matter of policy, to deter future police misconduct." *Id.* at 1193.
[224] *Id.* at 1194.

misconduct requires the trial judge to exercise his or her discretion to order an in camera hearing where the defendant by affidavit asserts facts which cast a reasonable doubt on the veracity of material representations made by the affiant concerning a confidential informant."[225]

h)   Access to Records

Although one may think that the keeping and access of judicial records is uniquely within the province of the court, other legal rights, including those found in state constitutions, state statutes, and the common law, can bear on the question: King County, Washington, in an effort to save costs, required the county's judicial administration to "limit file check-out to a prior appointment basis only."[226] An attorney sued, alleging that the new policy violated Washington's public disclosure act (PDA), common law right to access, and both the state and federal constitutions. The attorney was challenging the policy *itself*, and not a specific refusal of the clerk's office to provide access to records. Following a stipulation of facts, the trial court found in favor of plaintiff based on the PDA and the common law right to access.

On review, the Washington Supreme Court approved of the common law right to access, basing its approval largely on federal case law.[227] Again relying in part on federal precedent, the court declined to declare an absolute right to the access of records, opting instead for a case-by-case analysis with trial court exercising discretionary control over court records.[228] Having so opted, the court held as a matter of law that the PDA did not apply to court case files. It based its holding in part upon the rationale that the Department of Judicial Administration, "[a]lthough its funding and directives place it within the executive realm," it belongs more properly to the "judicial realm" as the "custodian for court case files."[229] As such, the agency is subject to the courts' "inherent authority to control their records and proceedings."[230] Moreover, the PDA, if interpreted to include court case files, would run counter to the common law right of access to court files.[231]

---

[225]*Id.* at 1196.

[226] *Nast v. Michels*, 730 P.2d 54, 55 (Wash. 1986) ("The Superior Court Clerk replaced the existing policy permitting on-demand access to court case files with a procedure requiring 1-day advance notice...").

[227] *See id.* at 56.

[228] *Id.*

> Because of the difficulties inherent in formulating a broad yet clear rule to govern the variety of situations in which the right of access must be reconciled with legitimate countervailing public or private interests, the decision as to access is one which rests in the sound discretion of the trial court.

Id. (quoting *In re Nat'l Broadcasting Co.*, 653 F.2d 609, 612 (D.C. Cir. 1981)).

[229] *Id.* at 57.

[230] *Nast*, 730 P.2d 54 at 57 (internal quotations omitted).

[231] *Id.* at 58.

Justice Durham dissented, arguing that the PDA applied to court case files since the intent of the voters (as evidenced by the voters' pamphlet) was to include *all* public records.[232] Moreover, Justice Durham accused the majority of running "afoul of the principle that unambiguous statutes are to read in conformity with their obvious meaning, *without regard to previous common law.*"[233]

i)   Child Custody

Hearing a father's appeal from the trial court's order appointing the stepfather as guardian of father's two children following the death of mother, the Indiana Supreme Court eschewed any "hard and fast rules" for judicial "disposition of children," and relied instead on the "exercise of the sound discretion of the court confronted with the problem."[234] After setting out the abuse of discretion standard of review, the court criticized the methodology the intermediate appellate court had set forth in *Hendrickson v. Binkley.*[235] The *Hendrickson* court had "presumed it will be in the best interests of the child to be placed in the custody of the natural parent" and allowed the "attacking party" to "rebut this presumption" with a showing of (1) "unfitness," (2) "long acquiescence," or (3) "voluntary relinquishment."[236] Although the court did not adopt an "any evidence" standard under which a trial court could conclude that a party had rebutted the *Hendrickson* presumption (as some decisions of the intermediate court), it departed from the *Hendrickson* factors and required only that a party show "clear and convincing evidence that the best interests of the child require" placement outside the home of the biological parent.[237] Employing the clear and convincing standard, the court affirmed the trial court's decision, noting that its review under Indiana's abuse of discretion standard would be limited to "whether a reasonable trier of fact could conclude that the judgment was established by clear and convincing evidence."[238]

j)   Trial Court's Use of Hard–and–Fast Rules When Discretion Is Afforded

A Seventh Circuit case is one jurisdiction that includes a trial court's failure to exercise discretion in favor of a bright-line rule as itself constituting an abuse of discretion.[239] Plaintiff Robb filed an action against defendant railroad based on the alleged wrongful death of her husband. Following discovery, defendant moved for

---

[232] *Id.* at 60 (Durham, J., dissenting).

[233] *Id.* at 61(emphasis in original).

[234] *In re Guardianship of B.H.*, 770 N.E.2d 283, 286 (Ind. 2002) (internal quotations omitted).

[235] *Id.* at 286 ("Beginning with *Turpen v. Turpen*, 537 N.E. 2d 537 (Ind. Ct. App. 1989), however, several opinions by the Court of Appeals have avoided a strict application of the *Hendrickson* methodology.").

[236] *Hendrickson v. Binkley*, 316 N.E.2d 376, 381 (Ind. Ct. App. 1974), quoted in *In re Guardianship of B.H.*, 770 N.E.2d at 286.

[237] *In re Guardianship of B.H.*, 770 N.E.2d at 287.

[238] *Id.* at 288.

[239] *Robb v. Norfolk & W. Ry. Co.*, 122 F.3d 354 (7th Cir. 1997).

summary judgment. Plaintiff's counsel, although supposedly reaching an agreement with opposing counsel for an extension, failed to ask the trial court for additional time to file a response (based on a busy litigation schedule). Sixteen days after plaintiff's time to respond had elapsed, the trial court granted summary judgment to defendant on the grounds that plaintiff had failed to respond to the motion. Five days later, plaintiff filed a motion under Federal Rule of Civil Procedure 60(b), alleging that her oversight was due to counsel's "mistake" and "excusable neglect," both grounds for relief from judgment. Following a hearing, the trial court "reluctantly denied [plaintiff's] motion, concluding that [it] lacked discretion to grant relief because of what [it] saw as a firm rule in the Seventh Circuit 'unambiguously prohibiting a grant of a Rule 60(b) motion for attorney carelessness or negligence.'"[240]

Although the court stated that the abuse of discretion standard clearly applied to a Rule 60(b) decision, the court stated further that the standard "presents a conundrum in the present case, for here *the district judge concluded that he was without discretion to exercise*."[241] Thus, the court announced that it would review "the legal assumption underlying the district court's conclusion that it had no discretion."[242] The court acknowledged that in the past the Seventh Circuit had adopted a "narrow approach" to Rule 60(b) and implied that the district court's decision may have been justified under that approach.[243] However, the United States Supreme Court had rejected the "narrow approach" of the Seventh Circuit, opting instead for an approach that affords trial courts "discretion to consider the equities and then determine whether a missed filing deadline attributable to an attorney's negligence is (or is not) 'excusable neglect'."[244] Based on the fact that the trial court's decision "was based on the incorrect premise that he lacked discretion to do so" the court vacated so that the trial judge could "exercise his *discretion* in assessing whether the negligence of Robb's attorney amounts to 'excusable neglect' warranting relief from the entry of summary judgment."[245]

k)   Critique

The United States Supreme Court, in *Crawford v. Washington*, chose to curb the judicial discretion that state trial courts exercise when admitting or refusing to admit evidence.[246] Defendant was charged with assault with a deadly weapon when he attacked a man who supposedly had tried to rape the defendant's wife. Defendant's wife had led the defendant to the victim's location immediately prior to the attack. Defendant's wife witnessed the attack and gave a taped statement to the police.

[240] *Id.* at 357.
[241] *Id.* (emphasis in original).
[242] *Id.*
[243] *Id.* at 358 ("In order to qualify as 'excusable neglect' under our [now archaic] case law, an attorney's omission must have been attributable to some kind of 'exceptional circumstance' and not mere carelessness or negligence.").
[244] *Robb*, 122 F.3d at 359.
[245] *Id.* at 361.
[246] 541 U.S. 36 (2004).

Defendant's wife was unable to testify at trial because of the marital privilege, and the state therefore sought to admit the wife's taped statement as a statement "against penal interest" and thereby falling under a state hearsay exception. Defendant objected on the grounds that not having an opportunity to cross-examine the wife would violate his Sixth Amendment rights.[247] The dispute in the Washington courts centered around whether the taped statements bore "particularized guarantees of trustworthiness" sufficient to satisfy the Confrontation Clause. The Washington Supreme Court held that the statements satisfied the Confrontation Clause.

After reviewing the common law origins of the Confrontation Clause, the Court, per Justice Scalia, concluded that "the principal evil at which the Confrontation Clause was directed was the civil law mode of criminal procedure." The Court then focused on *ex parte* testimony such as statements to the police, depositions, and so on, reasoning that such testimony is uniquely within the purview of the Confrontation Clause.[248]

The Court held that the Confrontation Clause is violated when a trial court allows *ex parte* testimony unless the witness "was unavailable to testify" and "the defendant had had a prior opportunity for cross-examination."[249] Reasoning that the text of the Sixth Amendment did not allow for "open-ended exceptions,"[250] the Court overruled its prior precedent in *Ohio v. Roberts*, which allowed trial courts to admit hearsay if a firmly rooted hearsay exception applied to the evidence or if the evidence bore "particularized guarantees of trustworthiness."[251] The Court first criticized *Roberts* on grounds that it afforded judicial discretion at the expense of defendant's constitutional rights:

> Where testimonial statements are involved, we do not think the Framers meant to leave the Sixth Amendment's protection to the vagaries of the rules of evidence, much less to amorphous notions of "reliability." Certainly none of the authorities... acknowledges any general reliability exception to the common-law rule. Admitting statements deemed reliable by a judge is fundamentally

---

[247] *Id.* at 40.

Petitioner countered that, state law notwithstanding, admitting the evidence would violate his federal constitutional right to be "confronted with the witnesses against him." According to our description of that right in *Ohio v. Roberts*, 100 S.Ct. 2531, it does not bar admission of an unavailable witness's statement against a criminal defendant if the statement bears "adequate indicia or reliability." To meet that test, evidence must either fall within a "firmly rooted hearsay exception" or bear "particularized guarantees of trustworthiness."

[248] *Id.* at 51 ("An accuser who makes a formal statement to government officers bears testimony in a sense that a casual remark to an acquaintance does not. The constitutional text, like the history underlying the common-law right of confrontation, thus reflects an especially acute concern with a specific type of out-of-court statement.").

[249] *Id.* at 1354.

[250] *Id.*

[251] *Id.* at 60.

at odds with the right of confrontation. To be sure, the Clause's ultimate goal is to ensure reliability of evidence, but it is a procedural rather than a substantive guarantee. It commands, not that evidence be reliable, but that reliability be assessed in a particular manner: by testing in the crucible of cross-examination. The Clause thus reflects a judgment, not only about the desirability of reliable evidence (a point on which there could be little dissent), but about how reliability can best be determined.

The *Roberts* test allows a jury to hear evidence, untested by the adversary process, based on a mere judicial determination of reliability. It thus replaces the constitutionally prescribed method of assessing reliability with a wholly foreign one. In this respect, it is very different from exceptions to the Confrontation Clause that make no claim to be a surrogate means of assessing reliability. For example, the rule of forfeiture by wrongdoing (which we accept) extinguishes confrontation claims on essentially equitable grounds; it does not purport to be an alternative means of determining reliability.

The Court then attacked the *Roberts* test's unpredictability:

Reliability is an amorphous, if not entirely subjective, concept. There are countless factors bearing on whether a statement is reliable; the nine-factor balancing test applied by the Court of Appeals below is representative. Whether a statement is deemed reliable depends heavily on which factors the judge considers and how much weight he accords each of them. Some courts wind up attaching the same significance to opposite facts. For example, the Colorado Supreme Court held a statement more reliable because its inculpation of the defendant was detailed, while the Fourth Circuit found a statement more reliable because the portion implicating another was fleeting. The Virginia Court of Appeals found a statement more reliable because the witness was in custody and charged with a crime (thus making the statement more obviously against her penal interest)... while the Wisconsin Court of Appeals found a statement more reliable because the witness was *not* in custody and *not* a suspect. Finally, the Colorado Supreme Court in one case found a statement more reliable because it was given immediately after the events at issue, while that same court, in another case, found a statement more reliable because two years had elapsed.[252]

The Court concluded:

---

[252] 541 U.S. at 63

116

We have no doubt that the courts below were acting in utmost good faith when they found reliability. The Framers, however, would not have been content to indulge this assumption. They knew that judges, like other government officers, could not always be trusted to safeguard the rights of the people.... They were loath to leave too much discretion in judicial hands. By replacing categorical constitutional guarantees with open-ended balancing tests, we do violence to their design. Vague standards are manipulable, and, while that might be a small concern in run-of-the-mill assault prosecutions like this one, the Framers had an eye toward politically charged cases... great state trials where the impartiality of even those at the highest levels of the judiciary might not be so clear. [253]

Justice Rehnquist, joined by Justice O'Connor, concurred in the judgment of the court but dissented from its decision to overrule *Ohio v. Roberts*. With regard to whether the "Confrontation Clause categorically requires the exclusion of testimonial statements," the concurrence argued that the history of the Confrontation Clause was not as linear as the majority had supposed.[254] Based on its review of the history of the Confrontation Clause, the concurrence argued that "such a right was not absolute" and that "exceptions to the exclusionary component of the hearsay rule... had been introduced."[255] Justice Rehnquist continued, "Exceptions to confrontation have always been derived from the experience that some out-of-court statements are just as reliable as cross-examined in-court testimony due to the circumstances under which they were made. We have recognized, for example, that co-conspirator statements simply cannot be replicated...."[256]

l)   Conclusion

Some authorities have identified the preservation of the "functions and morale of the trial court" as a reason for affording trial courts judicial discretion.[257] Case authority in support of this rationale for judicial discretion is scarce. Moreover, the

---

[253] *Id.* at 67-68.

[254] *See id.* at 72 (Rehnquist, J., concurring in the judgment) (reviewing the history of the right to confrontation in English common law and under state constitutions).

[255] *Id.* at 73-74 (Rehnquist, J., concurring in the judgment). Justice Rehnquist cited to Chief Justice Marshall's opinion in *United States v. Burr*, 25 F. Cas. 187, 193 (CC Va. 1807).

[256] *Id.* (Rehnquist, J., concurring in the judgment). *See also, c.f., Kurth v. Iowa Dept. Trans.*, 628 N.W.2d 1, 5 (Iowa 2001) ("Generally, hearsay rulings are also reviewed for errors at law. However, when the basis for admission to hearsay evidence is the expert opinion rule, which provides no hard and fast rule regarding admissibility, we will employ an abuse of discretion standard.")

[257] For an example of these authorities, *see* Kelly Kunsch, *Standard of Review (State and Federal): A Primer*, 18 Seattle U. L. Rev. 11, 20 (1994); Todd E. Pettys, *Federal Habeas Relief and the New Tolerance of Reasonably Erroneous Applications of Federal Law*, 63 Ohio St. L. J. 731, 762 (2002).

rationale has been criticized.[258] Finally, the primary "function" of a trial court is to determine facts and credibility (having more than the so-called cold record for assistance) and to make decisions over which no clear rule governs or which require knowledge of the facts beyond that found in the cold record of the case. The way our appellate system works, the trial judge should not expect as a matter of its morale to have most all of its *legal* decisions upheld on appeal, since its primary function is not to decide questions of law.

§ 2.4.   Judicial Efficiency and Economy

a)   Generally:Efficiency and Justice

Much of the discretion a trial court enjoys in the interest of "judicial efficiency" comes with the expectation that the trial court will balance the interest that the court system has in deciding cases quickly and inexpensively and the interest both the parties and the system have in securing a just result. For example, when reviewing a shareholders' suit against a corporation and its directors, the Tenth Circuit remarked:

> In deciding the instant appeal, this court has reviewed a piece of litigation spanning a decade and a half and a trial lasting nearly three months. This court is well aware that in such litigation the discretion of the trial court is important to accomplish efficiency, notice, and fairness. In this context, however, we could not reasonably expect perfection in the district court's exercise of that discretion or in its overall handling of the case; rather, what this court expects from the district court is basic fairness to all parties. Having reversed the district court on but two of many issues presented on appeal, we are satisfied that the district court achieved fundamental fairness in its presentation of this vast and complex piece of litigation to lay fact finders.[259]

b)   Dismissal as a Discovery Sanction

A Minnesota appellate court, affirming a trial court's decision to enter default judgment for plaintiff based on defendant's noncompliance with discovery, held that although "a district court has broad discretion to enforce rules of court and ensure the efficient disposition of cases" the court would "give greater scrutiny" when the trial court's "sanction denies a party a trial on the merits."[260] Plaintiff had brought an action against defendant for fraud and conversion. She based her claim on the allegation that defendant had told her that she would be implicated in a drug ring unless she conveyed all of her assets to defendant.[261] Defendant was frequently late in meeting discovery deadlines and was even found in contempt of court for

---

[258] *See, e.g.*, Kunsch, *supra* note 120, at 20.
[259] *Koch v. Koch Ind. Inc.*, 203 F.3d 1202, 1239 (10th Cir. 2000).
[260] *Engel v. Ryan*, No. A03-1558. 2004 WL 1614877 at *3 (Minn. Ct. App. July 20, 2004).
[261] *Id.* at *1.

118

failing to disclose the location of the assets he had received from plaintiff.[262] The trial court entered default judgment after defendant responded to interrogatories after what the court characterized as "the final discovery deadline."[263]

The court enumerated three factors within which the trial court could exercise its discretion.[264] The court identified "prejudice to the parties" as its "guiding consideration" when reviewing the trial court's decision, but also considered "the effect of and reasons for delay" and "whether a party has a pattern of misconduct."[265] Although defendant on appeal argued that the trial court had an obligation to warn defendant of impending default (which the trial court did not do), the court reaffirmed its precedent that "such a warning is not a requirement but only a 'significant factor' in determining whether default is appropriate.[266]

c)   **Summary Judgment**

The Court of Appeals of New York has cited efficiency as a reason *not* to afford the trial court discretion to consider a summary judgment motion filed after deadline.[267] Defendant city moved for summary judgment against plaintiff, after the 120-day deadline prescribed by the relevant civil procedure rules and "close to a year after the trial calendar papers were filed."[268] The trial court accepted the motion "in the interests of judicial economy, and since [plaintiff] did not manifest any prejudice from the delay."[269] After a hearing on the merits, the trial court awarded defendant summary judgment.

The Court of Appeals reversed. Although the court acknowledged summary judgment's role in "avoiding needless litigation cost and delay,"[270] the court focused on the "problematic" nature of a summary judgment procedure operating in "the absence of an outside time limit" to end the process.[271] The court stated, "Eleventh-hour summary judgment motions, sometimes used as a dilatory tactic, left inadequate time for reply or proper court consideration, and prejudiced litigants who had already devoted substantial resources to readying themselves for trial."[272] The court then recounted that the state legislature had amended state procedural rules to

---

[262] *Id.* at *2.
[263] *Id.* at *3 (noting the district court's conclusions that defendant's responses were "evasive, vague and incomplete").
[264] *Engel,* 2004 WL 1614877 at *3.
[265] *Id.*
[266] *Id.* (citation omitted). ("We note that prior Minnesota Supreme Court cases do not support a warning requirement. Indeed, some have upheld defaults or dismissals based solely on a party's intransigence.").
[267] *Brill v. City of New York,* 814 N.E.2d 431 (N.Y. 2004) (slip-and-fall on city sidewalk).
[268] *Id.* at 433 ("The City gave no explanation for filing the motion after the 120-day limit....").
[269] *Id.*
[270] *Id.* ("Where appropriate, summary judgment is a great benefit both to the parties and to the overburdened... trial courts.") (citations omitted).
[271] *Id.*
[272] *Brill,* 814 N.E. 2d at 433.

require parties to file summary judgment motions within 120 days "after the filing of the note of issue, *except with leave of court on good cause shown.*"[273] The court concluded that the rule "struck a balance, fixing an outside limit on the time for filing summary judgment motions, but allowing courts latitude to set an alternative limit or to consider untimely motions to accommodate genuine need."[274] The court then acknowledged a split within the jurisdiction as to whether "good cause" required that the tardy movant offer a "satisfactory explanation" for its delay or whether "good cause" simply meant that the late motion "had merit" and that "there was no prejudice to the adversary."[275]

The Court of Appeals adopted the former view based on the language of the rule.[276] As to the "more vexing issue"[277] of whether the motion should be considered, the court made the following observations about the efficiency of the court system:

> ... [W]e affirmed the dismissal of a complaint for failure to respond to interrogatories within court-ordered time frames, observing that if the credibility of court orders and the integrity of our judicial system are to be maintained, a litigant cannot ignore court orders with impunity. The present scenario, another example of sloppy practice threatening the integrity of our judicial system, rests instead on the violation of legislative mandate.

> If this practice is tolerated and condoned, the ameliorative statute is, for all intents and purposes, obliterated. If, on the other hand, the statute is applied as written and intended, an anomaly may result, in that a meritorious summary judgment motion may be denied, burdening the litigants and trial calendar with a case that leaves nothing to try. Indeed, the statute should not provide a safe haven for frivolous or meritless lawsuits, which is precisely why practitioners should move for summary judgment within the prescribed time period or offer a legitimate reason for delay.[278]

Justice Smith dissented on the grounds that "there was good cause for the trial court to entertain this [summary judgment] motion and because the time of the litigants, jurors, lawyers, the judge and other court personnel should not be wasted in going through the motions of a trial which has no merit and must be

---

[273] *Id.* at 434 (quoting N.Y. C.P.L.R. 3212(a) (McKinney 2004)) (emphasis added).
[274] *Id.*
[275] *Id.*
[276] *Id.* ("Th[e] reading is supported by the language of the statute—only the movant can show good cause—as well as by the purpose of the amendment, to end the practice of eleventh-hour summary judgment motions. No excuse at all, or a perfunctory excuse, cannot be 'good cause.'").
[277] 814 N.E. 2d at 435.
[278] *Id.*

dismissed."[279] Justice Smith also stated pithily that "[t]he trial court did not abuse its discretion in entertaining the motion"[280] and that "nothing that the defendant did prejudiced the plaintiff."[281]

As the prior case shows, here is a distinction between an appellate court's review of the merits of a summary judgment motion (normally reviewed *de novo*) and the appellate court's review of the trial court's procedural decisions governing summary judgment. The Minnesota Court of Appeals had a slightly different question involving whether, as a matter of law, one insurance company would have to pay for a casualty on the grounds that the terms of its policy was "closest-to-the-risk" realized.[282] Insurance company General Casualty argued that under the "closest-to-the-risk" analysis, the trial court had to consider whether insurance company INA's coverage was "statutorily mandated."[283] The court held that it was "unnecessary" for the trial court "to determine whether INA's coverage was statutorily mandated" when deciding (on summary judgment) which insurance company would pay benefits to the insured.[284] The court reasoned, "Because the issue involved factual findings, the trial court analyzed the case using only the undisputed facts presented. The trial court's decision not to decide the issue of whether INA's coverage was statutorily mandated was, as a matter of judicial efficiency, within the court's broad discretion."[285]

d)   Continuance

Regarding continuances, the United States Supreme Court has stated the following:

> The matter of continuance is traditionally within the discretion of the trial judge, and it is not every denial of a request for more time that violates due process even if the party fails to offer evidence or is compelled to defendant without counsel. Contrariwise, a myopic insistence upon expeditiousness in the face of a justifiable request for delay can render the right to defend with counsel an empty formality. There are no mechanical tests for deciding when a denial of a continuance is so arbitrary as to violate due process. The

---

[279] *Id.* at 435–36 (Smith, J., dissenting).

[280] *Id.* at 436 (Smith, J., dissenting). Addressing the majority's argument regarding the intent of the legislature, Justice Smith stated, "What is clear from the legislative history is that the [l]egislature sought to give the trial court wide discretion in entertaining a motion for summary judgment." *Id.* at 436–37.

[281] *Id.* at 436 (Smith, J., dissenting) ("The clear fact is that the plaintiff cannot prove a prima facie case and thus that she is entitled to prevail.").

[282] *Northland Ins. Co. v. W. Nat'l Mut. Ins. Co.*, No. C5-92-324, 1992 WL 153094, at *1 (Minn. Ct. App., July 7, 1992). The court held that General Casualty was responsible for coverage under the "closest-to-the-risk" analysis.

[283] *Id.* at *2.

[284] *Id.*

[285] *Id.*

answer must be found in the circumstances presented to the trial judge at the time the request is denied.[286]

The Ohio Court of Appeals found that a the trial court presiding over a divorce case had abused its discretion when it denied husband's motion for a continuance so that he could determine the fair market value of horses that had been purchased during his marriage to wife.[287] Husband moved for a continuance on the grounds that wife "had transferred several horses to out-of-state third parties, in violation of [a] temporary restraining order."[288] Husband "contended that due to [wife's] actions, he was prevented from obtaining fair market values for the horses, and requested a continuance of the trial so that such values might be obtained."[289] The trial court passed over the motion and proceeded with the trial without explanation, although the trial court did indicate that it wanted to finish the case quickly in order to conform with a general mandate from the Ohio Supreme Court.[290]

The court stated that in "reviewing whether the trial court abused its discretion by denying a motion for a continuance" it "must apply a balancing test, weighing the trial court's interest in controlling its own docket, including facilitating the efficient dispensation of justice, versus the potential prejudice to the moving party."[291] Upon weighing the appropriate factors, the court concluded that "the potential prejudice to [husband] outweighed the interest in efficiency, and that the trial court abused its discretion by failing to grant [the] motion for a continuance."[292]

The Ohio Court of Appeals has taken a slightly more favorable approach to the concept of judicial efficiency when reviewing trial court decisions regarding the trial court's management of class actions. In *dicta*, the Court made the following observation's about its jurisdiction's rule for class actions:

> The legislature... did not enact a statute, which allowed a party to appeal every time a trial court modified the membership of a class. Instead, the legislature allowed an appeal following the initial finding that a class action, as opposed to an individual action, could be maintained. This decision of the legislature is consistent with the efficient operation of the trial courts. Maximum discretion for management of a class action once certified must be vested in the

---

[286] *Ungar v. Sarafite*, 376 U.S. 575, 589 (1964).
[287] *Schiesswohl v. Schiesswohl*, No. 21629. 2004 WL 626110 (Ohio Ct. App., March 31, 2004).
[288] *Id.* at *3.
[289] *Id.*
[290] *Id.* at *4.
[291] *Id.* (setting forth a multi-factor test in order to determine whether the trial court had abused its discretion).
[292] *Id.* at *5.

122

trial court so they can manage such complex litigation as efficiently as possible....[293]

Reviewing a trial court's order denying a continuance to plaintiffs in an age discrimination case, the Tennessee Court of Appeals stated that "[t]rial courts have wide discretion in granting or denying continuances but a trial court must exercise that discretion in an efficient manner."[294] The court identified the "age of the cause of action" as the "prime factor in considering a continuance."[295] Plaintiffs had argued that they were entitled to a continuance in order to conduct further discovery and because defendant had not provided them with documents, that plaintiff alleged would prove defendant's discriminatory conduct by virtue of inconsistent enforcement of defendant's rules.[296] The court rejected these arguments on the grounds that the trial court had allowed for further discovery for the four weeks between the time of the motion for continuance and the day before the trial.[297] More importantly, the court noted that "well over three years passed between the time the [p]laintiffs filed their complaints and commencement of trial."[298]

The Wisconsin Court of Appeals upheld the trial court's decision denying a homicide defendant a continuance in order to find and produce an additional alibi witness.[299] The appellate court concluded that "the trial court carefully considered and evaluated [Defendant's] interests and balanced those interests with the need for prompt and efficient justice" and "properly exercised its discretion in denying [Defendant's] request for a continuance."[300] Responding to Defendant's argument that "his interest in a fair trial outweighed that of the State in a fast trial" and that "his late disclosure was justified because of the unique circumstances of the second alibi," the court concluded that Defendant's "request for a continuance was inadequately supported by the evidence he presented."[301] The court found that: (1) Defendant had made no showing that his alibi would "be material to his case," (2) that Defendant "was negligent in waiting until the eve of trial to tell his defense attorney about his second alibi," and (3) that Defendant could not show that "the

---

[293] *Gabbard v. Ohio Bureau of Workers' Comp.*, No. 02AP-976. 2003 WL 21007091 (Ohio Ct. App., May 6, 2003) (holding that there is no right to appeal every time the trial court modifies the class' membership).

[294] *Jessee v. Amer. Gen. Life & Acc. Ins. Co.*, E2002-00182-COA-R3-CV, 2003 WL 165777, at *5 (Tenn. Ct. App., Jan. 24, 2003). For a published opinion citing the same standard, see *Coakley v. Daniels*, 840 S.W. 2d 367, 370 (Tenn. Ct. App. 1992).

[295] *Id.*

[296] *Id.* at *4.

[297] *Id.*

[298] *Id.* at *5 ("It is our conclusion that the [p]laintiffs had sufficient time for discovery and the [p]laintiff's argument that the [t]rial [c]ourt abused its discretion in failing to continue this case in order that they might engage in further discovery are not well taken.").

[299] *State v. King*, 541 N.W.2d 837 (Wis. App. Ct. 1995), *available at* 1995 WL 521859, at ***4.

[300] *Id.*

[301] *Id.* at ***2.

second alibi witnesses were capable of being produced."[302] With respect to efficiency, the court concluded:

> The trial court considered the need for efficient and speedy administration of justice. The record reflects that the trial court found that a continuance for [Defendant] at the "eleventh hour" would be inconsistent with the goal of speedy justice, which exits to serve not just the defendants, the State or the victims, but also the court system and community as a whole.

e) Timeliness of Motions

A Connecticut appellate court has held that when "parties have advanced substantive arguments on [a] motion to strike" portions of a pleading for failure to state a claim, "in the interest of judicial economy" the trial court may in its discretion "overlook, in part, the untimeliness of the motion."[303] Defendant Nationwide had filed a motion to strike portions of plaintiff's amended cross claim against it, but filed the motion one day past the filing deadline.[304] The court then noted that "well-established" precedent made clear that the trial "court has discretion as to whether it will consider the merits of an untimely motion."[305]

f) Discretion of Trial Court to Make Local Rules and General Orders

A pair of Ninth Circuit cases, *United States v. Gray* and *United States v. DeLuca*, illustrate the appellate court's concern for judicial efficiency when reviewing decisions based on the trial court's local rules or general orders.[306] In *Gray*, defendant alleged a due process claim based on the fact that the trial court had violated its local rules by reassigning his case to another judge.[307] Before determining that the local rules allowed for the transfer, the court stated: "We do not review a district court's determination of the scope and application of local rules and general orders because we give district courts broad discretion in interpreting, applying, and determining the requirements of their own local rules and general orders."[308] The court did not reach the due process claim since it concluded that

---

[302] *Id.* at ***3–4.

[303] *Langer v. Nationwide Mut. Ins. Co.*, No. CV020077564S, 2004 WL 575053, at *2 (Conn. Sup. Ct., Mar. 1, 2004).

[304] *Id.*

[305] *Id.* ("[A]lthough a motion to strike may appear untimely on its face, the court has discretion to permit a late pleading where the parties have both submitted arguments on the merits.") (internal quotations omitted).

[306] *United States v. Gray*, 876 F.2d 1411 (9th Cir. 1989).
United States v. DeLuca, 692 F.2d 1277 (9th Cir. 1982).

[307] 876 F.2d 1411, 1414 (9th Cir. 1989) ("General Rule Eight provides that: 'All actions, causes, and proceedings, civil and criminal, shall be assigned by the clerk to the respective judges of the court.'").

[308] *Id.*

there was neither a violation of the local rules nor a separate "impermissible reason" for reassigning the case.[309]

The *Gray* court cited to its holding in *United States v. DeLuca* when setting out the appropriate standard of review. Defendant DeLuca also challenged a reassignment to another judge based on a violation of local court rules and on alleged judicial bias.[310] The court held that even "if the transfer failed to satisfy the literal terms of the local rule," "it met minimum due process demands."[311] The court concluded, "Because general orders and local rules not only implement due process and other statutory rights but also promote efficiency, we permit the district court broad discretion in determining their requirements."[312]

g)   Procedures for *Daubert* Hearings

Affirming a trial court's decision to allow a *Daubert* hearing in the presence of the jury, the Third Circuit held that "the court exercised sound discretion in controlling the efficient and orderly disposition of this case to avoid unnecessary inconvenience to the jury."[313] Plaintiff Holbrook argued on appeal that the trial court had "failed in its gatekeeping responsibility by allowing the jury to hear the radiation testimony without first determining its admissibility."[314] The court rejected this argument, pointing out that the trial court had scheduled a pretrial *Daubert* hearing at plaintiff's request. "Inexplicably, [plaintiff's] counsel seemed unprepared to proceed with that hearing, and the court therefore did not hold one. Despite this, the court nevertheless indicated to [plaintiff's] counsel that it would entertain counsel's motion at trial to strike the expert testimony."[315] The court concluded that while *Daubert* would "ordinarily" "require that the court make the preliminary determination outside the jury's hearing," it could not say "that the [trial] court abused its discretion in the manner in which it adhered to the requirements" of *Daubert*.[316] The court also quoted the trial court's reasoning in making its decision: "I will not have a hearing of such length while a jury is waiting to be selected.... This was your opportunity for a *Daubert* hearing today and tomorrow. It is improper to have jurors waiting for several days to be selected in a case that might go on for weeks."[317]

---

[309] *Id.* at 1415 ("Judges may reassign cases for almost any reason, provided that the assignment is not an impermissible reason.").
[310] *DeLuca*, 692 F.2d 1277, 1281 (9th Cir. 1982).
[311] *Id.*
[312] *Id.*
[313] *Holbrook v. Lykes Bros. Steamship Co.*, 80 F.3d 777, 784 (3rd Cir. 1996).
[314] *Id.*
[315] *Id.*
[316] *Id.*
[317] *Id.*

h)   Discovery

The Ninth Circuit held in an unpublished disposition that a district court acted within its discretion in ordering plaintiff's "deposition be taken instead of allowing him to amend his complaint."[318] The court without further explanation concluded that trial courts "have broad discretion in promoting efficient and equitable case management."[319] The court cited to a prior Third Circuit case, *In re Fine Paper Antitrust Litigation* in support of its conclusion.[320] The *Fine Paper* court did not mention judicial efficiency as a reason for upholding the trial court's discretionary decision to cut off discovery and to set dates for trial. It did, however, weigh the trial court's interest in ending discovery against the interest of the parties in acquiring the evidence they needed to prepare for trial:

> "Appellants' primary argument is that they were afforded too little time for discovery and trial preparation. Appellants have a heavy burden to bear, however, as matters of docket control and conduct of discovery are committed to the sound discretion of the district court. We will not interfere with a trial court's control of its docket except upon the clearest showing that the procedures have resulted in actual and substantial prejudice to the complaining litigant. Similarly, we will not upset a district court's conduct of discovery procedures absent a demonstration that the court's action made it impossible to obtain crucial evidence, and implicit in such a showing is proof that more diligent discovery was impossible.

> "We find no abuse of discretion by the district judge in his scheduling of discovery or of the trial. After considering all of appellants' contentions and examining the 16-volume appendix that they have supplied to this court, we are not persuaded that the pre-trial rulings of the district court prejudiced the preparation or presentation of their case. The trial of their antitrust claims followed fifteen months of discovery, including approximately 270 depositions and production of nearly two million documents. The trial commenced four months after conclusion of discovery and one month after the date appellants had earlier set as the date on which they would be ready for trial.[321]

i)   Assignment of Cases to Multiple Judges

The Tenth Circuit had the opportunity to consider whether the district court could assign a case to multiple judges in the absence of a local rule authorizing the

---

[318] *Turner v. Fin. Corp. of Amer.*, 960 F.2d 152 (9th Cir. 1992), *available at* 1992 WL 33370, at **1.
[319] *Id.*
[320] 685 F.2d 810 (3rd Cir. 1982).
[321] *Id.* at 817-818.

126

practice.[322] Defendant Diaz argued on appeal that the assignment of his case to multiple judges violated his Fifth Amendment due process rights.[323] Although the court reviewed this issue *de novo* as a legal question, it cited to federal authorities conferring the decision to assign multiple judges to the discretion of the trial court.[324]

The court rejected defendant's contention "that the absence of a written policy or order renders the rotating assignment system invalid."[325] Noting evidence that the judges on the court had consented to the transfer, the court stated:

> It is obvious that the judges of the district in question regularly show up for work, and they seem to balance their assignments systematically, in all likelihood so that their more voluminous regular dockets in their resident chambers can proceed as efficiently as possible, given the necessity of traveling to other courthouses.

Addressing defendant's argument that it was "improper to justify the use of a rotating assignment system on the grounds of judicial efficiency," the court responded that the courts "have long considered judicial efficiency a proper justification for transferring cases between judges."[326] The court reserved to the trial court the question of whether reassignment was "actually efficient," concluding that "the judges need to be the ones to make that call."[327]

j)   Peremptory Challenges

The Supreme Court of Delaware held that a trial court acted within its discretion when it refused to allow defendant ten peremptory challenges during his assault trial (which ended in conviction).[328] The trial court had initially granted the state ten peremptory challenges and the joint defendants ten peremptory challenges, or five each. However, the trial court "realized that if each party were to exercise all of its challenges, there would be an insufficient number of veniremen remaining to constitute a jury."[329] Over defendant's objection, the trial court reduced the number

---

[322] *United States v. Diaz*, 189 F.3d 1239, 1243 (10th Cir. 1999).

[323] *Id.*

[324] *Id.* ("The business of a court having more than one judge shall be divided among the judges as provided by the rules and orders of the court.") (quoting 28 U.S.C. § 137). The court also quoted Fed. R. Crim. P. 57(b), which "provides that when there is no controlling law, '[a] judge may regulate practice in any manner consistent with federal law, these rules, and local rules of the district.'" *Id.* at 1244.

[325] *Id.* at 1244.

[326] *Id.* at 1244.

[327] 189 F.3d at 1244.

[328] *Williamson v. State*, 707 A.2d 350, 362 (Del. 1998) ("The trial court did not abuse its discretion, and [defendant] did not show how the exercise of discretion conferred an unfair benefit upon the State.")

[329] *Id.*

of peremptory challenges to eight per side, giving four to each defendant. When the state exercised only two peremptory challenges, defendants each requested an additional peremptory challenge. The trial court denied their request.

The court cited to the trial court's procedural rule providing that in noncapital cases, each side would have at least six peremptory challenges total, but that the trial court "may grant additional peremptory challenges in its discretion."[330] Although the trial court apparently complied with this rule, defendant argued that "the court should not have reduced the number of challenges from ten to eight merely because there may have been too few perspective jurors in the venire."[331] The court rejected this argument:

> This Court, however, has held that the number of jurors in a venire may be considered by a trial court when it determines the number of peremptory challenges it will award. That the low number of jurors on the venire was not discovered until the questioning of the venire had begun does not change our analysis. The trial court's decision not to grant the [defendants] two extra challenges was based on considerations of fairness, orderliness and efficiency.

k)   Right of Trial Court to Control Its Docket

In *Ahneman v. Ahneman*, the Connecticut Supreme Court reversed a trial court for abuse of discretion on the grounds that the trial court summarily declined to consider some of the wife's motions following issuance of the decree of dissolution.[332] After determining that the trial court's decision was a final appealable order and remanding to the intermediate appellate court for consideration of the merits, the court invoked its "supervisory powers" "to address the subject of the trial court's decision."[333] The court concluded that the trial court "lacked authority to refuse to consider the defendant's motions."[334] In doing so, it rejected plaintiff's contention that "the trial court's refusal was justified on the ground of efficiency in light of the alleged connection between the issues on appeal and the subject of the defendant's motions":[335]

> Although it may be efficient for a trial court not to expend judicial resources on a question that a pending appeal may subsequently render moot, that kind of efficiency has never been considered a

---

[330] *Id.*

[331] *Id.*

[332] 706 A.2d 960 (Conn. 1998) (reversing the intermediate appellate court's decision to dismiss defendant's appeal based on the lack of a final appealable order).

[333] *Id.* at 481 ("[B]ecause the trial court has not rendered any factual or legal conclusions regarding defendant's motions, the Appellate Court cannot perform that review [on remand]. Therefore, in order to avoid confusion, we will review the propriety of the trial court's decision ourselves.")

[334] *Id.*

[335] *Id.* at 966

128

justification for a trial court's refusal to consider a question. If anything, considerations of judicial efficiency point in the opposite direction, toward recognizing that a trial court may render moot an appeal by opening, and altering, the judgment that gave rise to it.

More fundamentally, basic principles of jurisprudence refute the plaintiff's proposition that a trial court has discretion, based on notions of efficiency, to decline to exercise its jurisdiction by refusing to consider certain motions. Courts are in the business of ruling on litigants' contentions...."[336]

The court went on to conclude that once a trial court establishes jurisdiction over the parties and over the subject matter, the trial court must address "every question which may arise in the cause."[337]

l)   Order and Mode of Interrogation at Trial

Defendant was convicted of charges stemming from multiple incidences in which defendant struck and threw objects at a child disabled by cerebral palsy.[338] At trial, because of the child's disability, the trial court permitted both parties to use leading questions during examination.[339] The appellate court affirmed, stating that trial "courts have broad discretion to decide when such special circumstances are present" so as to allow the use of leading questions.[340] The court found that the trial court acted within its discretion when it found that the child's disability constituted a special circumstance.[341] Although the court also found the child competent to testify (and without an interpreter), "her speech impediment precluded her from doing so efficiently."[342] The court concluded that the "trial court found the use of leading questions to be the most direct means of circumventing this obstacle":

> The court's decision is corroborated by the record itself, which demonstrates the use of leading questions allowed the victim to communicate her testimony effectively and efficiently. The trial court had the discretion to select the option it deemed most fair to all parties, including the victim. The evidence in the record substantiates the trial court's decision. We find no abuse of discretion.[343]

The Texas Court of Appeals upheld a criminal defendant's conviction for assault of a police officer despite comments the trial judge made during the

[336] *Id.*
[337] *Williamson*, 706 A.2d at 966 (quotation omitted).
[338] *People v. Augustin*, 5 Cal. Rptr.3d 171, 175 (Cal. Ct. App. 2003).
[339] *Id.*
[340] *Id.* at 175.
[341] *Id.* at 176.
[342] *Id.*
[343] 5 Cal. Rptr.3d at 176.

defendant's cross—examination of a prosecution witness.[344] Defendant argued that the trial court had violated his rights to a fair trial, due process, and effective assistance of counsel because "the trial court's comments during cross examination... demonstrated that the trial court failed to keep an open mind throughout the trial, [and] made a decision on guilt before all of the evidence had been submitted."[345] The court acknowledged defendant's constitutional right to a fair trial and stated that if "there exists in the mind of this court any doubt as to the fairness or impartiality of the trial, it becomes our duty to award a new trial."[346] However, the court also weighed the "broad discretion" of a trial court "to place reasonable limits on cross-examination" and its presumption that in "the absence of a clear showing to the contrary" a trial judge is a "neutral and detached officer."[347] Reviewing the record, the court concluded that the trial judge's comments "merely reflect[ed] the trial court informing defense counsel that the fall had already been covered and did not bear on how this officer was injured or appellant's intent with regard to that injury."[348] The court concluded that the trial court's "effort to conduct the trial efficiently was within the trial court's discretion and did not suggest a lack of objectivity."[349]

---

[344] *Sinegal v. State*, Nos. 14-95-00394-CR, 14-95-00395-CR, 14-95-00396-CR, 1997 WL 412533 at *3–*4 (Tex. Ct. App. July 24, 1997).

[345] *Id.* at *3.

[346] *Id.*

[347] *Id.*

[348] *Id.* at *4.

[349] Sinegal, 1997 WL 412533 at *4. The exchange upon which defendant appeals follows:

Defense counsel: Would that be consistent with your saying he's backing up, as I'm doing now, falling backwards and tripping over the curb?

The State: Objection, Your Honor. It's a misstatement of testimony. It's also a question that's been asked and answered.

The Court: *It strikes me that we've talked about this about ten times now.*

Defense counsel: I'm not sure we've asked the specific question if he's backed up and tripped over and fell over the curb.

The Court: *I guess I have this question.*

Defense counsel: Okay.

The Court: *Who cares?*

Defense counsel: Well, the purposes of this offense—I assume there has to be some intent on the part of the defendant to injure these officers.

The Court: I think that's already been testified to. *He's already injured these officers; or at least this one.*

Defense counsel: Well, I think in this particular instance, Your Honor, there's a question of whether or not he intended—of if he's walking back, they fall.

130

m)   Admissibility of Evidence

In *Shook v. Hancock*, the Missouri Supreme Court upheld a trial court's decision to allow defendant Shook to play videotaped excerpts of a third-party's deposition.[350] Although plaintiff Hancock had objected under the completeness doctrine, the trial court allowed the videotape but also permitted plaintiff to read in those portions of the depositions that the video omitted.[351] The Missouri Supreme Court affirmed, stating:

> The trial court's discretion over the admissibility of evidence extends to the admissibility of deposition testimony. The trial court faced a situation where it could postpone the presentation of the evidence and require the [defendants] to re-edit the videotape with Mr. Hancock's designations or let the evidence proceed with Mr. Hancock reading his designations to the jury. The trial court did not abuse its discretion in choosing the more efficient option.[352]

n)   Consolidation and Separation of Trials

Defendant convicted of two counts of rape appealed the trial court's decision to deny his motion to sever the charges relating for each alleged victim.[353] Defendant argued that "the trial had taken weeks, that each case involved different witnesses, that the jury probably co-mingled the two cases, and that each case enhanced the

---

The Court: Let's deal with Officer Spann and not this officer. *This officer got popped in the face and in the upper chest. That's what he testified to. According to the way this thing is pled, that's plenty.*

Defense counsel: Again, I still think that requires some kind of active state of mind on the part of the defendant.

The Court: I think that's already been testified to. I don't have any problem if you're going to talk about the guy falling down; let's not beat it into the ground. *I mean for purposes of this officer, he's already testified as to how it is he says he got injured. That's what I see.*
Id. (emphasis in original).
[350] 100 S.W. 3d 786, 801 (Mo. 2003) (affirming judgment on plaintiff's appeal from his negligence action against a feed supplier on allegations that the supplier sold plaintiff defective feed that killed plaintiff's livestock).
[351] *Id.* (Responding to plaintiff's objection, the court stated, "I'm not going to prevent [defendant] from playing the depo because you two didn't agree what should go in and what shouldn't.... [T]he problem is we're sitting here waiting for the jury to come in and watch it.... I don't know any way to fix it other than let [defendant] play [the] video and then let [plaintiff] read the parts that [plaintiff] want[s] to read.").
[352] *Id.*
[353] *State v. Cranshaw*, No. 26167-7-II. 2002 WL 1880768, at *2 (Wash. Ct. App., Aug. 16, 2002).

credibility of the victim in the other case."[354] The court stated that the trial court could sever "if it determines that severance will promote a fair determination of the defendant's guilt or innocence..." and stated that it would review such determination only "for manifest abuse of discretion."[355] The court stated that it would find such abuse if defendant could "show that one trial for both victims was so manifestly prejudicial as to outweigh the concern for judicial economy."[356] The court then listed a number of factors that would "offset any prejudicial effect" to defendant.[357] Weighing prejudice to defendant against the offsetting factors, the court concluded that the interest of judicial economy outweighed prejudice to defendant and that denying the motion for severance was within the trial court's discretion.[358]

The majority of the South Dakota Supreme Court held in *Christians v. Christians* that the wife had made out a cause of action against the husband for intentional infliction of emotional distress after the grounds for a divorce suit had been established.[359] Justice Konenkamp filed a special concurrence. In that concurrence, he noted that "the circuit court joined the divorce and tort actions in the same trial."[360] Justice Konenkamp then acknowledged that the trial court could join the two actions at its discretion, but catalogued a list of reasons as to why a trial court might refrain from doing so:

> In this case, the circuit court joined the divorce and tort actions in the same trial. This is permissible, but not mandatory. Circuit courts have general jurisdiction to hear all civil actions. Trial courts should carefully consider in each case whether to hear the tort and divorce in the same trial. To avoid prejudice and maintain efficiency, courts have the discretion to order separate trials in these proceedings. In many instances, a joinder of both actions will run contrary to considerations of public policy. When a divorce is brought on by irreconcilable differences, joinder of an intentional tort claim defeats the legislative intent in enacting no-fault divorce. Tort actions seek to compensate the injured and sometimes to punish the wrongdoer; divorce actions aim to provide for support, divide marital property, and restore the parties to unmarried status. A tort claim may include facts irrelevant to divorce issues,

[354] *Id.*
[355] *Id.* (quotation omitted).
[356] *Id.* (quotation omitted).
[357] *Id.* ("Certain factors offset any prejudicial effect, including (1) the strength of the State's evidence, (2) the clarity of defenses to each count, (3) whether the court instructed the jury to consider the counts separately, and (4) the cross-admissibility of the evidence if the cases had been tried separately.")
[358] 2002 WL 1880768, at *3 ("Where, as here, the State's evidence is fairly strong on all charges, the defenses are consistent, the court properly instructed the jury, and two trials would burden judicial economy and efficiency, the trial court does not abuse its discretion by refusing to sever the charges.")
[359] 637 N.W. 2d 377 (S.D. 2001).
[360] *Id.* at 386 (Konenkamp, J., concurring).

numerous witnesses, and other parties, such as joint tortfeasors. Combining tort claims with a divorce action may unduly lengthen and complicate a trial and result in delayed child custody and support rulings. Obviously, if a jury trial is demanded, the court will have to separate the trials.

On the other hand, counsel must be aware that these matters are subject to principles of res judicata and estoppel....

....An Ohio appeals court... ruled that the concern for judicial economy does not outweigh the fact that a domestic relations forum is not the proper forum in which to litigate a tort claim.

Contingency fees are common in tort actions. But the South Dakota Rules of Professional Conduct prohibit any fee in a domestic relations matter, the payment or amount of which is contingent upon the securing of a divorce or upon the amount of alimony or support, or property settlement in lieu thereof.... In *Simmons, supra,* the court considered the problem of apportioning attorneys' fees to be an additional policy reason for rejecting joinder. Combining divorce and tort claims presents difficulties in allotting time and fees in client billings....[361]

Consolidation and separation of claims in federal courts is governed by the Federal Rules of Civil Procedure. Federal Rule of Civil Procedure 42 provides:

(a) Consolidation. When actions involving a common question of law or fact are pending before the court, it may order a joint hearing or trial of any or all the matters in issue in the actions; it may order all the actions consolidated; and it may make such orders concerning proceedings therein as may tend to avoid unnecessary costs or delay.

(b) Separate Trials. The court, in furtherance of convenience or to avoid prejudice, or when separate trials will be conducive to expedition and economy, may order a separate trial of any claim, cross-claim, counterclaim, or third-party claim, or of any separate issue or of any number of claims, cross-claims, counterclaims, third-party claims, or issues, always preserving inviolate the right of trial by jury as declared by the Seventh Amendment to the Constitution or as given by a statute of the United States.

The federal appellate courts have acknowledged that Rule 42 confers discretion upon the trial court to separate or consolidate claims.[362] The Eleventh Circuit, in

---

[361] *Id.* at 386–87 (Konenkamp, J., concurring) (internal quotations and citations omitted).
[362] *See, e.g., Hangarter v. Provident Life & Acc. Ins. Co.*, 373 F.3d 998, 1021 (9th Cir. 2004) ("Rule 42(b) of the Federal Rules of Civil Procedure confers broad discretion upon

making a Rule 42(b) determination, focused on the "common core of allegations" alleged by class action plaintiffs claiming racial discrimination:

> Given the common core of allegations, the substantial overlap of the particular claims, and the logical interconnection of several of the different forms the alleged discrimination took, we are satisfied that the district court did not abuse its discretion in finding that the efficiency of a consolidated jury trial outweighed the potential for unfair prejudice or jury confusion.[363]

Acting under the state equivalent to Rule 42(b), a Utah trial court bifurcated a trial in which plaintiff landowner sued a neighboring gas station for trespass and private nuisance on allegations that gasoline had contaminated plaintiff's property.[364] The trial court ordered further that the damages portion of the trial be heard first.[365] The Utah Supreme Court reversed for abuse of discretion.[366] The court reaffirmed its prior precedent holding that "[r]egardless of convenience, however, an order to bifurcate a trial is an abuse of discretion if it is unfair or prejudicial to a party or if the issues are [not] clearly separable."[367] The court

---

the district court to bifurcate a trial, thereby deferring costly and possibly unnecessary proceedings. A district court's refusal to bifurcate a trial is accordingly reviewed for an abuse of discretion."); *Alexander v. Fulton County*, 207 F.3d 1303, 1324–25 (11th Cir. 2000). The *Alexander* court stated:

> Alternatively, the Defendants argue that even if the district court did not abuse its discretion in finding proper joinder under Rule 20(a), it did err in failing to sever the Plaintiffs' cases for trial under Fed. R. Civ. P. 42(b). As Rule 42(b) requires the district court to balance considerations of convenience, economy, expedition, and prejudice, the decision to order separate trials naturally depends on the peculiar facts and circumstances of each case. Again, we disturb a district court's decision not to order separate trials only upon a showing of abuse of discretion.*Id.*

[363] *Id.* at 1325–26.

[364] *Walker Drug Co. v. La Sal Oil Co.*, 972 P.2d 1238, 1244 (Utah 1998). Utah R. Civ. P. 42(b) provides: "The court in furtherance of convenience or to avoid prejudice may order a separate trial of any claim, cross-claim, counterclaim, or third-party claim, or of any separate issue or of any number of claims, cross-claims, counterclaims, third-party claims, or issues."

[365] *Id.*

[366] *Id.* ("Rule 42(b) of the Utah Rules of Civil Procedure gives the trial court considerable discretion to administer the business of its docket and determine how a trial should be conducted.")

[367] *Id.* A Virginia trial quote, relying on the precedents of the state's supreme court, stated the following regarding separation of contract and tort claims:

> Ordering separate trials is a matter of procedure within the discretion of the trial court. In exercising its discretion, the Court must balance efficiency, convenience and economical use of resources against possible prejudice. As the [Virginia Supreme Court] noted: "needless

concluded that plaintiffs had suffered prejudice because the issue of damages was too closely connected both to the issue of private nuisance and to the trespass action itself.[368] The court concluded:

> Because the issues of damages and liability were not clearly separable in this case, the bifurcation of the trial inescapably resulted in jury confusion that prejudiced plaintiffs and undermined the fairness of [the] trial. The trial court's discretion under rule 42(b) to improve efficiency or convenience of trial must always yield to its more fundamental duty to ensure that the trial be fair and impartial.[369]

o) Binding Precedent

The Ninth Circuit in *Hart v. Massanari* (per Judge Kozinski) discussed the constitutionality of an order to show cause why an attorney who had cited to an unpublished opinion in violation of a local court rule should not be sanctioned.[370] The attorney argued that the rule against unpublished opinions violated the constitution.[371] Although the court discharged the show cause order on other grounds, it concluded that the rule against unpublished opinions did not violate Article III of the constitution. In concluding thus, the court devoted considerable time discussing the concept of "binding authority." The court stated:

> delay, expense and consumption of the court's time would have been involved in separate trials. It is the policy of the law to avoid this wherever possible. The claims present common issues of fact which derive from the agreement of the parties. As Defendant has pointed out, the principal witnesses for all the claims are the parties themselves. Severance of the claims, therefore, would be both inefficient and uneconomical. To require Defendant to present his case first for one claim and then to return for the remaining claims would be inconvenient as well as inefficient. Effective jury instructions will allocate and distinguish the different burdens of proof, thus reducing possible prejudice.

[368] *Id.* at 1244–45. With regard to the trespass issue, the court stated, "While proof of damages is not required for a plaintiff to establish liability in an action for trespass, the amount of damages recoverable for trespass . . . is integrally related to the extent of the defendant's interference with both the land and the plaintiff's possessory interests." *Id.* at 1244.

[369] 972 P.2d at 1245. The court sharply criticized the trial court's bifurcation order in its footnotes. It stated, "Bifurcation of a trial can seriously interfere with the proper adjudication of closely related issues. Furthermore, bifurcation does not allow the jury to award nominal damages in the event that substantial damages are not proved." *Id.* at 1244, n.6. In another footnote, the court stated, "While bifurcation of trial on the issues of liability and damages is perhaps the most common application of rule 42(b), reverse bifurcation is much less common and has been used only in complex asbestos-related litigation. To our knowledge, so drastic a technique has never been employed in Utah." *Id.* at 1244, n.7.

[370] 266 F.3d 1155 (9th Cir. 2001).

[371] *Id.* at 1159.

That the binding authority principle applies only to appellate decisions, and not to trial court decisions, is yet another policy choice. There is nothing inevitable about this; the rule could just as easily operate so that the first district judge to decide an issue within a district, or even within a circuit, would bind all similarly situated district judges, but it does not. The very existence of binding authority principle is not inevitable. The federal courts could operate, though much less efficiently, if judges of inferior courts had discretion to consider the opinions of higher courts, but "respectfully disagree" with them for good and sufficient reasons.[372]

p)   *Habeas Corpus*

As a matter of first impression, the Ninth Circuit held that a district court had discretion to dismiss a petition for procedural default "before the state custodian is served with the petition or files an answer, when the default is obvious on the face of the petition"[373] and held further that "a habeas court has discretion to raise procedural default sua sponte to further the interests of comity, federalism, and judicial efficiency."[374] The court began its analysis by reaffirming its precedent that "clearly holds that a habeas court is not required to raise procedural default or failure to exhaust available state remedies when the [s]tate has waived the defenses."[375] However, the court distinguished the case before it because the state "was not required to appear before the district court and thus did not waive the defense of procedural default."[376] Nevertheless, the court relied on the fact that "a habeas court may, in its discretion, reach the merits of a habeas claim or may insist on exhaustion of state remedies despite a [s]tate's waiver" so long as the court exercised its discretion "to further the interests of comity, federalism, and judicial efficiency."[377] The court concluded that "a habeas court also should exercise discretion to raise procedural default sua sponte if doing so furthers these interests."[378]

---

[372] *Id.* at 1174.

[373] *Boyd v. Thompson*, 147 F.3d 1124, 1127 (9th Cir. 1998).

[374] *Id.* at 1128 (affirming the district court's sua sponte dismissal because it "furthered the equitable considerations of comity, federalism, and judicial efficiency" and because it "was easily identifiable on the face of the petition").

[375] *Id.* at 1127.

[376] *Id.*

[377] *Id.*

[378] 147 F.3d at 1127. The court also cited to federal procedural rules for habeas proceedings in support of its position that "Congress envisioned district courts taking an active role in summarily disposing of facially defective habeas petitions." *Id.* The court also cited to the opinions of other circuits in support of its claims that every "circuit to consider the issue holds that a habeas court has discretion to raise procedural default sua sponte to further the interests of comity, federalism, and judicial efficiency." *Id.* at 1128.

q)   Compelling Arbitration

In *Kamaya Co. v. American Property Consultants*, plaintiff Japanese investors sued defendant American corporations on a fraud-in-inducement claim.[379] Defendants moved the trial court to compel arbitration, and the trial court granted the motion with respect to one group of defendants but not the others. Plaintiff raised two arguments on appeal: (1) that the order to compel arbitration was reversible error and (2) that if compelled arbitration were proper, the court should have ordered it against all defendants.[380]

The court affirmed with respect to the first issue but found that the trial court had abused its discretion with respect to the second issue. With regard to the second action, the court rejected defendants' argument that that plaintiff should arbitrate with only those defendants that had actually moved to compel arbitration.[381] The court also rejected defendants' argument that "the trial court's order staying the proceedings against all the defendants but only compelling arbitration between [p]laintiffs and [some] defendants was within the trial court's discretion to efficiently manage the case."[382] With regard to defendants' second argument, the court responded:

> As [defendants] point out, however, trial courts are afforded considerable discretion in managing their civil caseloads "to achieve the orderly and expeditious disposition of cases." But once a party moves to compel arbitration of a particular dispute and the court determines that the parties have agreed to arbitrate that dispute, the court *must* order the parties to proceed to arbitration save upon such grounds as exist at law or in equity for the revocation of any contract....
>
> ....The Grancorp Defendants have not asserted any legal or equitable grounds for revoking the partnership agreement as a whole or the arbitration clause in particular. Therefore, because the trial court properly found that the partnership agreement required arbitration of [p]laintiffs' fraud-in-the-inducement claims, the trial court abused its discretion by not compelling arbitration between [p]laintiffs and the Grancorp Defendants.[383]

r)   Sequestration of a Witness

Reviewing defendant's appeal from a vehicular homicide conviction, the Colorado Court of Appeals affirmed the trial court's decision to allow a toxicologist to hear witness's testimony and to respond to defendant's claim on cross—examination that

---

[379] 959 P.2d 1140 (Wash. Ct. App. 1998).
[380] *Id.*
[381] *Id.* at 1148.
[382] *Id.*
[383] *Id.*

"he had two to three beers at about 3:00 p.m. on the day of the collision."[384] In response, the toxicologist claimed "that defendant's five measured blood alcohol levels were inconsistent with his testimony regarding either the chronology of events or the quantity of alcohol consumed, or both."[385]

The court stated that issues "relating to witness sequestration are entrusted to the sound discretion of the trial court, and we will not overturn the court's decisions absent an abuse of that discretion."[386] The court stated further that "to constitute an abuse of discretion, the defendant must show that he was prejudiced by the decision of the trial court."[387] The court found that defendant had not suffered prejudice because of the court's decision in part because "there [was] no hint of witness collusion or fabrication of testimony."[388] It then discussed judicial efficiency:

> Furthermore, the toxicologist's testimony was based in part upon defendant's testimony, and allowing his presence during defendant's testimony was therefore a reasonable exercise of the trial court's discretion to promote courtroom efficiency.
>
> Had the toxicologist been excluded from the courtroom, the trial would have been delayed by the reading of the relevant portions of defendant's testimony and further delayed while the toxicologist performed his calculations based on that testimony. We therefore hold that no prejudice to defendant resulted from that exercise of the court's discretion.[389]

s)   Efficiency and the Superior Vantage Point of the Trial Judge

Federal appellate courts review a "district court's grant of class certification for an abuse of discretion."[390] Regarding judicial efficiency, the court stated,

> Determining whether a class action is manageable, and thereby a superior method of fair and efficient adjudication, is committed to the discretion of the district court because that court generally has greater familiarity and expertise with the practical... and primarily... factual problems of administering a lawsuit than does a court of appeals.[391]

---

[384] *People v. Scarlett*, 985 P.2d 36, 40 (Colo. 1998).
[385] *Id.*
[386] *Id.* at 41. (noting that the "purpose of a sequestration order is to prevent a witness from conforming his testimony to that of other witnesses and to discourage fabrication and collusion").
[387] *Id.*
[388] *Id.*
[389] 985 P.2d at 41.
[390] *Andrews v. AT&T*, 95 F.3d 1014, 1022 (11th Cir. 1996)
[391] *Id.* Fed R. Civ. P. 23 provides:

t)   Finality in the Administration of Justice

Closely related to judicial efficiency and economy, the rationale of finality in administration of justice suggests that a trial court should exercise discretion in order to prevent litigation from continuing for an inordinate amount of time. The most common context in which finality arises is when the trial court exercises its discretion to deny a motion to open a final judgment.

> Federal Rule of Civil Procedure 60(b) provides:
>
> On motion and upon such terms as are just, the court may relieve a party or a party's legal representative from a final judgment, order, or proceeding for the following reasons: (1) mistake, inadvertence, surprise, or excusable neglect; (2) newly discovered evidence which by due diligence could not have been discovered in time to move for a new trial under Rule 59(b); (3) fraud (whether heretofore denominated intrinsic or extrinsic), misrepresentation, or other misconduct of an adverse party; (4) the judgment is void; (5) the judgment has been satisfied, released, or discharged, or a prior judgment upon which it is based has been reversed or otherwise vacated, or it is no longer equitable that the judgment should have prospective application; or (6) any other reason justifying relief from the operation of judgment.... A motion under this subdivision (b) does not affect the finality of a judgment or suspend its operation.

(a) One or more members of a class may sue or be sued as representative parties on behalf of all only if (1) the class is so numerous that joinder of all members is impracticable, (2) there are questions of law or fact common to the class, (3) the claims or defenses of the representative parties are typical of the claims or defenses of the class, and (4) the representative parties will fairly and adequately protect the interests of the class.

(b) An action may be maintained as a class action if the prerequisites of subdivision (a) are satisfied, and in addition:
....

(3) the court finds that the questions of law or fact common to the members of the class predominate over any questions affecting only individual members, and that a class action is superior to other available methods for the fair and efficient adjudication of the controversy. The matters pertinent to the findings include: (A) the interest of members of the class in individually controlling the prosecution or defense of separate actions; (B) the extent and nature of any litigation concerning the controversy already commenced by or against members of the class; (C) the desirability or undesirability of concentrating the litigation of the claims in the particular forum; (D) the difficulties likely to be encountered in the management of a class action.

Interpreting Rule 60(b), Judge Easterbrook, writing for the Seventh Circuit Court of Appeals in *Metlyn Realty Corp. v. Esmark*, elaborated on the importance of finality in the administration of justice and its relevance to judicial discretion:

> Judgments in civil cases fix the rights of parties and entitle them to go about their lives....
>
> There are good reasons for the stringent limits on reopening a final judgment. The rule that the final judgment governs the future induces the parties to focus all of their efforts in a single proceeding. If they know that the judgment will establish their rights once and for all, they will bring to bear the information and energies necessary to produce an informed decision. If they believe that they can have a second try, they are more likely to skimp the first time around, and as a result the judicial process will become less accurate.
>
> True, mistakes are bound to occur. There are few perfect trials. But the inevitable shortfalls of the legal system do not call for revisiting judgments. Second proceedings have problems of their own. The passage of time dims memories and makes evidence harder to find and assess. The knowledge that comes with hindsight is a mixed blessing at best; new knowledge may color the evaluations of what people knew (or should have known) at an earlier time, though the judicial process must focus on the information available at the time of the underlying events or the first trial. And of course there may be new mistakes in the second proceeding even as the parties and the court cure the blunders of the first. So even if the first proceeding was flawed, there is no assurance that the second proceeding will come closer to the truth. These considerations inform the development of the law under Rule 60(b), as they inform principles of issues and claim preclusion, the interpretation of statutes of limitations, and other doctrines of repose in civil and criminal litigation.
>
> These considerations have led us to say... that judgments may not be reopened under Rule 60(b) except in compelling and extraordinary circumstances. The objectors remind us that we have also said that the provisions of Rule 60(b) should be liberally construed to avoid injustice. But... when reviewing same cases using the "liberal construction" language, this simply is a reminder that the purpose of Rule 60(b) is to authorize some limited review of judgments. A court ought not let the interests of finality lead it to decline to afford the sort of review Rule 60(b) authorizes. It does not mean that relief from a final judgment should be freely given; to the contrary, our review of the cases... ineluctably led to the

140

conclusion that Rule 60(b) relief is an extraordinary remedy and granted only in exceptional circumstances.

This conclusion is reinforced by the standard of review. The decision of a district court declining to reopen a judgment under Rule 60(b) may be reviewed only for abuse of discretion... and we have held that to find an abuse of discretion the court of appeals must conclude that no reasonable man could agree with the district court. When the district judge reviewing the Rule 60(b) motion also rendered the underlying judgment and concludes that any error complained of did not affect the earlier decision, the movant's task on appeal is more difficult still. It is perhaps conceivable that a moving party could establish that no reasonable man could find that an error did not affect the result when the judge rendering the original decision has found no effect, but there cannot be many such cases.

There is discretion and then there is discretion. The scope of the district court's discretion is greatest when there is no strictly legal rule of decision, when there is no standard against which to compare the district court's decision. When there is no right answer, it becomes difficult to speak of "error," and the scope of review shrinks accordingly.

A motion under Rule 60(b) often puts to a court a question without a right answer. The district judge must weigh incommensurables— the value of finality, the probability that an error affected the outcome of the proceeding, the probability that a second go-round would produce a "better" outcome, the costs of that second proceeding to the parties (and ultimately to society as the finality of judgments is undercut). Dealing with these intersecting planes of legal argument is a task of great subtlety, calling on all skills of the district judges. It is not, however, a task that gives rise to "error" (as opposed to questionable exercise of judgment), unless the judge leaves something important out of his analysis. This is why we have been so deferential in Rule 60(b) cases to decisions not to reopen. [392]

---

[392] *Metlyn Realty Corp. v. Esmark*, 763 F.2d 826, 830–31 (1985). Although Judge Easterbrook's opinion might suggest otherwise, cases that address finality as a distinct grounds for judicial discretion are somewhat rare. For an example of other finality cases, see *Minton v. Nat'l Assoc. of Sec. Dealers, Inc.*, 336 F.3d 1373, 1379 (holding that a court was "well within its discretion" to deny a motion for reconsideration under Fed. R. Civ. P. 59(e)) (Fed. Cir. 2003); *In re Marriage of Landry*, 699 P.2d 214, 215 (Wash. 1985) (refusing to reverse trial court decisions in divorce cases except on rare occasions) ("[T]he emotional and financial interests affected by such decisions are best served by finality.")

In *United States v. Horne*, the D.C. Circuit upheld a district court's decision not to allow defendant to withdraw his guilty plea prior to sentencing.[393] The court reiterated its three factor test it used to review "whether there is any fair and just reason to withdraw a guilty plea."[394] Regarding whether allowing withdrawal of the guilty plea would prejudice "the public's legitimate interests," the court stated:

> If withdrawal of the guilty plea would substantially prejudice the Government's ability to prosecute the case or unduly inconvenience the court, then the movant's reasons must meet exceptionally high standards, and withdrawal is almost never allowed. Although the Government alleges no such difficulty in this case, this court is always properly reluctant to find that a district court abused its discretion in denying a motion to withdraw a guilty plea because withdrawal of a guilty plea is inherently in derogation of the public interest in finality and the orderly administration of justice. As the Supreme Court observed in *Hill*, permitting withdrawal of a guilty plea "undermines confidence in the integrity of our procedures..., increases the volume of judicial work, [and] inevitably delays and impairs orderly administration of justice." For this reason, the judicial system consecrates the guilty plea as a grave and solemn act, and this court must have a compelling reason indeed before it can say that a district court abused its discretion in upholding the finality of a guilty plea.[395]

u)   Conclusion

The reasons the trial court has discretion in a wide range of contexts, as discussed in this chapter, serve to preserve the morale of trial courts. The trend is to require the trial judge to state on the record his or her reasons for exercising discretion in a certain way. This serves to inform the litigants of the basis for the trial court's decesion and to explain to the reviewing court the reasoning of the first decider.

---

[393] 987 F.2d 833 (D.C. Cir. 1993).
[394] *Id.* at 837. The three factors are: (1) whether the defendant asserts innocence; (2) whether granting defendant's request would "prejudice" "the public's legitimate interests," and (3) "most importantly," "whether there was some defect in the original plea." *Id.*
[395] *Id.* (quoting *Hill v. Lockhart*, 474 U.S. 52, 58 (1985)) (other quotations omitted).

3

Different Levels of Discretion

§ 3.1.   Overview of the Degrees of Discretion

To the extent that the level of discretion a trial court enjoys can be measured at all, it is helpful to do so by referring to four specific degrees of discretion: (1) unfettered discretion; (2) discretion which is presumptively valid; (3) discretion which must be justified on the record; and (4) discretion which receives mere lip service obeisance from the reviewing court.

One must not, however, think that each time a trial court exercises discretion, that discretion will fit neatly into one of what Rosenberg calls the four-degrees of discretion.[1] Justice Richard Wallach offers the helpful analogy of the various colors in a traffic light.[2] "Red" would signify the point at which the trial court retains nominal discretion only, even if appellate courts continue to classify the trial court's decision as discretionary as opposed to a question of law.[3] "Green" would signify the starting point of judicial discretion, the point at which the appellate court defers without reservation to the trial court's decision.[4] The colors in between represent points at which the trial court decision receives some deference, but not total deference.[5] Unlike a traffic light, there is more than one "in between" shade; in fact there are several, ranging from broad discretion approaching unfettered discretion to cases in which the appellate court imposes strict guidelines

---

[1] Maurice Rosenberg, *Judicial Discretion of the Trial Court, Viewed from Above*, 22 Syracuse L. Rev. 635, 650–51 (1971) (describing discretion as a color-spectrum with four general grades of discretion).

[2] Wallach, Richard W., *Judicial Discretion: How Much.* In J. Eric Smithburn, Judicial Discretion 8 (successor ed. 1991). Wallach's model is essentially the same as Rosenberg's, but employs more concise labels to describe the degrees of discretion).

[3] *See id.* at 12. "Many appellate decisions may be found which state that applications for injunctions... are addressed to the sound discretion of the trial court. However, it is demonstrable that this is pure legal formulary insofar as true judicial discretion is concerned. In fact, equitable remedies are granted and withheld on strictly legal principles".

[4] *See id.* at 9 (describing this type of discretion as "impervious to review").

[5] *See id.* at 10–11 (so describing).

144

that rarely but nonetheless do allow a trial court to exercise discretion without showing extraordinary circumstances.[6]

Unfettered discretion does not give the trial court the right to do whatever it wants. The trial court must still follow the law, and to the extent that its decision runs afoul of the law, the trial court cannot validly make that decision. [7] On a related note, a trial court cannot use discretion to infringe upon the fundamental rights citizens enjoy by virtue of the state and federal constitutions.[8]

Presumptively valid discretion describes a situation in which the judge has no preestablished guidelines from higher courts (other than the ever-present rule that the trial court must follow the law).[9] Unlike in a case of unfettered discretion, however, the appellate court will review the trial court's decision *post facto* to determine whether the trial court's decisionmaking process was reasonable.[10] The trial court need not use a specific rubric for making its decision, so long as the rubric it does use meshes with so-called legal principles and common sense.[11] Since the presumption is that the trial court has exercised its discretion appropriately, the appellate court will only reverse when it cannot after its own inquiry find a valid basis for the trial court's decision.[12]

The problem with the label "must appear on the record" is that it does not even so much as hint as to why the appellate court would want the reasons for making the decision to appear on the record in the first place. The reason the trial judge has to put reasons for its discretionary decision on the record is because the appellate court (or a statute) has established certain considerations that a trial court

---

[6] *See, e.g., id.* at 9 (admitting the possibility of "an infinite number of shadings" in the traffic light analogy).

[7] *See People v. Mason*, 411 N.Y.S.2d 970, 975 (N.Y. Sup. Ct. 1978) (Wallach, J.) (finding no discretion to break the law). *But see* Rosenberg, *supra* note 1 at 640 ("The law does not authorize judges to make up the rules to suit themselves any more than sports allow officials to extemporize the score according to whim. Still, neither law nor athletics tries to review every decision made by an official.")

[8] *See id.* (stating that no court has the discretion to violate constitutional rights).

[9] *See* Henry J. Friendly, *Indiscretion about Discretion*, 31 Emory L. J. 747, 772 (1982)
> When circumstances are either so variable or so new that it is not yet advisable to frame a binding rule of law, trial courts may be given discretion until the factors important to a decision and the weight to be accorded them emerge from the montage of fact patterns, which arise. Often, in time, the contours of a guiding rule or even principle may develop as the courts begin to identify the policies, which should control.

[10] *See* Wallach, *supra* note 2 at 10 (listing types of cases in which the appellate court will presume that the trial court's decision is correct "except where a clear abuse of discretion appears").

[11] *See id.*

[12] *See id.*

must weigh when exercising its discretion.[13] It is the duty of the trial court to show the appellate court that it has investigated the appropriate questions in reaching its decision.[14] The trial court fulfills this duty by ensuring that the reasons for its decision appear on the record. This type of discretion would more appropriately be described as discretion preguided by the appellate court or by statute.

Identifying the third type of discretion with whether or not reasons for exercising it appear on the record may lead one to believe that so long as the trial court documents its reasoning, its decision will stand undisturbed. This is not the case. Even setting due process concerns aside, a trial court could not protect from review a decision it made based on the flip of a coin simply by noting in writing that the court had other matters to tend to and needed to reach its decision quickly.

The problem with the label "must appear on the record" is that it does not even so much as hint as to why the appellate court would want the reasons for making the decision to appear on the record in the first place. The reason the trial judge has to put reasons for its discretionary decision on the record is because the appellate court (or a statute) has established certain considerations that a trial court must weigh when exercising its discretion. It is the duty of the trial court to show the appellate court that it has investigated the appropriate questions in reaching its decision. The trial court fulfills this duty by ensuring that the reasons for its decision appear on the record. This type of discretion would more appropriately be described as discretion preguided by the appellate court or by statute.

Lip service obeisance situations occur when the trial court must decide a case in a particular way unless it can show a good reason not to do so.[15] A lip service decision in some respects presents a situation opposite to the one presented in a decision reviewed as presumptively valid. With respect to decisions that are presumptively valid, the appellate court must determine that the trial court had no valid basis for making the decision that it did. With respect to lip service situations, it is for the trial court to find (1) a valid reason to deviate from the norm and (2) no valid reason not to deviate from the norm.[16] The trial court has to do more than

---

[13] See Friendly, *supra* note 9 at 770 ("Once it has been deemed appropriate to limit the range of discretion... it becomes necessary that the trial court articulate the basis for its decision.").

[14] See id.

> The rulemakers gave the district courts discretion; but after enough of them had decided always to exercise it the same way... the channel of discretion had narrowed, and a court of appeals should keep a judge from steering outside it rather than allow disparate results on the same facts.

[15] See Friendly, *supra* note 9, at 771 ("The case for full appellate review is particularly strong when a settled practice has developed in cases of the type sub judice and the trial court has departed from it.").

[16] See Wallach, *supra* note 2 at 12 (describing declaratory judgments as a lip service situation) ("Here again, although the verbiage of discretion may be used by appellate courts, there are fixed legal criteria which must support a declaratory judgment."). Wallach does not discuss whether a trial court could deny entering a declaratory judgment even where the plaintiff satisfies all the legal criteria.

146

simply follow the guidelines of the appellate court; it has to overcome a presumption that its departure from the norm is an abuse of discretion.

Rosenberg's comparison of discretion to a pasture with fences illustrates the distinction between an appellate court or legislature's making law and simply limiting the trial court's discretion.[17] Trial court discretion is like an animal in an open pasture in that the trial court has range of results it can reach in making a decision.[18] An appellate court–or legislature–fences off part of the pasture each time it establishes a new rule of law.[19] On the other hand, the higher lawmaking authority limits discretion not by prohibiting the trial court from reaching a potential outcome but by controlling how the trial court reaches *any* outcome with respect to a particular type of case.[20] At times, however, it is tricky to determine when a lawmaking authority has imposed broad imitation on discretion and when it has created a rule of law that prohibits discretion in the area that the rule covers. Hopefully, the following materials will shed some light on that question.

§ 3.2. Unfettered Discretion

a) Definition

The Supreme Court of Kansas, relying heavily on New York Judge Richard Wallach's article *Judicial Discretion: How Much?*, illustrated the concept of "unfettered discretion" as distinct from matters in which the appellate court affords less deference to the trial court:

> The trial judge has unfettered discretion when the ruling is not subject to appellate review. In this situation, the trial judge is much like the fictional king of common law who can do no wrong. An example is the judge's right to grant or to refuse to grant probation where there is no statutory presumption for or against probation.
>
> A high degree of appellate deference is allowed a trial judge's exercise of discretion in assessing the texture and feel of the trial, the credibility of witnesses, and the perceived impact of an allegedly prejudicial event. In these circumstances, appellate decisions often recognize a presumption of validity in the exercise of discretion because of the superior vantage point of the trial

---

[17] Maurice Rosenberg, *Appellate Review of Trial Court Discretion*, 79 F.R.D. 173, 180 (1978) ("The area of discretion is a pasture in which the trial judge is free....").
[18] *See id.*
[19] *Id.*
[20] Since Rosenberg does not make this distinction, a common example may be helpful. Fed. R. Civ. P. 15(a) requires a federal district court to allow freely amendments to complaints. There is no legal *right* to amend a complaint in that a particular set of facts would compel the court to accept an amendment; at the same time, the language of the rule suggests that the district court would have to cite a compelling reason to deny leave to amend in order to avoid reversal.

judge. The judge's decision will be affirmed even though the appellate tribunal might otherwise be inclined to take a precisely opposite view of the matter. An example of this presumptive validity of the trial judge's ruling includes orders sustaining a jury verdict and denying motions for a mistrial in a civil case particularly where the unsuccessful challenger relies upon the alleged insufficiency of the evidence to sustain the jury verdict. Another example is the trial judge's conclusion that the misconduct of counsel, or some other untoward event in the course of the trial was not sufficiently grave to disturb the verdict. A third example is the judge's granting or denying adjournments and/or continuances.

If a constitutional or statutory right has been violated, the trial judge's use of discretion is limited. Under these circumstances there is a greater need for articulation by the trial judge of the reasons for his "discretionary" decision. Discretion must be exercised, not in opposition to, but in accordance with, established principles of law. It is not an arbitrary power. In its practical application in this state, judicial discretion is substantially synonymous with judicial power.[21]

b)   Special versus General Verdicts

The watershed case is *Skidmore v. Baltimore & Ohio Ry. Co.*[22] Skidmore filed under FELA to recover for injuries he sustained working for the railroad. At the close of trial, the railroad requested that the jury return a special verdict specifying whether and to what extent Skidmore's own negligence contributed to his injuries. The trial court denied that request and directed the jury to bring a general verdict. (The trial court's charge to the jury discussed the denied request.) The jury awarded Skidmore thirty thousand dollars and the railroad appealed.

The court spoke critically of the trial court's refusal to allow a special verdict. The court claimed that the trial judge had given the jury a "right" to decide a case according to what the jury thought the law should be rather than what the law actually was.[23] General verdicts, the court stated, call the integrity of the civil jury system in to doubt, since a civil jury has a clean slate upon which to write new law.[24] The court believed that the general verdict in this case allowed the jury to act on its own prejudices and biases rather than to serve as a neutral factfinder.[25]

---

[21] *Saucedo v. Winger*, 850 P.2d 908, 918–19 (Kan. 1993) (internal quotation marks omitted).

[22] 167 F.2d 54 (2d Cir. 1948 reprinted in *J. Eric Smithburn, Judicial Discretion* 263–65 (successor ed. 1991).

[23] *Judicial Discretion* at 264.

[24] *See id.* at 263.

[25] *Id.* at 264.

The court determined, however, that Federal Rules of Civil Procedure. 49(a), unlike some state procedural rules, did not require the trial judge (in this case, the federal district judge) to direct the jury to render a special verdict.[26] The trial judge had "full, uncontrolled discretion in the matter."[27] No matter how misguided the trial judge may have been to order a general verdict, the reviewing court felt compelled to affirm such orders until Rule 49 was amended.

A later case, *Davis v. Ford Motor Co.*,[28] held that under Rule 49, the discretion of the trial court to order or not to order a special verdict is "'not ordinarily reviewable.'" The facts of *Davis* were similar to those of *Skidmore*. Plaintiff Davis sued Ford when her Ford vehicle rolled over her foot. The transmission had been in "park." Ford alleged that Davis failed to set her parking break, and thus, was contibutorily negligent. At the close of trial, Ford requested a special verdict in which the jury would apportion fault between Ford and Davis. The trial court denied Ford's request.

Despite calling this type of case "not ordinarily reviewable," the trial court proceeded to explain why the trial court acted within its discretion. Ford failed to show prejudice resulting from the general verdict.[29] The jury's award to plaintiff (substantially less than what plaintiff claimed) showed that it had applied the comparative fault principles as the trial judge had instructed them. One judge concurred in order to "encourage" trial judges in their exercise of discretion to require special verdicts.[30]

c)   Dismissals, Mistrials, and New Trials

The traditional rule is that a trial judge in a civil case has unfettered discretion to grant or deny a motion for a mistrial in civil cases.[31] On the other hand, judgment as a matter of law, summary judgment, dismissal for failure to state a claim, and motions for judgment on the pleadings are reviewed as questions of law.[32] The trial judge may order a new trial at his or her discretion, but that discretion is not unfettered.[33]

---

[26] (Rule 49(a) reads in part, "The court may require a jury to return only a special verdict....").

[27] *Id.* at 265.

[28] 128 F.3d 631, 633 (8th. Cir 1997)

[29] 128 F.3d at 633.

[30] *Id.* at 635.

[31] *See Menningmann v. Indep. Fire Ins. Co.*, 369 S.E.2d 295, 296 (Ga. Ct. App. 1988) ("Thus, unless it is apparent that a new trial is essential to the preservation of the right of a fair trial, this court will not interfere with the discretion of the trial court.") (internal quotations and citations omitted).

[32] *See, e.g., Spain v. Brown & Williamson Tobacco Corp.*, 363 F.3d 1183, 1187 (11th Cir. 2004) (motion to dismiss); *Bodett v. CoxCom, Inc.*, 366 F.3d 736 (9th Cir. 2004) (summary judgment); *Howard v. Bd. Educ. Memphis City Schs.*, 70 Fed. Appx. 272, 279 (6th Cir. 2003) (judgment as a matter of law).

[33] *See, e.g., Manley v. Ambase Corp.*, 337 F.3d 237 (2d Cir. 2003) (so demonstrating).

The standard for motions for a new trial in criminal cases is similar to that of civil cases.[34] In criminal cases, the granting of a motion to dismiss *once the prosecutor has opened the case* are in fact committed entirely to the discretion of the trial court. The criminal is free from further prosecution under the double jeopardy rule. Denials of motions to dismiss in a criminal case are matters of law subject to *de novo* review.[35]

In criminal cases, the denial of a motion for a mistrial is reviewed for a "clear abuse of discretion."[36] The appellate court will also defer to the trial court's decision to grant a mistrial; double jeopardy issues may make the trial court's decision effectively unreviewable.[37]

This raises the question as to why motions for mistrials in civil cases are normally granted or denied at the unfettered discretion of the trial judge. The Maryland Court of Appeals' recent decision in *Tierco Maryland, Inc. v. Williams*[38] affords some insight. An African-American family sued an amusement park after some members of the family were forcibly restrained, handcuffed, and publicly escorted to the amusement park's security office. One of the children attempted to get on a ride with the rest of her family, but theme park personnel refused to start the ride, claiming that the child was too short. The family alleged that the theme park had let white kids ride the ride despite being under the required height. A confrontation ensued, and the arrests followed. Although the family sued for assault and battery, false imprisonment, and negligent supervision, plaintiff frequently emphasized the racial overtones of the case at trial. The jury found for plaintiffs, and the trial court entered judgment accordingly.

The *Williams* court reversed for a new trial. It held that, although "an appellate court does not generally disturb the trial court's discretion" in denying a motion for a mistrial, in this case "the prejudice was so great that it denied Tierco a fair trial."[39] The court found that the references to race were irrelevant to the causes of action plaintiff pursued and served only "to inflame the passions of the jury" and

---

[34] *See, e.g., United States v. Ward*, 274 F.3d 1320, 1323 (11th Cir. 2001).

[35] *See State v. Lassiter*, 588 S.E.2d 488, 496 (N. C. App. 2003) (so demonstrating).

[36] *See United States v. Carlson*, 423 F.2d 431, 439 (9th Cir. 1970):

Since the jury had only a fleeting view of the articles, since there was much other testimony and some exhibits pertaining to other weapons, and since no misconduct is chargeable to Government counsel, we hold that the trial court did not abuse its discretion.

While a cautionary instruction on these items might have been appropriate, defendants did not request one, and the court was not obliged to give such an instruction on its own motion.

[37] *See United States v. Atisha*, 804 F.2d 920, 925 (6th Cir. 1986) (stating that double jeopardy would preclude further review if the government moves for a mistrial without showing a manifest necessity for doing so) (stating that when defendant moves for a mistrial, double jeopardy generally will not apply).

[38] 849 A.2d 504 (Md. 2004).

[39] *Id.* at 526.

to "attack... the social glue that helps bind society together...."[40] The court did not comment on the reasonableness of the trial judge's decision as such; it held only that the trial judge's refusal to grant a mistrial had denied defendant its fundamental right to a fair trial.

d)   Bifurcated Trial

Historically, a trial judge has unfettered discretion to bifurcate a trial. Whether that is still the case is disputable.[41] The Connecticut Supreme Court has held that the "bifurcation of trial proceedings lies solely in the discretion of the trial court."[42] Applying that standard, the Connecticut Appellate Court held that in an automobile accident case, the trial court acted within its discretion by denying the defendant police officer's motion to bifurcate plaintiff's negligence and due process claims.[43] Plaintiff Dumas sued Mena, another Hartford police officer, and the City of Hartford after Officer Mena's car collided with Dumas's car. The appellate court found that a jury "reasonably could have found" that Dumas first stopped at a stop sign and then attempted to turn left into a southbound lane.[44] Officer Mena, who was on duty driving a police car, crossed from the northbound lane in to the southbound lane and collided with Dumas.[45] Both drivers sustained injuries.[46] Co-defendant DiStefano, another Hartford police officer investigated the accident and issued a ticket to Mena for running the stop sign.[47] The court rejected defendant's arguments that trying the two claims together distracted the jury and allowed plaintiff to launch "a wholesale attack" on defendant's witnesses.[48] The court noted that in "determining whether the [trial] court has abused its discretion, we must make every reasonable presumption in favor of the correctness of its action.[49] The court could not "conclude that the [trial] court's denial of the defendants' motion, based on principles of convenience and judicial economy, infected the fairness of the trial so as to amount to an abuse of discretion."[50]

The recent decisions of other courts show some discomfort with the New Hampshire Supreme Court's conclusion. In *Hendrickson v. State*, a mother sued a state university on account of injuries her son sustained when he slipped off of a

---

[40] *Id.* at 528.

[41] *See, e.g., John Middleton, Inc. v. Swisher Int'l, No. Civ. A.* 03-3908, 2004 WL 792762 at *1 (E.D. Pa. Apr. 8, 2004) ("The decision to bifurcate is a 'matter to be decided on a case-by-case basis and must be subject to an informed discretion by the trial judge in each instance.'") (*quoting Lis v. Robert Packer Hosp.*, 579 F.2d 819, 824 (3rd Cir. 1978)).

[42] *Barry v. Quality Steel Prods., Inc.*, 820 A.2d 258, 273 (Conn. 2003).

[43] *Dumas v. Mena*, 842 A.2d 618, 620 (Conn. 2004).

[44] *Id.* at 619.

[45] *Id.*

[46] *Id.*

[47] *Id.*

[48] *Id.* at 620 ("Nothing in the record persuades us that the court abused its broad discretion.").

[49] *Id.*

[50] *Id.* at 621.

staircase, fell twenty feet, and broke his skull.[51] The mother alleged the fall caused both injuries to herself and injuries to her son. The trial court bifurcated both the liability and damages issues, and also bifurcated the son's damages and the mother's damages.[52] In determining that the trial court had acted within its discretion, the Montana Supreme Court stated that the "decision whether to bifurcate claims... is a matter left to the broad discretion of the [trial] court."[53] The court, however, noted that as a rule it would not allow bifurcation either when "the issues are so intertwined that if they are separated it will create confusion and uncertainty" or when "the issue of exemplary damages [is] so interwoven with proving negligence and malice or oppression that to have separate trials would lead to extended and needless litigation."[54] In *Allstate Insurance Co. v. Wade*, the Virginia Supreme Court reaffirmed the "inherent authority to consolidate claims for trial and have been given specific authority to order separate trials in certain circumstances."[55] Although the court noted that the "decision to order separate trials or to consolidate claims" was "left to the trial court's discretion," the court reaffirmed its precedent that "[w]hen considering a request for separate trials, the trial court must also consider any resulting unnecessary delay, expense, or use of judicial resources that would flow from separate trials of the claims at issue."[56]

Michigan has limited its trial courts' discretion to bifurcate trials for a number of years. The Michigan Supreme Court held in *Peasley v. Quinn* that the trial court could not order "separate submission of issues unless the issues are in fact separable in the sense that they may be proved independently of other issues."[57] When bifurcation interferes "with a party's presentation of proofs in the customary fashion," the party seeking bifurcation must make a strong showing of "compelling necessity" "in the interest of convenience or the avoidance of prejudice."[58]

The Supreme Court of New Mexico held that a trial court had no discretion *not* to bifurcate a negligence case involving an insurance carrier.[59] The trial court had originally granted defendant insurer's motion to bifurcate and prevent plaintiff from mentioning defendant Reid's insurance coverage until the damages portion of the trial. It did so in order to uphold the policy behind a state rule of evidence preventing tort victims from admitting the alleged tortfeasor's insurance coverage into evidence.[60] On reconsideration, the trial court withdrew the bifurcation order,

---

[51] 84 P.3d 38 (Mont. 2004).

[52] *Id.* at 47.

[53] *Id*

[54] *Id.*

[55] 579 S.E.2d 180, 185 (Va. 2003) (upholding trial court's decision to deny defendant car owner and intoxicated driver's motion to bifurcate compensatory and punitive damages sought by personal injury plaintiff).

[56] *Id.*

[57] 128 N.W.2d 515, 517 (Mich. 1964)

[58] *Id.* at 517–18.

[59] *Martinez v. Reid*, 46 P.3d 1237 (N.M. 2002). (State Farm was also a defendant.).

[60] *Id.* at 1238. N.M. R. Evid. 11-411 provides,

finding that bifurcation would expend too much time and would have a negative effect on the judiciary.[61]

On appeal, defendant argued for a hard—and—fast rule in favor of "bifurcation of a negligence case involving insurance," and, apropos, "preventing the jury from hearing about the presence of insurance until liability and damages have been established."[62] The court discussed two lines of cases, the first addressing the situation in which the insurance company acts as defendant's liability insurer, the second addressing the situation in which the insurance company acts as the plaintiff's subrogated insurer.[63] In the former line, the case law suggested that joinder of an insurance company would require disclosure of the fact that a party carried insurance.[64] The second line of cases, of which *Safeco Ins. Co. v. United States Fid. & Guar. Co.* controls, held that when procedural rules require joinder of subrogated insurers, the existence and identity of the insurer would not be disclosed to the jury.[65]

In response to defendant's argument that Rule 11-411 and *Safeco* should control, plaintiff argued (1) that Rule 11-411 "as a rule of evidence, does not affect the decision to let the jury know the parties to a lawsuit, (2) that "*Safeco* only requires the bifurcation of a trial involving subrogated insurers, and (3) that "modern realities minimize the alleged prejudice" to defendant.[66] The court rejected these arguments. The court reasoned that "the rules of evidence are designed to regulate the information presented to the jury, whatever the form."[67] Moreover, the existence of "modern realities" is irrelevant to the inquiry because Rule 11-411, as a "particularized application" probative value / undue prejudice balancing test of Rule 11-403, requires exclusion: "Because the presence of absence of insurance is not relevant to the issues of liability or damages in the ordinary negligence case, any prejudice of confusion of the issues, no matter how slight, would require exclusion under ordinary concepts of relevancy."[68]

Evidence that a person who was or was not insured against liability is not admissible upon the issue whether the person acted negligently or otherwise wrongfully. This rule does not require the exclusion of evidence of insurance against liability when offered for another purpose, such as proof of agency, ownership or control, or bias or prejudice of a witness.

[61] *Id.* at 1239.

[62] *Id.* at 1240.

[63] *Id.*

[64] *Id.* at 1241.

[65] *Martinez,* 46 P.3d at 1241 (citing *Safeco,* 679 P.2d 816 (N.M. 1984)).

[66] *Id.* at 1242.

[67] *Id.* at 1243. ("In any event, Rule 11-411 can be read as a strong articulation of the policy that in an ordinary negligence case the presence or absence of insurance is not relevant to the issues that need to be decided by the jury.").

[68] *Id.*

After rejecting the trial court's holding that bifurcation would "increase the burden on" the dockets of trial courts,[69] the court addressed plaintiff's observation that "the decision whether to bifurcate a trial ordinarily rests in the sound discretion of the trial court":

> We could, therefore, simply allow trial judges to make these decisions and review them for an abuse of discretion. We decline to do so, and instead we choose to adopt the bright-line rule of *Safeco* in cases such as this one.
>
> In the order certifying this matter to us, the Court of Appeals noted, "It has come to the Court's attention that trial courts across the State are divided in their application of *Raskob*, with some holding that the fact of an insurer's joinder should be disclosed to the jury and others holding to the contrary ...." We think that we are called on in this case to provide guidance to the lower courts, and we cannot provide that guidance by simply affirming or reversing trial decisions as an exercise of abuse of discretion. Additionally, *Safeco* itself created a rule of bifurcation that did not allow for a trial court's discretion in the normal case, and we can see no reason to treat a defendant's insurance company differently.[70]

The dissent would not have conferred discretion on the trial court but opted instead for a rule requiring disclosure of insurance.[71]

The Supreme Court of Wisconsin held that a trial court had no discretion to bifurcate on account of a state statute.[72] Plaintiff Waters, a minor acting through his guardian *ad litem*, sued following a sledding accident on defendant Pertzborn's property. Defendant filed a motion to bifurcate trial into separate liability and damages proceedings. The trial court granted the motion over plaintiff's objection, stating that it was "swayed by the time and expense that might be saved by bifurcation and the potential that bifurcation would facilitate settlement."[73] The trial court's order provided that the liability and damages issues would be tried by separate juries. On interlocutory appeal, plaintiffs argued that bifurcation had deprived them of his right to a trial by jury and also argued that the Wisconsin rules of civil procedure prohibited bifurcation.

---

[69] *Id.* at 1244.
> Although we are reluctant to increase the burden on our District Courts' dockets, we are not persuaded that the increased burden of bifurcation is significant enough to outweigh the complication of the issues that inevitably result from revealing to the jury the presence of insurance, or to overcome the policy embodied in Rule 11-411.

[70] *Id.*

[71] *Id.* at 1247 (Serna, C.J., dissenting).

[72] *Waters v. Pertzborn*, 627 N.W. 2d 497 (Wis. 2001).

[73] *Id.* at 501.

154

The court addressed only the statutory argument and concluded that under the Wisconsin rules of civil procedure, bifurcation of issues was prohibited.[74] The court concluded:

> In prior cases we have explained that § 805.09(2) codifies the constitutional guarantee of a five-sixths jury verdict of Article I § 5 of the Wisconsin Constitution. While the first sentence of the statute codifies the constitutional protection, the second sentence provides protection more explicit than the constitutional guarantee. The second sentence of § 805.09(2) requires the same five-sixths of a jury to agree to all questions necessary to sustain a claim in order for a jury's verdict to be valid. We have explained that this language requires a "claim-by-claim" review of a verdict. Thus, when we subject a verdict to scrutiny, we examine each question necessary to sustain a claim to insure that the same five-sixths of the jury agrees on all the issues necessary to sustain that claim.

> We believe that the circuit court's order to bifurcate the issues of liability and damages and to try them before different juries cannot be reconciled with the requirements of the § 805.09(2) five-sixths verdict protection. In the context of a negligence claim, in order for a jury to render a valid verdict under the plain language of § 805.09(2), the same five-sixths of the jury must agree on all questions necessary to sustain that claim of negligence. Because of the requirement that the same five-sixths of the jury must agree on all questions cannot be met where the questions are answered by an entirely different jury panel, we conclude that the circuit court's order in this case is invalid.

> In light of the statutory provisions and statutory history that we believe wholly undermine the validity of the circuit court's order to bifurcate, we only briefly address several arguments raised by defendants in support of their position.

> In advancing their statutory argument, the defendants rely to a large degree on the court of appeals decision in *Zawistowski*. In *Zawistowski*, the court of appeals approved of a circuit court's order to bifurcate issues in a defamation trial. After examining numerous statutory provisions, including § 805.09(2), the court of appeals concluded that § 906.11(1) provided the circuit court with the "inherent discretion to bifurcate issues for reasons of judicial economy."

> In *Zawistowski*, the court of appeals concluded that while § 805.05(2) does not authorize bifurcating individual issues of trial,

---

[74] *Id.* at 503–504 (relying on legislative history to reach result).

"neither does it prohibit the trial court from taking such an action." This conclusion cannot stand in light of the statements of intent to disallow bifurcation revealed in the statutory history of § 805.05(2) presented above. While it is unclear from the *Zawistowski* decision whether the circuit court contemplated trials before the same or different juries, to the extent that opinion is inconsistent with today's decision, it is overruled.

Moreover, while we agree that evidentiary rule § 906.11(1) provides the circuit court with broad discretion in its control over the presentation of evidence at trial, that discretion is not unfettered. It must give way where the exercise of discretion runs afoul of other statutory provisions that are not discretionary. In the context of bifurcation of issues for trial before different juries, § 805.05(2) and § 805.09(2) limit that discretion.

....

Finally, we note defendants have raised numerous policy arguments advancing the merits of bifurcated trials on separate issues. Because we have concluded that the question of bifurcation raised in this case is addressed by § 805.05(2) and § 805.09(2), we will not entertain these policy arguments to reach a result contrary to that required by the statutes. To do so on appeal would be an inappropriate exercise of our rule-making power....[75]

The District of Columbia Court of Appeals upheld a trial court's discretion to bifurcate an adoption proceeding. The trial court specified in the pretrial order that, during the first stage of the trial, the trial court would hear evidence as to the fitness of the biological parents in order to determine whether the parents were withholding their consent to the adoption contrary to the best interests of the child.[76] The trial court would then proceed to decide the remaining issues in the adoption. The bifurcation issue arose when the birth parents sought to compel the adopting parents to submit to answer questions on their family backgrounds. The trial court denied the birth parents' request, ruling that the issue of the adoptive parents' family backgrounds could be addressed at the next stage in the proceeding.[77] Birth mother argued on appeal that the trial court's decision preventing her from exploring whether her withholding consent to the adoption was contrary to the best interest of the child was an abuse of discretion.

---

[75] *Id.* at 505–07.
[76] *In re A.W.K.*, 778 A.2d 314, 323 (D.C. 2001).
[77] *Id.* at 324 (ruling further that the first stage of the proceeding would proceed similar to a termination of parental rights).

The court observed initially that "generally the trial court has considerable discretion in determining how it shall proceed in a particular case."[78] The court then noted that bifurcation has advantages to all parties in an adoption proceeding:

> There are advantages for the birth parents as well as for the petitioning adoptive parents in a procedure which separates the consideration of the birth parents' fitness from the remainder of the proceedings. A significant advantage for the birth parents is that it avoids any tendency to base a decision on the relative merits of the birth parents compared with those of the adoption petitioners.... [W]e warned that the outcome of a [termination of parental rights] proceeding could be called into question if it appeared that all the court had done was to make a direct comparison of the natural parent and the foster home.[79]

Turning to the factors that the trial court considered when it determined that the birth parents had withheld consent contrary to the interests of their child, the court concluded that the trial court's "focus was in keeping with the manner in which it bifurcated the proceedings" and "was shaped by its concern that to allow any substantial inquiry into the lives and backgrounds of the [adoptive parents] would frustrate the purpose of bifurcation and make the show cause hearing the equivalent of a plenary hearing on the adoption petition."[80]

e) Family Law Matters

The Vermont Supreme Court, addressing whether its state's custody guidelines in the divorce context also applied when unwed parents were litigating over the custody of their child, made a decision that curtailed the broad discretion of a family court to make custody decisions.[81] Mother and father, unmarried, had reared the child together from the child's birth in October 1999 until the parents separated in August 2000. Mother filed a parentage action, and the court awarded primary physical custody to mother, allowing father visitation between 3:30 P.M. and 7:00 P.M. weekdays, three weekends a month, three weeks in the summer, and alternating holidays. The court awarded the parents joint legal custody. On the first appeal, the intermediate appellate court remanded, stating that under Vermont statutes applying to divorces of married couples, a family court had to award sole legal custody to one parent. On remand, the trial court awarded sole legal custody to the mother. Father appealed on the grounds that the Vermont statute that the intermediate court considered did not apply to unmarried couples.

The court rejected father's argument: "We cannot agree that the Legislature intended to create a detailed, mandatory set of guidelines for our courts to apply only when resolving custody disputes in divorce and other dissolution

---

[78] *Id.* at 325.

[79] *Id.* at 326 (internal quotations omitted).

[80] *Id.*

[81] *Heffernan v. Harbeson*, 861 A.2d 1149, 1152 (Vt. 2004).

proceedings, while giving the courts unfettered discretion to resolve the same issues between unwed parents. Accordingly, we affirm."[82]

Interestingly, when considering father's argument that the family court had not given him a "greater degree of equalization" in visitation time "by extending father's contact through dinner and after dinner time, including more overnight contact . . .," the court recited the traditional abuse of discretion standard: "The family court has broad discretion in custody matters. We will not reverse a family court's order absent a showing that the court abused its discretion or exercised it in a manner that was clearly unreasonable in light of the evidence."[83]

f)   Revocation of Driver's License

Defendant Stoletz was convicted of DUI and felony driving with a suspended license.[84] The charges stemmed from a fatal accident in which the defendant struck and killed a person aiding a victim of a separate car accident. The court sentenced her to five years imprisonment, nine months in jail, and permanent revocation of her driver's license. Defendant appealed the revocation.

Defendant argued that although a trial court has the discretion under a Florida statute to revoke a driver's license based on a "totality of the circumstances" test, a more specific statute, applying to situations in which a driver is convicted of two DUIs, limits the length of a revocation to five years.[85] As she falls within the more specific statute, the defendant concluded that the permanent revocation of her license was unlawful.[86]

Addressing a split within the intermediate court of appeal, the Florida Supreme Court held that the specific statute applied only a five-year mandatory minimum on license revocation when the driver is convicted of a second DUI.[87] The court held further that "[w]hen a defendant is convicted of another offense in chapter 316 or any other law of this state regulating motor vehicles, and the totality of the circumstances merits a suspension or revocation, a trial court may utilize [Florida law] to suspend or revoke the defendant's license."[88] Either holding alone sustained the judgment of the trial court.

Judge Pariente, concurring in the result, disagreed with the majority's first holding, relying instead only on the general power of the trial court to revoke a

---

[82] *Id.*

[83] *Id.* at 1154. ("We think the [family] court succeeded in achieving a reasonable balance in its amended order with respect to contact, recognizing that only so much contact is feasible when one parent retains sole physical custody. Accordingly, we see no abuse of discretion in the court's amended parent-child contact schedule.").

[84] *Stoletz v. State*, 875 So.2d 572 (Fla. 2004).

[85] *Id.* at 573.

[86] *Id.*

[87] *Id.* at 575.

[88] *Id.* at 576.

158

license for an offense other than a second DUI.[89] Judge Pariente wrote, "I thus disagree with the majority that a trial court has unfettered discretion [under the two DUI statute] to permanently revoke a driver's license based solely on a second DUI conviction without regard for the circumstances of the offense."[90] The concurrence was concerned that "without articulated criteria, there [would be] no basis for an appellate court to determine whether a trial court abused its discretion in permanently revoking a license under section 322.28(2)."[91]

g)   **Case Management**

When an appellate court almost dismisses out of hand one of appellant's contentions, it is possible that it does so out of a sense of extraordinary deference to the trial court. Consider the following examples:

> Following a nine-month delay resulting from five previous continuances, on the first day of trial the district court denied a further request for continuance to permit Ademaj to obtain new counsel and conduct additional discovery. In response to an inquiry by the district court as to why he was requesting new counsel, Ademaj stated simply: "[H]e think I'm guilty.... He's trying to cop me out." When the district court asked what additional evidence he sought, Ademaj adverted vaguely to "my evidence."
>
> We accord "extraordinary deference" to trial court rulings on "last-minute requests for a continuance. The instant challenge is frivolous.[92]
>
> ....
>
> Broaddus states that the district court should have allowed several continuances due to the poor quality of representation she was receiving from her attorney. However, the district court has complete discretion to manage its litigation schedule. The record establishes that despite Broaddus's failing to file documents in a timely manner, the district court still entertained the documents. The district court was more than generous in Broaddus's prosecution of her case.[93]

---

[89] *Id.* at 577 (Pariente, J., concurring in the result).

[90] *Id.* (Pariente, J., concurring in the result).

[91] *Id.* at 579 (Pariente, J., concurring in the result) ("I do not believe the Legislature intended this result in authorizing commensurately longer revocations for repeat DUI offenders.").

[92] *United States v. Ademaj*, 170 F.3d 58, 64–65 (1st Cir. 1999).

[93] *Blue v. Coca-Cola Enterps.*, 43 Fed. Appx. 813 (6th Cir. 2002) *available at* 2002 WL 1792192 at **2.

Although a trial court customarily has unfettered discretion to manage the order and mode of proof at trial, the Sixth Circuit held that a trial court abused its discretion when it disregarded the parties' stipulation when conducting a *Daubert* challenge:

> The landowners argue that it was unfair for the district court to rule on the motion to strike [expert] Simanek's affidavit (and Columbia Gas's motion for reconsideration of the court's prior ruling denying summary judgment to Columbia Gas) without giving the landowners an adequate opportunity to cross-examine Columbia Gas's proposed experts and to submit a supplemental proffer bolstering Simanek's qualifications, especially because the parties had stipulated, and the district court had agreed, that the landowners would have both opportunities. Indeed, the district court, in failing to consider the evidence that it had agreed to let the landowners defer submitting, effectively granted Columbia Gas's motion to strike Simanek's affidavit without an opportunity for the landowners to be heard in opposition. Although the district court enjoys broad discretion in matters of pretrial management, scheduling, and docket control, we believe that the district court abused its discretion under the present circumstances.[94]

Sims v. ANR Freight Systems, Inc.[95] shows that, at least in the Fifth Circuit, the notion that the trial court has broad discretion to control its cases may enjoy continued popularity. What follows are the facts of this Title VII and tort case alleging sexual harassment and retaliatory discharge as set out by the court:

> Prior to the trials, all parties agreed on an estimate that the cases would require 5 to 7 days total to try. Nevertheless, the district court gave the parties only 1 day for each trial. Furthermore, the district court imposed strict time limits on each party: 5 minutes each for opening statements, 2 hours for Plaintiff's case in chief, 2.5 hours for Defendant's case, and .5 hour for Plaintiff's rebuttal (5 hours of testimony for each case). The district court granted extra time over these limits in the bench trial but still forced the parties to complete each of the trials in less than a day, far less than half the time any of the parties estimated was necessary for a fair trial.

> The district court required the parties to submit extremely detailed statements as to the facts they intend to prove at trial.... The district court then refused to allow the parties to introduce any evidence as to the uncontested issues, including background facts such as the witnesses' work experience and education. The district court later

---

[94] *Columbia Gas Transmission Corp. v. Gwin*, 198 F.3d 244 (6th Cir. 1999) *available at* 1999 WL 1023728 at **4.
[95] 77 F.3d 846 (5th Cir. 1996).

denied a request to read certain stipulated facts to the jury, and the record is not clear how many or which ones were actually read to the jury.

The district court ordered [plaintiff] to call her witnesses in a specific order. Throughout both trials, the district court repeatedly limited both direct and cross examination, frequently ordering counsel to "move on," and continually reminded counsel of the time limits.[96]

The court recognized "that a district judge has broad discretion in managing his docket, including trial procedure and the conduct of trial."[97] The court stated:

Furthermore, although a trial judge must be neutral, he should not be a passive spectator. When in his sound discretion he deems it advisable, a judge may comment on evidence, question witnesses, elicit facts not yet adduced, or clarify those previously presented. He may maintain the pace of trial by interrupting or setting time limits on counsel. However, discretion has its limits.[98]

Despite the court's warning, the court affirmed, based on the harmless error doctrine. The trial court had bifurcated the proceedings so that a jury could hear plaintiff's tort claims while the court heard the Title VII claim. With respect to the jury trial, the court held that "the evidence is so overwhelming against [plaintiff] that there is no reasonable possibility that the outcome would be different if the case were re-tried, even if [plaintiff] were allowed to present fully her evidence in a comprehensible manner."[99] With respect to the bench trial, the court held that because "of the lengthy pre-trial history of this case, it is clear that [the trial court] was familiar with the issues and evidence."[100] The trial court "did not require the same structured presentation of evidence that the jury did."[101]

With regard to the jury trial, the court found that even if the trial court had not committed reversible error, it had abused its discretion even though it had discharged what the court saw as its duty to expedite the litigation by taking an active role in the management of the case.[102] The court described a trial as "a proceeding designed to be a search for the truth" and that "role played by lawyers" in pursuing the truth at trial "is paramount."[103] In light of these considerations, the court held, "Essential to the endeavor [of a trial] is an opportunity for the parties through their lawyers to present information in a manner that is comprehensible to a

---

[96] *Id.* at 848.
[97] *Id.* at 849.
[98] *Id.*
[99] *Id.*
[100] *Id.* at 850.
[101] *Id.*
[102] *Sims*, 77 F.3d at 849.
[103] *Id.*

judge or jury."[104] The court held further that "[w]hen the manner of the presentation of information to a jury is judicially restricted to the extent that the information becomes incomprehensible then the essence of the trial itself has been destroyed."[105] Applying its holding to the facts, the court concluded that "the methodology imposed on this trial by the court and the restrictions that were placed on the lawyers regarding the manner of the presentation of evidence adversely impacted on the comprehensibility of the evidence to the point that [plaintiff] was denied a trial."[106]

h)   Discovery

Trial courts traditionally enjoy broad discretion when managing discovery.[107] The Washington Court of Appeals, however, has held that a trial court must at a minimum review the contents of a police investigation report *in camera* before shielding such information from a criminal defendant's efforts at discovery.[108] Defendant was indicted on several counts stemming from a chase and standoff with police. After the chase, the police department prepared an internal report in light of the fact that the police had shot defendant during the encounter. When defendant served a subpoena for "any information or material regarding the internal investigation," the police department moved to quash on the grounds that the investigation reports were privileged and fell within one of the exemptions to Washington's Public Disclosure Act.[109] The trial court granted the police department's motion to quash, but the record was silent as to whether the trial court actually conducted an *in camera* review of the report (as it promised to do). Defendant was convicted and appealed the trial court's order quashing the subpoena.

The court began by noting that the "scope of discovery is within the discretion of the trial court."[110] Reviewing its own precedents, the court concluded first that the police's privilege to keep its investigation reports secret was "conditioned upon a finding that the public interest will suffer by disclosure."[111] The court concluded further that in order to determine whether the public interest

---

[104] *Id.*

[105] *Id.*

[106] *Id.* For another example of the broad discretion a trial court enjoys in matters of case management, see *United States v. Hopkins*, 310 F.3d 145, 151 (4th Cir. 2002) (noting that a trial court's decision to admit expert testimony "is given the broadest degree of latitude").

[107] *See, e.g., In re Carp*, 340 F.3d 15, 22 (1st Cir. 2003) ("We review bankruptcy court's discovery decisions for abuse of discretion—and that discretion is very wide."); *Ayala-Gerena v. Bristol Myers-Squibb Co.*, 95 F.3d 86, 91 (1st Cir. 1996) ("It is well settled that the trial judge has broad discretion in ruling on pre-trial management matters, and we review the district court's denial of discovery for abuse of its considerable discretion.").

[108] *State v. Jones*, 979 P.2d 898, 902 (Wash. Ct. App. 1999).

[109] *Id.* at 900.

[110] *Id.* at 901.

[111] *Id.*

will suffer by disclosure, the trial court must conduct an *in camera* review of the material in question.[112] Discussing a case from the Washington Supreme Court, the court noted that "while the [Supreme] Court permitted discovery of the internal files, the Court also emphasized the trial courts' use of protective orders to limit discovery and minimize any potential harm."[113] The court of appeals concluded that the trial court had no discretion not to conduct an *in camera* review but could fashion protective orders in order better to serve the public's interest in keeping police investigations private:

> We conclude that under *Cook* and *Barfield*, the trial court must, at a minimum, conduct an *in camera* examination of the contested material and determine whether the public interest would suffer by [its] full disclosure where the government invokes privilege under RCW 5.60.060(5). If the trial court allows discovery following the in camera review, then the court may fashion appropriate judicial controls to minimize any potential harm from disclosure.[114]

The court remanded for an *in camera* review because the record was silent as to whether the trial court had conducted one.

i)   Interpreters

One area in which several courts have affirmed the wide discretion of a trial court is the decision whether to appoint an interpreter. The First Circuit's discussion in *United States v. Carrion* is instructive:

> Because the determination is likely to hinge upon various factors, including the complexity of the issues and testimony presented during trial and the language ability of the defendant's counsel, considerations of judicial economy would dictate that the trial court, coming into direct contact with the defendant, be granted wide discretion in determining whether an interpreter is necessary. It would be a fruitless and frustrating exercising for the appellate court to have to infer language difficulty from every faltering, repetitious bit of testimony in the record. But precisely because the trial court is entrusted with discretion, it should make unmistakably clear to a defendant who may have a language difficulty that he has a right to a court-appointed interpreter If the court determines that one is needed, and, whenever put on notice that there may be some

---

[112] *Id.* at 902.

[113] 979 P.2d at 902.

[114] *Id. See also Duncan v. Duncan*, 789 S.W.2d 557, 561 (Tenn. Ct. App. 1990) ("However, a trial court's discovery decisions are not immune from appellate review simply because they are discretionary.")

significant language difficulty, the court should make such a determination of need.[115]

j)   Warrants

Defendant Clark was convicted of the murder and rape of child after the police searched his van and home and seized incriminating evidence. Defendant's motion to suppress the evidence was denied, and defendant appealed. Before the Washington Supreme Court, defendant argued that the "search warrant" upon which the evidence was seized was unsupported by probable cause.[116] The court stated the following rule:

> In determining whether probable cause exists, a magistrate is entitled to draw reasonable inferences from the facts and circumstances set forth in the affidavit, and his determination is given great deference by a reviewing court and will not be reversed absent an abuse of discretion. The affidavit must be read in a common-sense manner and doubts should be resolved in favor of the warrant.[117]

After reviewing defendant's specific claims, the court concluded,

---

[115] 488 F.2d 12, 14–15 (1st Cir. 1973). *See also Valladres v. United States*, 871 F.2d 1564, 1566 (11th Cir. 1989).

> The use of an interpreter under § 1827 is committed to the sound discretion of the trial judge. Because the proper handling of translation hinges on a variety of factors, including the defendant's knowledge of English and the complexity of the proceedings and testimony, the trial judge, who is in direct contact with the defendant, must be given broad discretion.
>
> Appellant's constitutional claims under the Fifth and Sixth Amendments are subject to a similar standard. As a constitutional matter the appointment of interpreters is within the district court's discretion. The trial court must balance the defendant's rights to confrontation and effective assistance against the public's interest in the economical administration of criminal law, and the court's balancing is reversible only on a showing of abuse.

[116] *State v. Clark*, 24 P.3d 1006, 1014 (Wash. 2001) (claiming that "the warrant merely mentioned that Clark had a previous criminal history involving a similar crime, and that Clark had failed a polygraph test). Defendant claimed further that "the affidavit contained intentional or recklessly made material omissions, and was merely a boilerplate affidavit." *Id.* Defendant further claimed that "the warrant, once issued, was overbroad and lacked the particularity with respect to evidence to be seized." *Id.* The court noted that defendant also argued that since "further search warrants... relied on evidence seized from the van and had supporting affidavits indistinguishable in basic form from the first objectionable warrant" "virtually every piece of physical evidence found in this case should be suppressed as tainted fruit of the illegal van search." *Id.*

[117] *Id.*

While [defendant] may be correct that no single one of these evidentiary bases may have been enough to establish probable cause per se, there is no basis for believing that, taking this information on the whole, the issuing magistrate could form no reasonable belief that [defendant] was probably involved in the criminal activity under investigation.[118]

k)   Disqualification of Counsel and the Sixth Amendment

The Sixth Circuit discussed the amount of judicial discretion that a criminal trial court enjoys when granting a motion to disqualify defendant's counsel.[119] The United States moved to disqualify defendant's counsel because of an alleged conflict of interest.[120] (Defendant's counsel had apparently represented several government witnesses before the grand jury.) The trial court granted the motion after counsel failed to file a brief in opposition to the motion.

On appeal, defendant argued "that the disqualification of his chosen attorney was without meaningful inquiry into the alleged conflict of interest and without inquiry into the [defendant's] right to waive conflict-free representation, thus mandating reversal."[121] The court found these arguments to be without merit. It reasoned:

Our standard of review of a district court's decision regarding disqualification of counsel is a generous one. The district court is to be given wide latitude. On the other hand, evidence that a defendant was denied his right to retained counsel arbitrarily and without adequate reasons is sufficient to mandate a reversal without a showing of prejudice. But in this case, the District Court's disqualification was not arbitrary nor without adequate reasons. The government's representations that [defendant's counsel] had represented seven government witnesses during the grand jury investigation and had represented two of [defendant's] co-defendants were undisputed. Such representations, which the District Court was entitled to accept as truthful, support an inference of actual or potential conflict of interest warranting disqualification.

When presented with a motion to disqualify, the district court must make a careful inquiry, balancing the constitutional right of the defendant to representation by counsel of his choosing with the court's interest in the integrity of the proceedings and the public's interest in the proper administration of justice. The inquiry will ordinarily require a hearing at which both parties will be permitted

---

[118] *Id.* at 1015.
[119] *United States v. Mays*, 69 F.3d 116 (6th Cir. 1995).
[120] *Id.* at 121.
[121] *Id.*

to produce witnesses for examination and cross-examination. However, when the facts alleged in the motion to disqualify disclose an actual or potential conflict of interest and are uncontested, a hearing is not required.[122]

The court also concluded that, contrary to defendant's claim, "a district court, in certain situations, can disqualify an attorney despite a defendant's voluntary, knowing, and intelligent waiver of his constitutional right to conflict-free counsel."[123]

l) **Judicial Notice**

Quoting from Wright and Miller's treatise, the Eighth Circuit recently stated that "the [trial] court has complete discretion to determine whether or not to accept any material beyond the pleadings that is offered in conjunction with a Rule 12(b)(6) motion."[124] Even though the court's language is limited to motions to dismiss for failure to state a claim, the continued viability of this position is tenuous. The Federal Rules of Evidence provide,

> Rule 201. Judicial Notice of Adjudicative Facts
>
> (a) Scope of rule. This rule governs only judicial notice of adjudicative facts.
>
> (b) Kinds of facts. A judicially noticed fact must be one not subject to reasonable dispute in that it is either (1) generally known within the territorial jurisdiction of the trial court or (2) capable of accurate and ready determination by resort to sources whose accuracy cannot reasonably be questioned.
>
> (c) When discretionary. A court may take judicial notice, whether requested or not.
>
> (d) When mandatory. A court shall take judicial notices if requested by a party and supplied with the necessary information.[125]

Interpreting this rule, the Ninth Circuit held that a trial court had abused its discretion when it took judicial notice of "[defendant] Trott being named as a defendant in a complaint which included a vague reference to 'H.O.' and named neither Trott nor any Doe defendants in the caption."[126] The court wrote,

---

[122] *Id.*

[123] *Id.* at 122.

[124] *Stahl v. United States Dept. of Agriculture*, 327 F.3d 697, 700 (8th Cir. 2003).

[125] Fed. R. Evid. 201.

[126] *Rodgers v. Horsely*, 123 Fed. Appx. 281 (9th Cir. 2005), available at 2005 U.S. App. LEXIS 1761, at *9.

Determinations regarding the status of unnamed parties to a litigation are not within the realm of judicially noticeable facts. Such facts are neither 'generally known within territorial jurisdiction' nor 'capable of accurate and ready determination by resort to sources whose accuracy cannot reasonably be questioned." Fed R. Evid. 201(b); compare *United States v. Daychild*, 357 F.3d 1082, 1099 (9th Cir. 2004) (district court permitted to take judicial notice that indictment was properly returned because it would be 'capable of accurate and ready determination'); *Ritter v. Hughes Aircraft Co.*, 58 F.3d 454, 458–59 (9th Cir. 1995) (district court permitted to take judicial notice that layoffs had been made in Southern California because it 'would be generally known... and capable of sufficiently accurate and ready determination").

The district court, therefore, abused its discretion by taking judicial notice of a disputable fact pursuant to Rule 201. Because we reject the judicially noticed fact, we must review the record to determine whether Trott was actually a party to the initial timely filed complaint, or alternatively whether the relation back doctrine saves the subsequent complaint from a statute of limitations bar.[127]

Reviewing a trial court's judgment on the pleadings in favor of the defendant, the Supreme Court of Rhode Island vacated on grounds that plaintiff had not had the opportunity to refute defendant's *res judicata* claim.[128] Regarding the Department of Children's motion for judgment on the pleadings, the court noted that "the record upon which the Superior Court ruled contained no evidence of any final judgment" that might raise a *res judicata* defense.[129] The court then concluded that "because it is well established that, although the superior court may in its discretion take judicial notice of prior judgments, the party seeking the benefit of *res judicata* has the burden to plead and prove the judgment upon which it relies."[130] The court remanded so that the trial court could allow plaintiff's the opportunity to rebut defendant's *res judicata* claim "because a determination of res judicata generally requires the court to look beyond the pleadings to the judgment and other pertinent portions of the record in the prior action" and thus the "motion should more appropriately have been treated as a motion for summary judgment."[131]

m)   Appealability versus Immunity from Review

One must be careful not to confuse true immunity from review from a situation in which an *appellate* court in *its* broad discretion chooses not to review a case because of a party's failure to preserve error or some other defect. For example, a

---

[127] *Id.*
[128] *DiBattista v. Dept. Children, Youth & Families*, 771 A.2d 640, 642 (R.I. 1998).
[129] *Id.*
[130] *Id.*
[131] *Id.* (citing to state rules of civil procedure).

federal appellate court may "[determine] for itself whether to grant permission to appeal an interlocutory order certified by a trial court."[132] The Hawaii Supreme Court has afforded broad discretion to its jurisdiction's intermediate appellate courts to hear or refuse to hear an appeal with procedural defects.[133] The court stated:

> In this case, the Petitioners did not comply with HRAP Rule 28(b)(4) by failing to provide a quotation of the grounds urged for the objection in the points error section of the opening brief. The ICA's conclusion that the petitioners failed to present this issue properly because they did not quote the grounds urged for the objection and the full substance of the evidence admitted or rejected is a correct statement of fact and application of law. That the ICA then quoted a portion of the discussion section of the opening brief is inconsequential and does not amount to grave error.

> It should be noted that the ICA disregarded this point of error but chose to review other points of error that also failed to comply with HRAP Rule 28(b)(4). Under HRAP Rule 28(b)(4), it is entirely within the discretion of an appellate court to do so. It should also be noted that the record on appeal in this case contained twenty-two volumes of court records, twenty-eight transcripts, and numerous exhibits, perhaps emphasizing the need for compliance with HRAP Rule 28(b)(4). Nonetheless, inasmuch as the ICA had the discretion to do under HRAP Rule 28(b)(4), it did not gravely err by electing not to address a point of error.[134]

n)   Unfettered Discretion and the Trial Court's Findings of Fact

It is common knowledge that a trial court's findings of fact are not reviewed for abuse of discretion but under the more deferential clearly erroneous standard. The Texas Court of Criminal Appeals' holding in *Guzman v. State* raises a question as to whether this deference is due to the trial court having unfettered discretion to make

---

[132] *Testwuide v. United States*, 73 Fed. Appx. 395 (Fed. Cir. 2003), *available at* 2003 WL 21949547 at **1.

[133] *Sprague v. Calif. P. Bankers & Ins. LTD*, 74 P.3d 12, 19 (Haw. 2003).

[134] *Id.* For a slightly more restrictive view of the appellate court's discretion to consider an unpreserved argument, see *Jones v. State*, 843 A.2d 778, 784. (Md. 2004). The *Jones* court, although it declined to establish a "fixed formula for determination" as to when an appellate court should exercise its discretion to consider an unpreserved argument, it offered "principles to guide the courts when consideration of unpreserved issues might be proper." *Id.* The court stated as a matter of principles that the intermediate court should (1) consider whether reviewing an unpreserved error would work prejudice on either party, and (2) consider whether "the exercise of its discretion [would] promote the orderly administration of justice" *Id.* The court noted that it would not reverse unless the intermediate court clearly abused its discretion. *Id.*

findings of fact.[135] When analyzing the appropriate standard of review for mixed questions of law and fact, the court first articulated a policy that the "amount of deference a reviewing court affords to a trial court's ruling on a mixed question of law and fact (such as the issue of probable cause) often is determined by which judicial actor is in a better position to decide the case."[136] After citing United States Supreme Court precedent requiring some measure of independent appellate review, the court applied *de novo* review to the intermediate appellate court's decision and reversed on grounds that the intermediate court misapplied the totality of circumstances test.[137]

The court then critiqued the position of the concurring and dissenting opinion (hereinafter, the dissent). The dissent argued that under prior precedent, a higher court reviews a lower court's application of law to facts for abuse of discretion and gives the trial court "proper deference."[138] The majority argued that the precedent upon which the dissent relied allowed an appellate court to reverse for abuse of discretion when "no reasonable view of the record could support the trial court's ruling" on an application of law to facts question.[139] The court found that the "no reasonable view" approach amounted to de novo review and that the precedent upon which the dissent relied "mandated almost total deference with one hand then took it away with the other hand."[140] The court explained further:

> [A]s a general rule, the appellate courts... should afford almost total deference to a trial court's determination of the historical facts that the record supports especially when the trial court's fact findings are based on an evaluation of credibility and demeanor. The appellate courts . . . should afford the same amount of deference to trial courts' rulings on "application of law to fact questions,"... if the resolution of those ultimate questions turns on an evaluation of credibility and demeanor. The appellate courts may review *de novo* "mixed questions of law and fact" not falling within this category.

---

[135] 955 S.W.2d 85 (Tex. Crim. App. 1997) (holding that the appellate court reviews the trial court's ultimate finding on the issue of probable cause *de novo* and the trial court's finding of other historical facts with great deference).

[136] *Id.* At 87.

> If the issue involves the credibility of a witness, thereby making the evaluation of that witness' demeanor important, compelling reasons exist for allowing the trial court to apply the law to the facts. On the other hand if the issue is whether an officer had probable cause to seize a suspect, under the totality of the circumstances, the trial judge is not in an appreciably better position than the reviewing court to make that determination.

Id.

[137] *Id.* The intermediate court had on *de novo* review reversed a trial court's decision that the probable cause requirement had been satisfied with respect to the evidence at issue.

[138] *Id.* at 95 (Meyers, J., dissenting in part).

[139] *Id.* at 88.

[140] *Id.*

This Court may exercise its discretion to review *de novo* these decisions by the intermediate appellate courts....

Our decision also is meant to reaffirm the longstanding rule that appellate courts should show almost total deference to a trial court's findings of fact especially when those findings are based on an evaluation of credibility and demeanor—i.e., in reviewing a trial court ruling on an "application of law to fact question," the appellate courts should view the evidence in the light most favorable to the trial court's ruling. Our decision does not call into question the "very definition of abuse of discretion." We merely decide that an abuse of discretion standard does not necessarily apply to "application of law to fact questions" whose resolution does not turn on an evaluation of credibility and demeanor.[141]

Judge Meyers began his dissent pointing out that "since the reviewing court won't afford any deference to the trial court's ruling in conducting a *de novo* review, the defendant gets a wholly new opportunity to have the evidence suppressed."[142] In support of his position, Judge Meyers quoted the majority opinion of a prior case in which the court vacated an appellate court judgment on grounds that the appellate court did not apply the deferential abuse of discretion review:

At a suppression hearing, the trial judge is the sole and exclusive trier of fact and judge of the credibility of the witnesses, as well as the weight to be given their testimony. The trial judge is also the initial arbiter of the legal significance of those facts. The court of appeals is to limit its review of the trial court rulings, both as to the facts and the legal significance of those facts, to a determination of whether the trial court abused its discretion. Even if the court of appeals would have reached a different result, so long as the trial court's rulings are at least within the zone of reasonable disagreement, the appellate court should not intercede.[143]

Judge Meyers considered whether the majority misunderstood the abuse of discretion standard and explained abuse of discretion thus:

The majority says I interpret [former precedent] as "requiring the intermediate appellate courts to show almost total deference to a trial court's ruling on an application of law to fact question." I do not know what is meant by the "almost total deference" standard. [Former precedents] hold that an abuse of discretion standard should be applied.... It is a deferential standard in that the

[141] *Id.* at 89.

[142] *Id.* at 92, n.1 (Meyers, J., dissenting in part).

[143] *Id.* at 93 (Meyers, J., dissenting in part) (quoting *Dubose v. State*, 915 S.W.2d 493, 495 (Tex. Crim. App. 1996).

170

reviewing court is not to substitute its own view of the question so long as the lower court's decision or ruling on the issue is a reasonable one. A case should not be reversed simply because the reviewing court disagrees with the conclusion of the lower court, assuming the lower court is within the zone of reasonable disagreement....

....

... The majority further asserts that [former precedent] left the door open to *de novo* review when no reasonable view of the record supports the trial court's ruling. But that is what an abuse of discretion is all about—whether the lower court's conclusion was reasonable. If no reasonable view of the record would support its ruling, then it has abused its discretion. This has long been our understanding of abuse of discretion. The majority's opinion appears to call into question the very meaning of abuse of discretion.[144]

The dissent also questioned whether the majority's distinction between mixed questions that go to credibility or demeanor and other mixed questions of law and fact.[145]

o)   Justification for Unfettered Discretion

Although not clearly a case of unfettered discretion, the Texas Court of Criminal Appeals offered a rationale as to why appellate courts are particularly reluctant to overturn certain trial court decisions. When considering whether the trial court erred

---

[144] *Id.* at 94 (Meyers, J., dissenting in part). On a similar point as in The Supreme Court of Utah had a fairly detailed discussion of findings of fact and standard of review in *RHN Corporation v. J. Alton Veibell & Willow Creek Water Co.*:

> While it is settled that in cases at law, an appellate court will review a trial court's findings of fact under a clearly erroneous standard, in cases in equity, some confusion still exists over the proper standard of review for a trial court's findings of fact. In equity cases, appellate courts have often applied a clear preponderance standard. Nevertheless, there is also a recent trend in equity cases to review findings of fact under the clearly erroneous standard. Truth be told, there is little, if any, difference between these two standards. In the interests of simplicity, therefore, we hold that the proper standard of review for a trial court's findings of fact for cases in equity is the same as for cases at law, namely the clearly erroneous standard. Moreover, in both equity and law, we review the trial court's conclusions of law for correctness. 96 P.3d 935, 944 (Utah 2004).

[145] *Id.* at 95 (Meyers, J., dissenting in part) ("There will be little dispute on what constitutes historical facts. The ambiguity arises on what exactly is a mixed question of law and fact the resolution of which turns on an evaluation of credibility and demeanor.").

in denying a capital murder defendant's motion challenging a juror for cause, the court stated:

> When reviewing a trial court's decision to grant or deny a challenge for cause we look at the entire record to determine if there is sufficient evidence to support the court's determination. Great deference is given to the trial court's decision because the trial judge is present to observe the demeanor of the venireperson and to listen to his tone of voice.
>
> [The court then discussed how venireperson Drake told the prosecutor on voir dire that he would assume that the alleged killer, if guilty, would kill again.]
>
> In response to this comment, the prosecutor told Drake that while he could base the answer to the future dangerousness issue purely on the evidence presented at the guilt stage of trial, Drake needed to consider all of the evidence presented at the punishment stage of trial as well.... Drake indicated that he could see that there might be instances in which the future dangerousness question should be answered in the negative. Drake also reiterated his belief that the death penalty was appropriate in certain cases, but that there were also situations where he did not believe that it was appropriate.
>
> During defense counsel's questioning, Drake expressed his feeling that in particular fact situations, such as with a premeditated murder, he felt that the death penalty was *the* appropriate punishment. Indeed, he noted on his questionnaire that, "Anyone who would take another human being's life in a premeditated manner is a sick animal and should be put to sleep." However, he also continued to assert that he would listen to all of the evidence before making his decision.
>
> Although this exchange shows that Drake had very strong feelings in favor of the death penalty in particular circumstances, it did not establish that he would automatically answer the future dangerousness issue in the affirmative in every case.... Given the totality of the voir dire, the judge was within her discretion in determining that the venireperson was not challengeable for cause.[146]

---

[146] *Gullen v. State*, No. 73491. 2003 WL 21401956 at *3–*4 (Tex. Crim. App., June 18, 2003). The cases gathered in this chapter are only illustrative of unfettered discretion. *See, e.g.*, *United States v. Bullock*, 48 Fed. Appx. 913 (4th Cir. 2002) *available at* 2002 WL 31415733 ("Courts consistently confer upon the district courts unfettered discretion for a breach of a plea agreement.").

§ 3.3. Presumed Validity

a)   Distinguishing No Reason from Bad Reasons

In *Valley Steel Products Co. v. Howell*, the Texas Court of Appeals distinguished a situation in which a trial court gives no specific reason for its decision and a situation in which the trial court gives an improper reason for its decision.[147] Following a bench trial, the trial court had initially entered judgment for plaintiff in a contract dispute in which the question was whether plaintiff had delivered products that defendant ordered. On defendant's motion to vacate and modify, the trial court vacated the original judgment and entered judgment for the defendant because plaintiff "did not produce *any* evidence that... [defendant] delivered the goods."[148] The Court of Appeals had to decide whether the court's modified judgment was the equivalent to an initial jury verdict or, rather, to a judgment notwithstanding the verdict.[149] The court concluded that the trial court had granted what amounted to a judgment not withstanding the verdict because the trial court had stated that there was *no* evidence of delivery.[150] In doing so, the court found "a better analogy in the review of a trial court's authority to grant a new trial," stating that at the time the trial court "rendered the second judgment" "it still had plenary power over its judgment" and could either alter the judgment or grant a new trial.[151] The court noted that in "both instances," the trial court had "broad discretion, and its acts are treated with great deference on appeal."[152] Explaining the trial court's broad discretion, the court stated: "In deciding whether to grant a new trial, the trial court has broad discretion and need not specify the reason for... its order. When, however, it states a prohibited reason for granting a new trial, the appellate courts assume the court granted it on the prohibited ground...."[153]

b)   Family Law

The Wisconsin Court of Appeals adheres to a rule that "[w]hile a failure to specify the reasons for the exercise of discretion, we may examine the record to determine whether there is a sufficient basis to support the court's discretionary determination."[154] The court affirmed the trial court's order reducing the incarcerated father's child support obligation, stating that "the [trial] court had the

---

[147] 775 S.W. 2d 34, 36 (Tex. App. 1989).

[148] *Id.* at 35.

[149] *Id.*

[150] *Id.* at 36.

[151] *Id.*

[152] *Id.*

[153] *Id.* ("If the trial court had merely entered a second judgment without stating the reason, we would... review the record as if the trial court rendered the judgment considering all the evidence, pro and con. We cannot, however, ignore the trial court's language in its judgment.").

[154] *Voecks v. Voecks*, 491 N.W.2d 107, 110 (Wis. Ct. App. 1992).

power to modify child support and the reduction was a proper exercise of judicial discretion."[155] Although the trial court did not specifically list the factors it considered when granting the father's request, the court held that, based on the findings of the court that *did* appear on the record, the trial court's modification order was proper.[156]

The California Supreme Court's ruling in *Marriage of Lamusga* followed (implicitly) and expanded on the Wisconsin rule.[157] Mother had been awarded primary physical custody in the original dissolution decree. When Mother proposed to move the couple's two sons to Ohio, she sought an order in the trial court allowing the move. Father contested this order and sought primary physical custody in the event that Mother moved to Ohio. The trial court held that a move to Ohio would be "detrimental" to the children on account of "a tenuous and somewhat detached relationship with the boys and their father."[158] On Mother's appeal, the intermediate appellate court reversed, concluding that the trial court "neither proceeded from the presumption that Mother had a right to change the residence of the children, nor took into account this paramount need for stability and continuity in the existing custodial arrangement. Instead, it placed undue emphasis on the detriment that would be caused to the children's relationship with Father if they moved."[159]

On review, the California Supreme Court reversed the intermediate court and reinstated the trial court's order. Regarding the trial court's discretion to issue its order, it stated:

> We reaffirm our statement... that the paramount need for continuity and stability in custody arrangements—and the harm that may result from disruption of established patterns of care and emotional bonds with the primary caretaker weigh heavily in favoring ongoing custody arrangements. But there is nothing in the record before us that indicates that the superior court failed to consider the children's interest in stable custodial and emotional ties with their mother. The court carefully considered the comprehensive reports prepared by Dr. Stahl and the evidence submitted by both parties. The court placed primary importance on the effect the proposed move would have on what is now a tenuous and somewhat detached relationship with the boys and their father, concluding that the proposed move would be extremely detrimental to the children's welfare because it would disrupt the progress being made by the children's therapist in promoting this relationship. The superior court found that it was realistic to be concerned that the

---

[155] *Id.* at 108.
[156] *Id.* at 110.
[157] *In re Marriage of Lamusga*, 88 P.3d 81 (Cal. 2004).
[158] *Id.* at 89 (awarding Father primary custody of the children in the event that Mother moved to Ohio).
[159] *Id.*

174

proposed move could result in the relationship between the father and the children being lost. In future cases, courts would do well to state on the record that they have considered this interest in stability, but the lack of such a statement does not constitute error and does not indicate that the court failed to properly discharge its duties.

Contrary to the conclusion of the Court of Appeal, the superior court did not place undue emphasis on the detriment to the children's relationship with their father that would be caused by the proposed move. The weight to be accorded to such factors must be left to the court's sound discretion. The Court of Appeal erred in substituting its judgment for that of the superior court.[160]

Judge Kennard dissented, stating that she would prefer an approach that would require the trial court to specify its reasons for altering the custody arrangement on the record:

When it explained its ruling, the trial court said that moving the children to another state could damage the children's relationship with their father, but the court never mentioned the potential harm to the children from losing their mother as their primary caretaker, despite undisputed evidence that this harm would be significant. The majority acknowledges that the trial court was required to consider this detriment—indeed it acknowledges the paramount need for continuity and stability in custody arrangements—but it assumes the trial court adequately considered this point.

In a matter of this importance, involving the custody and welfare of minor children, a reviewing court should not make such a speculative assumption. When a trial court's explanation for exercising its discretion in a particular way does not mention a critical matter that the court was bound to consider, and does not accurately state the controlling legal standard, a reviewing court cannot simply ignore these omissions. When, as here, the appellate record raises substantial doubts that the trial court applied the proper legal principles and policies that should have guided its decision, reversal is required.[161]

A recent family law case out of Maryland illustrates the distinction between presumed validity and the narrower degrees of judicial discretion. In *Goldberg v. Miller*, plaintiff Goldberg sought to collect guardian *ad litem* fees from the husband in the underlying child custody dispute.[162] (Husband had opposed Goldberg's

---

[160] *Id.* at 94–95.

[161] *Id.* at 100 (Kennard, J., dissenting).

[162] *Goldberg v. Miller*, 810 A.2d 947 (Md. 2002).

appointment as guardian and had alleged that he was biased toward the child's mother.) In order to collect, the plaintiff filed a motion with the trial court seeking to treat his *ad litem* fees as child support. The trial court granted his motion. On appeal, the intermediate court reversed on grounds that *ad litem* fees were not covered in the state's child support guidelines and thus the trial court had no authority to treat the fees as child support.[163] Affirming the intermediate court, the Maryland Court of Appeals made the following observation:

> Not only does Goldberg lack support for his position [that *ad litem* fees are child support] in the structure of the statute, but the purpose of the Guidelines also undermines his position. As we noted..., the Legislature sought to promote consistency in child support awards by requiring the use of a limited universe of variables to determine award amounts. The Legislature, through these provisions, deliberately restricted the trial court's discretion in determining a child support award.
>
> Inapposite to the restrictive purposes of the Guidelines, the statute governing guardian *ad litem* fees does not reflect the same specificity of the Guidelines as to the reasonableness of the expenses or income limits. Section 1-202, which provides for the appointment of the guardian *ad litem*, offers the Circuit Court no guidance regarding what considerations should govern the extent of the award of guardian *ad litem* fees. The award of guardian *ad litem* fees, furthermore, is not determined based on financial resources available to the parents. Had the Legislature intended the court to include guardian *ad litem* fees in an order to pay child support, it could have created specific measuring devices, like those under the Guidelines, to define how fees of the guardian *ad litem* would be computed as child support.[164]

On the opposite end of the spectrum, a Tennessee case involving child custody illustrates the contrast between unfettered discretion and presumed validity. The trial court, granting a decree of divorce to the mother based on inappropriate marital conduct, also awarded custody to the mother and supervised visitation rights to the father.[165] Affirming the trial court, the court rejected the father's argument that supervised visitation was inappropriate absent evidence of abuse. The court explained its position:

> In determining whether or not supervision of visitation is necessary, courts are directed by Tenn. Cod. Ann. § 36-6-301 (2001). That section states that "[i]f the court finds that the non-custodial parent has physically or emotionally abused the child, the

---

[163] *Id.* at 950.

[164] *Id.* at 957, n.6.

[165] *Dirr v. Dirr*, No. M2001-03049-COA-R3-CV, 2003 WL 22345479, at *2 (Tenn. Ct. App. Oct. 15, 2003).

court may require that visitation be supervised or prohibited until such abuse has ceased or until a there is no reasonable likelihood that such abuse will recur." When considering a decision of the trial court, we are reminded that "[t]he trial court is accorded broad discretion in deciding issues of custody and visitation, and appellate courts will not interfere with the trial court's decisions absent a showing that the trial court abused its discretion." In addition, though the statute mentions situations of abuse in ordering supervised visitation, Tennessee courts, refusing to unduly restrict a trial court's discretion, have held previously that this statute does not prevent courts from ordering supervised visitation in the absence of physical or emotional abuse.[166]

c)   Withdrawal of Plea Bargains

Under Texas Code of Criminal Procedure Article 26.13, a defendant has a right to withdraw his or her guilty or no contest plea in a felony case when the court announces that it will not accept the terms of the underlying plea bargain.[167] The Texas Court of Criminal Appeals has held that Article 26.13 only applies narrowly

---

[166] *Id.* ("We are mindful that with cases involving custody arrangements, the details of custody of and visitation with children are peculiarly within the broad discretion of the Trial Judge whose decisions are rarely disturbed.").

    Trial courts also hold discretion when deciding whether or not to appoint a guardian. The District of Columbia Court of Appeals has discussed this discretion:

> The decision to appoint a guardian or conservator is committed to the [trial] court's considerable discretion and we review it on appeal only for abuse of that discretion. However, an exercise of discretion must be founded upon correct legal standards. Whether the trial court abused its discretion in declining to appoint a guardian or conservator for [petitioner] depends upon an interpretation of the trial court's jurisdiction under the District of Columbia Guardianship, Protective Proceedings, and Durable Power of Attorney Act of 1986. This is a legal issue we review *de novo*.

In re Uwazih, 822 A.2d 1074, 1077 (D.C. 2003).

[167] Code of Criminal Procedure Article 26.13 provides:

> (a) Prior to accepting a plea of guilty or a plea of nolo contendere the court shall admonish the defendant of:
>
> ....
>
> (b) (2) the fact that the recommendation of the prosecuting attorney as to punishment is not binding on the court. Provided that the court shall inquire as to the existence of any plea bargaining agreements between the state and the defendant and, in the event that such an agreement exists, the court shall inform the defendant whether it will follow or reject such agreement in open court and before any finding on the plea. Should the court reject any such agreement, the defendant shall be permitted to withdraw his plea of guilty or nolo contendere....

Tex. Crim. Proc. Ann. § 26.13 (Vernon 1989).

to felony cases and not to misdemeanors or revocation proceedings.[168] In *Gutierrez v. State*, the defendant Gutierrez had pleaded guilty (in a 1991 proceeding) to attempted sexual assault and was sentenced to ten years' imprisonment to be served on probation. In January 2000, the state moved to revoke probation. Defendant agreed not to contest the motion in exchange for the state's recommendation of three years' imprisonment. However, when the trial court revoked probation, it imposed the ten-year sentence. Defendant appealed. The intermediate appellate court reversed, relying on the United States Supreme Court's opinion in *Santobello v. New York*:

> This phrase of the process of criminal justice, and the adjudicative element inherent in accepting a plea of guilty, must be attended by safeguards to insure the defendant what is reasonably due in the circumstances. Those circumstances will vary, but a constant factor is that when a plea rests in any significant degree on a promise or agreement of the prosecutor, so that it can be said to be part of the inducement or consideration, *such promise must be fulfilled.*[169]

The court, disagreeing with the intermediate appellate court, distinguished *Santobello*, reaffirming its precedent:

> The promise that was not fulfilled in *Santobello*, in violation of the Due Process Clause, was the prosecution's promise to make no recommendation as to punishment. It was not a promise that the defendant would receive a certain punishment. *Santobello* does not require a state court to enforce a prosecutor's recommendation as to punishment. After considering all the policy arguments for plea bargaining, we decided not to restrict the trial court's discretion to grant or deny a motion to withdraw a guilty plea. This traditional discretion obtained in cases in which defendants entered guilty pleas, both in felony and misdemeanor prosecutions.[170]

Since the court had already reaffirmed its precedent that Article 26.13 did not apply to revocation proceedings, the logical conclusion was that the court of appeals had undermined the trial court's discretion. In this regard, the court stated:

---

[168] *Gutierrez v. State*, 108 S.W.3d 304, 309 (Tex. Crim. App. 2003) ("Therefore... in the context of revocation proceedings, the legislature has not authorized binding plea agreements, has not required the court to inquire as to the existence of a plea agreement or admonish the defendant pursuant... and has not provided for withdrawal of a plea after sentencing.").

[169] *Gutierrez v. State*, 65 S.W.3d 362, 364–65 (Tex. App. 2001) (en banc) (quoting *Santobello v. New York*, 404 U.S. 257, 262 (1971)). The emphasis appeared in the Texas Court of Appeals' opinion. The Texas Court of Appeals read *Santobello* as a due process case bearing on the defendant's right to fundamental fairness. *Id.*

[170] *Id.* at 309.

We are mindful that the benefits of plea-bargaining are not so great in probation-revocation hearings. The principal justification for plea-bargaining is the conservation of scarce judicial resources, and our judicial system relies heavily on avoidance of trials by jury in felony cases. But a probation-revocation proceeding requires fewer judicial resources than a trial by jury; there is none of the time and expense that attends a jury trial on guilt or punishment, the fact issues are usually less complex than those in a criminal trial, and the burden of proof is lower. Such considerations may be one reason why the legislature has not bestowed on probationers a right to withdraw a plea of true.

This does not mean that, in probation-revocation proceedings, plea-bargaining and the resulting punishment recommendations are worthless. A recommendation by the State gives the trial judge some indication of what justice requires based on the specific circumstances of a case, and it may serve to persuade the judge that a particular sentence is appropriate. Although the law requires the State to make the agreed-upon recommendation to the court, it does not give a probationer the right to withdraw a plea, and the court of appeals erred in holding otherwise.[171]

Judge Meyers dissented, arguing that the trial court's refusal to accept the recommendation violated defendant's due process rights:

By urging the rejection of "other policy reasons" for enforcing plea bargain agreements, the majority completely ignores the basic premise of the *Santobello* holding: that the waiver of fundamental rights inherent in the plea bargaining process necessarily implicates due process concerns. The premise is equally applicable in a situation like this one, when an individual waives his or her right to a hearing and pleads true during a motion to revoke community supervision.[172]

d)   The Jury

Appellate courts will often zealously protect the trial court's discretion in its dealings with the jury. In *State v. Clark*, the Supreme Court of Connecticut reviewed a case in which the trial court had read an improper jury instruction that imposed an "additional element that the state was not required to prove" in a manslaughter case. Defendant appealed, arguing, *inter alia*, that the court should "adopt a bright line rule that, in the limited circumstance in which an initial improper instruction is corrected and a recharge is later requested by the jury, the

---

[171] *Id.* at 310.

[172] *Id.* at 310–11 (Meyers, J., dissenting).

trial court must provide only the proper instruction in its recharge."[173] Defendant argued that his proposal "would avoid jury confusion because it would provide a means of ensuring that a recharge on a previously corrected instruction" would "remove whatever mistaken impression remained in the mind of the jury."[174] The court rejected defendant's argument, stating:

> We decline to adopt such a rule because the trial court is best suited to determine, on a case-by-case basis, the proper means for reorienting the jury to the proper legal standard. The rule that the defendant proposes would unduly restrict the trial court's discretion in situations that will inevitably vary in degree and circumstance, and would be as likely to create, as to limit, jury confusion.[175]

Deciding whether to adopt a *per se* rule requiring a trial judge to *voir dire* all remaining jurors when it excuses an individual juror for partiality, the Supreme Court of New Jersey took a more nuanced approach to the same question.[176] At the beginning of defendant's trial on charges stemming from defendant's alleged molestation of his granddaughter, the trial court selected a jury and admonished the jurors not to discuss the case among themselves until after they had heard all of the evidence. Following the testimony of victim's mother, a juror told the court that he had cared for the victim's mother while she was in the hospital for a week, had received some pertinent information about the case, and felt that he could no longer serve as an objective juror. The court excused the juror, but did not *sua sponte* question the remaining jurors.[177] Defendant was convicted on most counts and appealed. Reviewing under the plain error doctrine, the intermediate appellate court reversed on grounds that the trial court should have questioned the panel.

The New Jersey Supreme Court reversed the intermediate court and reinstated the guilty verdict, "applying an abuse of discretion standard to the trial court's determination that a *voir dire* of the remaining jurors was not required."[178] Citing to both the United States and New Jersey constitutions, the court began by affirming that the defendant has a fundamental right to a fair trial by an impartial jury.[179] The court then outlined the steps that a trial court must take in a case of potential jury taint.[180] Despite the fact that the trial court must take certain steps to

---

[173] 826 A.2d 128, 137 (Conn. 2003).

[174] *Id.*

[175] *Id.*

[176] *State v. R.D.*, 781 A.2d 37 (N.J. 2001).

[177] *Id.* at 40 ("Neither counsel asked the court to question the remaining jurors."). The excused juror had told the court that he had not discussed his familiarity with the victim's mother or his opinion of the case with the other jurors. *Id.*

[178] *Id.* at 39.

[179] *Id.* at 41. ("The trial court must use appropriate discretion to determine whether the individual juror, or jurors, are capable of fulfilling their duty to judge the facts in an impartial and unbiased manner, based strictly on the evidence presented in court.").

[180] *Id.* ("The court is obliged to interrogate the juror, in the presence of counsel, to determine if there is a taint; if so, the inquiry must expand to determine whether any other

investigate taint, the court stated that the decision as to whether or not to "grant a new mistrial resides in the discretion of the trial court" and that a "new trial is not necessary in every instance where it appears an individual juror has been exposed to outside influence."[181] The court explained:

> Ultimately, the trial court is in the best position to determine whether the jury has been tainted. That determination requires the trial court to consider the gravity of the extraneous information in relation to the case, the demeanor and credibility of the juror or jurors who were exposed to the extraneous information, and the overall impact of the matter on the fairness of the proceedings. The inquiry about whether extraneous information had the *capacity* to influence the result of the jury requires an examination of whether there was at least an opportunity for the extraneous information to reach the remaining jurors when that extraneous information is knowledge unique to one juror who is excused mid-trial.
>
> The abuse of discretion standard of review should pertain when reviewing such determinations of a trial court. Application of that standard respects the trial court's unique perspective. We traditionally have accorded trial court deference in exercising control over matters pertaining to the jury. Many state and federal courts also apply an abuse of discretion standard of review to a trial court's decision not to *voir dire* remaining members of the jury following the excusal of a single juror.
>
> An appropriate *voir dire* of a juror allegedly in possession of extraneous information mid-trial should inquire into the specific nature of the extraneous information, and whether the juror intentionally or inadvertently has imparted any of that information to other jurors. Depending on the juror's answers to searching questions by the court, the court must then determine whether it is necessary to *voir dire* individually other jurors to ensure the impartiality of the jury. That determination should be explained on the record to facilitate appellate review under the abuse of discretion standard. But the decision to *voir dire* individually best remains a matter for the sound discretion of the trial court. No *per se* rule should obtain. The court may learn through its questioning of the excused juror that circumstances made it impossible for that juror to impart impermissible information to the other jurors even unintentionally. Although the court should not simply accept the juror's word that no extraneous information was imparted to the

jurors have been tainted thereby.) (The trial court must then determine whether the trial may proceed after excusing the tainted juror or jurors, or whether a mistrial is necessary.").

[181] *Id.* at 41–42. The court noted, however, that the trial court must explore the possibility of potential taint as well as actual taint. *Id.* at 41.

others, the court's own thorough inquiry of the juror should answer the question whether additional *voir dire* is necessary to assure that impermissible tainting of the other jurors did not occur. In same instances, the court may find that it would be more harmful to *voir dire* the remaining jurors because, in asking questions, inappropriate information could be imparted.[182]

Although the court noted that the trial court's "determination should be explained on the record," the court relied not on the trial judge's explanation but on the fact that (1) there "was no chance for the excuse juror to communicate his extraneous information about the witness to the other jurors," (2) the "court repeatedly instructed the jurors not to discuss the case with each other," and the excused juror denied discussing the case, and (3) the trial court "had sufficient opportunity to observe the juror during [its] two exchanges with him and form an opinion concerning the juror's credibility and reliability, particularly in light of the corroborating circumstances."[183]

Judge Stein dissented:

In my view, the majority errs in declining to acknowledge that once a tainted juror is identified mid-trial, the trial court is required to *voir dire* the remaining jurors even if the likelihood of contact with the tainted juror is minimal. Consistent with our strong common-law tradition of securing a fair and impartial jury, trial courts should not merely rely on a juror's word that he or she did not share information with other jurors. Trial courts must aggressively weed out the possibility of juror taint, and if courts fail to take appropriate action juror taint should be presumed and a mistrial declared....

In reversing the Appellate Division's disposition, the Court is unwisely diminishing the responsibility of trial courts to verify that a tainted juror has not influenced other jurors and to assure that defendants are tried by fair and impartial juries. Here, the trial court undoubtedly made two errors. As the majority acknowledges, the court failed to adequately interrogate juror number two to determine the extent of his taint. After concluding that the juror was tainted and excusing him, the court failed to question the remaining jurors concerning their exposure to potentially damaging information adverse to defendant. Polling the jurors operates to safeguard the rights of the accused and vindicate societal interests

---

[182] *Id.* at 42–43.
[183] *Id.* at 43–44 ("Although we conclude that in applying an abuse of discretion standard here, the court did not err in failing to *voir dire* the remaining jurors *sua sponte* after excusing juror number two, we would have preferred further inquiry of the excused juror.").

in the fair and efficient administration of the criminal justice system.[184]

e)   Proceedings in Federal Courts *In Forma Pauperis*

Twenty-eight U.S.C. § 1915(e) (*formerly* §1915(d)) provides:

> (1) The court may request an attorney to represent any person unable to afford counsel.

> (2) Notwithstanding any filing fee, or any portion thereof, that may have been paid, the court shall dismiss the case at any time if the court determines that—

> (A) the allegation of poverty is untrue; or

> (B) the action or appeal -

> (i) is frivolous or malicious;

> (ii) fails to state a claim on which relief may be granted; or

> (iii) seeks monetary relief against a defendant who is immune from such relief.

Plaintiff Barnhill filed an action under 28 U.S.C. § 1983 in the Southern District of Illinois, alleging that he had been subject to interrogation in violation of his civil rights while serving prison time on an unrelated charge. The magistrate hearing plaintiff's action summarily denied plaintiff's request for appointed counsel under § 1915. The magistrate cited to the Seventh Circuit's opinion outlining "five nonexclusive factors to be considered when ruling on requests for appointed counsel" but "simply concluded—without explanation—that appointment of counsel [was] not warranted."[185] When defendants filed motions to dismiss, plaintiff renewed his request for counsel. The trial court granted the motions to dismiss and denied plaintiff's request; however, the court gave plaintiff sixty days to amend his complaint.

On appeal, plaintiff argued that the trial court "per se abused its discretion by not specifying any reasons for denying his motions."[186] The court disagreed:

> [Defendant's] first argument has no basis in law. While we have indeed held that a district court abuses its discretion when it identifies the proper standards for evaluating § 1915(d) motions but fails to explain a denial of counsel, we have never foreclosed our

---

[184] *Id.* at 47–48 (Stein, J. dissenting).

[185] *Barnhill v. Doiron*, 958 F.2d 200, 201 (7th Cir. 1992).

[186] *Id.* at 202.

ability to independently examine § 1915(d) requests. Quite the contrary, we have repeatedly pointed out that our expertise is as great as the district court's with respect to ruling on § 1915(d) motions. Holding otherwise makes little sense; we need not squander scant judicial resources when it is apparent that the district court has acted within—or beyond—its discretion when ruling on § 1915(d) motions.[187]

f) Dismissal of Case Based on Defendant's Sentence Being Executed

An unusual set of facts emerged in *State v. Corchado.*[188] Defendant had been convicted of manslaughter and had served his sentence. Defendant had been convicted in 1980, but the court overturned the conviction in 1982. In 1984, the state sought to retry the defendant, and the defendant filed a motion to dismiss. The court upheld the trial court's discretionary decision to dismiss the charges (effectively ending the state's efforts to retry defendant). In doing so, the court stated:

> The question that emerges at this point is what standard should be used to evaluate the action of the trial court in dismissing this case with prejudice. Upon analysis, it becomes evident that the notion of fairness permeates the considerations to be given to the trial court's decision in this unique case. Thus, a balancing process must occur which weighs the interests of the state and society in having defendant again stand trial against the interest of the defendant, who has already served his sentence, in not being subject to a new trial. Such process, with its core concern of fairness, prescribes the standard that inheres in discretionary choice—that of abuse of discretion. We need not reach any question of whether constitutional principles of due process or fundamental fairness may be the basis for the inherent judicial authority to dismiss with prejudice a criminal case in the posture of the one before us....[189]

Nevertheless, the court emphasized several times that a trial court should only dismiss with prejudice for lack of "cause" "with great caution."[190]

g) Bonds

The Supreme Court of Georgia held that the decision "[w]hether to require the posting of a bond by [mother] to assure the return of the children is a matter within the trial court's discretion."[191] The court upheld the trial court's decision to require

---

[187] *Id.* § 1915(d) is now § 1915(e).

[188] 512 A.2d 183 (Conn. 1986).

[189] *Id.* at 186.

[190] *Id.* at 187.

[191] *Moon v. Moon*, 589 S.E.2d 76, 79 (divorce proceeding) (reviewing trial court's rulings on child custody).

184

mother to post $100,000 bond in light of mother's "earlier refusal to return the children to Georgia as ordered by court in both Georgia and Kansas."[192]

In order to preserve the discretion of its small claims courts, the Indiana Court of Appeals took what is arguably an expansive interpretation of its jurisdiction's landlord-tenant statutes. Indiana landlord-tenant law appears to require that the landlord post bond when seeking an order for immediate possession independent of a final judgment.[193] The statute provides:

> A court may not issue an order of possession in favor of a plaintiff other than an order of final judgment until the plaintiff has filed with the court a written undertaking in an amount fixed by the court and executed by surety to be approved by the court binding the plaintiff to the defendant in an amount sufficient to assure the payment of any damages the defendant may suffer if the court wrongfully ordered possession of the property to the plaintiff.[194]

Despite the statutory language, the court rejected a tenant's argument that "[i]nasmuch as the trial court fixed no bond in the present case, and the Landlord offered no security" "the order of ejectment is void and unenforceable, and therefore pre-judgment, until the Landlord posts bond."[195] Regarding the discretion of the trial court to require a bond, the court stated:

> ... [T]he present case remained upon the small claims docket of the trial court. Therefore, the trial of the Landlord's claim remained informal, with the sole objective being to dispense speedy justice between the parties according to the rules of the substantive law of evictions. The trial court was not bound by the statutory provisions on the formal procedures related to evictions. We therefore conclude that the order of the trial court constituted a final judgment for possession of the real estate and that the trial court properly issued an order of possession in the Landlord's favor even the Landlord had not executed a surety under I.C. 32-6-1.5.-6 [now IC 32-30-3-6].[196]

h)   Attorney Fees

There is authority from the Supreme Court of Georgia suggesting that the trial court's award of attorney fees is presumptively valid.[197] However, the *Mitchell* case

---

[192] *Id.*
[193] Ind. Code Ann. § 32-30-3-6 (West 2005).
[194] *Id.*
[195] *Stout v. Kokomo Manor Apts.*, 677 N.E.2d 1060, 1068 (Ind. Ct. App. 1997).
[196] *Id.*
[197] *Mitchell v. Mitchell*, 311 S.E.2d 456, 459 (Ga. 1984) ("As to the trial judge's failure to award [litigation] expenses to the former wife, this is a matter lying within the trial judge's discretion. While the awarding of these expenses to the former wife certainly would have

did not consider the award of attorney fees *per se*, but as part of former wife's argument "that the superior court erred in imposing the prohibitions against either parent from taking either of the sons out of Georgia, from procuring passports, and from making passport applications."[198] Other authority suggests that appellate courts carefully scrutinize trial court's rulings on attorney fees, even if such rulings remain nominally discretionary. In *Moon v. Moon*, the Supreme Court of Georgia remanded a trial court's attorney fee award "for a statement of the statutory basis for the award of attorney fees and any finding that must be made to support it."[199] The trial court had awarded father over fourteen thousand dollars in attorney fees to cover father's litigation costs in a multijurisdictional custody dispute. In remanding, the court stated:

> Generally, an award of attorney fees is not available in Georgia unless authorized by statute or contract. OCGA § 19-6-2(a)(1) authorizes the grant of attorney fees in a divorce action "[w]ithin the sound discretion of the court, except that the court shall consider the financial circumstances of both parties as a part of its determination of the amount of attorney's fees, if any, to be allowed against either party...." OCGA § 9-15-14(b) authorizes an award of reasonable and necessary attorney fees upon a finding that an action or any part thereof lacked substantial justification... was interposed for delay or harassment, or... an attorney or party unnecessarily expanded the proceeding by other improper conduct...." The purpose of an award of attorney fees pursuant to § 19-6-2 is to ensure effective representation of both spouses so that all issues can be fully and fairly resolved. The damages authorized by § 9-15-14 are intended not merely to punish or deter litigation abuses but also to recompense litigants who are forced to expend their resources in contending with [abusive litigation]. If the award of attorney fees to [father] was predicated on OCGA § 9-15-14, it must be vacated because the findings necessary to support such an award were not made. If the award was predicated on OCGA § 19-6-2, it must be vacated because the only evidence of the parties' financial circumstances contained in the trial court's order is the parties' gross monthly income which shows that [mother] has one-half the income of [father]. Such evidence does not support the conclusion that the award of attorney fees was to ensure that the recipient spouse could afford effective representation.[200]

---

been authorized, we cannot say that the refusal to award these expenses constitutes an abuse of discretion.").

[198] *Id.* at 458.

[199] *Moon*, 589 S.E.2d 76 at 81 (Ga. 2003).

[200] *Id.* at 89. For yet another take on the attorney fee question, see *Bhattacharya v. Copple*, 898 F.2d 766, 769 (10th Cir. 1990).

> This court has recently held that a calculation of attorney's fees in a diversity case is reviewed only for an abuse of discretion. We can find no abuse of discretion in awarding fees based on an hourly rate in this

186

i)   Case Management

The Indiana Court of Appeals announced that it would "set aside a trial court ruling made in the exercise of discretion" denying a criminal defendant's motion to reopen a case to present additional evidence "if the decision was unreasonable in light of all of the circumstances and prejudiced the defendant's rights."[201] The court then listed factors that a trial court could consider when exercising its discretion to deny a motion to reopen, but did not limit the trial court to those factors:

> Factors that may be considered in determining whether a motion to reopen should be granted are possible prejudice to the opposing party, whether the party raising the motion rested inadvertently or purposely, the stage of the proceedings at which the request was made and whether confusion or inconvenience would result from granting the request. While a defendant's motion should be given serious consideration in light of the state constitutional right to testify, it is not per se an abuse of discretion to deny such a request.[202]

The *White* court relied heavily on *Flynn v. State*, an Indiana Supreme Court case in which one justice dissented.[203] The dissent concluded that the denial of defendant's motion to reopen "insofar as it denied the defendant" "himself the chance to testify" "was an unreasonable exercise of the trial court's authority."[204] Because the trial court's ruling touched on defendant's constitutional right to present a viable defense, the case called for "closer judicial scrutiny."[205] Applying his reasoning to the case at bar, the dissent concluded that "[W]hen the personal right of the defendant is viewed in this heightened fashion and added to the detailed

---

case. Plaintiff's attorneys have not cited any authority to indicate that the district court was without power under § 7-121b to set aside the contingent fee agreement. In fact, the express language of § 7-121b clearly indicates that the essential inquiry in setting a fee is reasonableness, regardless of any attorney-client relationship. Under § 7-121b a fee arrangement can be of evidentiary value but it does not displace a court's responsibility to determine a reasonable fee. In the absence of any suggestion in this case that the district court misapplied the factors under § 7-121b and made erroneous factual findings, it is difficult to see how the district court exceeded the bounds of permissible choice simply by rejecting the request of plaintiffs' attorneys for in excess of forty percent... of the total settlement package... and awarding fees based on an hourly rate.

[201] *White v. State*, 726 N.E.2d 831, 835 (Ind. Ct. App. 2000) ("The decision to allow a defendant to reopen her case lies within the trial court's discretion.").
[202] *Id.*
[203] 497 N.E.2d 912 (Ind. 1986).
[204] *Id.* at 916 (DeBruler, J., dissenting).
[205] *Id.* (DeBruler, J., dissenting).

circumstances set forth in the majority opinion, it reveals that the ruling of the trial court was unreasonable and an abuse of discretion."[206]

Although the trial court's decision to deny a continuance is presumptively valid, the Alabama Supreme Court in *Ex Parte Jacobs* clarified that such "discretion is not without limitations."[207] Husband had filed for divorce and sought custody of his minor daughter. Wife, who resided in Germany, moved for a continuance in January 1992, arguing that she "needed time to return to the United States with the child."[208] The trial court granted the motion and continued the divorce trial until March 18. On March 18, the wife moved for a second continuance, arguing that she "had been unable to accumulate sufficient funds for travel from Germany to the United States."[209] The trial court denied the motion, held the trial in the wife's absence, and awarded the husband custody.

In determining whether the trial court had abused its discretion in denying the continuance, the court quoted the state's intermediate appellate court's holding that "continuances are not favored, and a denial of a continuance will not be reversed without a showing of gross abuse of discretion."[210] Reviewing the record, the court noted that the husband had given the wife $450 for airfare, but that one ticket from Germany to Alabama cost $915 and that the wife made the equivalent of $850 a month at her job.[211] The court concluded that the "evidence in the record" suggested "that the wife was financially unable to afford air fare, even with the husband's $450 contribution," that "wife's counsel was prepared for trial and tried the case without the wife or child being present," and that the "record does not suggest that the wife was trying to avoid the proceeding."[212] In concluding that the trial court abused its discretion, the court distinguished an earlier case decided by the intermediate appellate court:

> The facts underlying Owens are distinguishable from those in this case. In Owens, the trial court had granted at least three continuances. After being told that the court would grant no more continuances, the wife went to Tennessee. On the day of trial, the wife claimed that repairs on her automobile had not been completed and that she therefore could not return to Alabama, and she claimed that she lacked the funds to secure other transportation to Alabama. The court noted in Owens that no witnesses had been

---

[206] *Id.* (DeBruler, J., dissenting).
[207] 636 So. 2d 410, 411 (Ala. 1994) ("We conclude that the trial court erred in denying the second motion for a continuance.").
[208] *Id.*
[209] *Id.*
[210] *Id.*
[211] *Id.*
[212] *Id.*

188

subpoenaed for trial and that neither the wife nor her counsel had made any preparation for trial.[213]

Judge Maddox provided the lone dissent:

> In reversing judgment of the Court of Civil Appeals, this Court is substituting its judgment for that of the judge, who saw the witnesses, heard the testimony, and was familiar with the events surrounding the controversy.
>
> One of the issues presented here is whether the trial court's denial of the wife's second motion for a continuance was an abuse of discretion. The granting of a motion for a continuance is a matter within the discretion of the trial court. The wife requested a second continuance for the same purpose as the first continuance, which had been granted two months earlier, and the motion was made at the time of the trial by the wife's counsel because she was not present. The trial court concluded that the wife was attempting to avoid the proceeding. This Court should not question its judgment under these circumstances.[214]

Although a denial of a motion to amend is presumptively valid, an appellate court may be "mindful" of the "admonition that 'leave shall be freely given'" to amend a pleading "'when justice so requires.'"[215] As a result, "unless there appears to be an adequate reason for the denial (*e.g.*, undue delay, bad faith, dilatory motive on the part of the movant, futility of the amendment,)" the court concluded that it would "not affirm the denial."[216] The court explained that it would give even less deference to the court because the plaintiff had unsuccessfully sought to amend in an employment discrimination case:

> We also are aware that Title VII plaintiffs often lack access to statistical evidence such as the racial composition of the job applicant pool until after they have filed their complaints and engaged in discovery. For this reason, we think that a denial of leave to amend to add Title VII claims supported by statistics should be evaluated with some caution. Too casual a review of such a denial might encourage the abandonment of (or failure to pursue) potentially meritorious claims. It might also precipitate an increase in unsubstantiated pleading.

---

[213] *Id.* Addressing what it identified as a separate issue, the court also held that "the wife was denied an opportunity to be heard."
[214] *Id.* at 412.
[215] *Grant v. News Gr. Boston, Inc.*, 55 F.3d 1, 5 (1st Cir. 1995).
[216] *Id.* ("We review a denial of leave to amend under Fed. R. Civ. P. 15 for an abuse of discretion, and defer to the district court if any adequate reason for the denial is apparent on the record.").

Having carefully evaluated the court's lateness determination in lights of the record, we discern no abuse of discretion in this case. At the time [plaintiff] filed his motion, discovery was already complete, and [plaintiff] all but concedes that it would have to have been reopened in order for [defendant] to defend itself properly against the claims asserted in the amended complaint.[217]

j) Dismissal for Failure to Prosecute

The Supreme Court of Appeals of West Virginia reversed the trial court for abuse of discretion after the trial court *sua sponte* dismissed plaintiff's case for failure to prosecute. In doing so, the court declined to follow what has become a landmark case on judicial discretion.[218]

Plaintiff filed a personal injury suit on May 19, 1992, following an automobile accident on defendant's property. From the date of the complaint until July 14, 1993, plaintiff did nothing, but defendants filed a discovery request and a notice to take plaintiff's deposition. On January 31, 1995, the trial court dismissed the action for failure to prosecute.[219] The trial court denied the plaintiff's motions to reinstate the case.

The court framed the issue as "a challenge to the procedural requirements and the breadth of discretion enjoyed by the circuit court in making rulings pursuant to Rule 41(b)."[220] Aligning the reasons for and against judicial discretion in this context, the court stated:

> The judicial authority to dismiss with prejudice a civil action for failure to prosecute cannot seriously be doubted. This power to invoke this sanction is necessary in order to prevent undue delays in the disposition of pending cases, and to avoid congestion in the calendar of the circuit court. In the course of discharging their traditional responsibilities, circuit courts are vested with inherent and rule authority to protect their proceedings from the corrosion that emanates from procrastination, delay, and inactivity. Thus, the

---

[217] *Id.* at 5–6.

[218] *Dimon v. Mansy*, 479 S.E.2d 339 (W. Va. 1996). In finding an abuse of discretion, the court called in to question the viability of *Link v. Wabash Railroad Co. Id.* at 348.

[219] Rule 41(b) of the West Virginia Rules of Civil Procedure provides:

> Any court in which is pending an action wherein for more than one year there has been no order or proceeding... may, in its discretion, order such action to be struck from its docket; and it shall thereby be discontinued. The court may direct that such order be published in such newspaper as the court may name. The court may, on motion, reinstate on its trial docket any action dismissed under this rule... within three terms after entry of the order of dismissal[.] W. Va. Code § 56-8-9 (1995) (hereinafter, Rule 41(b)).

[220] 479 S.E.2d at 343.

190

determination whether the plaintiff has failed to move the case in a reasonable manner is a discretionary call for the circuit court. The power to resort to the dismissal of an action is in the interest of orderly administration of justice because the general control of the judicial business is essential to the trial court if it is to function. To this extent, Rule 41(b) is still good law in that granting authority to trial judges to control their dockets through dismissals is consistent, not debilitative, of sound judicial administration. It is equally clear that it is the plaintiff's obligation to move his or her case to trial, and where the plaintiff fails to do so in a reasonable manner, the case may be dismissed as a sanction for the unjustified delay. To be clear, we squarely hold that a plaintiff has a continuing duty to monitor a case from the filing until the final judgment, and where he or she fails to do so, the plaintiff acts at his or her own peril.

The extent of this discretionary authority, however, must be delimited with care, for there is always the unseemly danger of overreaching when the judiciary undertakes to define its own power and authority. Guided by this limitation, we have suggested that a circuit court's sanction authority be a reasonable response to the problems and needs that provoked its use. In other words, a court's authority to issue dismissals as a sanction must be limited by the circumstances and necessity giving rise to its exercise. The sanction of dismissal with prejudice for the lack of prosecution is most severe to the private litigant and could, if used excessively, disserve the dignitary purpose for which it is invoked. It remains constant in our jurisprudence that the dignity of a court derives from the respect accorded its judgment. To often, that dignity is eroded, not enhanced, by too free of a recourse to rules foreclosing considerations of claims on the merit.

...

It is our task to supervise the administration of justice in the circuit courts, and to that end, we must ensure that fair standards of procedure are maintained. Judicial supervision and responsibility implies the duty of establishing and maintaining civilized standards of procedure and evidence. Our supervisory and rulemaking authority extends to issuance of sanctions under Rule 41(b), particularly when we are dealing with a procedure for which a uniform practice is desirable. As suggested below, other appellate courts have found that exercise of their authority is appropriate when needed to guarantee litigants fair access to the courts to have their grievances heard on the merits. Of course, our supervisory and rulemaking authority is not a form of free-floating justice, untethered to legal principle. Attempts by an appellate court, for example, to use broad supervisory and rulemaking authority as a way to control the property vested discretion of the trial court should be squarely rejected. But, on occasion, and we think this is one, we must act to secure rights and fairness when we are persuaded a procedure followed in a trial court is wrong.[221]

The court's holding left "intact the standard upon which we review Rule 41(b) dismissals" but altered "the procedural requirements to require pre-dismissal notice and an opportunity for the parties to be heard on the court's proposed action."[222] In stating the additional procedural requirements for Rule 41(b) dismissals, the court did not clearly specify whether the trial court had abused its discretion by not affording sufficient procedural safeguards to plaintiff or whether the trial court had violated as a matter of law the plaintiff's right to notice and opportunity to be heard.[223]

Adopting the plaintiff's proposal that the law should afford him an opportunity to be heard prior to dismissal for failure to prosecute, the court acknowledged a precedent in which it had questioned *Link v. Wabash Railroad Co.*[224] The court stated:

> In support of this argument, the plaintiff cites note 2 of our decision in *Taylor*, 171 W.Va. at 666, 301 S.E.2d at 623, wherein we said:
>
> "It has been suggested that after the bench and bar have had experience with the operation of the new Rules, it may be desirable to eliminate entirely the second paragraph of Rule 41(b), which paragraph is not in the Federal rule. All such involuntary dismissals could be made under the first sentence in Rule 41(b), on motion or on the court's own initiative. Our statutory rules now embraced in Rule 41(b) were borrowed from Virginia. Virginia modified its statute in 1932 to provide that the clerk of the court shall notify the parties in interest if known, or their counsel of record, if living, at his last known address, at least fifteen days before the entry of the order of dismissal, so that all parties may have an opportunity to be heard on the matter. We are inclined to think our rule should be modified for some form of notice of dismissal.

---

[221] *Id.* at 344–45 (noting also the "harshness" of dismissing a case for failure to prosecute).

[222] *Id.* at 345.

[223] *Id.* Specifically, the court stated:

> To effectuate this procedural change, we hold that once the circuit court determines that a case has been inactive for an unreasonable period of time, the court, after serving notice on counsel and the parties and after affording them an opportunity to be heard, may dismiss the action unless good cause for the delay is presented at the hearing provided for that purpose.

[224] *Id.* at 347.

We note at the outset that the United States Supreme Court upheld, in the face of a due process challenge, the practice of dismissing an action, without notice and an opportunity to be heard, for want of prosecution. *Link v. Wabash Railroad Co.*, 370 U.S. 626 (1962). While addressing the due process issue inherent in such a disposition, the Court in *Link* said the following:

"Nor does the absence of notice as to the possibility of dismissal or the failure to hold an adversary hearing necessarily render such a dismissal void. It is true, of course, that the fundamental requirement of due process is an opportunity to be heard upon such notice and proceedings as are adequate to safeguard the right for which the constitutional protection is invoked. But this does not mean that every order entered without notice and a preliminary adversary hearing offends due process. The adequacy of notice and hearing respecting proceedings that may affect a party's rights turns, to a considerable extent, on the knowledge which the circumstances show such party may taken to have of the consequences of his own conduct...."

"In addition, the availability of a corrective remedy such as is provided by Federal Rule of Civil Procedure 60(b)... renders the lack of prior notice of less consequence." 370 U.S. at 632.[225]

The *Dimon* court adopted as its holding its footnote from the earlier *Taylor* case, concluding that "the time has arrived to disassociate the civil practice in this State with the position taken in *Link*, and the dicta of any of our previous decisions which indicated that notice prior to dismissal for failure to prosecute is not required."[226] The court also cited to several other states that had departed from the *Link* holding.[227]

k) Evidentiary Rulings

Federal Rule of Evidence 401 provides: "'Relevant evidence' means evidence having any tendency to make the existence of any fact that is of consequence to the action more probable or less probable than it would be without the evidence."[228] Federal Rule of Evidence 403 provides: "Although relevant, evidence may be excluded if its probative value is substantially outweighed by the danger of unfair prejudice, confusing of the issues, or misleading the jury, or by considerations of

---

[225] *Id.* at 347–48.

[226] *Id.* at 348 ("Although it is true that either an interested party, or the circuit court on its own motion, may move to dismiss, fundamental fairness dictates that notice and a hearing be afforded prior to a determination by the trial court.").

[227] *Id.* ("The decision we reach today moves our civil practice forward and in lock-step with the manner in which the majority of jurisdictions address this issue.").

[228] Fed. R. Evid. 401.

undue delay, waste of time, or needless presentation of cumulative evidence."[229] Trial courts consider Rules 401 and 403 in tandem, and their decisions under both rules are reviewed for abuse of discretion.[230] Discussing its abuse of discretion standard, the Tenth Circuit stated:

> We review a district court's exclusion of evidence under an abuse of discretion standard, reversing only if we have a firm and definite belief that the trial court made a clear error in judgment.
>
> Our deferential review applies both to a trial court's threshold determination of relevance under Rule 401 and to its conclusion under Rule 403 that relevant evidence should nonetheless be excluded due to its tendency to cause jury confusion or unfair prejudice. But it is not only our deferential standard of review that diminishes the likelihood of remand for a new trial based on a trial court's admission or exclusion of evidence; even if we were to find an error that amounted to abuse of discretion, reversible error may be predicated only upon errors that affect a party's substantial rights. Remand for a new trial is a blunt instrument with which to address the many and multifarious evidentiary rulings made during any trial; a deferential standard of review coupled with the distinction between harmless and reversible error ensures that that instrument will be wielded only as necessary to protect litigants' rights to a fundamentally fair adjudication of their disputes.[231]

The same deferential standard of review also applies to hearsay rulings.[232] Operating under this standard of review, Judge Buchwald of the Southern District of New York had the opportunity to discuss the famous case of *Dallas County v. Commercial Union Assurance Co.* The court denied the plaintiff's request to admit a news article "to prove that [defendant] uttered the allegedly defamatory statements at issue."[233] In doing so, it stated:

---

[229] Fed. R. Evid. 403.

[230] *See, e.g., Tanberg v. Sholtis*, 401 F.3d 1151, 1162 (10th Cir. 2005).

[231] *Id.*

[232] *See Dallas County v. Commercial Union Assurance Co.*, 286 F.3d 388 (5th Cir. 1961) (admitting hearsay statements within a half-century old newspaper to prove that lightning had hit a building). Federal Rule of Evidence 807 provides:
> A statement not specifically covered by Rule 803 or 804 but having equivalent circumstantial guarantees of trustworthiness, is not excluded by the hearsay rule, if the court determines that (A) the statement is offered as evidence of a material fact; (B) the statement is more probative on the point for which it is offered than any other evidence which the proponent can procure through reasonable efforts; and (C) the general purposes of these rules and the interests of justice will best be served by admission of the statement into evidence. Fed. R. Evid. 807.

[233] *Jacobson v. Deutsche Bank, A.G.*, 206 F. Supp. 590, 594 (S.D.N.Y. 2002).

First, [plaintiff] analogizes the present circumstances to *Dallas County v. Commercial Union Assurance Co.*. The Dallas County Court, after acknowledging that "a newspaper article is hearsay, and in almost all circumstances is inadmissible," admitted a half-century old newspaper account of a courthouse fire because the circumstances surrounding the article indicated its trustworthiness. In the sagacious words of Judge Wisdom,

> [I]t is inconceivable... that a newspaper reporter in a small town would report there was a fire in the dome of the new courthouse—if there had been no fire. [The reporter] is without motive to falsify, and a false report would have subjected the newspaper and him to embarrassment in the community. The usual dangers inherent in hearsay evidence, such as lack of memory, faulty narration, intent to influence the court proceedings, and plain lack of truthfulness are not present here.

The present case, however, is clearly distinguishable from *Dallas County*.

The difference between the hearsay evidence offered in case at bar and *Dallas County* becomes evident when we recall that the Second Circuit has instructed us to analyze the trustworthiness of a piece of evidence offered under the residual exception with respect to whether, and to what extent, it minimizes the four classic hearsay dangers, namely, insincerity, faulty perception, faulty memory, and faulty narration. [Therefore,] we are obliged to look closely at the proposition for which hearsay is being offered. In *Dallas County*, the proponent of the newspaper article was merely trying to prove that there had been a fire in the county courthouse nearly sixty years previously. *Dallas County* concerned what might be called a "binary event"—either there was a fire, or there was not. The specifics of the temperature of the fire, exactly what time it started, et cetera, were not relevant to the case at hand. Thus, the binary nature of the proposition in *Dallas County* itself provides as circumstantial guarantee of trustworthiness because even if the author's perception, memory, or narration... were less than perfect, it truly is inconceivable that he would have misreported the simple occurrence of a fire in the courthouse.

Whereas the proponent in *Dallas County* sought to prove a simple "binary" proposition, [plaintiff] seeks to prove that [defendant] uttered certain specific statements at a specific time. We face a situation where every word, their placement, order, and translations from German to English, are highly relevant to [plaintiff's] defamation suit. As [plaintiff's] case truly rises and falls on the details, the classic hearsay dangers of faulty perception, memory, and narration are inherent....[234]

The Maryland Court of Appeals, reviewing a trial court's decision to allow a state witness to testify following the defendant's case-in-chief when the defendant had no notice that the witness would appear, described the discretion trial court's enjoy both to receive evidence in rebuttal and to alter the order of proof in a trial:[235]

> To understand why we agree with the Court of Special Appeals that the judgments... must be reversed, we believe it helpful to review briefly the evidentiary principles regarding the admissibility of testimony offered by the State at the rebuttal stage. It should be made clear from the outset that there are two distinct types of evidence which may be adduced at this point in the proceedings: (1) rebuttal evidence, which the State ordinarily has a right to have received, and (2) evidence which should have been adduced during the State's case in chief, but which the trial court, in the exercise of its discretion to vary the order of proof, may allow at the rebuttal stage.... Our cases are clear that the question of what constitutes rebuttal testimony rests within the sound discretion of the trial court, and that the court's ruling should be reversed only where shown to be both manifestly wrong and substantially injurious. Even if the trial court clearly rules that certain testimony is not rebuttal evidence, the court may nonetheless exercise its discretion to vary the order of proof and admit it as part of the case in chief at the rebuttal stage in order to meet the requirements of a particular case, so long as this action does not impair the ability of the defendant to answer and otherwise receive a fair trial. Such deviations from the general rule regarding the order of presentation of evidence are likewise in the sound discretion of the trial court.[236]

Applying this analysis, the court held that the trial court had erred in admitting the testimony as rebuttal evidence, concluding that the testimony could "by no stretch of the imagination be said to explain, reply to, or contradict the testimony of... the defense's only witness."[237] Regarding the trial court's discretion to alter the order of proof, the court concluded:

---

[234] *Id.* at 595–96.

[235] *State v. Hepple*, 368 A.2d 445, 449 (Md. 1977).

[236] *Id.* at 448–49.

[237] *Id.* at 450. ("The mere denial... of the State's accusation together with an assertion that he was engaged in different activities than those sought to be proved by the prosecution does not necessarily constitute 'new matter' entitling the State to present additional evidence....").

We further point out that it is of no consequence that the trial judges might have allowed the testimony pursuant to their discretion to deviate from the conventional order of producing evidence, because we are convinced that in both cases this discretion was not exercised. The fact that the prosecution made no motion to reopen in either case is not dispositive, of course, since the court could have invoked its discretionary power *sua sponte*; because there is no indication here, however, that either court was exercising its discretion to vary the normal mode of presentation of evidence, we cannot uphold admission of the disputed testimony, even if we were convinced, looking at the record in retrospect, that the trial court could have properly allowed that testimony pursuant to this discretionary authority. This is so because if testimony is admitted at the rebuttal stage, but only pursuant to the trial court's discretion to vary the order of proof, the defense must be afforded the same opportunity to investigate and attempt to impeach or otherwise respond to the State's witness as it would have had had the evidence been offered in chief. Our decision today in no way restricts the exercise of the trial court's discretion to allow non—rebuttal evidence at the rebuttal stage of a trial—it merely requires that a change in the normal order of presentation of evidence be *in fact* an exercise of the court's discretion.[238]

§ 3.4. Discretion Requires Explicit Rationale

a) Statutes Requiring Courts to Consider Particular Factors

Generally speaking, the legislature may curtail a trial court's discretion by listing specific factors that the trial court must consider when making its decision. Upholding a trial court's decision to waive juvenile jurisdiction and try the accused as an adult, the Wisconsin Court of Appeals affirmed that the decision rested with "the sound discretion" of the trial court.[239] However, the court stated required that the trial court state its reasons for exercising its discretionary decision on the record.

[The relevant statute] requires that the juvenile court base its decision whether to waive jurisdiction on the criteria specified in the statute. [The statute] provides that "if the court determines on the record that it is established by clear and convincing evidence that it would be contrary to the best interests of the juvenile or of the public to hear the case, the court shall enter an order waiving jurisdiction. Whether to waive jurisdiction is within the juvenile court's sound discretion, and this court will uphold a discretionary determination if the record reflects that the juvenile court exercised its discretion and that there was a reasonable basis for its decision.

---

[238] *Id.* at 450–51.

[239] *In re Todd D.S.*, 621 N.W.2d 386 (Wis. Ct. App. 2000) *available at* 2000 WL 1665061.

The court's discretionary determination will not be upset unless there is an erroneous exercise of discretion. It is an erroneous exercise of discretion if the trial court fails to specify the reasons supporting the discretionary determination made, or if the trial court misapplies the law, unless by searching the record, we can find reasons to support the court's exercise of discretion.

The paramount consideration in determining waiver is the best interests of the child. In making its discretionary determination, the trial court must apply the statutory factors identified, but need consider only those factors that are relevant to the specific case. The weight to be accorded each of the relevant statutory factors in a specific case is a matter submitted to the trial court's discretion. The trial court's determination will be affirmed as long as there is a reasonable basis for the court's determination.[240]

In *Rose v. Rose*, the Ohio Court of Appeals demonstrated that when the legislature establishes specific guidelines for the court, the appellate courts will not necessarily require the trial court to discuss each factor specifically when making a record of its decision:

Through his first assignment, appellant maintains the trial court abused its discretion in failing to adequately specify the reasons behind the award of spousal support, pursuant to [Ohio statute]. That section sets forth fourteen separate factors that the court shall consider in determining whether spousal support is appropriate and reasonable. Those factors must also be considered in determining the nature, amount, and terms of payment, and duration of the award.

Contrary to appellant's assertion, the trial court specifically stated that it did consider the factors set forth.... There is nothing in this record that demonstrates the trial court did not consider all of the factors listed in that section or that it based its award upon any one of those factors taken in isolation. Instead, it appears that court considered all those factors and made specific comment on only those factors that applied to the evidence presented in this case. We cannot conclude that this [is] an abuse of discretion as that term is defined....[241]

A trial court may have discretion to depart from guidelines that the legislature establishes to govern certain matters only insofar as the trial court justifies its departure on the record. The Arizona Court of Appeals held that a trial

---

[240] *Id.*
[241] *Rose v. Rose*, No. 91-DR-90646, 1994 Ohio App. LEXIS 3851, at *5–*6 (Ohio Ct. App. July 28, 1994).

198

court had "erred by failing to specify its reasons for imposing" highly restrictive at-home supervision on a delinquent.[242] Nevertheless, the court affirmed "despite the absence of specific findings" because the record demonstrated that the trial court had considered the "statutory factors."[243] The court explained that although the statue requires specific findings, the statute only offered "guidelines" with respect to juvenile supervision.[244] As such, the statute proposed guidelines that were "not mandatory" and not binding on the court.[245]

Another context in which a court must "go on record" in order to support its departure from statutory guidelines is child support. The court summarized its holding thus:

> When Samuel and Kimberly Bell divorced in 1998, a King County Superior Court ordered Samuel to pay $400 in monthly child support for the couple's two children. In arriving at this amount, the court deviated [in favor of the father] more than 50 percent from the standard support calculation largely because of Samuel's support obligations to two other children from a previous relationship. While the court's basic decision to deviate was proper under the circumstances of this case, its reasons for doing so violate the purpose of the child support laws and were therefore an abuse of discretion.[246]

The court reasoned that its holding accurately carried out the purpose behind the state statute allowing for deviation from standard child support calculations:

> RCW 26.19.075 sets forth a nonexclusive list of grounds on which a court may deviate from the standard child support calculation. That section reads in pertinent part: "The court may deviate from the standard calculation when either or both of the parents before the court have children from other relationships to whom the parent owes a duty of support. A court must provide specific reasons for deviation in written findings of fact and the evidence must support those findings. Deviation is a discretionary matter[.] When reasons exist for deviation, the court shall exercise discretion in considering the extent to which the factors would affect the support obligation. Here, the trial court's determination that deviation was warranted based on the earnings of each party [and] the support obligations paid, received, and owed was proper in light of Samuel's income and his other significant support obligations.

---

[242] *In re J.G.*, 993 P.2d 1055, 1058 (Ariz. 1999).
[243] *Id.*
[244] *Id.*
[245] *Id.*
[246] *Bell v. Bell*, 4 P.3d 849, 851 (Wash. Ct. App. 2000).

But the court's basis for calculating the amount of deviation, i.e., Samuel's preexisting support obligations to other children, was improper. In creating a child support schedule the Legislature intended to insure that child support orders are adequate to meet a child's basic needs and to provide additional child support commensurate with the parent's income, resources, and standard of living. A [recent] case... summed up the goal of child support as follows: Child support is designed with the primary goal of preventing a harmful reduction in a child's standard of living, in the best interests of children whose parents are divorced. The Legislature has also instructed that deviations based on a parent's obligations to children from other relationships shall be based on consideration of the total circumstances of both households.[247]

The court concluded that the trial court had abused its discretion because "the court simply subtracted Samuel's other support obligations from his available net income to determine child support for Sammy and Marquese."[248]

b) Specification on Record Promotes Meaningful Appellate Review

Applying the state equivalent to Federal Rule of Civil Procedure 23, the Ohio Supreme Court partially reversed an intermediate appellate court's decision on class certification.[249] The trial court had summarily denied plaintiffs' motion for class certification, and the intermediate court reversed the trial court in part and allowed certification of some members of the prospective class. Before reaching its holding, the court explained the difficulty of reviewing Rule 23 decisions in the absence of specific findings:

> While there is no explicit requirement in Civ. R. 23 that the trial court make formal findings to support its decision on a motion for class certification, there are compelling policy reasons for doing so. Aside from the obvious practical importance, articulation of the reasons for the decision tends to provide a firm basis upon which an appellate court can determine that the trial court exercised its discretion within the framework of Civ. R. 23, and discourages reversal on the ground that the appellate judges might have decided

---

[247] *Id.* at 853.

[248] *Id.* The court continued:

> While there is no explicit requirement that courts treat each child equally, it would violate the purpose of the statute to create a situation in which two children receive less than half of their support needs solely or primarily because an earlier order granting full support to other children is already in place. Child support is not a first-come, first-served proposition.

[249] *Hamilton v. Ohio Savings Bank*, 694 N.E. 2d. 442, 459 (Ohio 1998) ("[W]e hold that this cause shall proceed as a class action, [and] that the entire class be certified with respect to all claims.").

200

differently had they been the original decisionmakers. On the other hand, the failure to provide an articulated rationale greatly hampers an appellate inquiry into whether the relevant Civ. R. 23 factors were properly applied by the trial court and given appropriate weight, and such an unarticulated decision is less likely to convince the reviewing court that the ruling was consistent with the sound exercise of discretion.

It is exceedingly difficult to apply an abuse-of-discretion standard to Civ. R. 23 determinations where, as here, the trial court fails not only to articulate its rationale, but also fails to disclose which of the seven class action prerequisites it found to be lacking with respect to the various alleged claims for relief. Accordingly, we suggest that in determining the propriety of class certification under Civ. R. 23, trial courts make separate written findings as to each of the seven class action requirements, and specify their reasoning as to each finding.[250]

c) Failure to Specify as Failure to Exercise Discretion

Reviewing the trial court's decision not to enforce a divorce settlement agreement between husband and wife, the Georgia Supreme Court reversed and remanded because the court could not determine whether the trial court had exercised its discretion in doing so.[251] Husband and wife had reached a handwritten agreement during mediation, but the wife later refused to sign the subsequent typewritten version because of her "concern with regard to the possibility that, in advising wife" her attorney "had been influenced by his close personal relationship with Husband's attorney."[252]

---

[250] *Id.* at 447–48. For another example of the "meaningful review" policy, see *State v. Francis*, 820 N.E.2d 355, 365 (Ohio 2004). The *Francis* court stated:

> [T]his court [has] acknowledged the importance of a hearing to aid in developing a record that could be examined by a reviewing court to determine whether a trial court properly exercised its discretion in ruling on a motion to withdraw a plea.... [U]nless it is clear that denial of the motion is warranted, a trial court should hold a hearing.... In some situations when a hearing should have been held, a trial court's failure to have held a hearing amounts to an abuse of discretion. We find this case to be one in which a hearing should have been held.
>
> Furthermore, the trial court's failure to specify any reasons in its journal entry denying the motion severely hampers any consideration of whether an abuse of discretion occurred. There is no specific requirement that the trial court issue findings of fact and conclusions of law. However, the failure to explain the reasoning places significant obstacles in the way of meaningful appellate review when, as here, so many variables are potentially relevant to a trial court's consideration.

Id. at 364–65.
[251] *Mathes v. Mathes*, 483 S.E.2d 573, 575 (Ga. 1997).
[252] *Id.* at 574.

The court first explained that the close relationship between the two attorneys did not deprive the wife of a legal right:

> [T]he trial court opined that Wife's attorney may have been "subconsciously unable to render [Wife] effective assistance of counsel." However, the constitutional right to effective assistance of counsel does not extend to participants in a civil dispute. A deficient performance on the part of Wife's attorney, in his capacity as her agent, would not, by itself, provide her a defense to enforcement of the settlement agreement, although it would give rise to a possible claim against him personally. Moreover, it is clear that, in this case, the enforceability of the settlement agreement is in no way dependent upon the apparent authority of Wife's attorney to bind her to that agreement, since it is undisputed that Wife herself agreed to the settlement which Husband seeks to enforce.... Thus, the possibility that Wife's attorney was influenced by his close relationship with Husband's attorney did not, without more, authorize the trial court to deny the motion to enforce the settlement agreement.[253]

The court went on to explain that it could not determine whether the trial court had exercised its discretion:

> A review of the transcript of the hearing shows... that the trial court did not address [wife's] contentions, but that it did continually express concern over the possibility that Wife's attorney was unduly influenced by Husband's attorney, and at one point, it explicitly declined to consider any issue of fairness. The final order does not specify the reason or reasons why the trial court denied Husband's motion to enforce the settlement agreement. Therefore, we cannot conclude that the trial court did, in fact, exercise its discretion to approve or reject the settlement in this divorce case. To the contrary, it appears that the trial court may not have exercised its discretion, because it was under the erroneous impression that the agreement was unenforceable merely by virtue of the relationship between the attorneys. In these circumstances, the appropriate remedy is to remand the case to the trial court....[254]

d)   Preliminary Injunctions

The relatively low level of deference that appellate courts give to decisions on preliminary injunctions requires a trial court to specify its reasons for issuing or not

---

[253] *Id.*
[254] *Id.* at 574–75.

202

issuing the injunction on the record.[255] When ruling on a preliminary injunction, a trial court normally considers four factors:

> (1) whether the plaintiff's remedies at law are inadequate, causing irreparable harm pending resolution of the substantive action; (2) whether the plaintiff has at least a reasonable likelihood of success at trial; (3) whether the plaintiff's threatened injury outweighs the potential harm to the defendant resulting from the granting of the injunction; and (4) whether the public interest will be disserved.[256]

Citing to Rule 52(a) of the Federal Rules of Civil Procedure, the Federal Circuit in *Chemlawn Services Corp. v. GNC Pumps, Inc.* adopted a Fifth Circuit holding that in the absence of specific findings of fact and conclusions of law supporting the trial court's decision, the court would remand the case.[257] Federal Rule of Civil Procedure 52(a) provides:

> In all actions tried upon the facts without a jury or with an advisory jury, the court shall find the facts specially and state separately the conclusions of law thereon, and judgment shall be entered pursuant to Rule 58; and in granting or refusing interlocutory injunctions the court shall similarly set forth both the findings of fact and conclusions of law which constitute the grounds of its action.[258]

The *Chemlawn* court applied the "meaningful review" rationale to a situation in which the trial court "eventually and belatedly entered findings of fact and conclusions of law" over two months after issuing a preliminary injunction.[259] In doing so, the court held that the belated entry "did not cure the defect of failing to do so at the time the preliminary injunction first issued and cannot retroactively legitimate that injunction."[260] Rejecting *Chemlawn's* request to allow the order to stand in the interest of "judicial economy," the court explained:

> [T]he findings of fact and conclusions of law are improper because they were entered at a time when the District Court no longer had jurisdiction over the case. Furthermore, considerations of these illegitimate findings and conclusions would be contrary to Fifth

---

[255] *See generally Chemlawn Services Corp. v. GNC Pumps, Inc.*, 823 F.2d 515 (5th Cir. 1987).
[256] *Fumo v. Med. Gr. of Mich. City Inc.*, 590 N.E.2d 1103, 1107 (Ind. Ct. App. 1992).
[257] 823 F.2d at 517. ("full and fair compliance with Rule 52(a) is one of the highest importance to a proper review of a court in granting or refusing a preliminary injunction") (internal quotation marks and citations omitted).
[258] Fed. R. Civ. P. 52(a).
[259] 823 F.2d at 517.
[260] *Id.* The court continued, "The District Court's delay in entering its findings of fact and conclusions of law is defective for another reason. By delaying... the court attempted to act at a time when it no longer had jurisdiction over the case because GNC had already filed a notice of appeal to this Court." *Id.* at 518.

Circuit law, to which we defer in this instance. It would be improper to accept, in the name of economy of judicial resources, these invalid determinations; other district courts might well be encouraged to circumvent the requirements of Rule 52(a) and enter preliminary injunctions without supporting findings of fact and conclusions of law.[261]

e)   Default Judgment

Federal Rule of Civil Procedure 60(b) provides:

> ... On motion and on upon such terms as are justice, the court may relieve a party or a party's legal representative from a final judgment, order or proceeding for the following reasons: (1) mistake, inadvertence, surprise, or excusable neglect; (2) newly discovered evidence which by due diligence could not have been discovered in time to move for a new trial under Rule 59(b); (3) fraud (whether heretofore denominated intrinsic or extrinsic), misrepresentation, or other misconduct of an adverse party; (4) the judgment is void; (5) the judgment has been satisfied, released, or discharged, or a prior judgment upon which it is based has been reversed or otherwise vacated, or it is no longer equitable that the judgment should have prospective application; or (6) any other reason justifying relief from the operation of the judgment. The motion shall be made within a reasonable time.... This rule does not limit the power of a court to entertain an independent action to relieve a party from a judgment, order, or proceeding....[262]

Appealing a default judgment in a divorce, the wife contended that relief from default was proper under Rule 60(b) because she had not received personal service regarding the husband's underlying suit.[263] The husband failed to serve the wife personally for many months, and then filed a motion seeking permission to serve by publication. The court granted the motion, the wife did not appear, and the court entered default against the wife. When the wife learned of the default some months later, she moved under Rule 60(b)(4) for relief. At the hearing on the wife's motion, the trial court concluded that "both parties were difficult to find" and had taken steps to conceal their whereabouts.[264] Because of that, the court concluded that the service by publication was appropriate and denied the wife's motion.[265]

The D.C. Court of Appeals reversed. In doing so, the court first explained the counters of the trial court's power to set aside default judgments:

---

[261] *Id.*
[262] Fed R. Civ. P. 60(b).
[263] *Cruz v. Sarmiento*, 737 A.2d 1021, 1025 (D.C. 1999).
[264] *Id.*
[265] *Id.*

204

>The power of a trial court to vacate or otherwise relieve a party from a prior judgment or order, other than merely for clerical mistakes, is circumscribed by Rule 60(b). When a timely motion is made under the rule, the decision to grant or deny it is committed to the sound discretion of the court. In exercising its discretion, the trial court must choose what is right and equitable under the circumstances and the law and state the reasons which support its conclusion. However, because there is a strong judicial presumption favoring adjudication on the merits, this court carefully reviews a trial court's refusal to set aside a default judgment....[266]

The court stated further that "despite the discretion generally afforded to trial judges when ruling on Rule 60(b) motions, this court must reverse when confronted with a denial of a motion to vacate if it decides that the judgment is void for lack of sufficient service of process."[267] The court reversed for abuse of discretion on the ground that service by publication was void because the plaintiff had not made the requisite showing under the so-called *Bearstop* factors.[268]

f)   Dismissal as a Discovery Sanction

Although a trial court normally enjoys wide discretion to regulate discovery, appellate courts may take a narrower view of that discretion when the trial court's discovery sanctions include severe remedies like dismissal of the case. A leading case in this regard is *Wilson v. Volkswagen of America*.[269] In *Wilson*, the trial court

---

[266] *Id.* at 1025–26.

[267] *Id.* at 1026.

[268] *Id.* at 1027. Quoting *Bearstop v. Bearstop*, 377 A.2d 405, 408 (D.C. 1977), the court identified the "additional information" "a plaintiff in a divorce proceeding must furnish" "before an order authorizing substituted service may be entered":

>(1) the time and place at which the parties last resided together as spouses; (2) the last time the parties were in contact with each other; (3) the name and address of the last employer of the defendant either during the time the parties resided together or at a later time if known to the plaintiff; (4) the names and addresses of those relatives known to be close to the defendant; and (5) any other information which could furnish a fruitful basis for further inquiry by one truly bent on learning the present whereabouts of the defendant.

Id.
Sarmiento pertained to a Rule 60(b)(4) motion. In a Rule 60(b)(2) context, the Sixth Circuit reiterated its abuse of discretion review but made no mention of a requirement that the trial court justify its decision on the record. *Gould v. Wood/Chuck Chipper Corp.*, 229 F.3d 1151 (6th Cir. 2000) *available at* 2000 WL 1234334. The *Gould* court's opinion implied further that the court would not reverse a denial of a Rule 60(b)(6) motion absent "extraordinary circumstances." *Id.*

[269] *See generally* 561 F.2d 494 (4th Cir. 1977) (products liability) (finding an abuse of discretion and reversing trial court's default judgment as a sanction for a discovery violation).

imposed a default judgment against defendant Volkswagen when it failed to comply with a discovery request. (The record indicated that plaintiff had also been less than diligent about complying with defendant's discovery requests.)

The Fourth Circuit offered the following explanation as to why a trial court must justify its actions on the record when it imposes severe discovery sanctions on a party:

> The power to impose sanctions under Rule 37(b) for failure, after court order in discovery proceedings to produce documents, is discretionary with the Trial Court. It is not, however, a discretion without bounds or limits but one to be exercised discreetly and never when it has been established that failure to comply has been due to inability, and not to willfulness, bad faith, or any fault of [the non-complying party]. Particularly is the Court to act cautiously when the sanction imposed is that of default judgment, which is the most severe in the spectrum of sanctions provided by statute or rule. In that situation the Trial Court's range of discretion is more narrow than when the Court is imposing other less severe sanctions. The reason for this narrower range of discretion is that the sanction of a default judgment, though a rational method of enforcement of the discovery rules, in an appropriate case, represents in effect an infringement upon a party's right to trial by jury under the seventh amendment and runs counter to sound public policy of deciding cases on their merits, and against depriving a party of his fair day in court. Because of the importance of these constitutional and policy considerations, a leading text has stated that the exercise of the power should be confined to the flagrant case in which it is demonstrated that the failure to produce materially affect(s) the substantial rights of the adverse party and is prejudicial to the representation of his case. This is so because a default judgment should normally not be imposed so as to foreclose the merits of controversies as punishment for general misbehavior save in that rare case where the conduct represents such flagrant bad faith and callous disregard of the party's obligation under the Rules as to warrant the sanction not simply for the purpose of preventing prejudice to the discovering party but as a necessary deterrent to others. Even in those cases where it may be found that failure to produce results in the discovering party's being jeopardized or prejudiced, it is the normal rule that the proper sanction must be no more severe . . . than is necessary to prevent prejudice to the movant. Accordingly, in determining whether to impose such sanction, the needs of the discovery party must be evaluated as well as the nature of the non-compliance and the Trial Court must consider how the absence of such evidence [not produced] would impair [the other party's] ability to establish their case and whether the non-complying party's conduct [in not

producing documents] would deprive [the other party] of a fair trial. And since every exercise of judicial discretion must find its basis in good reason, the Trial Court, when granting such sanction, should clearly state its reasons so that meaningful review may be had on appeal.[270]

In *In re Spear*, the Third Circuit considered the validity of the Tax Court's partial judgment with prejudice against a taxpayer for failure to comply with an IRS subpoena for her testimony.[271] The record showed that the taxpayer suffered serious mental problems in April 1991. Accordingly, the Commissioner sought to videotape taxpayer's deposition in July 1991, contending that her condition could prevent her from testifying at trial. The court eventually ordered the deposition, and taxpayer complied without suffering mental trauma. Thereafter, the Commissioner sought to compel taxpayer's presence at trial. The week before trial, taxpayer notified the Commissioner that, given her prior deposition and her mental condition, she would not testify. After the taxpayer failed to appear in defiance of a court order, the Tax Court imposed sanctions, resolving several contested issues of fact in favor of the Commissioner. The Third Circuit acknowledged that, with respect to the Tax Court's finding of taxpayer fraud, "the imposition of sanctions may well have been critically important to the result."[272]

The court first reviewed United States Supreme Court precedent requiring that "the sanction of deeming facts to be established" be 1) just and 2) "related to the particular claim which was at issue in the order to provide discovery."[273] Concluding that the High Court had "not elaborated on or applied" its standard, the Third Circuit turned to its own precedent:

> In [*Ali v. Sims*, 788 F.2d 954 (1986)], we held that where a district court sanctioned defendants by deeming allegations in plaintiff's complaint to be admitted and granted summary judgment for plaintiff, the ruling was equivalent to a default judgment and thus required application of the standards we had set for issuing a sanction of dismissal. More specifically, we held in *Ali* that, under the factors we had articulated... the sanctions constituted an abuse of discretion. In [*Poulis v. State Farm Fire & Casualty Co.*, 747 F.2d 863 (3d Cir. 1984)] we had explained that our review of a district court's dismissal with prejudice is guided by the manner in which the trial court balanced [six] factors... and whether the record supports its findings. The six factors are:

---

[270] *Id.* at 503–05.

[271] 41 F.3d 103, 105 (3rd Cir. 1994) (limiting the court's discussion to the validity of the Tax Court's sanction) (noting that the "sanction was a linchpin of the tax court's decision").

[272] *Id.* at 108.

[273] *Id.* at 109 (quoting *Ins. Corp. of Ireland v. Compagnie Des Bauxites*, 456 U.S. 694, 707 (1982)).

(1) the extent of the party's personal responsibility; (2) the prejudice to the adversary caused by the failure to meet scheduling orders and respond to discovery; (3) a history of dilatoriness; (4) whether the conduct of the party or the attorney was willful or in bad faith; (5) the effectiveness of sanctions other than dismissal which entails an analysis of alternative sanctions; and (6) the meritoriousness of the claim or defense.

In *Ali* we applied these factors to reverse a sanction deeming certain facts to be true. We held that, even if there was inexcusable delay by the defendants in that case, there was no bad faith, no history of dilatoriness, little prejudice from the delay that was caused, and less severe sanctions were probably available. Under those circumstances, sanctions that were equivalent to dismissal constituted an abuse of discretion. We explained that, in *Poulis*, we established the strong presumption against sanctions that decide the issues of a case.[274]

The court distinguished *Ali* because "the tax court's sanction did not end the case," but, at the most, "the tax court deemed certain key facts admitted and reversed the burden of proof."[275] The court explained that while "this is a severe sanction," "it is not the same as deeming allegations in a complaint to be admitted or granting a default judgment."[276] The court therefore applied a standard of review that afforded more deference to the trial court, stating that it would uphold the decision if it's independent "weighing and balancing exercise" resulted in the conclusion that the sanction was "just."[277] Employing an approach more generous to the trial court's decision, the court concluded that the Tax Court need not have made a finding of willfulness or bad faith before imposing the sanction that it did.[278] The court explained further:

---

[274] *Id.* at 109–10.

[275] *Id.* at 110.

[276] *Id.*

[277] *Id.* at 111. The court stated,

> In sum, in reviewing a trial court order deeming evidence admitted as a sanction for litigation misconduct, we will engage in a weighing and balancing exercise in which we consider: (1) culpability (including willfulness and bad faith, and whether the client was responsible or solely the attorney); (2) prejudice; and (3) whether lesser sanctions would have been effective. In making the actual balancing we utilize a sliding scale, so that bad faith, for example[,] will have to be quite high to tip the balance if other factors strongly favor the taxpayers.

Id.

[278] *Id.* at 112 ("Although we have held that dismissals are an extreme sanction reserved for cases... where there was flagrant bad faith, we have sometimes upheld a court's sanction of dismissal even when there was no willfulness or bad faith.").

208

Although... we do not have to decide the issue, we assume that, when the sanction of deeming facts to be true is not the equivalent of dismissal, willfulness and bad faith are not prerequisites for imposing that sanction. When a party does not provide information to another party to which that party is entitled, a court is certainly permitted to "even out" the proceedings by shifting a burden of proof in a fair way even in the absence of bad faith. Moreover, in *Insurance Corp. of Ireland*, the Supreme Court upheld a sanction of deeming facts to be established even though the court had made no explicit finding of bad faith, finding repeated violations of discovery orders to constitute sufficient fault to justify the sanction.

Nonetheless, the presence of willfulness and bad faith certainly enhances the case for sanctions. Shifting the burden of proof, as the tax court seems to have done here when it deemed certain facts to be established, is a fairly extreme sanction. It significantly changes the likely outcome at trial. In the absence of willfulness or bad faith, other factors have to weigh strongly in the favor of such a severe sanction to justify it.[279]

Apparently dedeciding that the other factors in the case did not weigh strongly in favor of the Tax Court's sanction, the court concluded that the Tax Court had abused its discretion in imposing it.[280]

---

[279] *Id.*

[280] *Id.* at 116–17. The Texas Court of Appeals gave little deference to a trial court when it imposed sanctions on a defendant law firm in an action to recover a legal fee with a legal malpractice counterclaim, *Carlton Firm v. Elwakil*, No. 05-98-00379-CV, 2000 WL 378521, at *2 (Tex. App. Mar. 31, 2000).

> The decision to impose sanctions is within the sound discretion of the trial judge, and we will set aside that decision only upon a showing of a clear abuse of discretion. In awarding sanctions, a trial court must state in its order the particular reasons for granting sanctions. This requirement serves two purposes: (1) it invites the trial court to reflect carefully on its order before imposing sanctions and (2) it informs the party of the offensive conduct so that he can refrain from committing the same or similar conduct in the future. The failure to comply with this requirement constitutes an abuse of discretion and renders the order unenforceable.

> ... The trial court did not give any reasons for issuing the sanctions order or otherwise describe the particular conduct that warranted sanctions. The trial court's failure to specify its reasons in the sanctions order constitutes an abuse of discretion and renders the sanctions order unenforceable. Further, contrary to Elwakil's assertion that this error was not preserved, Carlton specifically pointed out this lack of particularity in a motion for a new trial. Under the facts of this case, Carlton preserved the right to complain of the sanctions order defect....

g)   Trial in Absentia

Deciding whether a rape defendant, who had failed to appear at a pretrial hearing and did not appear during the following two years, had been "deprived of his constitutional and statutory right to be present at his trial," the intermediate appellate court in New York employed a two-part analysis.[281] First, the court asked whether there was "evidence" that defendant "was aware that a trial would proceed in his absence."[282] The court stated further that "it must also appear from the record that [the] County Court considered the appropriate factors including, *inter alia*, the possibility of locating defendant within a reasonable period of time before it exercised its discretion to try defendant in absentia."[283] Finding that the trial court had satisfied both prongs of the analysis, the court held that the trial court had not abused its discretion.[284]

h)   Appointed Counsel

Indiana courts have had the opportunity to address the amount of discretion a trial court has to deny an indigent party the right to appointed counsel. In *Moore v. State*, defendant Moore appealed his conviction on charges stemming from drug activity because the trial court denied him the right to appointed counsel.[285] The prosecutor had objected to defendant's request for appointed counsel because he was "employed and apparently a part owner in a business."[286] The trial court denied defendant's motion "without any further inquiry as to defendant's actual income or the amount of equity defendant had in his home or the drilling equipment."[287] At trial, defendant had his pastor represent him, and the pastor presented a defense that defendant had been "born again" and had changed his life. The jury didn't buy it, perhaps given the "innumerable instances during the trial of irregularities caused by the legal inexperience" of the pastor.[288]

In reversing the trial court's refusal to appoint counsel, the court explained:

Id. at *1–2.

[281] *People v. Sumner*, 681 N.Y.S.2d 611, 612 (N.Y. App. Div. 1998).

[282] *Id.*

[283] *Id.*

[284] *Id.* ("The fact that the People discovered defendant's whereabouts through his sister's subpoenaed telephone records shortly after the sentencing does not diminish the reasonableness of their previous efforts.").

[285] *See generally* 401 N.E.2d 676 (Ind. 1980).

[286] *Id.* at 677.

[287] *Id.* On defendant's request for reconsideration in light of his allegedly changed financial circumstances, the trial court again denied defendant's request for counsel because "defendant did own real estate and had some equity in that as well as in [some well-drilling] equipment." *Id.* at 678. "However, there [was] no evidence in the record of the actual amount of equity defendant had and there is no evidence of any attempt to evaluate defendant's income or total assets and liabilities." *Id.*

[288] *Id.*

There is no doubt that we are dealing here with one of the most fundamental of our constitutional guarantees. A defendant charged with a crime is guaranteed the right to be represented by counsel [by the state and federal constitutions]. A failure to permit a defendant to have counsel amounts to a denial of due process, and there can be no valid criminal trial unless a defendant is represented by counsel if he desires counsel.

The guarantee of the right to be represented by counsel includes the right for an indigent defendant in a criminal prosecution to have counsel provided for him at state expense. It is a judicial function to determine whether counsel shall be appointed at public expense, and this determination is within the sound discretion of the trial judge. While it is not possible to set specific monetary guidelines which would determine a defendant's indigency, there are several factors which must be considered. Since we are dealing with such a fundamental constitutional right, the record in each case must show that careful consideration commensurate with the right at stake has been given to the defendant....

First, it appears clear that the defendant does not have to be totally without means to be entitled to counsel. If he legitimately lacks the financial resources to employ an attorney, without imposing substantial hardship on himself or his family, the court must appoint counsel to defend him.

The determination as to the defendant's indigency is not to be made on a superficial examination of income and ownership of property but must be based on as thorough an examination of the defendant's total financial picture as is practical. The record must show that the determination of ability to pay includes a balancing of assets against liabilities and a consideration of the amount of the defendant's disposable income or other resources reasonably available to him after the payment of his fixed or certain obligations. The fact that the defendant was able to post a bond is not determinative of his non-indigency but is only a factor to be considered. The court's duty to appoint competent counsel arises at any stage of the proceedings when the defendant's indigency causes him to be without the assistance of counsel.[289]

The court concluded that "the record" did not "show an adequate determination of the factual question of defendant's ability to afford counsel prior to trial" and reversed for abuse of discretion.[290]

---

[289] *Id.* at 678–79.

[290] *Id.* at 679. ("There is nothing in the record to show a balancing of defendant's assets against his liabilities and a consideration of the amount of defendant's disposable income or other resources reasonably available to him.").

Judge Pivarnik dissented, arguing that "defendant did not come forward with any figures or facts to show that" his "assets would not, in fact, pay an attorney to defend him."[291] Arguing in support of the trial judge's discretionary decision, Judge Pivarnik explained:

> Probably most people in our society who have real and personal assets and a regular income have difficulty in raising money to meet particular obligations. They must budget carefully and choose priorities to sustain themselves and their families in the midst of difficult economic problems. They should not be required, through the use of their contributions to the public funds, to pay for the obligations of someone who is allowed to retain his own assets rather than liquidate them to meet his own obligations.[292]

Under Indiana statute, indigent civil litigants may have court-appointed counsel as well.[293] The Indiana Supreme Court interpreted the 34-10-1-2 in *Sholes v. Sholes*, a

---

[291] *Id.* at 680 (Pivarnik, J., dissenting). (finding significant the fact that defendant "hired paid counsel to bring this appeal).

[292] *Id.* (Pivarnik, J., dissenting).

[293] Ind. Code § 34-10-1-2 provides:

(b) If the court is satisfied that a person who makes an application... does not have sufficient means to prosecute or defend the action, the court:

(1) shall admit the applicant to prosecute or defend as an indigent person; and

(2) may, under exceptional circumstances, assign an attorney to defend or prosecute the cause.

(c) The factors that a court may consider under subsection (b)(2) include the following:

(1) The likelihood of the applicant prevailing on the merits of the applicant's claim or defense.

(2) The applicant's ability to investigate and present the applicant's claims or defenses without an attorney, given the type and complexity of the facts and legal issues in the action

(d) The court shall deny an application... if the court determines any of the following:

(1) The applicant failed to make a diligent effort to obtain an attorney before filing the application.

(2) The applicant is unlikely to prevail on the applicant's claim or defense.

divorce case. Husband had filed for appointment of counsel, and the trial court denied the motion "without making any findings."[294] Although the court agreed that "the statute does not confer discretion on the trial court to deny counsel,"[295] it followed its holding in *Moore v. State* with respect to the trial court's requisite finding of "indigence" under section b of the statute.[296] In doing so, the court concluded that the "determination as to the defendant's indigency is not to be made on a superficial examination of income and ownership of property but must be based on as thorough an examination of the defendant's total financial picture as is practical."[297] The court explained further:

> Whether the applicant has "sufficient means" goes beyond a mere snapshot of the applicant's financial status. Rather, the court must examine the applicant's status in relation to the type of action before it. If the action is of the kind that is often handled by persons of means without counsel, the court may find that even an indigent applicant has "sufficient means" to proceed without appointed counsel. For example, many forms of small claims actions are typically prosecuted and defended *pro se* even by persons of means. Similarly, cases that have their own ability to fund counsel are another general category where appointed counsel may be inappropriate. The marketplace for lawyer services can value cases often handled on a contingent fee basis. The same is true of litigation governed by fee shifting statutes. In these cases, an indigent may well be found to have sufficient means to prosecute or defend the action.

The statute has been found unconstitutional insofar as it requires attorneys to represent indigents without compensation. *See generally Sholes v. Sholes*, 760 N.E.2d 156 (Ind. 2001).

[294] 760 N.E.2d at 158.

[295] *Id.* at 159. The court stated further:

> We agree with the Court of Appeals that the statute does not confer discretion on the trial court to deny counsel. And, as explained below, amici are correct that the Indiana Constitution requires that appointed counsel be compensated. However, in the absence of any legislatively prescribed source of funding, a court's ability to direct that counsel be appointed is circumscribed by the doctrines surrounding the court's ability to order the expenditure of public funds. Ultimately, then, the decision to appoint counsel for an indigent litigant in a civil case turns on the court's assessment of the nature of the case, the genuineness of the issues, and any other factors that bear on the wisdom of mandating public funds for that purpose.

Id.

[296] *Id.* at 161.

[297] *Id.* ("The record must show that the determination of ability to pay includes a balancing of assets against liabilities and a consideration of the amount of the defendant's disposable income or other resources reasonably available to him after the payment of his fixed or certain obligations.").

We do not mean to create blanket categories of cases in which counsel should never be appointed. Rather, the court should look to the particular issues presented in the action and make a determination of whether the indigent applicant requires appointed counsel. A routine landlord-tenant dispute may present such straightforward issues that the ordinary litigant requires no counsel. In such a dispute, the indigent applicant has "sufficient means" to prosecute or defend the action without appointed counsel. On the other hand, the same dispute might present complexities or involve such significant precedent that proceeding pro se would disadvantage the ordinary litigant, and appointed counsel may be appropriate.[298]

i) Restraints and the Role of Harmless Error

Hearing defendant's appeal from a conviction on charges related to a robbery, the Connecticut Supreme Court reaffirmed the trial court's discretion to order a defendant restrained by shackles or other means.[299] After the first day of trial, the court informed defendant that he would wear shackles around his ankles for the remainder of the trial. When defendant asked for an explanation, the court simply stated that it had a right to order defendant restrained "based upon reliable information received from law enforcement officers or correctional officers" and that it had "received information" to that effect.[300] The court allowed defendant to testify without shackles, excused the jury whenever defendant entered or left the courtroom, and ordered both counsel tables covered with brown paper so that the jury would not see the restraints.[301] In response to defendant's argument that the record did "not establish the existence of a reasonable necessity to support the court's decision to shackle him" and thus denied him a fair trial, the court first explained the law governing the use of restraints in the courtroom:

As a general proposition, a criminal defendant has the right to appear in court free from physical restraints.... Grounded in the common law, this right evolved in order to preserve the presumption favoring a criminal defendant's innocence, while eliminating any detrimental effects to the defendant that could result if he were physically restrained in the courtroom. The presumption of innocence, although not articulated in the Constitution, is a basic component of a fair trial under our system of criminal justice. Nonetheless, a defendant's right to appear before the jury unfettered is not absolute. A trial court may employ a reasonable means of restraint upon a defendant if, exercising its

[298] Id.
[299] See generally State v. Tweedy, 594 A.2d 906 (Conn. 1991) (finding an abuse of discretion but affirming based on the harmless error doctrine).
[300] Id. at 914.
[301] Id.

broad discretion in such matters, the court finds that restraints are reasonably necessary under the circumstances.

In reviewing a shackling claim, our task is to determine whether the court's decision to employ restraints constituted a clear abuse of discretion. While appellate review is greatly aided when a court develops the record by conducting an evidentiary hearing concerning the necessity for restraints, such hearing is not mandatory. A record in some fashion disclosing the justification for using restraints, however, is essential to meaningful appellate review of a shackling claim. This is particularly so because of the potential for prejudice in the use of shackles. Accordingly, a trial court must ensure that its reasons for ordering the use of restraints are detailed in the record.[302]

After concluding that the trial court had "denied the defendant a meaningful opportunity" to contest his shackling and had not developed the record adequately, the court indicated that it would affirm because there was "no evidence in the record that the jury saw or otherwise knew of the defendant's restraints."[303] In doing so, the court explained the harmless error doctrine as applied to decisions about leg restraints:

In order for a criminal defendant to enjoy the maximum benefit of the presumption of innocence, our courts make every reasonable effort to present the defendant before the jury in a manner that does not suggest, expressly or impliedly, that he or she is a dangerous character whose guilt is a foregone conclusion. There is no doubt that the sight of shackles and gags might have a significant effect on the jury's feelings about the defendant. The negative connotations of restraints, nevertheless, are without significance unless the fact of the restraints comes to the attention of the jury. As the present record is devoid of competent evidence that the jury was aware of the defendant's shackles at any time during his trial, it is clear beyond a reasonable doubt that the presumption of innocence was not abridged by the court's decision to shackle him.[304]

j) Motions for a New Trial

Federal Rules of Civil Procedure Rule 59 provides:

---

[302] *Id.* at 914–15.

[303] *Id.* at 915.

[304] *Id.* at 915–16. *See also Cox v. State*, 931 S.W.2d 349, 352 (Tex. App. 1996) (finding an abuse of discretion for failure to specify reasons for restraints but holding that the error was harmless because the "sole evidence that jurors even noticed the device" was that they sent the judge a question about it during deliberations).

(d) On Court's Initiative, Notice, Specifying Grounds. No later than 10 days after entry of judgment the court, on its own, may order a new trial for any reason that would justify granting one on a party's motion. After giving the parties notice and an opportunity to be heard, the court may grant a timely motion for a new trial for a reason not stated in the motion. When granting a new trial on its own initiative or for a reason not stated in a motion, the court shall specify the grounds in its order.[305]

The California Code of Civil Procedure's provision governing new trials provides that whenever "a new trial is granted, on all or part of the issues, the court shall specify the ground or grounds upon which it is granted and the court's reason or reasons for granting the new trial upon each ground stated."[306]

The granting of a new trial does not *ipso facto* require a trial court to specify its reasons for doing so on the record. In *Clementi v. Procacci*, the Superior Court of Pennsylvania explained how specifying reasons could in fact mean that the trial court's decision gets less deference from an appellate court:

> When reviewing an order granting a new trial, a matter within the discretion of the trial court, we are called upon initially to determine whether the trial court would have ordered a new trial for any other reason but the one cited. If the trial court would have granted a new trial for reasons other than those it cited, a broad scope of review applies. In that situation, we examine the entire record, and using an abuse of discretion standard, we must affirm if there is any valid reason in the record for granting a new trial.

> However, where, as here, it is apparent that the reason given by the trial court is the only basis upon which it ordered a new trial, a narrower scope of review applies. In such a case, using an abuse of discretion standard, we examine only the stated reason the trial court ordered the new trial. Thus, if the trial court specifies the reasons for which it ordered a new trial, then an appellate court can only affirm the decision if at least one of the reasons specified is an adequate one.[307]

k)   Amendment of Complaint

Some states require that a trial court, although acting within its discretion when doing so, must specify its reasons for denying a motion to amend a pleading. The Michigan Court of Appeals held as such in *Terhaar v. Hoekwater*.[308] Compiling its

---

[305] Fed. R. Civ. P. 82(b).
[306] Cal. Civ. Pro. Code § 657 (West 2005).
[307] *Clementi v. Procacci*, 762 A.2d 1086, 1090 (Pa. Super. Ct. 2000).
[308] 452 N.W.2d 905, 907 (Mich. Ct. App. 1990).

own precedents and those of the Michigan and United States supreme courts, the court explained its position:

> In *Ben P. Fyke & Sons v. Gunter Co.*, 390 Mich. 649213 N.W.2d 134 (1973), our Supreme Court set forth the policy for amendment of pleadings. The Court stated:
>
> "Our rule... as the Federal rule, is designed to facilitate the amendment of pleadings except where prejudice to the opposing party would result. A motion to amend ordinarily should be granted and denied only for particularized reasons[.]
>
> In the absence of any apparent or declared reason—such as undue delay, bad faith or dilatory motive on the part of the movant, repeated failure to cure deficiencies by amendments previously allowed, undue prejudice to the opposing party by virtue of allowance of the amendment, futility of amendment, etc. —the leave sought should, as the rules require, be "freely given."
>
> ....
>
> To safeguard and implement the policy favoring amendment, this Court has directed that upon denial of a motion to amend such exercise of discretion should be supported by specific findings as to *reasons* for the same."
>
> The discretion confided to trial judges under the standard, "leave shall be freely given when justice so requires," is not boundless. In *Burg v. B & B Enterprises*, 2 Mich. App. 496, 500, 140 N.W.2d 788 (1966), Judge (now Justice) T.G. Kavanagh wrote, "[W]e believe that [this] language... imposes a limitation on the discretion of the court necessitating a finding that justice would not be served by the amendment."
>
> While admittedly the parameters of the judge's discretion are incapable of being precisely delineated, a judge abuses this discretion when he utilizes it to obviate a recognized claim or defense.
>
> A court must specify one of the *Fyke* reasons in its denial, and a failure to do so constitutes error requiring a reversal unless such amendment would be futile.
>
> ....
>
> On the record before us, we find that the trial court abused its discretion in denying plaintiff's motion to amend her complaint. First, the trial court failed to find that justice would not be served

by the amendment. Second, the court's ruling obviated a recognized claim in the absence of actual prejudice to defendant.[309]

l) *Forum Non Conveniens*

After reaffirming its precedent that trial courts hearing a motion to dismiss on *forum non conveniens* grounds should defer to the trial court and that defendant had the burden of showing that such grounds exist, the New Mexico Supreme Court explained its requirement that the trial court should justify decisions on *forum non conveniens* with clear findings on the record:

> The trial court has broad discretion in deciding a motion to dismiss based on forum non conveniens. On appellate review, the trial court may be reversed only when there has been a clear abuse of discretion; where the court has considered all relevant public and private interest factors, and where its balancing of these factors is reasonable, its decision deserves substantial deference. In order for the appellate court to effectively determine whether the trial court should make findings and conclusions supporting its ruling on the forum non conveniens motion, either set out in writing or clearly stated in the record. The court below did not clearly state the rationale for its ruling on the motion to dismiss, but because it did not have the benefit of this opinion we will—in this case—resolve the forum non conveniens issues ourselves. Ordinarily, however, it will be considered an abuse of discretion if the court summarily grants or denies a motion to dismiss on forum non conveniens grounds without oral or written explanation or if the court does not supply specific reasons and develop adequate facts to support its decision.[310]

§ 3.5. Lip Service Obeisance to the Trial Court

a)   Lip Service Obeisance as Distinct from "Court Must Show Compliance" Standard

In a criminal case raising a double jeopardy issue, the Wisconsin Supreme Court held that a trial court must exercise "'sound discretion' in concluding that the State satisfied its burden of showing a 'manifest necessity' for the mistrial" when defense counsel objected to the state's motion for mistrial.[311] In the first trial, the state moved for mistrial following defense counsel's opening statement to the jury, in which he allegedly violated an order *in limine* by alluding to the prior bad acts of the state's key witnesses. The trial court granted the motion, and the state retried the case. The jury convicted Seefeldt of possession of marijuana. On defendant's

---

[309] *Id.* at 906–07.
[310] *Marchman v. NCNB Texas Nat. Bank*, 898 P.2d 709, 721 (N.M. 1995) (affirming the trial court's decision to dismiss on *forum non conveniens*).
[311] *State v. Seefeldt*, 661 N.W.2d 822, 830 (Wis. 2003).

petition for postconviction relief, the intermediate appellate court held that the second trial violated double jeopardy. In doing so, "the court determined that it should give strict and searching scrutiny to the [trial] court's mistrial order because the mistrial request was made by the prosecutor over the objection of the defense."[312]

The Wisconsin Supreme Court affirmed. In doing so, the court first emphasized the importance of the defendant's constitutional right to avoid being tried twice for the same offense:

> The protection against double jeopardy limits the ability of the State to request that a trial be terminated and restarted. This protection is important because the unrestricted ability of the State to terminate and restart a trial increases the financial and emotional burden on the defendant, extends the period during which the defendant is stigmatized by an unresolved accusation of wrongdoing and may increase the risk that an innocent defendant may be convicted.
>
> However, the prohibition against retrial is not a mechanical rule to be applied to prevent any second trial after the first trial is terminated prior to judgment. We have recognized that criminal trials can be complicated and lengthy. Numerous technical or otherwise unforeseen eventualities may arise that necessitate terminating a trial. Treating the prohibition against retrial as a mechanical rule that prevents a second trial in all circumstances would be too high a price to pay for the added assurance of personal security and freedom from governmental harassment which such a mechanical rule would provide.
>
> A defendant's right to have his or her trial concluded by a particular tribunal can be, under certain circumstances, subordinated to the public interest in affording the State one full and fair opportunity to present its evidence to an impartial jury. Nevertheless, given the importance of the constitutional protection against double jeopardy, the State bears the burden of demonstrating a "manifest necessity" for any mistrial ordered over the objection of the defendant.... "Manifest necessity" means a "high degree" of necessity.[313]

---

[312] *Id.* At 826. ("According to the court, there was no showing of a manifest necessity because evidence regarding the existence of the 15 warrants ultimately would have been admissible during trial.") ("Thus, the jury was not tainted and there was no manifest necessity to terminate the trial.").

[313] *Id.* at 828.

The court then addressed the "level of deference that attends a circuit court's mistrial order."[314]

Discussing the United States Supreme Court's precedent in *Arizona v. Washington*,[315] the court commented on the difficulty with applying a uniform "level of deference" to all mistrial motions:

> In discussing the appropriate level of deference to apply in reviewing the mistrial order, the Washington court noted that the question of whether a manifest necessity has been shown is answered more easily in some kinds of cases than in others. It described two ends of the spectrum of deference. At one end are those cases in which the basis for the mistrial is the unavailability of critical prosecution evidence or there is reason to believe that the prosecutor is using the State's superior resources to harass the defendant or to achieve a tactical advantage. In such cases, an appellate court applies the strictest scrutiny to a trial judge's mistrial order.
>
> At the other end of the spectrum are cases in which the basis for the mistrial is the trial judge's belief that the jury is unable to reach a verdict. Often in such cases, the jury has been unable to reach a verdict after protracted and exhausting deliberations. Great deference is accorded to a trial court's exercise of discretion because the trial judge is best able to assess the risk that a verdict may result from pressures inherent in the situation rather than the considered judgment of all the jurors.
>
> Having described the ends of the spectrum, the Washington court then returned to the case before it in which the mistrial was ordered because defense counsel made improper comments during his opening statement. It determined that the situation before the trial judge was similar to a deadlocked jury. The court stated that it was persuaded that, along the spectrum of trial problems which may warrant a mistrial and which vary in their amenability to appellate scrutiny, the difficulty which led to the mistrial in this case also falls in an area where the trial judge's determination is entitled to special respect.
>
> However, the conclusion that the trial judge's decision was entitled to great deference did not end the inquiry. Rather, because of the constitutional implications of double jeopardy, the Washington court recognized its obligation to satisfy itself that the trial judge

---

[314] *Id.* ("We ultimately concluded, however, that regardless of the level of deference to be applied in this case, the [trial] court did not exercise sound discretion in ordering the mistrial.").
[315] 434 U.S. 497 (1978).

220

exercised "sound discretion" in declaring a mistrial. The court concluded that sound discretion was exercised. The trial judge had not acted hastily in response to the prosecutor's request for a mistrial. Rather, he gave both defense counsel and the prosecutor a full opportunity to explain their positions. The court found that the trial judge acted responsibly and deliberately, and accorded careful consideration to the [defendant's] interest in having the trial concluded in a single proceeding.[316]

The court then explained the meaning of "sound discretion":

Sound discretion means acting in a rational and responsible manner. Sound discretion includes, without limitation, acting in a deliberate manner taking sufficient time in responding to a prosecutor's request for a mistrial. It requires giving both parties a full opportunity to explain their positions and considering alternatives such as a curative instruction or sanctioning counsel. Sound discretion is not exercised when a [trial] court fails to consider the facts of record under relevant law, bases its conclusion on an error of law or does not reason its way to a rational conclusion.

Sound discretion also requires that the trial judge ensure that the record reflects there is an adequate basis for a finding of manifest necessity. As such, sound discretion is more than a review to ensure the absence of a mistake of law or fact. Rather, a review for sound discretion encompasses an assurance that an adequate basis for the finding of manifest necessity is on the record.[317]

The court found "two reasons" for holding that the trial court did not exercise sound discretion when granting the mistrial.[318] "First, the existence of [prior bad acts] would likely have been admissible during trial and the record does not reflect that the judge considered whether the evidence would ultimately be admissible."[319] "Second, the trial judge did not provide sufficient opportunity for the parties to present, and for the judge to consider, arguments regarding whether a mistrial should be ordered and the possible alternatives to a mistrial."[320]

A party has great leeway to continue a summary judgment motion in order to conduct additional discovery. Federal Rule of Civil Procedure 56(f) provides:

When Affidavits are Unavailable. Should it appear from the affidavits of a party opposing the motion that the party cannot for

[316] *Id.* at 829–30.
[317] *Id.* at 830–31.
[318] *Id.* at 831.
[319] *Id.*
[320] *Id.*

reasons stated present by affidavit facts essential to justify the party's opposition, the court may refuse the application for judgment or may order a continuance to permit affidavits to be obtained or depositions to be taken or discovery to be had or may make such other order as is just.[321]

The Fifth Circuit held that a trial court abused its discretion when it granted summary judgment while making no mention of plaintiff Tonnas's Rule 56(f) motion in its thirty—five word order.[322] The court explained that although "an abuse of discretion standard leaves a district court with a certain amount of freedom" "such discretion to deny the requested extension is not entirely unfettered."[323] The court explained that a "continuance for a motion for summary judgment for purposes of discovery should be granted almost as a matter of course [unless] the non-moving party has not diligently pursued discovery."[324] After noting that plaintiff appeared to satisfy a four-prong test that the Fifth Circuit had previously established, the court concluded that the trial court had "abused its discretion" by failing to include in its terse order an explanation for its holding with respect to plaintiff's Rule 56(f) motion:

> Even assuming, however, that a case may be made for denying the rule 56(f) motion, the district court failed to mention it. Its grant of the summary judgment contained no reference to the request for a delay in the summary judgment. Although a court has discretion to deny a rule 56(f) motion and could reason that Tonnas has failed to meet one of *International Shortstop*'s requirements, the court's reasoning normally should appear, in some form, in the judicial record. The fact that Tonnas apparently met all the requirements to receive a rule 56(f) extension makes the lack of a record of reasons for denying the extension even more perplexing. By acting without indicating why it apparently denied the otherwise valid rule 56(f) motion, the court abused its discretion.[325]

b)   The Separation of Powers and Lip Service Obeisance

The controversial case of Terri Schiavo, a woman of diminished capacity whose husband wished to remove her feeding tube against the wishes of her parents, reached a climax when the Florida Supreme Court reviewed Governor Jeb Bush's executive order to allow the governor to issue a "one-time stay to prevent the withholding of nutrition and hydration."[326] The order had been carefully crafted to

---

[321] Fed. R. Civ. P. 56(f).

[322] *Tonnas v. Stonebridge Life Ins. Co.*, 78 Fed. Appx. 966, 967 (5th Cir. 2003) (noting the courts "reluctance" to substitute its "judgment for that of the district court on matters such as this").

[323] *Id.* at 968.

[324] *Id.*

[325] *Id.*

[326] *Bush v. Schiavo*, 885 So. 2d 321, 328.

apply only to Ms. Schiavo and followed on the heels of a trial court order requiring that her feeding tube be removed. The trial court's order had been affirmed on appeal. The executive order also appeared to require the court to appoint a *guardian ad litem*, a function traditionally within the discretion of the trial court.[327]

The court focused on the issuance of the stay itself and concluded that Governor Bush's executive order as applied to Schiavo was an unconstitutional encroachment on the judicial branch.[328] The court quoted its precedent that the point of an independent judiciary was to prevent popular whim—under the guise of legislative enactments—should divest people of their legal rights as determined in a judicial proceeding.[329] The court also cited an advisory opinion to the governor, in which the court held that "the Governor does not have the power to review the judicial discretion and wisdom of a... Judge while he is engaged in the judicial process."[330] The court concluded:

> Under procedures enacted by the Legislature, effective both before the passage of the Act and after its fifteen-day effective period expired, circuit courts are charged with adjudicating issues regarding incompetent individuals. The trial courts of this State are called upon to make many of the most difficult decisions facing society. In proceedings [such as this], these decisions literally affect the lives or deaths of patients. The trial courts also handle other weighty decisions affecting the welfare of children such as termination of parental rights and child custody. When the prescribed procedures are followed according to our rules of court and the governing statutes, a final judgment is issued, and all post-judgment procedures are followed, it is without question an invasion of the authority of the judicial branch for the Legislature to pass a law that allows the executive branch to interfere with the final judicial determination in a case. That is precisely what

---

[327] *Id.* at 329.

[328] *Id.* 332. After determining that the order had encroached upon the authority of the judicial branch, the court held further that the order illegally delegated legislative authority to the chief executive of Florida.

[329] *Id.* At 329–30 (quoting *Trustees Internal Improvement Fund v. Bailey*, 10 Fla. 238, 250 (1863)) (noting that the United States Supreme Court had taken a similar view of the role of the judiciary).

[330] *Id.* at 331 (internal quotation marks and citations omitted). "In Advisory Opinion, the Governor asked the Court whether he had the 'constitutional authority to review the judicial accuracy and propriety of [a judge] and to suspend him from office if it does not appear... that the Judge has exercised proper judicial discretion and wisdom." *Id.* (quoting *In re Advisory Opinion to the Governor*, 213 So. 2d 716, 718 (Fla. 1968)). "The court agreed that the Governor had the authority to suspend a judge on grounds of incompetency 'if the physical or mental incompetency is established and determined within the Judicial Branch by a court of competent jurisdiction.'" *Id.* (quoting *Advisory Opinion*, 213 So. 2d at 720).

occurred here and for that reason the Act is unconstitutional as applied to Theresa Shiavo.[331]

c)   **Individual Constitutional Rights and Lip Service Obeisance**

Other sections of this book discuss cases in which the trial court's discretion conflicts with the constitutional rights of a party. The Connecticut Supreme Court, discussing a criminal defendant's right to cross-examination, suggested in *State v. Valentine* that an appellate court will pay lip service obeisance to a trial court's trial management decisions to the extent that those decisions bear on defendant's right to cross-examine:

> Although the trial court has broad discretion in determining the admissibility of evidence and the extent of cross-examination, the preclusion of sufficient inquiry into a particular matter tending to show motive, bias and interest may result in a violation of the constitutional requirements of the sixth amendment to the United States constitution. The sixth amendment to the United States constitution guarantees the right of an accused in a criminal prosecution to confront and cross-examine the witnesses against him. We have held that the primary interest secured by confrontation is the right to cross examination . . . and an important function of cross-examination is the exposure of a witness' motivation in testifying. Therefore, an accused's right to cross examination to elicit facts tending to show motive, interest, bias and prejudice may not be unduly restricted by the wide discretion of the trial court.... In order to comport with the constitutional standards embodied in the confrontation clause, the trial court must allow a defendant to expose to the jury facts from which [the] jurors, as the sole triers of fact and credibility, could appropriately draw inferences relating to the reliability of the witness.[332]

d)   **Meaning of "Lip Service"**

In *Drinkard v. State*, the majority found held that the trial court erred in "excluding" veniremember Nix from jury service in the penalty phase of a capital murder trial "without giving counsel for the defendant the option of questioning" him.[333] The court explained:

> The *voir dire* examination of Mr. Nix stretches across numerous pages of the record. Mr. Nix had substantial problems with the burden of proof and clearly indicated that he would hold the State to a standard higher than beyond a reasonable doubt. The portions

---

[331] *Id.* at 332.

[332] 762 A.2d 1278, 1284–85 (Conn. 2000).

[333] 776 S.W.2d 181, 188 (Tex. Crim. App. 1989) (upholding the trial court's judgment based on the harmless error doctrine).

of the examination excerpted above also demonstrate the veniremember's inability to follow the law in regards to the defendant's right to refuse to put on any evidence in his defense. In light of these factors, and the fact that the examination of Mr. Nix was both thorough and competent, involving both counsel for the State and the Court, we hold here that there was error in excluding him from jury service without giving counsel for the defendant the option of questioning veniremember.[334]

Judge Clinton dissented, arguing that the harmless error doctrine should not apply.[335] After concluding that "Nix's responses do indeed provide a basis from which a rational trial court could concluded he had a bias against the law which he was incapable of setting aside," Judge Clinton argued that the trial court's discretion to excuse a juror for cause was broad on paper but narrow in practice:

> In the past, and especially since the decision of the [United States] Supreme Court in *Wainwright v. Witt*,... then [sic] Court has paid lip service to the trial court's discretion in ruling upon State's challenges for cause....

> Having granted this discretion to trial courts, however, it seems to me we turn around and effectively revoke it when we continually conclude our discussion on these points of error with holdings that "we find" the venireman to have been substantially impaired, or that "clearly" he was so. At least in the context of what has been termed "equivocating" or "vacillating" veniremen, it seems to me that due deference to the trial court means that he has discretion to find such a venireman is *not* in fact impaired, in spite of some obvious difficulty he may have. Categorically to hold, or at least to imply as our holdings do, that such a venireman is in every case substantially impaired sends a message to trial courts that in fact they do *not* have the discretion to overrule State's challenges for cause in the premises. Rather, as a matter of appellate review, this Court should simply hold there is a reasonable basis in the record to support a finding by the trial court that the venireman will be impaired in his ability to abide by his oath as a juror. Such a standard of appellate review does not preclude the trial court from exercising its discretion to find that, what from a cold appellate record may appear to be a truly equivocating or vacillating venireman, has actually proven himself, by demeanor, tone or howsoever, able in fact to follow the law.

---

[334] *Id.*

[335] *Id.* (Clinton, J., dissenting). In a separate dissent, Judge Teague argued that the majority should not have applied the harmless error doctrine but should have reversed the trial court's judgment. Judge Teague otherwise agreed with Judge Clinton's dissent. *Id.* at 191 (Teague, J., dissenting).

> Having vested the trial court with this discretion to arbitrate challengability of veniremen who appear, "at least on a cold record, to be genuinely noncommittal, vacillating, equivocal, or uncertain", we should never allow it to exercise that discretion unilaterally; that is, without affording the opponent of the challenge to opportunity to rehabilitate the venireman....[336]

Judge Clinton concluded that the majority's approach, which allowed the trial court to excuse a juror on a *prima facie* showing of cause, both "insulated" the court from having to exercise its discretion and condoned "the trial court's abdication of its proper function in a capital voir dire."[337]

e)   Equitable Remedies

Believing that respondent Publisher's Clearing House, a magazine clearance company famous for its multi-million dollar sweepstakes was guilty of fraud, petitioner Attorney General of Iowa subpoenaed records from the organization as a part of consumer fraud investigation.[338] The trial court granted the subpoena in part, accepting respondent's argument that some of its records contained trade secrets.

On appeal, the court reversed, holding that the trial court's order "merely tracking the language of the [relevant] statute without particularized findings, presented facts that were merely stereotypical and conclusive, and thus insufficient" to justify the judicial protection of respondent's trade secrets.[339] The court held further that the trial court "failed to apply the three-part test for the protective order as required by *Farnum*."[340] Prior to reaching its holding, the court discussed the appropriate standard of review:

> The attorney general claims our review should be de novo because a civil action filed pursuant to the consumer fraud statute shall be by equitable proceedings. Under Iowa Rule of Appellate Procedure 4, appellate review in equity cases is de novo. The attorney general argues that the unique equitable remedies available under Iowa Code section 716.16(c) distinguish the enforcement of a subpoena under the consumer fraud act is subject to the same standard of review as agency subpoenas under chapter 17A and because

---

[336] *Id.* at 188–89 (Clinton, J., dissenting).
[337] *Id.* at 189 (Clinton, J., dissenting).
[338] *Miller v. Publisher's Clearing House, Inc.*, 633 N.W.2d 732, 735 (Iowa 2001).
[339] *Id.* at 740.
[340] *Id.* In *Farnum v. G.D. Searle & Co.*, 339 N.W.2d 384, 389 (Iowa 1983), the court held that when a trial court considered a protective order seeking to guard a trade secret, the trial court had to consider three factors: "(1) the harm posed by dissemination must be substantial and serious, (2) the order must be narrowly drawn and precise, and (3) there must be no alternative means of protecting the public interest that intrudes less directly on expression." *Miller*, 633 N.W.2d at 740 (quoting *Farnum*, 339 N.W.2d at 389–90).

agency subpoena power is essentially a discovery tool, our review is limited to abuses of trial court discretion.

We reject the attorney general's argument that, because the proceedings for an injunction under the consumer fraud statute are in equity, we should review collateral discovery issues de novo as well.... [T]his... is a discovery procedure, and the standard or review is for abuse of discretion, as in other administrative subpoena cases. In exercising such discretion, a court should keep in mind the broad scope of the attorney general's subpoena power under the consumer fraud statute. In an analogous case, involving an administrative subpoena, we noted the extensive powers of an investigating authority:

Administrative agencies are normally invested with broad investigative powers to enable them to effectively carry out their legislative mandates. Agencies with authority to conduct investigations for the purpose of ascertaining probable cause for the institution of a contested case have powers comparable to those of a grand jury. *Iowa Civil Rights Comm'n v. City of Des Moines / Personnel Dep't*, 313 N.W.2d 491, 495 (Iowa 1981).

When an agency has investigative and accusatory powers, courts have been cautious to interfere with agency subpoena powers except to preserve due process rights. Agency subpoenas are enforced if they are (1) within the statutory authority of the agency, (2) reasonably specific, (3) not unduly burdensome and (4) reasonably relevant to the matters under investigation. Subpoenas are not enforced if they do not meet these standards because... these standards mark the bounds of a permissible constructive search under the Fourth Amendment.[341]

f)   Speedy Trial Act

Eighteen U.S.C. § 3161(c) (1) provides that a defendant's trial, as a general rule, must begin within seventy days after the defendant's indictment has been filed and made public.[342] Discussing the Speedy Trial Act and its effect on the trial court's discretion to control its docket, Judge McKay on the Tenth Circuit stated:

The Act has not been uniformly popular among trial judges because it imposes strict time constraints that must be observed in conducting criminal trials. Under prior rules time constraints were much more flexible and better suited to the almost impossible

---

[341] *Id.* at 735–36.
[342] 18 U.S.C. A. § 3161(c) (1) (West 2005). The remainder of section §3161 and §3162, the Speedy Trial Act, set out exceptions to the general rule and other specific provisions governing the interim between when a defendant is arrested and brought to trial.

calendar management problems that constantly plague the district courts. Congress no doubt had this in mind when it not only drafted a strict rule with teeth, but in addition imposed the unusual requirement that trial courts specifically state their reasons for exercising the only important discretion available to them under the new Act. Congress recognized that legitimate counter-pressures inevitably would develop, allowing discretion in the granting of continuances to reduce the new rule to a carbon copy of the old flexible standard. Furthermore, it is not only the overworked trial courts that are hit hard by the strict new rule. Prosecutors have a vested interest in a return to the more relaxed standards of the past to accommodate their own excessive work loads. Congress was aware of all these matters and clearly showed that it intended there be no evasion of the new standards. Only vigilance by the Court of Appeals can prevent the erosion of the congressional mandate without Congress's consent.

... The evil lies in our approval of a form of order which permits undisciplined avoidance of the 70-day limit and undisciplined review of trial court orders extending the limits Congress imposed on courts and prosecutors.

This record shows little effort by the prosecutors to work out an arrangement that would meet both the demands of the Speedy Trial Act and the very sensitive situation presented by these peculiar facts. We are left with the impression that it could not be done. However, Congress clearly indicated that it did not intend that either this court or the trial court speculate when extending, over objection, the time a criminal defendant must wait to be brought to trial. I only hope that this case will be confined to its peculiar facts and will not be the harbinger of an eventual erosion of this important statute rooted in constitutional imperatives.[343]

g)   Family Law: Child Abuse and Custodial Matters

The Texas Court of Appeals, acknowledging that the "trial court is given wide latitude in determining custody issues," nonetheless has adhered strictly to a statutory requirement that "the trial court may not appoint joint managing conservators if credible evidence is presented of a history or pattern of past or present physical abuse by one parent directed against another parent."[344] The court concluded that in this case the trial court had not erred by making the husband and wife in a divorce action joint conservators of their child, despite wife's allegations of abuse. In doing so, the court found that there was "nothing in the record to show

---

[343] *United States v. Guerrero*, 667 F.2d 862 (10th Cir. 1981) (McKay, J., dissenting).
[344] *Burns v. Burns*, 116 S.W.3d 916 (Tex. App. 2003). ("While the trial court is given wide latitude in determining custody issues, the Texas Family Code places certain restrictions on the trial court's discretion when there are allegations of abuse.").

228

that the court did not consider [wife's] testimony."[345] Upholding the trial court's discretion to weigh wife's testimony in making its determination, the court made a key distinction: "A court abuses its discretion when it acts without reference to any guiding rules or principles". A trial court does not abuse its discretion when it makes a decision on conflicting evidence."[346]

h)   Temporary Restraining Orders

The Texas Supreme Court issued a writ of mandamus to a trial court effectively prohibiting the trial court from extending a temporary restraining order against defendant without defendant's consent.[347] Interpreting Tex. Rule of Civil Procedure 680, the court concluded that the trial court's extending a temporary restraining order by six weeks was improper.[348] Tex. Rule of Civil Procedure 680 provides:

> No temporary restraining order shall be granted without notice to the adverse party unless it clearly appears from specific facts shown by affidavit or by the verified complaint that immediate and irreparable injury, loss, or damage will result to the applicant before notice can be served and a hearing had thereon. Every temporary restraining order granted without notice shall be endorsed with the date and hour of issuance... shall define the injury and state why it is irreparable and why the order was granted without notice; and shall expire by its terms within such time after signing, not to exceed fourteen days, as the court fixes, unless within the time so fixed the order, for good cause shown, is extended for a like period or unless the party against whom the order is directed consents that it may be extended for a longer period. The reasons for the extension shall be entered of record. No more than one extension may be granted unless subsequent extensions are unopposed.... On two days' notice to the party who obtained the temporary restraining order without notice or on such shorter notice to that party as the court may prescribe, the adverse party may appear and move its dissolution or modification and in that event the court shall proceed to hear and determine such motion as expeditiously as the ends of justice require.[349]

Plaintiff argued that the language of Rule 680 limits its application to situations in which the opposing party has no notice prior to the granting of the restraining order. Rejecting the plaintiff's contention, the court reiterated its precedent that "all

---

[345] *Id.*

[346] *Id.* ("Based on the conflicting testimony and the implicit finds of the trial court, we conclude that the trial court did not abuse its discretion in appointing [husband] joint managing conservator with the exclusive right to establish the primary residence of the minor child.")

[347] *In re Tex. Natural Res. Conservation Comm'n*, 85 S.W.3d 201 (Tex. 2002).

[348] *Id.*

[349] Tex. R. Civ. P. 680.

temporary restraining orders are subject to Rule 680's limitations on duration."[350] The court pointed to Rule 687, which limits all temporary restraining orders to fourteen days.[351] The court then explained that "Rule 680 was originally taken almost verbatim from Rule 65(b) of the Federal Rules of Civil Procedure" and that "the federal courts have construed their rule as we do ours," holding (under federal rules) that twenty days was the longest a temporary restraining order could remain in effect absent the adverse parties consent.[352] The court continued:

> Moreover, if a party can obtained unlimited extensions of a temporary restraining order, there would be no reason to ever seek a temporary injunction, which has more stringent proof requirements. As our Court has explained:

> An applicant for a temporary injunction seeks extraordinary equitable relief. He seeks to immobilize the defendant from a course of conduct which it may well be his legal right to pursue. Crowded dockets, infrequent jury trial weeks, or trial tactics can often delay a trial of a case on its merits for many months. The applicant has, and in equity and good conscience ought to have, the burden of offering some evidence which, under applicable rules of law, establishes a probable right of recovery. If not, no purpose is served by the provisions of Rule 680... limiting the time for which a restraining order granted without a hearing can operate and requiring a hearing before a temporary injunction can issue. *Camp v. Shannon*, 348 S.W.2d 517, 519 (1961).

i)   Motion for Reconsideration

Lip service obeisance does not always work in favor of the party seeking to change a trial court's ruling. In *Ruggiero v. Fleming*, the Connecticut Superior Court denied defendant's motion for reconsideration in a personal injury case.[353] Defendant's motion came on the heels of the Connecticut Supreme Court's holding that "a vehicle owner cannot be vicariously liable for punitive damages."[354] The court held that the granting of a motion for reconsideration was within its sound discretion, but also that the trial court has no discretion to reconsider a case beyond a certain time:

> Unfortunately, the defendants did not file their request for review in a timely fashion. More significantly, they never filed a request for an extension of time to present their instant argument. Consequently, their request must be denied.

---

[350] 85 S.W.3d at 204.
[351] *Id.* ("Rule 680 provides the only method for extending a temporary restraining order beyond fourteen days.").
[352] *Id.*
[353] No. CV020398397, 2004 WL 944772, at *1 (Conn. Super. Ct. Apr. 15, 2004).
[354] *Id.*

The defendants argued that the interests of justice require reconsiderations. They ignore the fact that the Practice Book sets a limit upon time within which a trial court can exercise the type of discretion now sought. If the defendants were correct in their claim that the mandatory time frame for reconsideration was generally modifiable, no trial court decision would ever be final. Litigants would have endless opportunities to refine their positions.[355]

j)   Dismissals for Failure to State a Claim and Summary Judgment

Decisions on dismissals are traditionally within the discretion of the trial court.[356] Dismissals for failure to state a claim is a different matter. Federal Rule of Civil Procedure 12(b)(6) provides for dismissal of a complaint when the complaint fails to state a claim upon which relief can be granted.[357] Applying the 12(b)(6) standard, a district court in the Sixth Circuit stated the applicable standard of review in *In re Fernald Litigation*:

> [W]e will decline to consider the affidavits proffered by defendant and will be guided by a legal standard significantly different from the one applicable on motions for summary judgment. The Sixth Circuit has stated the standard of review of a motion under Rule 12(b)(6): (1) All allegations in the complaint are taken as true; the complaint is to be construed liberally in favor of the party opposing the motion; (2) The complaint need not set down in detail all particularities of plaintiff's claim; (3) Rule 8(a)(2) simply requires a short and plain statement of the claims showing that the pleader is entitled to relief; (4) The complaint need only afford the defendant fair notice of what plaintiff's claim is and the grounds upon which it rests; (5) A motion to dismiss under Rule 12(b)(6) should not be granted unless it appears beyond doubt that plaintiff can prove no set of facts in support of his claim which would entitle him to relief."[358]

In *Fernald Litigation*, the court denied defendant's motion to convert the 12(b)(6) motion to a motion for summary judgment and, accordingly, to submit affidavits in support of its contentions. Although appellate courts review decisions on summary judgment *de novo*, there is a lingering question as to whether the trial court has nominal discretion when making its findings of fact in support of a summary

---

[355] *Id.* at *2.

[356] *See, e.g., Link v. Wabash Railroad Co.*, 370 U.S. 626, 631–33 (1962) (stating that Fed. R. Civ. P. 41(b) codifies the inherent power of a court to control its docket by dismissing cases).

[357] *See* Fed. R. Civ. P. 12(b)(6). *See also* 28 U.S.C. § 1915(e)(2)(B)(ii) (habeas corpus proceedings *in forma pauperis*).

[358] *In re Fernald Litigation*, No. C-1-85-149, 1986 WL 81381, at *2 (S.D. Ohio, May 19, 1986) (quoting the standard of review employed in *Westlake v. Lucas*, 537 F.2d 857, 858 (6th Cir. 1976).

judgment order. The Indiana Supreme Court has opted for an approach offering no discretion:

> [I]n granting the motion for summary judgment, the trial court entered findings of fact and conclusions of law. We note that normally the requested entry of specific findings and conclusions triggers the appellate standard of review contained in Indiana Trial Rule 52. However, that rule governs only those cases which proceed to trial, not those cases disposed of in summary judgment proceedings. The entry of specific findings and conclusions does not alter the nature of summary judgment which is a judgment entered when there are no genuine issues of material fact to be resolved. Thus, in the summary judgment context, we are not bound by the trial court's specific findings of fact and conclusions of law. They merely aid our review by providing us with a statement of reasons for the trial court's actions.[359]

Another area of nominal trial court discretion arises under Rule 54(b) of the Federal Rules of Civil Procedure. Rule 54(b) provides:

> When more than one claim for relief is presented in an action, whether as a claim, counterclaim, cross-claim, or third-party claim, or when multiple parties are involved, the court may direct the entry of a final judgment as to one or more but fewer than all of the claims or parties only upon an express direction for the entry of judgment.[360]

The court in *W. L. Gore & Assocs. v. Int'l Med. Prosthetics Research Assocs.* stated that courts "analyzing whether Rule 54(b) applies must both focus on the finality of the judgment and the separateness of the claims for relief."[361] As to the "finality" prong, the court cited precedent from the United States Supreme Court that the "requirement of finality is a statutory mandate and not a matter of discretion."[362] The court explained, "While the district court's determination that there is no just reason for delay is reviewed under an abuse of discretion standard, the Supreme Court has emphasized that the 'District Court cannot, in the exercise of its discretion, treat as final that which is not ....'"[363] Again relying on Supreme Court precedent, the court concluded that the "separateness of the claims for relief" "is a

---

[359] *Rice v. Strunk*, 670 N.E. 2d 1280, 1281 (Ind. 1996). Ind. T. R. 52 requires that appellate court's apply a clearly erroneous standard of review to the trial court's findings of fact.
[360] Fed. R. Civ. P. 54(b).
[361] 975 F.2d 858, 862 (Fed. Cir. 1992).
[362] *Id.*
[363] *Id.* ("The Supreme Court has rejected the view that the mere recitation of finality and 'no just reason for delay' by the district court pursuant to Rule 54(b) automatically renders a judgment appealable as a final decision....").

232

matter to be taken into account in reviewing the trial court's exercise of discretion in determining that there is no just reason to delay the appeal."[364]

k) Rules of Relevancy

Although the discretionary decisions that a federal trial court makes pursuant to Federal Rules of Evidence 401 and 403 are presumptively valid, the subsequent rules in Article Four establish circumstances under which a trial court either *must* admit or exclude the evidence.[365] In many of these situations, however, the trial court retains discretion under Rule 403 to exclude otherwise relevant evidence if the evidence is unfairly prejudicied misleading or cummulative.

Rule 404(a) provides that evidence "of a person's character or a trait of character is not admissible for the purpose of proving action in conformity therewith on a particular occasion."[366] The rule provides an exception when the accused (*i.e.*, a criminal defendant) presents evidence of his own good character (and further allows the prosecution to rebut the accused's character evidence with other character evidence.[367]

Interpreting Rule 404(a), the court United States Court of Appeals for the D.C. Circuit reaffirmed that its standard of review for "a district court's exclusion of character evidence" is abuse of discretion.[368] Defendant, charged with conspiracy in connection with his involvement in illegal firearms trading, alleged as his sole claim on appeal that the court should have allowed him to present character evidence pertaining to his reputation in the community as an honest and truthful person. He claimed that the government had put his "reputation for law-abidingness, truthfulness, and honesty at issue by charging him with participating in a conspiracy" in which he "aided in the preparation of false statements filed with licensed gun dealers."[369] The court first upheld the trial court's decision allowing evidence of law-abidingness because "the general character trait of law-abidingness is pertinent to all criminal offenses."[370] Addressing defendant's argument squarely, the court added that evidence of honesty and truthfulness would be admissible "when the defendant is charged with an offense in which fraud or falsehood is one of its statutory elements."[371] The court explained further that under Rule 404(a), the

---

[364] *Id.*

[365] *See generally* Fed R. Evid. 404–414 (the so-called prepackaged rules of legal relevancy).

[366] Fed. R. Evid. 404(a).

[367] *Id.* at 404(a)(1). Rule 404(a) also provides other exceptions for character of a victim and the character of a witness. *Id.* at 404(a).

[368] *In re Sealed Case*, 353 F.3d 409, 411 (D.C. Cir. 2003).

[369] *Id.* ("The district court ruled that while character evidence regarding appellant's reputation for law abidingness would be admissible on all counts, character evidence regarding appellant's truthfulness and honesty would be inappropriate unless appellant testified.").

[370] *Id.* at 412.

[371] *Id.*

defendant could introduce evidence of his honesty and truthfulness even when not charged with fraud or another *crimen falsi*.[372] The court accepted the parties' contention "that the circumstances here are analogous to cases involving fraud or false statements in which courts have held that such character evidence is admissible." Having done so, it concluded that the conspiracy charge allowed defendant to introduce evidence of honesty and truthfulness because the indictment charged him with recruiting a third party to "knowingly make false and fictitious statements in order to purchase firearms."[373]

Although not addressing character evidence *per se*, Federal Rule of Evidence 404(b) provides that evidence "of other crimes, wrongs, and acts is not admissible to prove the character of a person in order to show action in conformity therewith."[374] However, the rule provides further that such evidence may "be admissible for other purposes, such as proof of motive, opportunity, intent, preparation, plan, knowledge, identity, or absence of mistake or accident."[375] Whether one of the exceptions to the general rule applies is a matter committed to the trial court's discretion.[376] In *Lazcano-Villalobos*, the court affirmed a trial court's decision that evidence of defendant's prior arrest on possession of marijuana with intent to distribute went to defendant's "knowledge."[377] The court quoted the four-part test it had developed for reviewing Rule 404(b) decisions:

> "(1) the evidence was offered for a proper purpose; (2) the evidence was relevant; (3) the trial court determined under Fed. R. Evid. 403 that the probative value of the evidence was not substantially outweighed by its potential for unfair prejudice; and (4) the trial court gave the jury proper limiting instructions upon request."[378]

After concluding that the trial court had correctly applied the first two prongs of its test to establish that the prior evidence was relevant to prove knowledge, the court acknowledged that "district court did not expressly state that under Rule 403, the probative value of the evidence substantially outweighed its potential for unfair prejudice."[379] Despite an apparent conflict with its own holding, which had required "on-the-record findings for a trial court's balancing under Rule 403 when the disputed evidence is offered pursuant to one of the specialized character evidence rules," the court found no abuse of discretion.[380] In doing so, it

---

[372] *Id.*

[373] *Id.* The court affirmed the trial court under the harmless error doctrine. *See id.*

[374] Fed. R. Evid. 404(b).

[375] *Id.*

[376] *See generally United States v. Lazcano-Villalobos*, 175 F.3d 838 (10th Cir. 1999).

[377] *Id.* at 845 (trial for possession with intent to distribute cocaine).

[378] *Id.* at 846.

[379] *Id.*

[380] *Id.* ("We have consistently upheld implicit Rule 403 determinations when the determinations are supported by the record.").

234

concluded that its "holding in [*United States v. McVeigh*][381] merely reaffirms our authority to conduct a *de novo* balancing where the trial court failed to make explicit findings to support a Rule 403 ruling."[382] The court explained further:

> Nonetheless, we are compelled to clarify the *McVeigh* footnote to which [defendant] refers, in which we state a requirement for on-the-record findings of a trial court's balancing test under Rule 403, when the disputed evidence if 404(b) evidence. The footnote cited by [defendant] relies on our holding in *United States v. Kendall*, 766 F.2d 1246 (10th Cir. 1985).... In *Kendall*, we stated the government must articulate precisely the evidentiary hypothesis for the admission of 404(b) evidence; the trial court must specifically identify the "*purpose*" for such evidence... (emphasis added). e noted that the specific articulation of the relevant purpose... will enable the trial court to more accurately make an informed decision and weigh the probative value of such evidence against the risks of prejudice specified in Rule 403. Thus, in *Kendall*, we required express articulation of the purpose for the evidence, but not express articulation of the district court's Rule 403 analysis on whether the probative value of the 404(b) evidence outweighed the prejudicial effect.[383]

I)   Damages

The trial court's decisions pertaining to the awarding of compensatory damages receive a presumption of validity.[384] With respect to punitive damages, however, the United States Supreme Court has held that a trial court's review of an award for "excessiveness" is a "constitutional issue" that "merits *de novo* review."[385] The

---

[381] 153 F.3d 1166 (10th Cir. 1998).

[382] *Id*

[383] *Id*. For an example of one of the prepackaged rules of relevancy allowing for a Rule 403 analysis, see Fed. R. Evid. 413 (evidence of defendant's prior sex offenses always admissible). Rule 412(c) provides that the rule "shall not be construed to limit the admission or consideration of evidence under any other rule").

[384] *Farley v. Nationwide Mut. Ins. Co.*, 197 F.3d 1322, 1335 (11th Cir. 1999) ("Our review of a trial court's decision to remit a jury's award of compensatory damages is highly deferential.") ("After a trial court has reviewed and remitted a jury award to a specific amount, we accord that decision a presumption of validity.").

[385] *Cooper Indus. v. Leatherman Tool Gr., Inc.*, 532 U.S. 424, 431 (2001). In announcing the issue before it, the Court noted that "[r]espondent and its *amicus* at times appear to conflate the question of the proper standard for reviewing the District Court's due process determination with the question of the substantive standard for determining the jury awards conformity with due process in the first instance." *Id.* at 531 n.4. "Thus, [the Court's] rejection in *TXO Production Corp. v. Alliance Resources Corp.* of heightened scrutiny of punitive damages awards is not only wholly consistent with [the] decision," it was "irrelevant to our resolution of the question presented." *Id.*

The language of *TXO* may lead one to believe otherwise:

Leatherman Court first clarified that when a trial court reviews a punitive damages award under state law or federal statutory law—that is, when "no constitutional issue is raised—"the role of the appellate court, at least in the federal system, is merely to review the trial court's determination under an abuse-of-discretion standard."[386] When the excessiveness of punitive damage does raise a constitutional issue, however, the analysis differs:

> Despite the broad discretion that States possess with respect to the imposition of criminal penalties and punitive damages, the Due Process Clause of the Fourteenth Amendment to the Federal Constitution imposes substantive limits on that discretion. That Clause makes the Eighth Amendment's prohibition against excessive fines and cruel and unusual punishments applicable to the States. The Due Process Clause of its own force also prohibits the States from imposing grossly excessive punishments on tortfeasors.

> The Court has enforced those limits in cases involving deprivations of life, deprivations of liberty; and deprivations of property.

> In these cases, the constitutional violations were predicated on judicial determinations that the punishments were grossly disproportional to the gravity [of the wrongdoer's conduct]. We have recognized that the relevant constitutional line is inherently imprecise rather than one marked by a simple mathematical formula. But in deciding whether that line has been crossed, we have focused on the same general criteria: the degree of the defendant's reprehensibility or culpability, the relationship between the penalty and the harm to the victim caused by the defendant's actions; and the sanctions imposed in other cases for comparable misconduct. Moreover, and of greatest relevance for the issue we address today, in each of these cases we have engaged in an independent examination of the relevant criteria.[387]

The only basis for criticizing the trial judge's review of the punitive damages award is that he did not articulate his reasons for upholding it. He did, however, give counsel an adequate hearing on TXO's postverdict motions, and during one colloquy indicated his agreement with the jury's appraisal of the egregious character of the conduct of TXO's executives. While it is always helpful for trial judges to explain the basis for their rulings as thoroughly as is consistent with the efficient dispatch of their duties, we certainly are not prepared to characterize the trial judge's failure to articulate the basis for his denial of the motions for judgment notwithstanding the verdict and remittitur as a constitutional violation.

509 U.S. 443, 464–65 (1993).
[386] 532 U.S. at 433.
[387] *Id.* at 434–35.

236

Analogizing to a case governing reasonable suspicion and probable cause determinations, the Court explained why its historical *de novo* review of constitutional questions should apply to punitive damages awards:

> Likewise, in *Ornelas*, we held that trial judges' determinations of reasonable suspicion and probable cause should be reviewed *de novo* on appeal. The reasons we gave in support of that holding are equally applicable in this case. First... the precise meaning of concepts like "reasonable suspicion" and "probable cause" cannot be articulated with precision; they are fluid concepts that take their substantive content from the particular contexts in which the standards are being assessed. That is, of course, also a characteristic of "gross excessiveness." Second, the legal rules for probable cause and reasonable suspicion acquire content only through application. Independent review is therefore necessary if appellate courts are to maintain control of, and to clarify, the legal principles. Again, this is also true of the general criteria set forth in *Gore* [reviewing the excessiveness of a punitive damages award for constitutional defect]; they will acquire more meaningful content through case-by-case application at the appellate level. Finally, *de novo* review tends to unify precedent and stabilize the law....[388]

Justice Scalia and Justice Thomas, in two separate concurring opinions, joined in the Court's judgment while questioning the wisdom of making the excessiveness of punitive damages awards a constitutional question.

Justice Ginsburg dissented, concluding that the Ninth Circuit "properly identified abuse of discretion as the appropriate standard in reviewing the District Court's determination that the punitive damages awarded against Cooper were not grossly excessive."[389] In her dissent, Justice Ginsberg, citing to the Court's opinion in *Gasperini v. Center for Humanities*, reiterated that under the Seventh Amendment appellate review of "a federal trial court's refusal to set aside a jury verdict as excessive" required a deferential abuse of discretion standard.[390] The dissent explained why the *Gasperini* holding should apply to the case at bar:

> But there can be no question that a jury's verdict on punitive damages is fundamentally dependent on determinations we characterize as factfindings—*e.g.*, the extent of harm or potential harm caused by the defendant's misconduct, whether the defendant acted in good faith, whether the misconduct was an individual instance or part of a broader pattern, whether the defendant behaved negligently, recklessly, or maliciously. Punitive damages are thus not unlike the measure of actual damages suffered, in cases

---

[388] *Id.* at 436.
[389] *Id.* at 450 (Ginsburg, J., dissenting).
[390] *Id.* at 444 (Ginsburg, J., dissenting).

of intangible, non-economic injury. One million dollars' worth of pain and suffering does not exist as a fact in the world any more or less than one million dollars' worth of moral outrage. Both derive their meaning from a set of underlying facts as determined by a jury. If one exercise in quantification is properly regarded as factfinding, it seems to me the other should be so regarded as well. In *Browning-Ferris Industries of Vt., Inc. v. Kelco Disposal, Inc.*, 492 U.S. 257, 109 S.Ct. 2909 (1989), we approved application of an abuse-of-discretion standard for appellate review of a district court's ruling on a motion to set aside a punitive damages award as excessive. *Browning-Ferris* reserved the question whether even such deferential appellate review might run afoul of the Seventh Amendment. At that time, the Court ha[d] never held expressly that the Seventh Amendment allows appellate review of a district court's denial of a motion to set aside an award as excessive. We found it unnecessary to reach the Seventh Amendment question in *Browning-Ferris* because the jury verdict there survived lower court review intact. *Browning-Ferris*, in short, signaled our recognition that appellate review of punitive damages, if permissible at all, would involve *at most* abuse-of-discretion review....[391]

The dissent also pointed to two "practical reasons" for employing an abuse of discretion standard.[392] First, the dissent noted that "district courts have an undeniably superior vantage over court of appeals," being experts "in the living courtroom context" rather than relying on "a cold paper record."[393] Second, the dissent critiqued the *de novo* standard as overly "complex" for these types of cases.[394] The dissented contended that *de novo* review required "lower courts to distinguish between ordinary common-law excessiveness and constitutional excessiveness and to separate out factfindings that qualify for clearly erroneous review."[395]

§ 3.6. Conclusion

The ranges of discretion described in this chapter provide the trial judge with a reasonable sense of predictability as to how much discretion will be allowed. The amount of freedom to decide the trial court enjoys in a given situation will, of course, depend upon the nature of the decision and other factors. To the extent that the matter is procedural and concerns *how* the trial is to be conducted, the trial judge can expect substantial appellate deference. If, however, the decidion is more of a

---

[391] *Id.* at 446–47 (Ginsburg, J., dissenting).

[392] *Id.* at 448 (Ginsburg, J., dissenting).

[393] *Id.* (Ginsburg, J., dissenting).

[394] *Id.* at 450 (Ginsburg, J., dissenting).

[395] *Id.* (Ginsburg, J., dissenting) ("The Court's approach will be challenging to administer. Complex as it is, I suspect that approach and mine will yield different outcomes in few cases.").

substantive nature, the trial, court should anticipate less deference, and in some situations, none at all. The trial courts freedom to characterize the issue as substantive or procedure will be affected by whether the appellate courts or the legislature have provided guidance for the trial court in exercising discretion. Should the issure be cast inconstitutional terms, the trial court's freedom to decide is further restricted.

4

The Abuse of Discretion Standard

a)   Introduction

The last word from the United States Supreme Court on the meaning of abuse of discretion was in *Koon v. United States*. Reviewing the federal sentencing guidelines, the Court stated that "an abuse of discretion standard does not mean a mistake of law is beyond appellate correction" and that a federal trial court "by definition abuses its discretion when it makes an error of law."[1]

The Sixth Circuit, apparently taking the Supreme Court's language in *Koon* as dicta, disagrees that an error of law is *ipso facto* an abuse of discretion.[2] Defendant newspaper companies claimed that documents which the National Labor Relations Board (NLRB) sought by subpoena were privileged. Defendants argued

---

[1] 518 U.S. 81, 100 (1996). The federal circuits have adopted the *Koon* holding. *See, e.g.*, *In re Superior Crewboats, Inc.*, 374 F.3d 330, 333 (5th Cir. 2004) ("However, an abuse of discretion standard does not mean a mistake of law is beyond appellate correction because a district court by definition abuses its discretion when it makes an error of law.") (internal quotation omitted).
[2] *NLRB v. Detroit Newspapers*, 185 F.3d 602, 605 (6th Cir. 1999).

further that "the court did not have the discretion to delegate the function of reviewing the documents for their privileged status to the ALJ (Adminstrative Law Judge)."[3] The NLRB argued in turn that "the proper standard [of] review in this case is whether the district court abused its discretion when it determined that the ALJ (Adminstrative Law Judge) should have the first opportunity to determine if subpoenaed documents were privileged."[4]

In response to the parties' arguments, the court offered the following analysis:

> As is evident from this back and forth between the parties, both sides seem to assume that the underlying question is whether the district court abused its discretion, and therefore, that abuse of discretion is our standard of review. It isn't but we cannot fault the parties for thinking it is.

> When a district court purports to exercise discretion in a matter with respect to which it has no discretion, it has misperceived what the law permits it to do, and therefore, commits an error of law. Now, it may be that such a court will have reached the right result, as a matter of law, but it will not have done so because it had discretion to go one way or the other, as it saw fit. In a situation like that, we would, upon review, conclude that we affirm the decision, not for the reason that the district court did not abuse its discretion (because it had none), but for the reason that the district court's decisional result was not an error of law.

> Entrenched in the strange lexicon of federal abuse of discretion jurisprudence is the notion that a district court abuses its discretion when it commits an error of law. It is too late in the day, and, in this case, would be too great a distraction, to examine how it can be that a district court can be said to have abused its discretion for failing to apply a rule of law it was without discretion to fail to apply. Once would think the failure to apply the rule of law would be an error of law, not an abuse of discretion.

> We decline the parties' invitation to incant once again the inaccurate rhetoric of federal abuse of discretion jurisprudence, and instead, declare simply that because the district court had no discretion to do what it did, but was obligated, as a matter of law,

---

[3] *Id.* at 604. Defendant argued further that "handing the documents over to the ALJ for an in camera review is the substantial equivalent to producing the documents to the General Counsel of the NLRB....." *Id.*

[4] *Id.* ("The NLRB also argues that the district court did not abuse its discretion because it was more efficient for the ALJ to review the documents first....").

either to decide the privilege issue itself or delegate the duty to an ALJ, we conduct de novo review of the court's decision."[5]

The Second Circuit examined the different standards of review carefully in *Zervos v. Verizon New York, Inc.*[6] Petitioner-Appellant Zervos argued that the appropriate standard of review for a preliminary injunction was *de novo* when the district court based its decision on the cold record without the aid of testimony.[7] Before rejecting petitioner's argument in favor of its traditional standard of review, the court described abuse of discretion, as well as the *de novo* and clearly erroneous standards of review:

> *De novo* review is review without deference. When we review a district court's decision *de novo*, we take note of it, and study the reasoning on which it is based. However, our review is independent and plenary; as the Latin term suggests, we look at the matter anew, as though it had come to the courts for the first time.
>
> Clear error is the standard under which appellate courts review a district court's factual findings. It is a deferential standard of review grounded, *inter alia*, on the belief that district courts have a good deal of "expertise" when it comes to fact-finding. A finding is clearly erroneous when although there is evidence to support it, the reviewing court is left with the definite and firm conviction that a mistake has been committed....
>
> Finally, there is abuse of discretion review. This is a second, more complicated, species of deferential appellate review. When a district court is vested with discretion as to a certain matter, it is not required by law to make a *particular* decision. Rather, the district court is empowered to make a decision—of *its* choosing—that falls within a range of permissible decisions. A district court "abuses" or "exceeds" the discretion accorded to it when (1) its decision rests on an error of law (such as application of the wrong legal principle) or a clearly erroneous factual finding, or (2) its decision—though not necessarily the product of a legal error or a clearly erroneous factual finding—cannot be located within the range of permissible decisions.[8]

---

[5] *Id.* at 605.

[6] 252 F.3d 163 (2nd Cir. 2001) (reviewing the trial court's denial of a preliminary injunction).

[7] *Id.* at 167–68.

[8] *Id.* at 168–69 (internal quotations omitted).

242

b) Harmless Error Distinguished

Indiana will find an abuse of discretion "if a trial court's decision is clearly against the logic and effect of the facts and circumstances before the court."[9] The court clarified that it would not reverse an evidentiary error if harmless, that is, "if the erroneously admitted evidence was cumulative of other evidence appropriately admitted."[10] Thus, Indiana contrasts "abuse of discretion" from the "harmless error" rule, which prevents appellate courts from reversing the trial court when an erroneous ruling does not prejudice the outcome of the case.

Other courts are not as clear about the distinction between the harmless error rule and abuse of discretion properly speaking. After explaining its reasons for adopting the abuse standard in *Daubert* rulings, the Vermont Supreme Court announced that when "reviewing a trial court's decision to either admit or exclude expert testimony," it would "consider whether the judge's decision was either made for reasons clearly untenable or was unreasonable."[11] The court continued:

> Absent a clear showing of judicial error, we will affirm the trial court's decision to admit or exclude the proffered testimony. This does not mean, however, that we will not engage in a substantial and thorough analysis of the trial court's decision and order to ensure that the trial court's decision was in accordance with *Daubert* and our applicable precedents.[12]

The Vermont Supreme Court described a "clear showing of judicial error" in harmless error language, suggesting that the court would in the same opinion affirm the trial court and criticize it for not following its precedent.

c) *De Novo* Review Distinguished

The Ninth Circuit, reviewing a district court's review of the Social Security Administration's decision regarding benefits, distinguished the abuse of discretion standard and the de novo standard of review.[13] Citing to Childress and Davis[14], the court concluded that "[n]ormally, the decision of the trial court is reversed under the abuse of discretion standard only when the appellate court is convinced firmly that the reviewed decision lies beyond the pale of reasonable justification under the circumstances."[15] "In contrast," the court stated that when it reviewed *de novo*, "the appellate court accords no deference to the trial court, but rather determines for

---

[9] *Iqbal v. State*, 805 N.E.2d 401, 406 (Ind. Ct. App. 2004) (citing *Joyner v. State*, 678 N.E.2d 386, 390 (Ind. 1997)).

[10] *Id.* at 406.

[11] *US Gen New England, Inc. v. Town of Rockingham*, 862 A.2d 269, 277 (Vt. 2004).

[12] *Id.*

[13] *Harman v. Apfel*, 211 F.3d 1172, 1175 (9th Cir. 2000).

[14] Childress and Davis, Federal Standards of Review, § 4.01, 4-13 (2d ed. 1992).

[15] *Id.*

itself whether the administrative decision should be reversed on the ground that it is arbitrary, capricious, an abuse of [administrative] discretion, or contrary to law."[16]

d)   Clearly Erroneous Distinguished

The Kentucky Supreme Court discussed the abuse of discretion standard in detail when reviewing a trial court's *Daubert* ruling on the admissibility of expert testimony.[17] The court reaffirmed its definition for abuse of discretion, "whether the trial judge's decision was arbitrary, unreasonable, unfair, or unsupported by sound legal principles."[18] The court went on to state that the definition is "nebulous" and difficult for intermediate courts to apply.[19] Specifically, the court expressed concern that some of the lower courts within its jurisdiction were "importing" a "clearly erroneous standard" into the abuse of discretion standard.[20] The court complained that these lower appellate courts would find an abuse of discretion whenever a trial court "relies on clearly erroneous findings of fact."[21] The court clarified that "clearly erroneous" is a distinct standard of review that applies to findings of fact only.[22] The court concluded that "abuse of discretion applies in other situations, where, for example, a 'court is empowered to make a decision—of *its* choosing—that falls within a range of permissible decisions.'"[23] The court determined that the trial court's decision regarding admissibility under *Daubert* is a matter subject to an abuse of discretion review and the clear error does not figure into the analysis with respect to that decision itself.

e)   Abuse of Discretion Not Immunity from Review

Reviewing the admissibility of an expert's testimony, the Rhode Island Supreme Court offered this definition of abuse of discretion, relying on prior case law:

> The determination of the admissibility of an expert witness's testimony rests within the sound discretion of the trial justice and will not be disturbed on appeal absent an abuse of that discretion. This is not to suggest however that a discretionary ruling is not reviewable. "What it does mean is that the ruling will be sustained provided the discretion has been soundly and judicially exercised, that is, if it had been exercised in the light of reason applied to all the facts and with a view to the rights of all the parties to the

---

[16] *Id.*
[17] *Miller v. Eldridge*, 146 S.W.2d 909, 914 (Ky. 2004).
[18] *Id.*
[19] *Id*
[20] *Id.* at 915.
[21] *Id*
[22] *Id*
[23] *Id.*

action... and not arbitrarily or willfully, but with just regard to what is right and equitable under the circumstances and the law."[24]

The court reversed the trial court for abuse of discretion. The expert had testified that "suicide was the only possibility" for a patient who had been granted grounds privileges at a mental health facility. Relying on the expert's one-time use of the word "possibility," the trial judge concluded that the expert was not testifying to knowledge that the expert held to an absolute certainty. Assuming that certainty was required, the trial court struck the expert's testimony.

f)   Abuse of Discretion Not Grounds for Mandamus

In reviewing the state's petition for a writ of mandamus, the Delaware Supreme Court offered a good description of what an abuse of discretion is *not*.[25] The court rejected the state's argument that the trial court had breached a "duty" to sentence a defendant "in accordance with the statutory provisions."[26] In doing so, the court stated, "Were we to characterize any error of law or abuse of discretion by a lower court as an arbitrary failure or refusal to act, and hence a 'breach of duty,' then the limitations on the mandamus jurisdiction of this Court would be meaningless."[27]

g)   "Abuse" as Unsustainable Exercise of Discretion

New Hampshire courts use the term "unsustainable exercise of discretion" instead of "abuse of discretion," although the two terms mean the same thing.[28] In announcing its new terminology, the New Hampshire Supreme Court offered some considerations bearing on the meaning of "abuse" of discretion: (1) it does not bear on the conduct or misconduct of a trial judge; (2) "[w]hen we determine whether a ruling made by a judge is a proper exercise of judicial discretion, we are really deciding whether the record establishes an objective basis sufficient to sustain the discretionary judgment made"; (3) in order for a party to show an "unsustainable" exercise of discretion, that party must both point to a ruling "clearly untenable or unreasonable" and make a showing of prejudice.[29] A subsequent case employed the same factors in order to determine whether the trial court had made a reversible decision rather than had made an unsustainable exercise of discretion.[30]

---

[24] *Morra v. Harrop*, 791 A.2d 472, 476–77 (R.I. 2002) (reversing trial court's decision to strike expert's testimony in an action in which plaintiff was alleging that defendant doctor had negligently granted suicidal decedent grounds privileges).

[25] *Matter of State*, 616 A.2d 292 (Del. 1992) (dismissing state's petition for mandamus for want of jurisdiction).

[26] *Id.* at 293.

[27] *Id.* at 294.

[28] *State v. Lambert*, 787 A.2d 175, 177 (N.H. 2001) ("Because the abuse of discretion standard may carry an inaccurate connotation, we will hereafter refer to it as the unsustainable exercise of discretion standard.").

[29] *Id.*

[30] *Arcidi v. Town of Rye*, 846 A.2d 535, 544 (N.H. 2004).

A Wisconsin appellate court also employed an "erroneous exercise of discretion standard" when reviewing a trial court's decision to compel a criminal defendant's alibi witnesses to testify at trial in prison clothes.[31] The court defined erroneous exercise of discretion thus: "If the trial court applied the correct law, after considering the pertinent facts and reaching a reasonable decision, we will not overturn the decision."[32] The court upheld the trial court's exercise of discretion because (1) the trial court had found as a practical matter that it would be too difficult both to transport the prisoners and have them change clothes once they reached the courtroom, (2) changing clothes would create security problems, (3) the trial court had explained in a written order that it did not believe the due process interest of a witness appearing in street clothes was equal to that of a criminal defendant, (4) the jury would likely learn that the witnesses had been convicted of a crime and had been incarcerated and thus the prison attire would reveal nothing new about the witnesses.[33]

h)   Complete Deference in Case of True Discretion

The Arizona Supreme Court has struggled to define "abuse of discretion." and recently equated "abuse of discretion" with a "clear and manifest error."[34] The court quoted a footnote from a prior decision, in which it complained about the term "abuse of discretion," calling it "unfortunate."[35] Although the court recognized that "the phrase as a whole has been interpreted to apply where the reasons given by the court for its action are clearly untenable, legally incorrect, or amount to a denial of justice," the court proposed some further "operative principles" with respect to how lower courts should understand "abuse of discretion."[36] The court distinguished between a "truly discretionary" decision, in which the trial court faces "an assessment of conflicting procedural, factual or equitable considerations which vary from case to case," and a "discretion" in which "the facts or inferences from them are not in dispute and where... the resolution of the question is one of law or logic."[37] The court announced that it would defer completely to the trial court in matters of "true discretion," because the trial court was in a better position to obtain the knowledge necessary to render a correct decision.[38] The court reserved for itself the right to review in full those "discretionary" decisions that involve a question of law or logic.[39]

---

[31] *State v. Reed*, 605 N.W.2d 885, 888 (Wis. Ct. App. 2002).

[32] *Id.*

[33] *Id.* at 889.

[34] *State v. Jones*, 49 P.3d 273, 277 (Ariz. 2002).

[35] *State v. Chapple*, 660 P.2ds 1208, 1224 at n.18 (Ariz. 1983) (en banc) ("In ordinary language, 'abuse' implies some form of corrupt practice, deceit or impropriety.").

[36] *Id.*

[37] *Id.*

[38] *Id.*

[39] *Id.*

i)   Misapplication of the Law

The federal Court of Appeals for the D.C. Circuit, hearing an appeal from a discovery dispute, reiterated that an "abuse of a discretion occurs when the court applies the wrong legal standard or relies on clearly erroneous facts" when making its decision.[40] Plaintiff was the father of a man killed by Contra rebels in Nicaragua, and had sued the leaders of the Contra groups. In the course of that litigation (the underlying action), plaintiff sought by subpoena information from the Department of Defense and CIA regarding the infrastructure and practices of the Contra armies. Eventually, after negotiations between plaintiff and the agencies and further court proceedings, a federal district court denied plaintiff's request for discovery beyond the information that the agencies had already provided. Under these facts, the court reversed and remanded the trial court's decision that the subpoena was "unduly burdensome" on the agencies.[41] The court reasoned that the CIA had provided no estimate as to how much time and labor compliance with the subpoena would require.[42] Moreover, the court concluded that "nothing in [the trial court's] order indicates that the court considered the relevance of the requested information to the second and third theories of [plaintiff's] case...."[43]

Reviewing the trial court's order for dismissal based on discovery abuse in a § 1983 action, the Tenth Circuit used the same "legal standard"/"erroneous facts" definition as the D.C. Circuit.[44] Although the court remanded because the trial judge had employed an incorrect legal standard when ordering dismissal, the court remanded so that the trial court could impose alternate sanctions and specifically declined to impose sanctions itself.[45]

The Court of Appeals for the Federal Circuit applies an "abuse" standard that may appear identical to those of the D.C. and Tenth Circuits but differs in one important respect. Rather than reversing upon a finding that the trial court relied on "clearly erroneous facts," the court will first determine whether the trial court made "a clearly erroneous assessment of the evidence" as a whole.[46] This difference may mean that a trial court *can* rely on a fact that is clearly erroneous so long as there are other factual bases for upholding its decision.

---

[40] *Linder v. Dept. of Defense*, 133 F.3d 17, 24 (D.C. Cir. 1998).

[41] *Id.*

[42] *Id.*

[43] *Id.*

[44] *Ashby v. McKenna*, 331 F.3d 1148, 1149 (10th Cir. 2003)

[45] *Id. Cp. Romstadt v. Allstate Ins. Co.*, 59 F.3d 608, 615 (6th Cir. 1995) ("An abuse of discretion exists when the reviewing court is firmly convinced that a mistake has been made. A district court abuses its discretion when it relies on clearly erroneous findings of fact, or when it improperly applies the law or uses and [sic] erroneous legal standard.") (internal citations and quotation marks omitted).

[46] *Precision Specialty Metals, Inc. v. United States*, 315 F.3d 1346, 1354 (Fed. Cir. 2003) (quotation omitted).

The 2004 New Jersey case *State v. Madan* afforded the intermediate appellate court the opportunity to revisit and compile prior New Jersey case law on both judicial discretion and the abuse thereof.[47] The court played with the possibility of describing abuse of discretion via a negative: namely, as a discretionary decision that is not "arbitrary and capricious."[48] The court instead settled on the following definition from one of its older precedents:

> Consequently, if the trial judge misconceives the applicable law or misapplies it to the factual complex, in total effect the exercise of legal discretion lacks a foundation and becomes an arbitrary act. When this occurs it is the duty of the reviewing court to adjudicate the controversy in the light of the applicable law in order that a manifest denial of justice be avoided.[49]

Virginia also employs the "legal error/clearly erroneous facts" standard. Reviewing a trial court's order denying a motion for a new trial based on after–discovered evidence, the Virginia Supreme Court synthesized its prior case law to hold that a "trial court may be found to have abused its discretion if the court uses an improper legal standard in exercising its discretionary function or makes factual findings that are plainly wrong or without evidence to support them."[50]

j)   Firm and Definite Conviction of Error

The Fourth Circuit, reviewing for an abuse of discretion, overturned a trial court's decision to abstain from a case over which it had jurisdiction (apparently because of the trial court's concern that the case also dealt with Virginia contract law).[51] The court began by noting that abstention "is the exception, not the rule" for federal trial courts and that the federal courts have "a virtually unflagging obligation" "to exercise the jurisdiction given them."[52] The court spelled out the six-factor test for determining whether a trial court should abstain, and stated that it would review the trial court's application of the six factors for an abuse of discretion.[53] The court indicated that "even if a district court applies the correct legal principles to adequately supported facts," it would reverse if it had "a definite and firm conviction that the court below committed a clear error of judgment in the conclusion it reached upon a weighing of the relevant factors."[54] Based on the "clear

---

[47] *State v. Madan*, 840 A.2d 874, 881–82 (N.J. 2004) (reversing a trial judge's decision to reject a plea agreement in the interests of justice because the trial court's decision had "insufficient factual underpinning" and had made "legal mistakes" in reaching its decision).
[48] *Id.* at 882 (citation omitted).
[49] *Id.* (internal quotation omitted).
[50] *Orndorff v. Commonwealth*, 605 S.E.2d 307, 320–21 (Va. Ct. App. 2004).
[51] *Gannett Co., Inc. v. Clark Const. Gr., Inc.*, 286 F.3d 737 (4th Cir. 2002).
[52] *Id.* at 741 (quotation omitted).
[53] *Id.*
[54] *Id.* (quotation omitted).

error of judgment" definition, the court concluded that it could find an abuse of discretion if the trial court did not "exercise its discretion in accordance with the [six-factor] test."[55]

The Alaska Supreme Court has indicated that whether the trial court abused its discretion depends upon the strength of the appellate court's conclusion that the trial court erred.[56] The court stated, "[w]e review [the trial court's] determination for abuse of discretion, reversing the superior court only when we are left with the definite and firm conviction, after reviewing the whole record, that it erred in its ruling."[57] Despite its relatively broad grant of authority to the reviewing court, Alaska's definition of "abuse of discretion" does not allow an appellate court to find an abuse whenever it has a strong distaste for the trial court's decision.[58] In *Lincoln v. Interior Regional Housing Authority*, the court reversed the trial court for an abuse of discretion because the trial court's summary judgment against plaintiff's intentional infliction of emotional distress claim was plainly unreasonable.[59] The court held the trial court's decision plainly unreasonable because the trial court had not made a proper "threshold determination" as to whether plaintiff's emotional distress was sufficiently serious to constitute a cause of action.[60] Instead, the court found that the trial court "had concluded that [plaintiff's] wrongful termination claims were without merit in the sense that they presented no fact issues requiring further adjudication."[61]

Nebraska defines "judicial abuse of discretion" as discretion exercised such "that the reasons or rulings of the trial judge are clearly untenable, unfairly depriving a litigant of a substantial right and denying a just result in matters submitted for disposition."[62] The court then distinguished the abuse standard from the burden of proof, adding that the "burden is on the party challenging a joint trial to demonstrate how and in what manner he or she was prejudiced."[63] Under its abuse standard, the court conducted a three-part analysis: (1) whether there was a legal right to a separate trial, (2) whether consolidation was proper in the present case; (3) whether a joint trial had prejudiced defendant.[64]

---

[55] 286 F.3d at 741.

[56] *See, e.g., City of Bethel v. Peters*, 97 P.3d 822, 828 (Alaska 2004).

[57] *Id.* (internal quotation omitted).

[58] *See Lincoln v. Interior Regional Housing Authority*, 30 P.3d 582, 589 (Alaska 2001) ("In the context of this sort of evidentiary sufficiency ruling, abuse of discretion means that the court's decision will not be disturbed unless plainly unreasonable.") (internal quotation marks omitted).

[59] *Id.* (wrongful termination).

[60] *Id.*

[61] *Id.*

[62] *State v. McPherson*, 668 N.W. 2d 488, 496 (Neb. 2003) (considering a trial court's ruling of a motion for consolidation of prosecutions).

[63] *Id.*

[64] *Id.* at 497.

k)   Preliminary Injunctions and Attorney Fees: Outside Legal Guidance

Overturning for abuse of discretion a district court's injunction prohibitingdefendant HMOs from arbitrating claims for medical expenses by plaintiff doctors, Judge Tjoflat, writing for the Eleventh Circuit, listed a variety of ways in which a trial court could abuse its discretion: (1) relying on clearly erroneous facts, (2) employing "improper procedures" when making a decision, (3) applying the wrong legal standard, (4) "applying the law in an unreasonable or incorrect manner," or (5) "impos[ing] some harm, disadvantage, or restriction upon someone that is unnecessarily broad or does not result in any offsetting gain to anyone else or society at large."[65] The final criterion appears to apply only to cases in which the trial court has used its discretion to grant an injunction. Of the five criteria, the most unique is the fourth, "applying the law in an unreasonable or incorrect manner." If this criterion is in fact distinct from the common notion that a trial court must follow the law in the exercise of its discretion, it would appear that a trial court could actually abuse its discretion while coming to a technically correct legal result. The door is open for the appellate court to reverse the trial court solely based on what the appellate court concludes is "incorrect" legal reasoning.

The First Circuit test for preliminary injunctions allows for no such result:

> Appellate review of an order granting or denying a preliminary injunction proceeds deferentially. The trial court's evaluation of the four elements embedded in the preliminary injunction calculus will stand unless the appellant can show an abuse of discretion. An error of law is, of course, an abuse of discretion. Apart from error of law, an abuse of discretion occurs when the district court considers improper criteria, ignores criteria that deserve significant weight, or gauges only the appropriate criteria but makes a clear error of judgment in assaying them.[66]

Reviewing the appropriateness of a preliminary injunction order, the Alabama Supreme Court made an important and often overlooked distinction between (1) the abuse of discretion standard proper and (2) a separate determination as to whether the trial court had discretion to exercise in the first place. Relying on prior case law, the court first noted that it had "defined an abuse of discretion as exceeding the bounds of reason, all the circumstances before the lower court being considered."[67] It disposed of the case, however, based on the fact that the trial court had ignored statutory "mandatory requirements" for the issuance of a preliminary injunction.[68] In doing so, the court observed that

---

[65] *Klay v. United Healthgroup, Inc.*, 376 F.3d 1092, 1096 (11th Cir. 2004).
[66] *See also Rosario-Urdaz v. Rivera-Hernandez*, 350 F.3d 219, 221 (1st Cir. 2003).
[67] *Appalachian Trans. Gr. Inc. v. Parks*, 738 So. 2d 878, 882 (Ala. 1999) (internal quotation omitted).
[68] *Id.*

"[d]iscretion exercised by the trial court with respect to a preliminary injunction is a legal or judicial one which is subjected to review for abuse or improper exercise, *as where there has been a violation of some established principle of law or principle of equity*, or a clear misapprehension of controlling law, and where an abuse of discretion is clearly made to appear, the appellate court will reverse the order or decree."[69] (Emphasis added by court.)

The West Virginia Supreme Court applied a similar definition of "abuse of discretion" outside the preliminary injunction context.[70] The court, reaffirming its precedent, stated that "an abuse of discretion occurs when a material factor deserving significant weight is ignored, when an improper factor is relied upon, or when all proper and no improper factors are assessed but the circuit court makes a serious mistake in weighing them."[71] The court remanded to the trial court because it did not make "adequate findings of fact and conclusions of law" such that the court could "intelligently discharge our limited appellate role to determine that the [trial] court did not abuse its discretion" by misapplying the jurisdiction's factors for determining attorney fees. [72] In another case involving the award of attorney's fees, the Nevada Supreme Court held that "where a trial court exercises its discretion in clear disregard of the guiding legal principles, this action *may* constitute an abuse of discretion."[73]

l)   Error of Law in the Circumstances

Colorado courts define "abuse of discretion" as "an error of law in the circumstances."[74] The Colorado state courts faced a problem with the terminology they used to articulate the abuse of discretion standard in the context of juror challenges. Addressing the "standard for appellate review of a trial's court's ruling on a challenge for cause to a prospective juror," the Colorado Supreme Court first "surveyed" how the courts under its jurisdiction defined that standard.[75] It found that some of the lower courts called the standard "gross abuse of discretion"; some called it "clear abuse of discretion"; and some called it simply "abuse of discretion."[76] In the case up on review, the intermediate appellate court had written

---

[69] *Id.* at 882–83 (internal quotation omitted). *But see Ex Parte Anonymous*, 803 So. 2d 542, 557 (Ala. 2001) (Lyons, J., concurring) (describing an abuse of discretion as "more than an error of law or of judgment" and as an "unreasonable, arbitrary, or unconscionable" attitude on the part of the trial court).

[70] *Shafer v. Kings Tire Serv. Inc.*, 597 S.E.2d 302, 311 (W. Va. 2004) (reversing a trial court's award of attorney fees because the trial court "simply made no findings under any of the [relevant] factors").

[71] *Id.* at 310.

[72] *Id.*

[73] *Bergmann v. Boyce*, 856 P.2d 560, 563 (Nev. 1993) (emphasis added).

[74] *Medina v. Dist. Ct.*, 493 P.2d 367, 368 (Colo. 1972) (internal quotation omitted). The court made clear that the term "abuse" does not reflect upon the trial judge's abilities or character but is simply a legal term of art. *Id.*

[75] *Carrillo v. People*, 974 P.2d 478, 485 (Colo. 1999).

[76] *Id.*

three opinions: the majority (upholding the trial court's denial of challenge for cause) had employed the "gross abuse of discretion" standard; the special concurrence had employed a "clear abuse of discretion" standard, and the dissent had employed a simple "abuse" standard.[77] The Supreme Court determined that the three standards "all have the same meaning," after pointing out the possibility that the concurring judge would have voted for reversal under a normal "abuse" standard, thus swinging the result in the intermediate court.[78] The court affirmed the decision of the both the trial court and the intermediate appellate court.[79]

m)   Substantial Evidence

Georgia's highest court has articulated a remarkably broad definition for "abuse of discretion" in a divorce action involving the custody of children.[80] Although the court unremarkably stated that it would not reverse absent a showing that the "trial court clearly abused its discretion," the court refused to find an "abuse of discretion" in cases "[w]here there is any evidence to support the decision of the trial court."[81] That definition, if taken on its face, would make a trial court virtually immune from review, since there is almost always some evidence supporting a trial court's decision. A narrower reading of this definition may still allow for cases traditionally thought to amount to an abuse of discretion, such as when the trial court does not follow the law; if the trial court looks to the wrong law (and hence, to evidence that is not apposite to the *correct* legal standard), then it will not have any *valid* evidence upon which to rest its decision.

Under Minnesota's abuse of discretion standard, appellate courts will affirm a judgment seeking a "just and equitable division of the material property" if the trial "court's determination has 'an acceptable basis in fact and principle.'"[82] It would appear that so long as the trial court can point to at least one fact and at least one point of law that lends support to its decision, the Minnesota appellate courts will not overturn for abuse of discretion. The court applied this highly deferential standard both because of prior case law "reviewing property distribution" and because "the legislature ha[d] afforded trial court considerable discretion between the parties."[83] An earlier decision from the Minnesota Supreme Court stated that the appellate court would not "disturb" "an award of alimony or support money or

---

[77] *Id.*

[78] *Id.* ("The use of these modifiers creates the appearance of inconsistency and unfairness.")

[79] *Id.* at 493.

[80] *Welch v. Welch*, 596 S.E.2d 134 (Ga. 2004) (affirming the trial court's decision to award custody of two children to husband).

[81] *Id.* at 135. South Carolina, Georgia's neighbor to the northeast, applied a similar standard when reviewing a motion to set aside default. *Stark Truss Co. v. Superior Const. Corp.*, 602 S.E.2d 99, 101 (S.C. 2004). The state supreme court concluded that "[a]n abuse of discretion occurs when the order was controlled by an error of law or when the order is without evidentiary support." *Id.* at 101–02.

[82] *In re Marriage of Rohling*, 379 N.W.2d 519, 523 (Minn. 1986).

[83] *Id.* at 522.

252

an adjudication as to property right" unless the trial court's decision was "manifestly and palpably contrary to the evidence as a whole."[84]

n)   Outside the Range of Permissible Choices

The Eighth Circuit stated that the "abuse of discretion standard *means* that a court has a range of choice, and that its decision will not be disturbed as long as it stays within that range and is not influenced by a mistake of law."[85] In the context of a preliminary injunction, the court stated further that an "abuse of discretion *occurs* if a relevant factor that should have been given significant weight is not considered, if an irrelevant or improper factor is considered and given significant weight, or if a court commits a clear of judgment in the course of weighing proper factors."[86] For the Eleventh Circuit, the meaning of "abuse of discretion" is definite, but the circumstances under which an abuse arises may depend on the factual context of the decision.

Reviewing the trial court's decision denying the state's motion for a mistrial of the penalty phase of a capital murder case, the Connecticut Supreme court defined discretion as (1) "a legal discretion, to be exercised in conformity with the spirit of the law" and (2) "in a manner to subserve and not to impede or defeat the ends of substantial justice."[87] As to the "conformity with the spirit of the law" element, the court stated: "In general, an abuse of discretion exists when a court could have chosen different alternatives but has decided the matter so arbitrarily as to vitiate logic, or has decided it based on improper or irrelevant factors."[88] As to the "subserve justice" requirement, the court clarified that it would reverse only when the abuse of discretion was "manifest" or when an injustice has resulted.[89]

The Illinois Supreme Court stated that, "[w]here discretion has been vested in the trial court, only a clear abuse of discretion or an application of impermissible legal criteria justifies reversal," and that a "reviewing court must look to the criteria on which the trial court should rely to determine if the trial court abused its discretion."[90] The court then went on to analyze whether the trial court had abused its discretion by allowing an expert witness to testify, employing a set of guidelines that the court had adopted previously.[91] The court's decision has three important

---

[84] *Kucera v. Kucera*, 146 N.W.2d 181, 183 (Minn. 1966).
[85] *Aaron v. Target Corp.*, 357 F.3d 768, 774 (8th Cir. 2004). (emphasis added).
[86] *Id.* (emphasis added).
[87] *State v. Peeler*, 857 A.2d 808, 860 (Conn. 2004) (quoting *State v. Onofrio*, 425 A.2d 560 (1979)).
[88] *Id.*
[89] *Id.* (citation omitted).
[90] *Boatman's Nat'l Bank of Belleville v. Martin*, 614 N.E.2d 1194, 1198–99 (Ill. 1993) (upholding trial court's discretion to allow plaintiff's expert to testify despite plaintiff's not notifying defendant about expert despite discovery request) ("The question of the appropriate sanction, if any, to be employed by the trial court for failure to list a witness is within the discretion of the trial court.").
[91] *Id.* at 1199.

elements to it: (1) the court requires trial court to follow the law when exercising discretion; (2) the court reserves the right to review the considerations upon which the trial court based its ruling, although the court did not state whether it would review the trial court's *weighing* of those considerations; and (3) although circular language obscures this point, the court seems to reserve its power to reverse the trial court when its decision is so bad that no appellate judge could debate that the trial court abused its discretion.[92]

Writing in dissent, Justice Rudman of the Supreme Judicial Court of Maine described that state's "abuse of discretion" standard:

> Discretion is not an absolute standard. The discretion accorded a trial court varies according to the principles identified as controlling a particular discretionary determination. When we say we review the court's determination for abuse of discretion we mean we have the responsibility to determine whether the court acted within the principles identified as bounding that discretionary determination. If the court acts within its principled bounds, its determination is entitled to deference. If, however, as here, the court's determination strays from these principles, that determination constitutes an abuse of the court's discretion.[93]

Justice Rudman identified the "controlling principles" in parental rights determinations as the "venerable" "general equity jurisdiction" of the trial court.[94] Although Justice Rudman agreed with the court as to the facts of the case, he disagreed with the court that a joint custody arrangement fell within the trial court's "guiding principle" "to act in the best interest of the child."[95]

The Utah Supreme Court adopted Judge Rudman's position with some insignificant variations.

> The phrase "abuse of discretion" has come into common usage in review of judicial proceedings. Although it has been seen by appellate courts as an efficient way of describing a more complex concept, it has also come to be seen by many as offensive. The phrase is used here simply to be consistent with prior case law regarding the standard of review to be applied to the trial court's actions. When a trial court abuses its discretion, it has exceeded the range of discretion allowed for the particular act under review.

---

[92] Six years earlier, a Justice Goldenhersh, writing in dissent, observed that Illinois' "long-standing definition of abuse of discretion" required that appellate courts not set aside the trial court's discretionary decision "unless the opposite conclusion is clearly apparent." *Bland v. Norfolk and W. Ry. Co.*, 506 N.E.2d 1291, 1298 (Ill. 1987).

[93] *Rodrigue v. Brewer*, 667 A.2d 605, 607–08 (Me. 1995) (Rudman, J., dissenting). The majority upheld the trial court's decision to award joint custody to the parents.

[94] *Id.* at 608

[95] *Id.* at 609.

When it does not abuse its discretion, it has stayed within the permitted range of discretion allowed. Use of the phrase "abuse of discretion" should not be misread to imply a conscious and intentional violation of the permitted discretion by the trial judge. Although such a willful disregard of the standards to be applied by the trial judge happens occasionally, it is certainly not the rule, and our use of "abuse" of discretion should not be read to imply such wrongful intent.[96]

o)   Arbitrary and Capricious

The intermediate courts of Massachusetts will "not consider" the trial court's discretion "abused unless its exercise has been characterized by arbitrary determination, capricious disposition, whimsical thinking, or idiosyncratic choice."[97] In a later case, however, a Massachusetts appellate court did not offer a blanket definition of abuse of discretion, pointing out that the standard "admits of numerous meanings in different contexts."[98] The case before the court, *Wojcik v. Boston Herald, Inc.*, involved a defamation action brought by a former employee of the State Lottery Commission whom the newspaper had accused of stealing lottery tickets. Plaintiff Wojcik requested production of those documents that would identify the sources of the *Herald*'s story. Upon the paper's refusal to produce, plaintiff successfully moved for an order to compel disclosure of the sources; the *Herald* appealed. The appellate court acknowledged that the standard of review for a discovery order was abuse of discretion, but noted that "in the present case, the judge's discretion is bounded by important values under the First Amendment to the United States Constitution."[99] Although the court agreed with the trial court's balancing of plaintiff's interest in gathering evidence against the paper's interest in protecting its sources, the court ultimately vacated "so much of the Superior Court order as compels disclosure of the identities of the reporters' sources."[100]

Judge Grasso dissented, arguing that "the motion judge did not abuse his discretion in ordering the defendants to disclose the identities of confidential sources."[101] Judge Grasso would have upheld the trial court's discretion because the trial court's "decision-making process was conducted within the established framework of relevant legal standards and took into account all the proper factors identified by relevant case law as necessary to inform the discretionary exercise."[102]

---

[96] *State v. Mead*, 27 P.3d 1115, 1124, n.4 (Utah 2001). The court concluded that the "trial court acted outside its discretion in refusing to allow [defendant] the opportunity to ask follow-up questions to the members of the jury panel who had prior knowledge of the case." *Id.* at 1124–25.

[97] *Greenleaf v. Mass. Bay Trans. Auth.*, 494 N.E.2d 402, 405 (Mass. Ct. App. 1986) (listing the factors that the trial court could "include" in the exercise of its discretion).

[98] *Wojcik v. Boston Herald, Inc.*, 803 N.E. 2d 1261, 1264 (Mass. Ct. App. 2004).

[99] *Id.*

[100] *Id.* at 1267.

[101] *Id.* (Grasso, J., dissenting).

[102] *Id.* (Grasso, J., dissenting) (internal quotation omitted).

Mississippi's abuse of discretion standard is broad, lacking an explicit requirement that the trial court must exercise discretion rationally. Reviewing the trial court's decision to exclude the testimony of defendant's expert, the court first "limited" its review to the question of whether or not the trial court abused its discretion.[103] The court stated that it would not determine whether the trial court "was 'right' or 'wrong' in our view."[104] The court qualified itself that it would "be authorized to reverse for an abuse of discretion" if the trial court's decision were "arbitrary and clearly erroneous" or if the trial based its decision on an erroneous review of law."[105]

North Dakota case law uses the words "arbitrary" and "unreasonable" in connection with "abuse of discretion," but it describes the standard in terms of the *attitude* as opposed to the actions or processes of the trial court.[106] The court clarified, however, that it would "'not overturn that [trial] court's decision merely because it is not the one we may have made if we were deciding the motion.'"[107] What constitutes an abusive attitude on the part of the trial court is not clear.

p)   Whether Reasonable Minds Could Differ

In *United States v. Henderson*, the Seventh Circuit reviewed the trial court's ruling allowing the government to introduce evidence of an informant's helpfulness in securing criminal convictions prior to the trial at hand.[108] Before discussing the "difference between bolstering a witness's credibility and rehabilitating that witness following an attack," the court stated that it would find an abuse of discretion "only when no reasonable person could take the district court's view."[109]

Another federal circuit applied the same "no reasonable person" standard when reviewing the trial court's decision to sanction a judgment-creditor.[110] Judgment-debtor K-Mart moved for sanctions after judgment-creditor's counsel— media in tow—attempted to seize money from cash registers at one of K-Mart's stores. After the execution of judgment was stayed, K-Mart moved for sanctions under Federal Rule of Civil Procedure 11, arguing that plaintiff had violated an automatic ten-day stay of execution provided for by Federal Rule of Civil Procedure. 62(f). K-Mart's motion also alleged that plaintiff's counsel had made

---

[103] *Detroit Marine Engineering v. McRee*, 510 So. 2d 462, 467 (Miss. 1987).
[104] *Id.*
[105] *Id.*
[106] *Gonzalez v. Tounjian*, 684 N.W.2d 653, 655 (N.D. 2004) (quoting *Production Credit Ass'n v. Dobrovolny*, 415 N.W2d 489, 491–92 (N.D. 1987)) (motion to vacate judgment) ("'An abuse of discretion is defined as an unreasonable, arbitrary, or unconscionable attitude on the part of the trial court.'").
[107] *Id.*
[108] 337 F.3d 914, 918 (7th Cir. 2003) (affirming the trial court's decision to overrule defendant's objection that the government was improperly "bolstering" a witness's credibility.
[109] *Id.*
[110] *Whitehead v. Food Max of Miss., Inc.*, 332 F.3d 796, 803 (5th Cir. 2003).

inflammatory comments to the press and had "paraded through" its store in an effort to damage K-Mart's reputation.[111] The trial court awarded sanctions on the grounds that counsel had "failed to make a reasonable inquiry" into the law governing execution of judgments and that his actions had "no basis whatsoever in fact or in law."[112]

The Fifth Circuit affirmed the trial court after reviewing for an abuse of discretion. It defined abuse of discretion thus:

> For this deferential review, the district court would necessarily abuse its discretion if it based its ruling on an erroneous view of the law or on a clearly erroneous assessment of the evidence. Generally, an abuse of discretion only occurs where *no reasonable person* could take the view adopted by the trial court.[113]

The majority criticized the dissent for failing to review the Rule 11 sanctions under the abuse of discretion standard that it set forth.[114] The dissent accused the majority of "short-circuiting" the inquiry that Rule 11 demands and argued that Rule 11 requires a threshold determination (apparently reviewed *de novo* by the appellate court) "on whether the filing at issue was warranted by existing law or a nonfrivolous argument for a change in the law."[115]

The leading case on the meaning of abuse of discretion in Florida describes the standard thus:

> Discretion... is abused when the judicial action is arbitrary, fanciful, or unreasonable, which is another way of saying that discretion is abused only where no reasonable man would take the view adopted by the trial court. If reasonable men could differ as to the propriety of the action taken by the trial court, then it cannot be said that the trial court abused its discretion.[116]

An article in the *Florida Bar Journal* questioned what may have been an unintended consequence of *Canakaris*, that "[a]buse of discretion, with a reflexive citation to *Canakaris*, has for no defensible reason become a shibboleth in far too many contexts."[117]The author of the bar journal article proposed that Florida apply a so-called bifurcated review to evidentiary questions, citing Hawaii's current

---

[111] *Id.* at 800.
[112] *Id.*
[113] *Id.* at 803.
[114] *Id.* at 803, n. 3.
[115] 332 F.3d at 809 (King, C.J., dissenting).
[116] *Canakaris v. Canakaris*, 382 So. 2d 1197, 1203 (Fla. 1980) quoted in *Emmer v. Brucato*, 813 So. 2d 264, 265, n.1 (Fla. Dist. Ct. App. 2002).
[117] Nancy Ryan, *Containing Canakaris: Tailoring Florida's One-Size-Fits-Most Standard of Review*, 78 FLA. B. J. 40, 42 (2004).

bifurcated standard and Florida's own use of the "bifurcated" standard in other contexts.[118] Under a "bifurcated" approach to evidentiary matters, the appellate court would review all relevant legal questions *de novo* and give near total deference to the trial court's factual findings.[119]

Kansas courts will find that "[j]udicial discretion is abused when no reasonable person would adopt the position taken by the district court."[120] Applying this standard to the trial court's award for attorney fees against an insurance company, the trial court quoted statutory language that allowed attorney fees when an insurer refuses to pay a claim "without just cause."[121] The court found no just cause because the district court had found that insurance company had no legal obligation to pay the claim at issue.[122] The court's decision raises two questions: (1) could the court have reached the same result on the grounds that the district court did not follow the relevant state statute, and (2) does the unreasonableness of the trial court's conclusion rest on the fact that it contradicts the trial court's other findings and conclusions.

Louisiana reviewed a *jury verdict* for general damages in excess of 5 million under the abuse of discretion standard.[123] Reaffirming its precedent, the court stated that it would overturn the jury verdict only if "the award is, in either direction, beyond that which a reasonable trier of fact could assess for the effects of the particular injury to the particular plaintiff under the particular circumstances."[124] The court reduced the damages because: (1) plaintiff would not need expensive medical treatment in the future and (2) plaintiff had suffered "no other physical or functional disabilities besides infertility and disfigurement."[125] The court did not inquire as to whether the trial court (affirming a jury verdict) could reasonably conclude that 5 million in damages was appropriate.

Texas courts will uphold a trial court's evidentiary rulings if they fall "within the zone of reasonable disagreement."[126] Defendant was on trial for the capital murder of his girlfriend's two-year-old daughter. At trial, the state over a

---

[118] *Id.* at 41.

[119] *Id.*

[120] *S. Cent. Kan. Health Ins. Gr. V. Harden & Co. Ins. Servs., Inc.*, 97 P.3d 1031, 1036 (Kan. 2004). Other decisions describe this "no reasonable person" standard as "another way of saying" that the trial court's "judicial action is arbitrary, fanciful, or unreasonable." *In the Matter of Marriage of Soden*, 834 P.2d 358, 367 (Kan. 1992). For an example of a federal court using the "no reasonable person" standard, *see In re PPI Enterprises (U.S.), Inc.*, 324 F.3d 197, 211 (3rd Cir. 2003) (bankruptcy proceeding) (reviewing a trial court's denial of creditor's motion to dismiss on grounds of debtor's "bad faith").

[121] *Id.*

[122] *Id.*

[123] *Cone v. Nat'l Emergency Servs.*, 747 So. 2d 1085 (La. 1999).

[124] *Id.* at 1089–90 (quoting *Youn v. Maritime Overseas Corp.*, 623 So.2d 1257, 1261 (La. 1993)).

[125] *Id.* at 1090 (noting that infertility and disfigurement are "extremely significant conditions").

[126] *Salazar v. State*, 38 S.W.3d 141, 153–54 (Tex. Crim. App. 2001).

hearsay objection offered evidence through victim's babysitter that victim had told babysitter that defendant had injured her upon babysitter's asking about a wound on victim's shoulder.[127] The trial court admitted the evidence as an excited utterance under the Texas equivalent to Rule 803. Although defendant argued that the statement (1) was made in response to a question and (2) that the statement was made some time after the requisite "startling event," the court held that neither of the considerations defendant raised were "dispositive" of the matter.[128] Rather, both were "simply factors to consider in determining whether the statement is admissible under the excited utterance hearsay exception."[129]

q)   Palpably and Grossly Violative of Fact and Logic

For the purpose of reviewing trial court decisions to depart from state sentencing guidelines, the Michigan Supreme Court clarified" that its "abuse" standard of review meant that "if, after consideration, the Court of Appeals discovers or perceives that the trial court did not have a substantial and compelling reason to justify its departure, the Court must remand the case for re-sentencing."[130] Interestingly, the Michigan Supreme Court disavowed the utility of Michigan's common understanding of abuse of discretion—"palpably and grossly violative of fact and logic that it evidences not the exercise of will but perversity of will..."—in the context of sentencing departures.[131] Distinguishing its definition from an outright *de novo* review, the court qualified that "*some* degree of deference is nevertheless owed the trial court's finding, and thus a *de novo* review is inappropriate."[132]

Ohio appellate courts will find an abuse of discretion when they determine that "the trial court's decision was so palpably and grossly violative of fact or logic that it evidences not the exercise of will but the perversity of will, not the exercise of judgment but the defiance of judgment, not the exercise of reason but instead passion or bias."[133] The court reversed the intermediate appellate court based on the

---

[127] *Id.* at 153.

[128] *Id.* at 154.

[129] *Id.*

[130] *People v. Babcock*, 666 N.W.2d 231, 241–42 (Mich. 2003).

[131] *Id.*

> This statute clearly does not require the Court of Appeals, in accord with *Spalding*, to affirm unless the result [is] so palpably and grossly violative of fact and logic that it evidences not the exercise of will but the perversity of will, not the exercise of judgment but defiance thereof, not the exercise of reason but rather of passion and bias.

(internal quotation omitted). For an example of Michigan's traditional standard of review, *see also People v. Hine*, 650 N.W. 2d 659, 664 (Mich. 2002) (evidentiary determination).

[132] *Id.* (noting the superior vantage point that the trial court holds when making decisions about sentencing departures). The court also subsequently noted the absence of a "single correct outcome" in sentencing decisions. *Id.* at 243.

[133] *Wilson v. Brush Wellman, Inc.*, 817 N.E.2d 59, 63 (Ohio 2004) (reversing the decision of the intermediate appellate court, which had in turn reversed the trial court's decision to deny class certification to a group of former employees).

fact that it had not given due deference to the trial court under the abuse of discretion standard.[134] On account of its role as a court "charged with considering issues of public or great general interest" the court also "examine[d] the propriety of the [intermediate] court's underlying legal analysis."[135]

r)   Against the Logic and Effects of the Case

Iowa employs the logic and effects definition of abuse of discretion.[136] In a workplace sexual harassment case, however, the Iowa Supreme Court defined "abuse of discretion" as trial court discretion exercised "on grounds or for reasons clearly untenable or to an extent clearly unreasonable."[137] One wonders whether the recent Iowa case law indicates that the meaning of "abuse of discretion" is evolving in Iowa, whether the court is articulating the "logic and effect" definition using more understandable language, or whether the court's articulation of two different standards was simply inadvertent.

The Missouri Supreme Court most recently offered a comprehensive definition of "abuse of discretion" just over ten years ago:

> Judicial discretion is abused when a trial court's ruling is clearly against the logic of the circumstances then before the court and is so arbitrary and unreasonable as to shock the sense of justice and indicate a lack of careful consideration; if reasonable men can differ about the propriety of the action taken by the trial court, then it cannot be said that the trial court abused its discretion.[138]

The Missouri standard requires an element other than Indiana's "against the logic and effects" test. The appellant also has to show what one could describe as gross negligence on the part of the trial court.

Although Oklahoma defines abuse of discretion as "clearly erroneous conclusion and judgment, one that is clearly against the logic and effect of the facts present in support of and against the application,"[139] the inquiry appears to rest on (1) whether the trial court erred, and (2) the magnitude of that error. When determining the admissibility of an expert's testimony, the court ended its inquiry and affirmed the trial court once it determined (1) that the expert had "demonstrated

---

[134] *Id.* ("[T]he appellate court held merely that the trial court 'erred'.").

[135] *Id.* (internal quotation omitted).

[136] *Glenn v. Farmland Foods, Inc.*, 344 N.W.2d 240, 244 (Iowa 1984) ("We consistently have defined 'abuse of discretion' as 'an erroneous conclusion of judgment, one clearly against the logic and effect of facts and circumstances before the court, or the reasonable, probable, and actual deductions to be drawn therefrom.").

[137] *Channon v. United Parcel Serv. Inc.*, 629 N.W.2d 835, 859 (Iowa 2001) (motion for a new trial).

[138] *Wingate v. Lester E. Cox. Med. Cent.*, 853 S.W.2d 912, 917 (Mo. 1993) (internal quotation omitted).

[139] *Lott v. State*, No. D-2002-88, 98 P.3d 318, 344 (Okla. Crim. App. 2004).

sufficient specialized knowledge to qualify him to testify as an expert on the subject [of sex crimes]," and (2) that the expert's testimony fit within his field of knowledge.[140] The court appeared not so much to be searching for abuse but for error.

s)   Jurisdictions Incorporating More Than One Abuse of Discretion Definition

In reviewing a trial court's discovery sanctions, New Mexico courts will find an abuse of discretion when one of four conditions is met: (1) the sanction is unfair; (2) it is arbitrary; (3) it is manifest error; or (4) it is not justified by reason.[141] The court upheld the trial court's decision to award attorney fees as a discovery sanction, even though the governing statute "specifically authorized" only dismissal as a possible sanction.[142] The court declined to limit the trial court "to either imposing the drastic sanction of default judgment or imposing no sanctions at all."[143]

Pennsylvania has four elements to its abuse of discretion standard: An abuse of discretion (1) transcends a mere error of judgment, and (2) misapplies the law, or (3) is "manifestly unreasonable," or (4) is the "result of partiality, prejudice, bias, or ill-will, as shown by the evidence or the record."[144] In this child support hearing, the court reversed because the trial court had misapplied the law when it found that a father had a legal obligation to support a son through college.[145] One judge dissented, stating without further explanation that the trial court's decision was not an abuse of discretion.[146]

The South Dakota Supreme Court conceded recently that "the term 'abuse of discretion' defies an easy description."[147] It described the phrase as "a fundamental error of judgment, a choice outside the range of permissible choices, a decision, which, on full consideration, is arbitrary or unreasonable."[148] The court concluded that the trial court had not overstepped its bounds by considering the father's handicap because its analysis had "centered on" which parent could better provide for the child.[149]

---

[140] *Id.*

[141] *Miller v. City of Albuquerque*, 540 P.2d 254, 261 (N.M. Ct. App. 1975).

[142] *Id.* at 260.

[143] *Id.*

[144] *Blue v. Blue*, 616 A.2d 628, 631 (Pa. 1992) (quoting *Kelly v. County of Allegheny*, 546 A.2d 608, 610 (Pa. 1988)).

[145] *Id.*

[146] *Id.* at 633 (Larsen, J., dissenting).

[147] *Arneson v. Arneson*, 670 N.W.2d 904, 910 (S.D. 2003) (upholding the trial court's decision to award custody to mother where father had cerebral palsy and needed assistance to perform certain daily functions).

[148] *Id.*

[149] *Id.* at 912 (eschewing a blanket rule that would preclude a handicapped parent from holding primary custody over his or her children).

t) Definition of Abuse of Discretion Varies with Type of Case

California's "abuse of discretion" standard can vary widely depending upon the type of case before the reviewing court. In a case involving the dismissal of a deliberating juror, Judge Werdegar, concurring, noted that the California Supreme Court had "on several occasions explained that a trial court's determination of good cause" "is subject to the deferential abuse-of-discretion standard, meaning that we will uphold the trial court's decision to discharge, or not discharge, a juror if there is substantial evidence supporting it."[150] In an earlier case involving the award of attorney fees, however, the court equated "abuse of discretion" with the trial court's being "clearly wrong."[151] Judge Werdegar joined the majority and did not write separately. Judge Baxter, dissenting from the court's decision to reverse the trial court's order denying a continuance, found no abuse of discretion. In reaching his conclusion, he acknowledged the difficulty of formulating a "precise definition" for abuse of discretion.[152] He instead relied on what he called the "generally accepted" test of "whether the trial court exceeded the bounds of reason, all of the circumstances before it being considered."[153]

The Supreme Court of Idaho has shown some reluctance to define "abuse of discretion" precisely, holding only that trial court must "carefully consider" the governing law and relevant facts:

> We decline to ascribe a definitive meaning to the amorphous phrase "abuse of discretion" solely for the purposes of this case, but it will suffice to say that where the trial court has exercised such discretion after a careful consideration of the relevant factual circumstances and principles of law, and without arbitrary disregard for those facts and principles of justice, we will not disturb the action.[154]

The rationale behind the Idaho Supreme Court's refusal to give a definition for "abuse of discretion" is different from that articulated by Justice Rudman on the Supreme Judicial Court of Maine. The Idaho Court declines to give a definition because the term is incapable of a general definition, whereas for Justice Rudman, the term "abuse of discretion" means that the trial court stepped outside the boundaries established by the substantive law for the case at hand.

---

[150] *People v. Cleveland*, 21 P.3d 1225, 1239 (Cal. 2001) (Werdegar, J., concurring).

[151] *PLCM Group, Inc. v. Drexler*, 95 Cal. Rptr. 2d 198, 206 (Cal. 2000) ("The experienced trial judge is the best judge of the value of professional services rendered in his court, and while his judgment is of course subject to review, it will not be disturbed unless the appellate court is convinced that it is clearly wrong"—meaning that it abused its discretion.").

[152] *Rappleyea v. Campbell*, 884 P.2d 126, 133 (Cal. 1994).

[153] *Id.*

[154] *Lisher v. Krasselt*, 538 P.2d 783, 786 (Idaho 1975) quoted by *State ex rel. Ohman v. Ivan H. Talbot Family Trust*, 820 P.2d 695, 696 (1991) (motion to reopen case).

The Oregon Supreme Court has shown its reluctance to offer a general definition for abuse of discretion. Reviewing the trial court's decision not to disqualify a juror after plaintiff's voir dire revealed potential bias, the court began by noting "[i]nnumerable court decisions covering a wide spectrum of jurisdictions" that had offered "a variety of definitions of the term 'abuse of discretion.'"[155] It then settled on the definition offered by Bouvier's Law Dictionary: "Abuse of discretion: A discretion exercised to an end or purpose not justified by, and clearly against, reason and evidence."[156]

The court proceeded to fashion an abuse of discretion standard particular to the context of reviewing a trial court's decision not to disqualify a juror that had exhibited bias. In light of the party's right to trial by an impartial juror, the court concluded that the trial court "in exercising discretion must find from all of the facts that the juror will be impartial and fair and not be biased consciously or subconsciously."[157] Based on the record of the voir dire examination, the court held "that there was a *substantial probability of bias* on the part of juror Brandt and therefore the plaintiffs were deprived of the right to have their issues determined by an impartial juror."[158]

Twenty-three years later, the court defined offered "several principles" for understanding the meaning of "abuse of discretion":[159]

> First, in the context of evidentiary rulings, "discretion," as this court has used that term, refers to the authority of a trial court to choose among several legally correct outcomes. If there is only one legally correct outcome, "discretion" is an inapplicable concept. It follows that we first must review evidentiary rulings without deference to determine whether proper principles of law were applied correctly. Next, and also without deference, we must determine whether the application of those principles leads to only one correct outcome. If there is only one legally correct outcome, and the trial court arrived at that outcome, it did not err; conversely, if the trial court arrived at a different outcome, it did err. Only if we determine that application of the correct legal principles leads to more than one correct outcome do we continue to review whether the trial court abused its discretion in choosing an outcome. If the trial court's decision was within the range of legally correct discretionary choices and produced a permissible, legally correct outcome, the trial court did not abuse its discretion.[160]

---

[155] *Id.* at 265–66.
[156] *Lambert v. Sisters of St. Joseph of Peace*, 560 P.2d 262, 266 (Or. 1977).
[157] *Id*
[158] *Id.* at 266–67.
[159] *State v. Rogers*, 4 P.3d 1261, 1277 (Or. 2000).
[160] *Id.* at 1278.

Despite the detail of that description, the court again limited its context to the trial court's rulings on evidentiary matters.[161]

u)   Discretion Exercised without Due Consideration

For evidentiary rulings, Arkansas defined "abuse of discretion" as "a discretion improvidently improvised, *i.e.*, exercised thoughtlessly and without due consideration."[162] A standard of review analysis from this definition logically begins with the question of whether the trial court had discretion in the first place. If the trial court has discretion and does not exercise it, it is a "thoughtless" exercise of discretion. If the trial court attempts to exercise discretion it does not have, that discretion is by its nature "improvidently improvised."

The Arkansas Supreme Court began its analysis of the trial court's decision by noting an error of law on the trial court's part.[163] The court then considered what *effect* the trial court's decision to exclude evidence would have on the proponent's theory of the case.[164] The court concluded that the trial court had erred by excluding the evidence in question, and that the error was grounds for reversal.[165] One should note that this approach effectively swallows up the "harmless error" doctrine into the meaning of "abuse of discretion."

Montana courts will not find an abuse of discretion unless "a district court acts arbitrarily without conscientious judgment or exceeds the bounds of reason."[166] One judge dissented in *Simmons Oil Corp.*, stating that the evidentiary ruling in issue was erroneous.[167] Considering that controversial ruling in tandem with false testimony offered by respondent's expert, the dissent concluded that appellant Standard Oil had been denied its right to a fair trial.[168] The dissent did not mention an abuse of discretion.

v)   Gross or Manifest Abuse Distinguished

Upholding a trial court's decision to deny the criminal defendant's motion for a continuance, the Supreme Court of North Carolina clarified that "a motion for continuance is ordinarily addressed to the sound discretion of the trial court" and that the court would not disturb the trial court's decision "unless it is manifestly unsupported by reason, which is to say it is so arbitrary that it could not have been

---

[161] *Id.*

[162] *So. Farm Bureau Cas. Ins. Co. v. Daggett*, 118 S.W. 3d 525, 532 (Ark. 2003).

[163] *Id.* ("We first note that, to the extent the trial court agreed that Daggett could not 'impeach' his own witness, such a ruling was incorrect.").

[164] *Id.* ("As the Knights' defense was premised on their contention that the truck was properly maintained, such evidence was highly relevant.").

[165] *Id.*

[166] *Simmons Oil Corp. v. Wells Fargo Bank*, 960 P.2d 291, 294 (Mont. 1998) (relevance of evidence).

[167] *Id.* at 297–98 (Trieweiler, J., dissenting).

[168] *Id.* (Trieweiler, J., dissenting).

the result of a reasoned decision."[169] The court recognized "that numerous decisions of the appellate courts of this state have indicated that, in such situations, the appealing party must demonstrate a 'gross abuse' or 'manifest abuse' of discretion.[170] The court stated that the terms "gross abuse" and "manifest abuse" had been employed before the "term 'abuse of discretion' "had been given any definitive meaning."[171] The court concluded that under the present "manifestly unsupported standard," there was "but one type of abuse of discretion" because any ruling of the trial court (1) would be given "great deference" and (2) would be upset "upon a showing that it was so arbitrary that it could not have been the result of a reasoned decision."[172]

w)   Clearly against Reason

A leading case on the concept of discretion, as well as on the meaning of abuse of discretion, is *Johnson v. United States*. The District of Columbia Court of Appeals was hearing defendant's appeal from the trial court's denial of a motion to sever the trials of defendant Johnson and his codefendants.[173] The record showed that one of the codefendants planned to offer and did offer a theory inconsistent with that of defendant. (The codefendant's theory implicated defendant in the crime.) The court begins with the premise that the trial judge "has the ability to choose from a range of permissible conclusions."[174] "Although the act of choosing will be guided by various legal and other considerations, the decision-maker, and not the law, decides."[175] However, the court determined that it must play a supervisory role to insure that the trial court's "judgment reflects a discretion exercised not arbitrarily or willfully but with regard to what is right and equitable under the circumstances and the law, and directed by the reason and conscience of the judge to a just result."[176] In light of these considerations, the court adopted a definition of abuse of discretion originally promulgated by the Supreme Court of Delaware: "Abuse of discretion is a discretion exercised to an end or purpose not justified by and clearly against reason and evidence."[177]

The court then set out a four-factor test for it to determine whether the trial court had abused its discretion under the Delaware definition: (1) whether "the determination" of the trial court "was committed to the trial court's discretion,"[178]

---

[169] *State v. T.D.R.*, 495 S.E.2d 700, 708 (N.C. 1998) (holding that the trial court's decision was reasonable because defendant offered no explanation on the record as to why the time he had been afforded to gather additional evidence was not sufficient).

[170] *Id.*

[171] *Id.*

[172] *Id.* ("Any such abuse of discretion is *a fortiori* 'gross' or 'manifest' as those terms have been used in prior cases of the appellate courts of this state.").

[173] *Johnson v. United States*, 398 A.2d 354 (D.C. 1979).

[174] *Id.* at 361.

[175] *Id.*

[176] *Id.* (internal quotation omitted).

[177] *Id.* at 363 (internal quotation omitted).

[178] *Johnson*, 398 A.2d at 363.

(2) whether the trial court "recognized" that "it had this discretion" and whether it "purport[ed] to exercise it;"[179] (3) whether the record "reveal[s] sufficient facts upon which the trial court's determination was based";[180] (4) whether "the trial court's action was within the range of permissible alternatives."[181]

The District of Columbia Court of Appeals has continued to adhere to *Johnson*. In a recent case involving the appointment of a guardian for a woman suffering from dementia, the court noted that the relevant statute "committed" "the appointment decision" to the trial court's "considerable discretion."[182] Relying on *Johnson*, the *Orshansky* court proposed a two-prong test to determine whether the trial court had abused its discretion: (1) "whether there is a sufficient factual predicate in the record for the determination that the trial court made" and (2) whether "the reasoning by which the trial court reached its determination" falls "within the range of permissible alternatives under the law and given the facts presented."[183]

Ruling on the admissibility of evidence under the state equivalent to Federal Rule of Evidence 403, the Hawaii Supreme Court found that the decision of legal relevance is "eminently suited to the trial court's exercise of its discretion because it requires a cost-benefit calculus and a delicate balance between probative value and prejudicial effect."[184] Because this necessarily entails a "judgment call" on part of the trial judge, the court employed what it called "the traditional abuse of discretion standard."[185] Under the "traditional standard," a trial court "may not be reversed on appeal unless the trial court clearly exceeded the bounds of reason or disregarded rules or principles of law or practice to the substantial detriment of a party litigant."[186] One should note that some of the jurisdictions discussed in this chapter treat the "substantial detriment" element separately, as a "harmless error" rule. Also, although the court is not alone in finding that a trial court's misapplication of the law is *ipso facto* an abuse of discretion, one wonders what general principles of *practice* a trial court would have to violate before an appellate court would find an abuse. Does this, mean, for example, that an appellate court

---

[179] *Id.*

[180] *Id.* at 364.

[181] *Id.* at 365. The court also set out a fifth factor, whether the abuse of discretion is "of a magnitude to require reversal," but that factor more appropriately falls under the harmless error doctrine. *Id.* at 366.

[182] *In re Orshansky*, 804 A.2d 1077, 1092 (D.C. 2002)
> Thus, on appeal this court "does not render its own decision of what judgment is most wise under the circumstances presented." "Rather, it examines the record and the trial court's determination for those indicia of rationality and fairness that will assure it that the trial court's action was proper."

Id. (quoting *Johnson*, 398 A.2d at 362).

[183] *Id* at 1093.

[184] *State v. McCrory*, 87 P.3d 275, 279 (Haw. 2004).

[185] *Id.*

[186] *Id.*

266

could find an abuse simply because the trial judge employed some unorthodox techniques when presiding over a trial?

Maryland's highest court applied an "abuse of discretion" standard to a case in which a special master recommended that a juvenile delinquent and his mother pay restitution to an insurance company that had paid for damage to a car that juvenile had burglarized.[187] Reaffirming prior case law, the court stated,

> Judicial discretion is a composite of many things, among which are conclusions drawn from objective criteria; it means a sound judgment exercised with regard to what is right under the circumstances and without doing so arbitrarily or capriciously. Where the decision or the order of the trial court is a matter of discretion it will not be disturbed on review except on a clear showing of abuse of discretion, that is, discretion manifestly unreasonable, or exercised on untenable grounds, or for untenable reasons.[188]

The *In re Don Mc..* analysis is two-fold: (1) the judge must exercise discretion, which, when boiled down, amounts to "good judgment" and (2) in order to find abuse, the judge must employ its discretion in a "manifestly unreasonable" way, or employ "untenable" grounds or reasons upon which to base discretion. Subsequent case law simplified the *Don Mc.* analysis, describing the abuse of discretion standard as a "reasoned decision based on the weighing of various alternatives."[189]

Considering the intermediate appellate court's decision to reverse the trial court's order changing the primary custodian of a child from the former wife to the former husband, the Washington Supreme Court reinstated the trial court's ruling and reversed the court of appeals because it found on the record that "the Court of Appeals substituted its judgment for that of the trial court."[190] The court noted the disruptive nature of custodial changes and the "strong presumption in favor of custodial continuity and against modification," but it declined to reverse the trial court for abuse of discretion "unless the court exercised its discretion in an untenable or manifestly unreasonable way."[191] The court concluded that the trial court's order was not manifestly unreasonable and cited to *inter alia*, wife's leaving the state with the child after denying that she would do so and wife's obstruction of husband's visitation rights.[192] Chief Justice Anderson dissented, arguing that "in proceedings to modify a child's *residential placement*" (original emphasis), the trial

---

[187] *In re Don Mc.*, 686 A.2d 269, 272 (Md. 1996).
[188] *Id.* (internal quotations omitted).
[189] *Metheny v. State*, 755 A.2d 1088, 1104 (Md. 2000).
[190] *In re Marriage of McDole*, 859 P.2d 1239, 1243 (1993).
[191] *Id.* at 1242.
[192] *Id.* at 1243.

court's "discretion is more limited and must be exercised with caution and within the bounds of established legal principles."[193]

x)   Exceeds the Bounds of Reason

Having its first opportunity to adopt the appellate standard of review for motions to sever offenses under the state's rules of criminal procedure, the Tennessee Supreme Court adopted the abuse of discretion review.[194] It did so based on the plain language of the relevant rules and on the fact that no hard–and–fast rule governs a motion to sever.[195] The court concluded that "a trial court's refusal to sever offenses will be reversed only when the court applied an incorrect legal standard, or reached a decision which is against logic and reasoning that caused an injustice to the party complaining."[196] The plain language of the definition quoted by the court appears to apply the prejudice requirement from the harmless error rule to those situations in which the court acts unreasonably; there is no mention of a similar requirement when the trial court misapplies the law.

In Wyoming, a "court does not abuse its discretion unless it acts in a manner which exceeds the bounds of reason under the circumstances."[197] The Wyoming Supreme Court offered two criteria for appellate courts to use when determining whether or not the trial court had abused its discretion: (1) "whether or not the court could reasonably conclude as it did" and (2) whether the trial court committed "an error of law... under the circumstances."[198] Other Wyoming decisions do not mention an error of law explicitly but add to the analysis a third element: "whether any facet of [the trial court's ruling] is arbitrary or capricious."[199]

---

[193] *Id.* (Andersen, J., dissenting). Judge Anderson went on to conclude that "the trial court's ruling in the present case did not satisfy the standard set forth in the modification statute." *Id.* It is unclear whether Judge Andersen here has concluded that the modification statute requires a heightened standard of review or if the nature of "residential placement" itself requires it. The modification statute to which Judge Anderson refers provides:

> (1) the court shall not modify a prior custody decree or parenting plan unless it finds, upon the basis of facts that have arisen since the prior decree of plan that were unknown to the court at the time of the prior decree or plan, that a substantial change has occurred in the circumstances of the child or the nonmoving party and that the modification is in the best interest of the child....

Wash. Rev. Code Ann. § 26.09.260 (West 2004). For an example of Washington's use of the "unreasonable" definition for abuse of discretion, *see Ellison v. Process Sys. Constr. Co.*, 50 P.3d 658, 660 (Wash. Ct. App. 2002).
[194] *State v. Shirley*, 6 S.W. 3d 243, 247 (Tenn. 1999).
[195] *Id.*
[196] *Id.*
[197] *Martinez v. State*, 611 P.2d 831, 838 (Wyo. 1980) (upholding the trial court's discretion to allow a state witness to testify by deposition rather than at trial).
[198] *Id.*
[199] *E.g., Ingersoll v. State*, 96 P.3d 1046, 1050 (Wyo. 2004).

y)   Conclusion

This chapter illustrates the wide-ranging nomenclature used by appellate courts to describe the standards for review of trial court discretion. These tests for abuse of discretion focus on whether the trial judge (1) misunderstood the law, which includes applying an improper legal standard or disregarding the applicable law or (2) rendered a decision that was devoid of logic. Notwithstanding that some of the terms used to garnish the abuse standard are vague and confusing, the courts' focus is on whether the trial court's decision was unreasonable. Stated differently, under this deferential standard, the appellate court will find abuse of discretion only if no reasonable judge could have concluded as the trial court did. Therefore, if reasonable judges could differ on the decision, the appellate court won't find abuse of discretion. It follows that under the abuse standard the trial court has the limited right to be wrong and that the reviewing court will refrain from substituting its judgment for that of the trial court. In this way, the abuse of discretion standard is an effective review-restraining device.

TABLE OF CASES

271

272

Table of Law Review Articles

Index

A

B

D

286

F

G

H

L

M

N

O

Opening Statements

296

Q

R

S

T

W